SUICIDE SQUAD
BLAZE

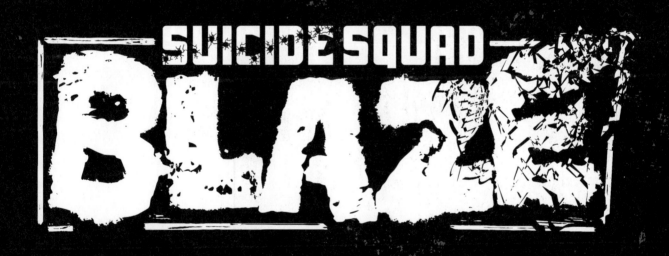

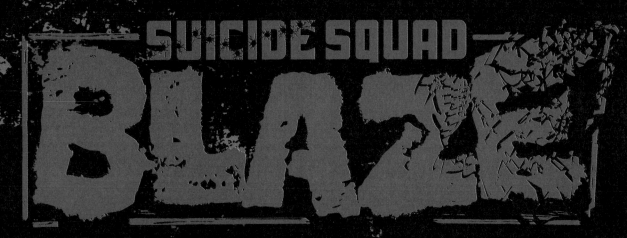

SUICIDE SQUAD BLAZE

SIMON SPURRIER
Writer

AARON CAMPBELL
Artist

JORDIE BELLAIRE
Colorist

ADITYA BIDIKAR
Letterer

AARON CAMPBELL
Series & collection cover artist

SUPERMAN created by
JERRY SIEGEL
& JOE SHUSTER.

By special arrangement with
the Jerry Siegel Family.

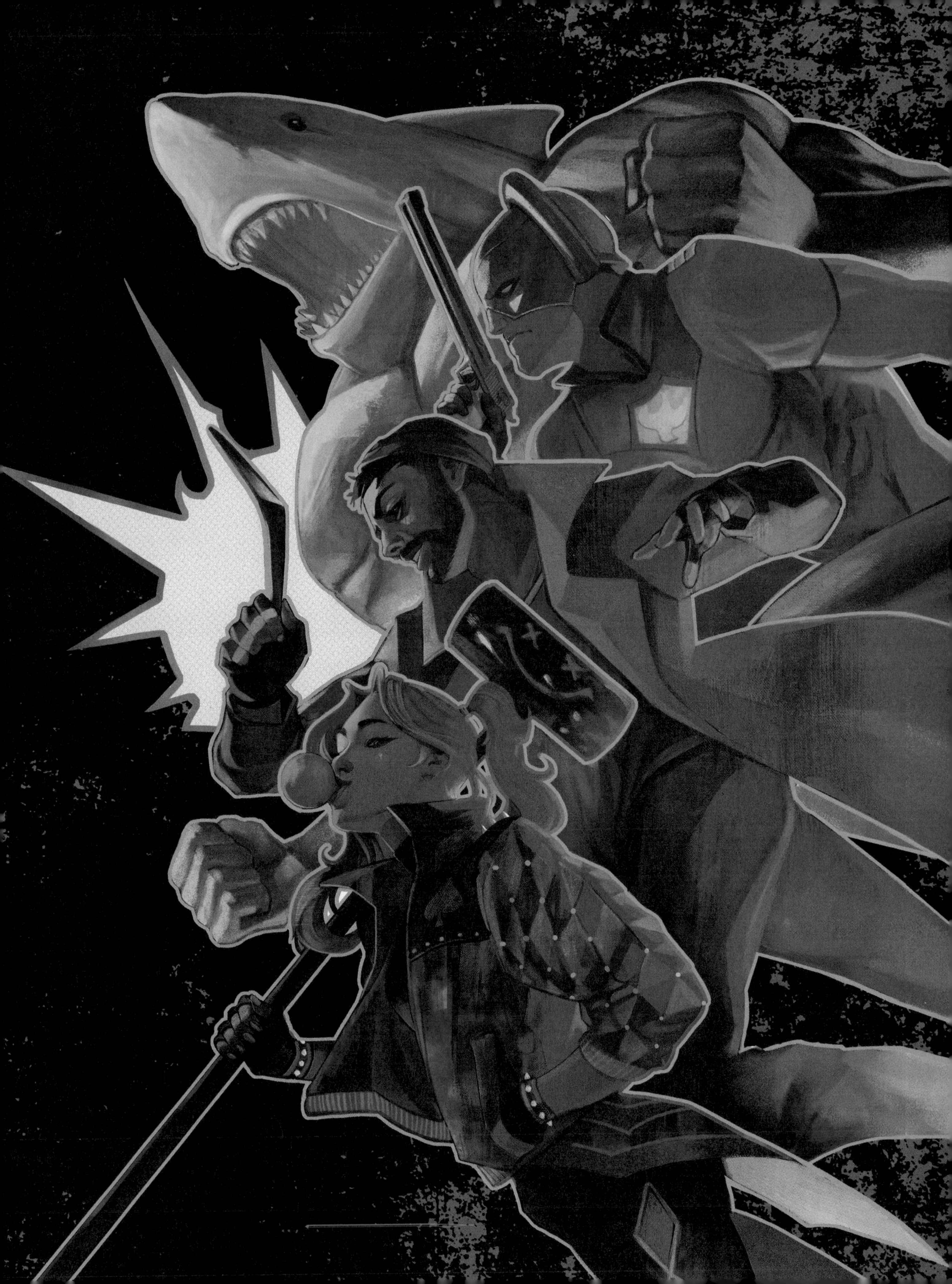

Chris Conroy Editor – Original Series & Collected Edition
Matthew Levine Associate Editor – Original Series
Steve Cook Design Director – Books
Megen Bellersen Publication Design
Emily Elmer Publication Production

Marie Javins Editor-in-Chief, DC Comics

Anne DePies Senior VP – General Manager
Jim Lee Publisher & Chief Creative Officer
Don Falletti VP – Manufacturing Operations & Workflow Management
Lawrence Ganem VP – Talent Services
Alison Gill Senior VP – Manufacturing & Operations
Jeffrey Kaufman VP – Editorial Strategy & Programming
Nick J. Napolitano VP – Manufacturing Administration & Design
Nancy Spears VP – Revenue

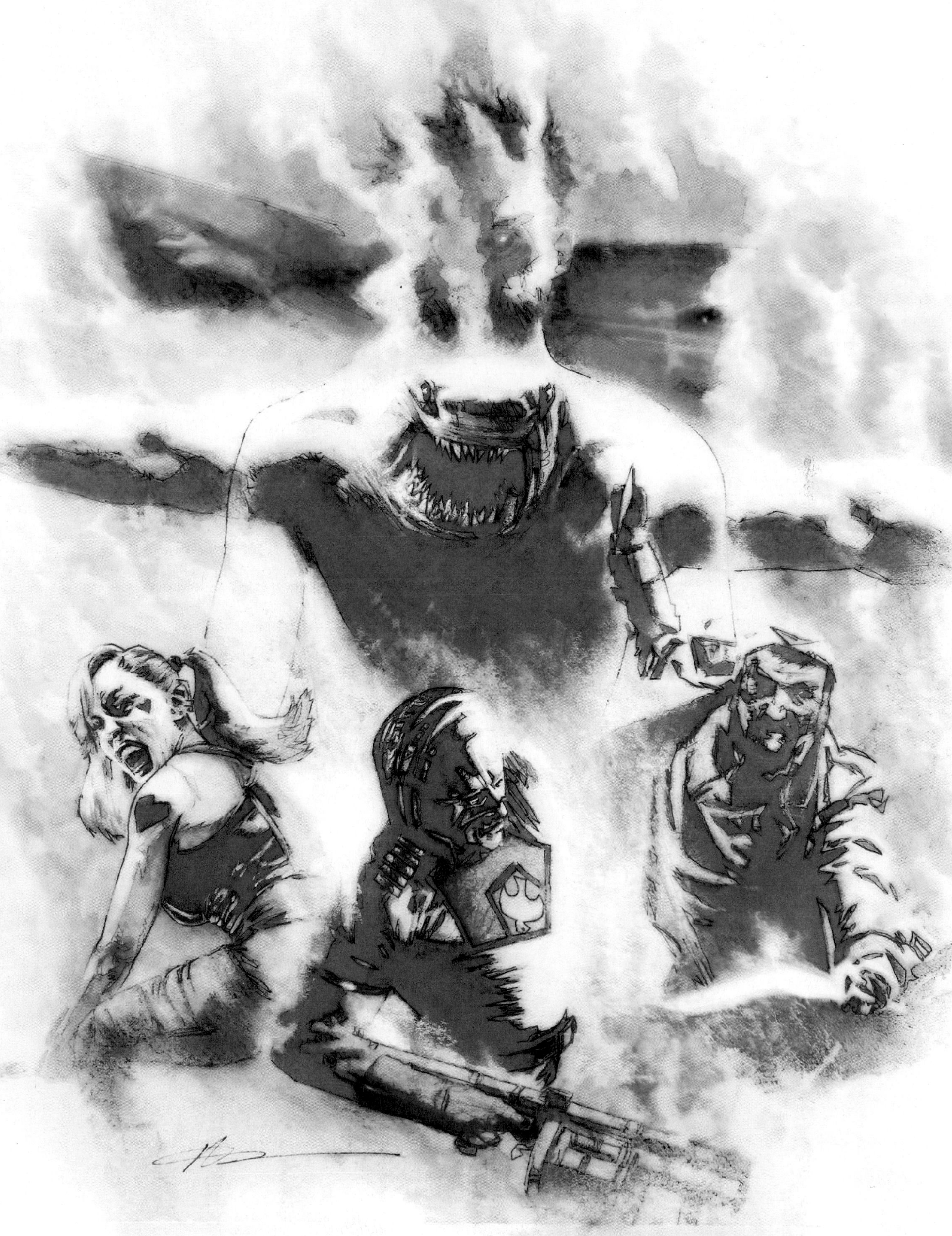

***Suicide Squad: Blaze* #1**
variant cover by MATÍAS BERGARA

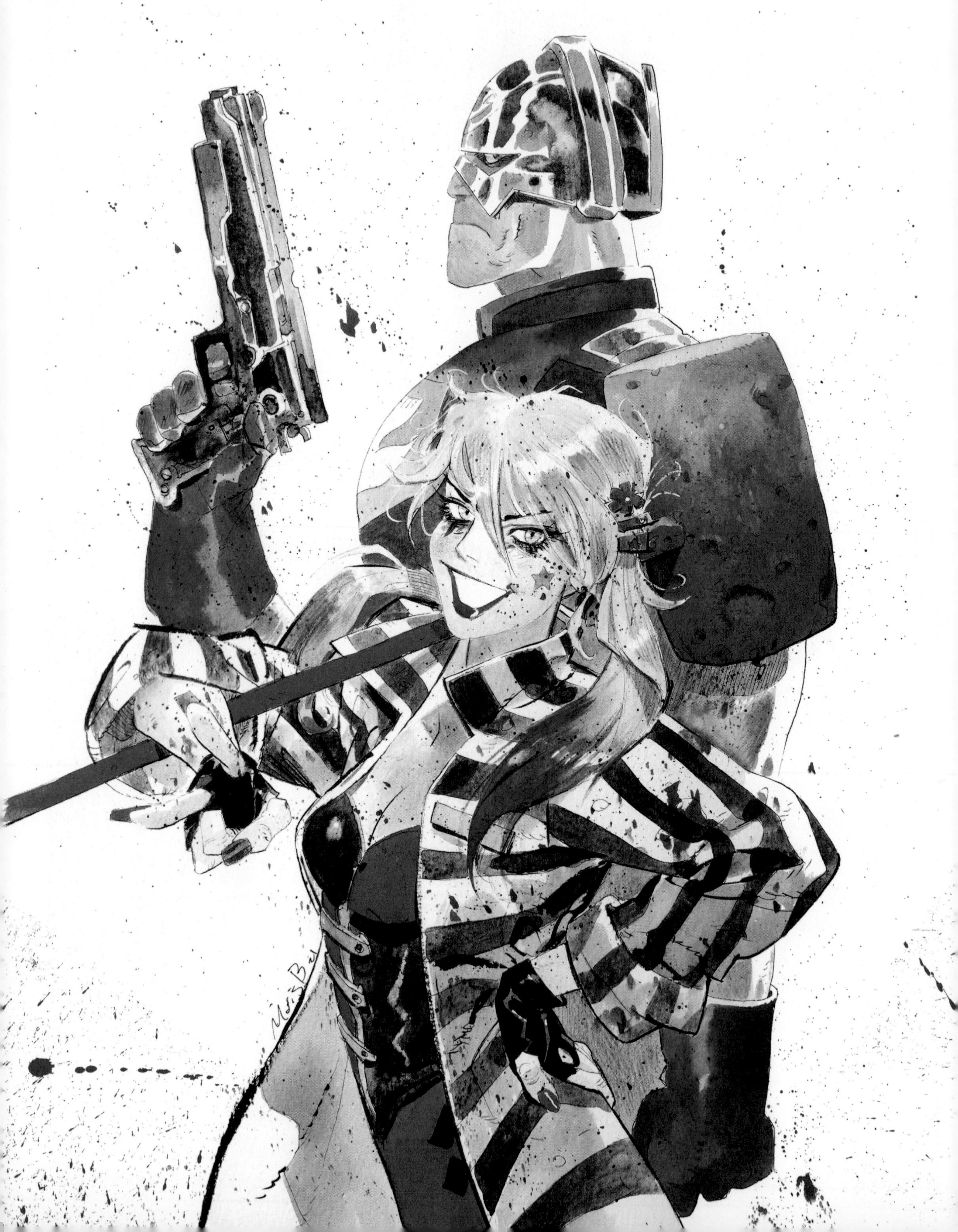

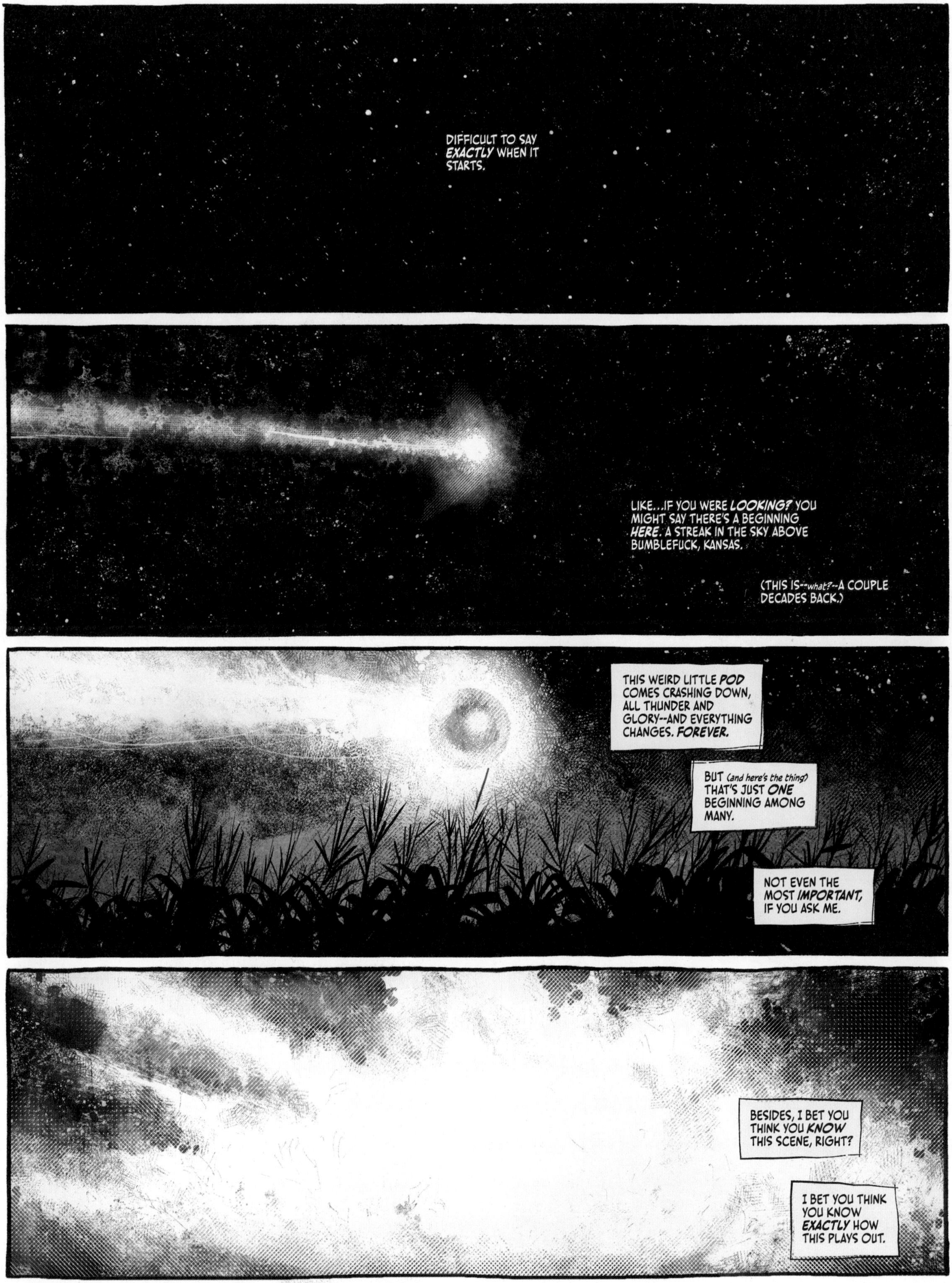
DIFFICULT TO SAY *EXACTLY* WHEN IT STARTS.
LIKE...IF YOU WERE *LOOKING?* YOU MIGHT SAY THERE'S A BEGINNING *HERE.* A STREAK IN THE SKY ABOVE BUMBLEFUCK, KANSAS.
(THIS IS--*what?*--A COUPLE DECADES BACK.)
THIS WEIRD LITTLE *POD* COMES CRASHING DOWN, ALL THUNDER AND GLORY--AND EVERYTHING CHANGES. *FOREVER.*
BUT *(and here's the thing)* THAT'S JUST *ONE* BEGINNING AMONG MANY.
NOT EVEN THE MOST *IMPORTANT,* IF YOU ASK ME.
BESIDES, I BET YOU THINK YOU *KNOW* THIS SCENE, RIGHT?
I BET YOU THINK YOU KNOW *EXACTLY* HOW THIS PLAYS OUT.

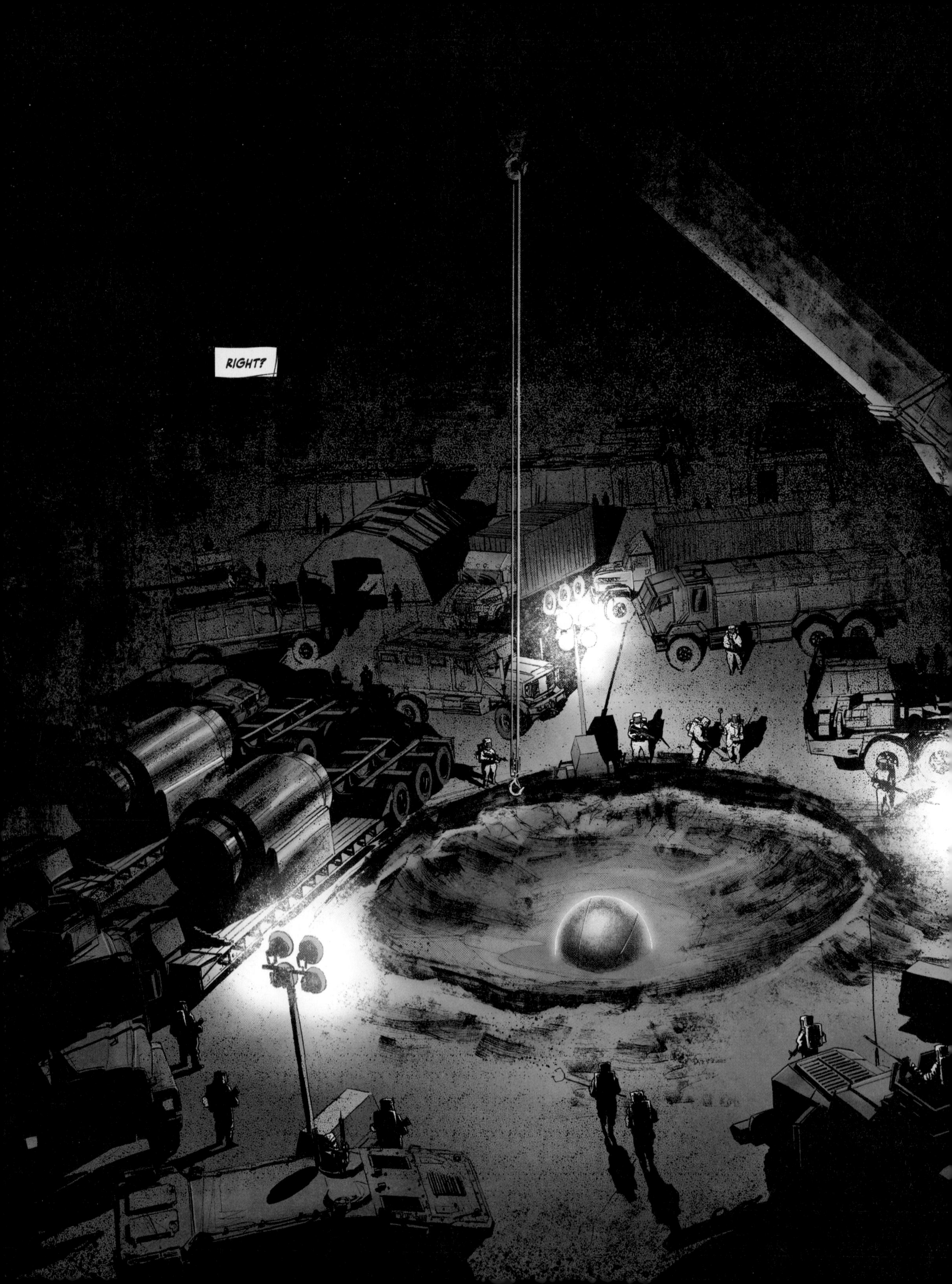
RIGHT?

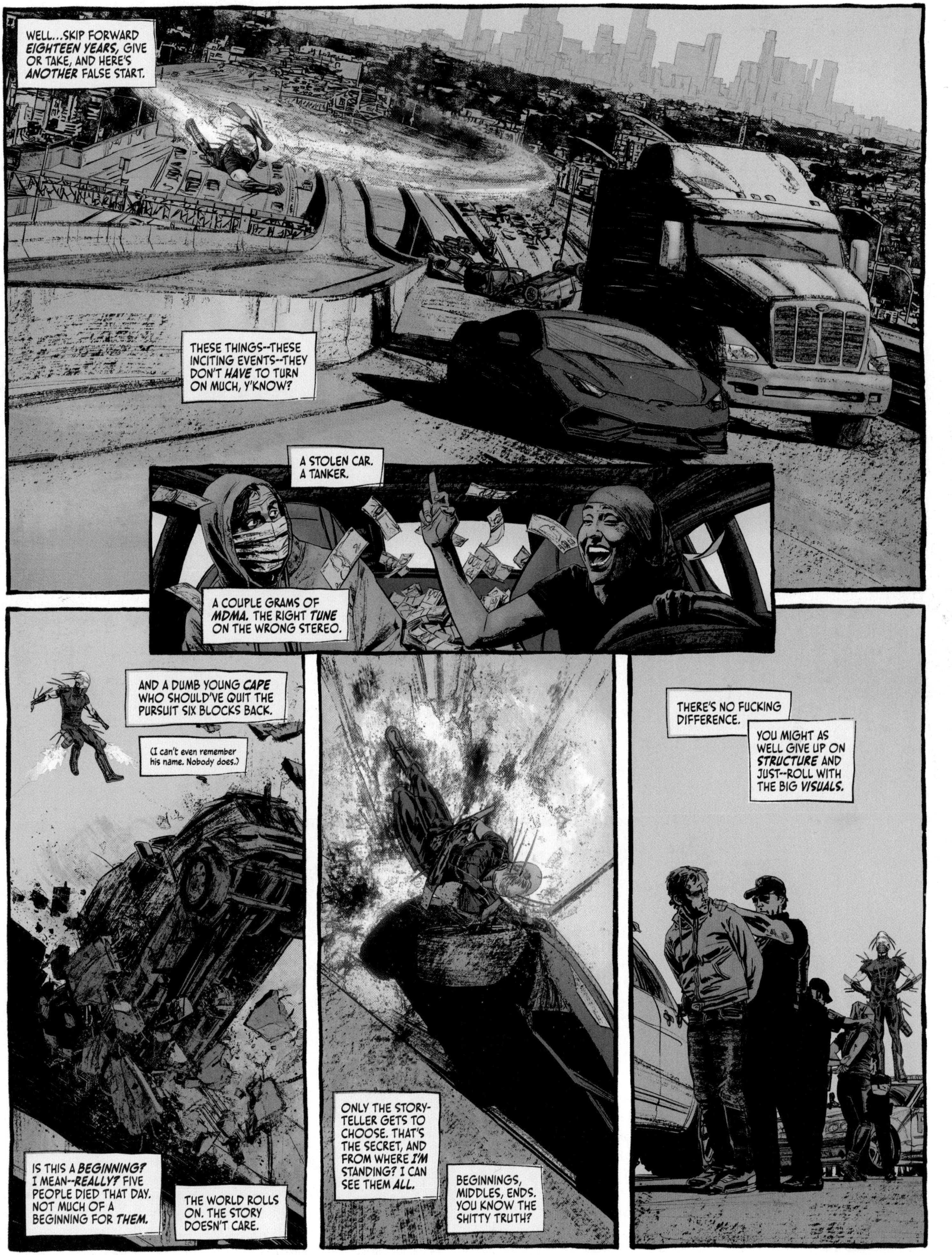
WELL...SKIP FORWARD EIGHTEEN YEARS, GIVE OR TAKE, AND HERE'S ANOTHER FALSE START.
THESE THINGS--THESE INCITING EVENTS--THEY DON'T HAVE TO TURN ON MUCH, Y'KNOW?
A STOLEN CAR. A TANKER.
A COUPLE GRAMS OF MDMA. THE RIGHT TUNE ON THE WRONG STEREO.
AND A DUMB YOUNG CAPE WHO SHOULD'VE QUIT THE PURSUIT SIX BLOCKS BACK.
(I can't even remember his name. Nobody does.)
IS THIS A BEGINNING? I MEAN--REALLY? FIVE PEOPLE DIED THAT DAY. NOT MUCH OF A BEGINNING FOR THEM.
THE WORLD ROLLS ON. THE STORY DOESN'T CARE.
ONLY THE STORY-TELLER GETS TO CHOOSE. THAT'S THE SECRET, AND FROM WHERE I'M STANDING? I CAN SEE THEM ALL.
BEGINNINGS, MIDDLES, ENDS. YOU KNOW THE SHITTY TRUTH?
THERE'S NO FUCKING DIFFERENCE.
YOU MIGHT AS WELL GIVE UP ON STRUCTURE AND JUST--ROLL WITH THE BIG VISUALS.

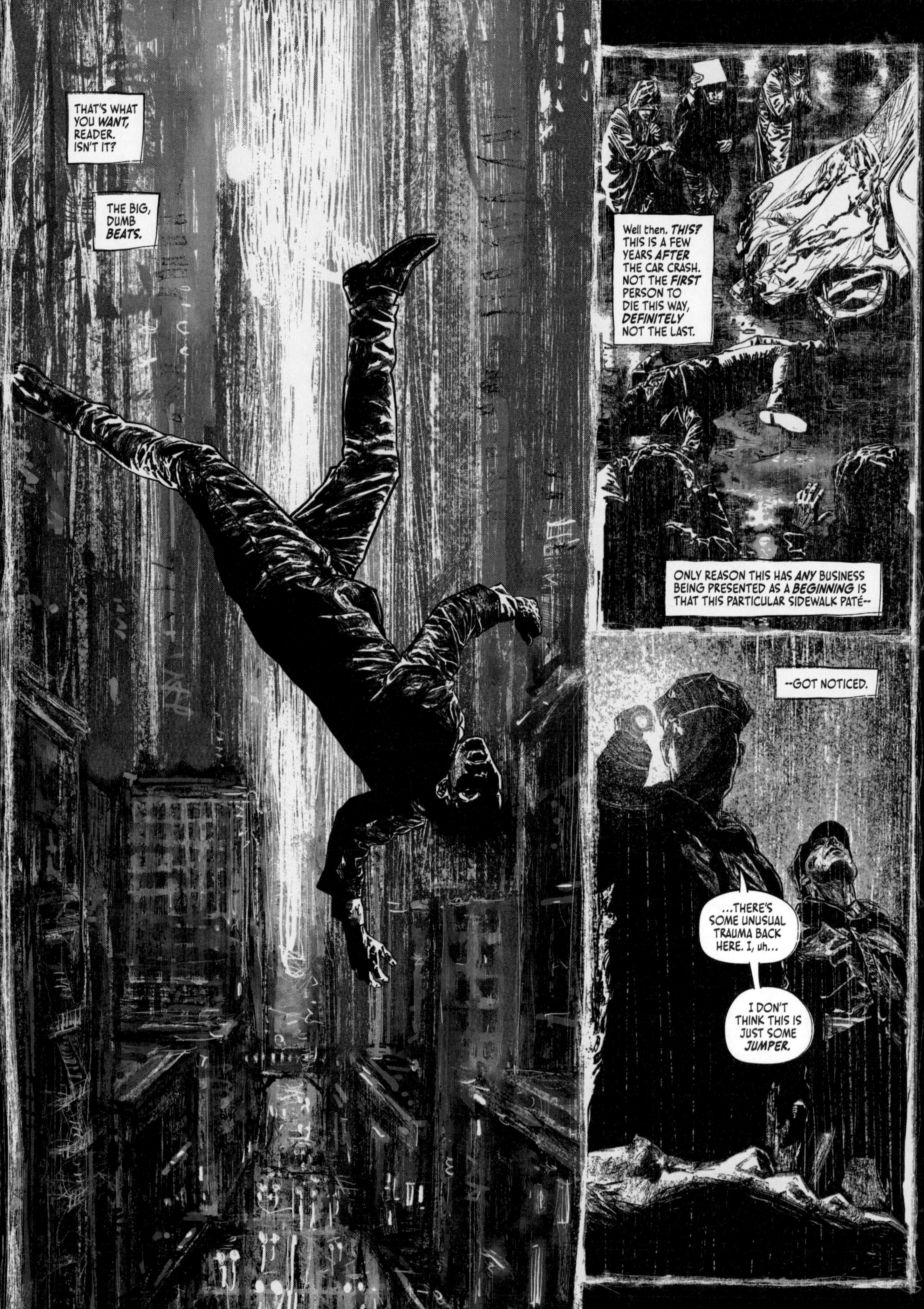
THAT'S WHAT YOU *WANT*, READER. ISN'T IT?
THE BIG, DUMB *BEATS.*
Well then. *THIS?* THIS IS A FEW YEARS *AFTER* THE CAR CRASH. NOT THE *FIRST* PERSON TO DIE THIS WAY, *DEFINITELY* NOT THE LAST.
ONLY REASON THIS HAS *ANY* BUSINESS BEING PRESENTED AS A *BEGINNING* IS THAT THIS PARTICULAR SIDEWALK PATÉ--
--GOT NOTICED.
...THERE'S SOME UNUSUAL TRAUMA BACK HERE. I, uh...
I DON'T THINK THIS IS JUST SOME *JUMPER.*

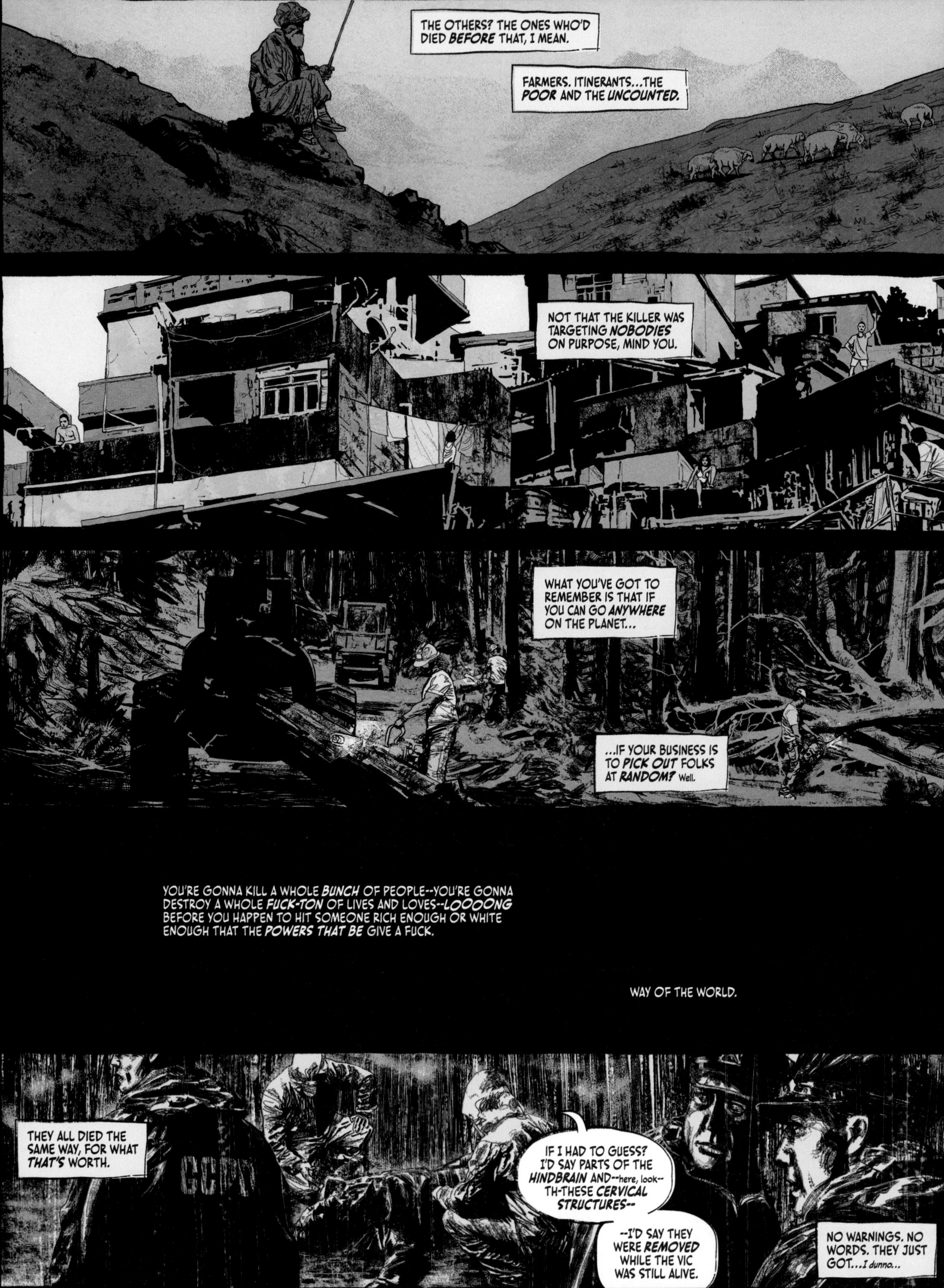
THE OTHERS? THE ONES WHO'D DIED BEFORE THAT, I MEAN.
FARMERS. ITINERANTS...THE POOR AND THE UNCOUNTED.
NOT THAT THE KILLER WAS TARGETING NOBODIES ON PURPOSE, MIND YOU.
WHAT YOU'VE GOT TO REMEMBER IS THAT IF YOU CAN GO ANYWHERE ON THE PLANET...
...IF YOUR BUSINESS IS TO PICK OUT FOLKS AT RANDOM? Well.
YOU'RE GONNA KILL A WHOLE BUNCH OF PEOPLE--YOU'RE GONNA DESTROY A WHOLE FUCK-TON OF LIVES AND LOVES--LOOOONG BEFORE YOU HAPPEN TO HIT SOMEONE RICH ENOUGH OR WHITE ENOUGH THAT THE POWERS THAT BE GIVE A FUCK.
WAY OF THE WORLD.
THEY ALL DIED THE SAME WAY, FOR WHAT THAT'S WORTH.
IF I HAD TO GUESS? I'D SAY PARTS OF THE HINDBRAIN AND--here, look--TH-THESE CERVICAL STRUCTURES--
--I'D SAY THEY WERE REMOVED WHILE THE VIC WAS STILL ALIVE.
NO WARNINGS. NO WORDS. THEY JUST GOT...I dunno...

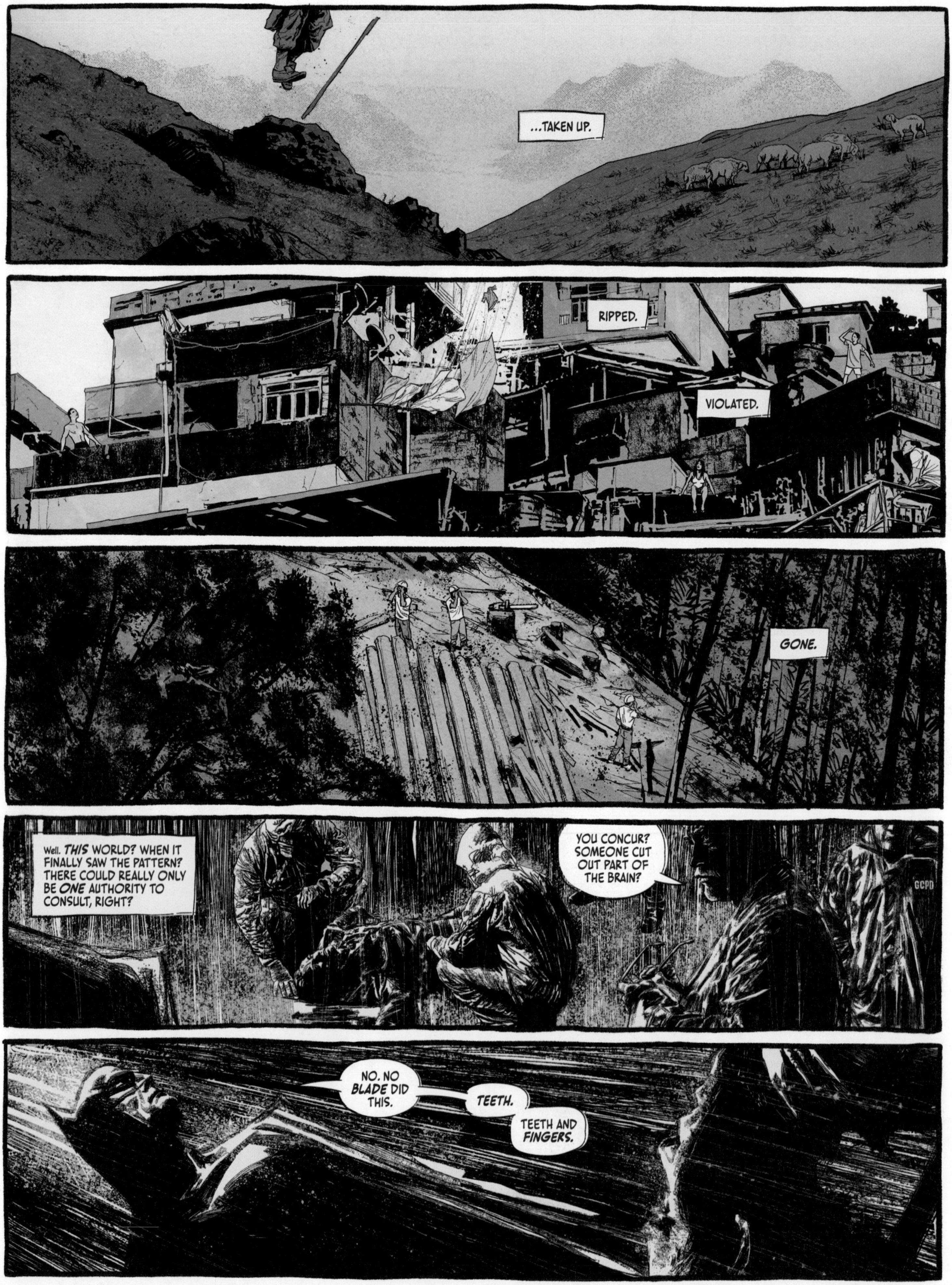

...TAKEN UP.
RIPPED.
VIOLATED.
GONE.
Well. THIS WORLD? WHEN IT FINALLY SAW THE PATTERN? THERE COULD REALLY ONLY BE ONE AUTHORITY TO CONSULT, RIGHT?
YOU CONCUR? SOMEONE CUT OUT PART OF THE BRAIN?
GCPD
NO. NO BLADE DID THIS.
TEETH.
TEETH AND FINGERS.

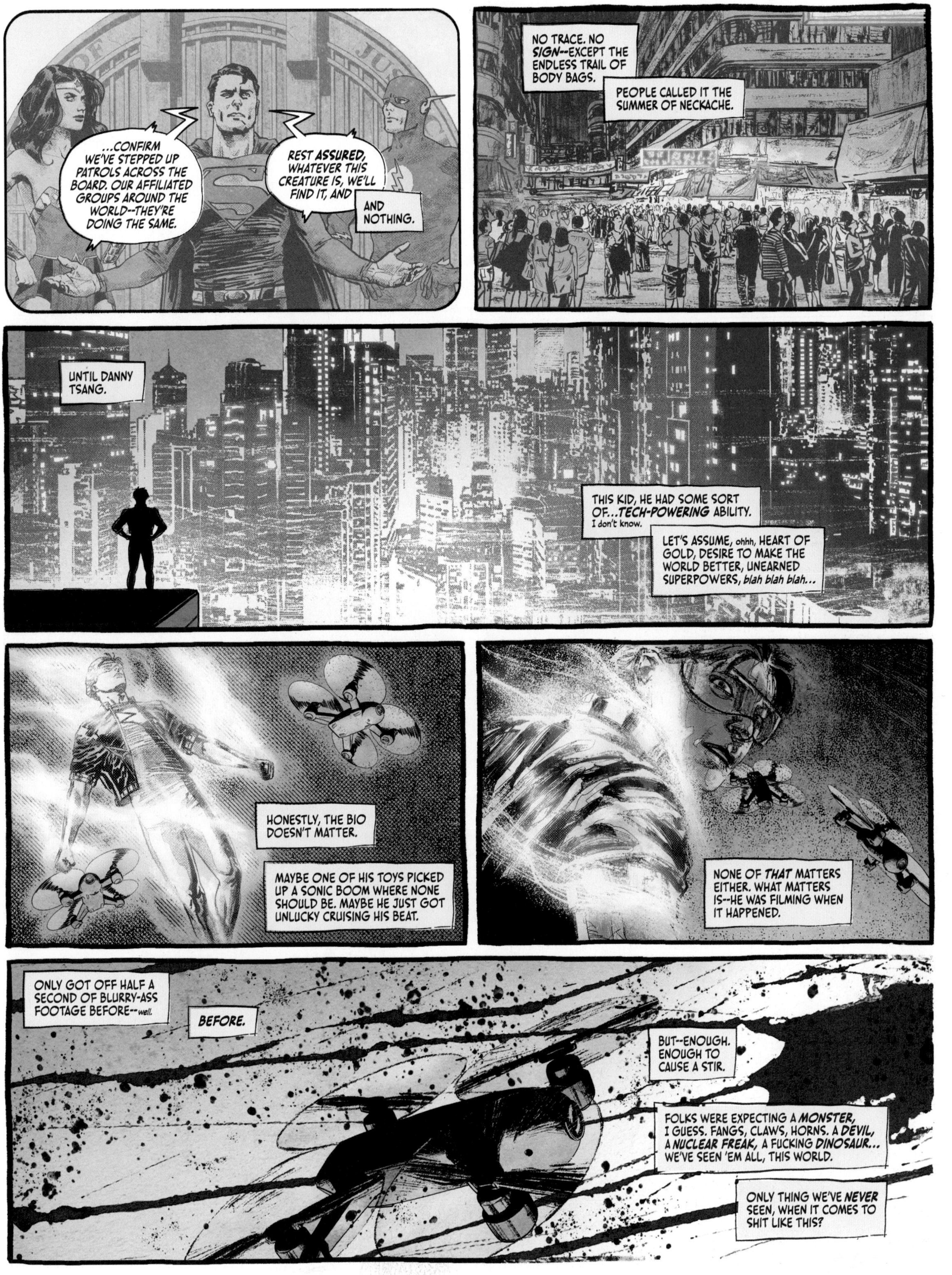
...CONFIRM WE'VE STEPPED UP PATROLS ACROSS THE BOARD. OUR AFFILIATED GROUPS AROUND THE WORLD--THEY'RE DOING THE SAME.
REST ASSURED, WHATEVER THIS CREATURE IS, WE'LL FIND IT, AND
AND NOTHING.
NO TRACE. NO SIGN--EXCEPT THE ENDLESS TRAIL OF BODY BAGS.
PEOPLE CALLED IT THE SUMMER OF NECKACHE.
UNTIL DANNY TSANG.
THIS KID, HE HAD SOME SORT OF...TECH-POWERING ABILITY. I don't know.
LET'S ASSUME, ohhh, HEART OF GOLD, DESIRE TO MAKE THE WORLD BETTER, UNEARNED SUPERPOWERS, blah blah blah...
HONESTLY, THE BIO DOESN'T MATTER.
MAYBE ONE OF HIS TOYS PICKED UP A SONIC BOOM WHERE NONE SHOULD BE. MAYBE HE JUST GOT UNLUCKY CRUISING HIS BEAT.
NONE OF THAT MATTERS EITHER. WHAT MATTERS IS--HE WAS FILMING WHEN IT HAPPENED.
ONLY GOT OFF HALF A SECOND OF BLURRY-ASS FOOTAGE BEFORE--well.
BEFORE.
BUT--ENOUGH. ENOUGH TO CAUSE A STIR.
FOLKS WERE EXPECTING A MONSTER, I GUESS. FANGS, CLAWS, HORNS. A DEVIL, A NUCLEAR FREAK, A FUCKING DINOSAUR... WE'VE SEEN 'EM ALL, THIS WORLD.
ONLY THING WE'VE NEVER SEEN, WHEN IT COMES TO SHIT LIKE THIS?

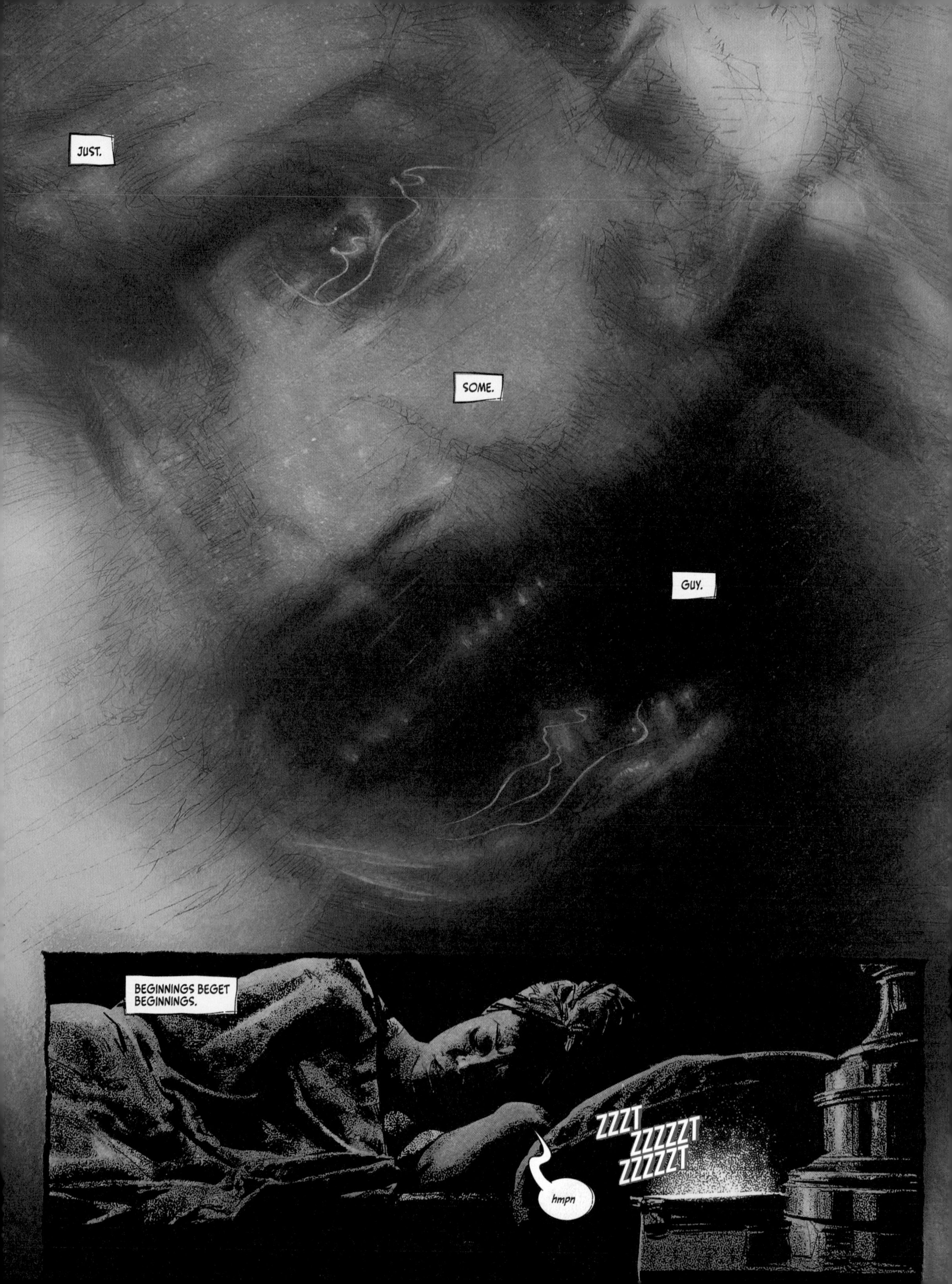
JUST.
SOME.
GUY.
BEGINNINGS BEGET BEGINNINGS.
hmpn
ZZZT ZZZZZT ZZZZZT

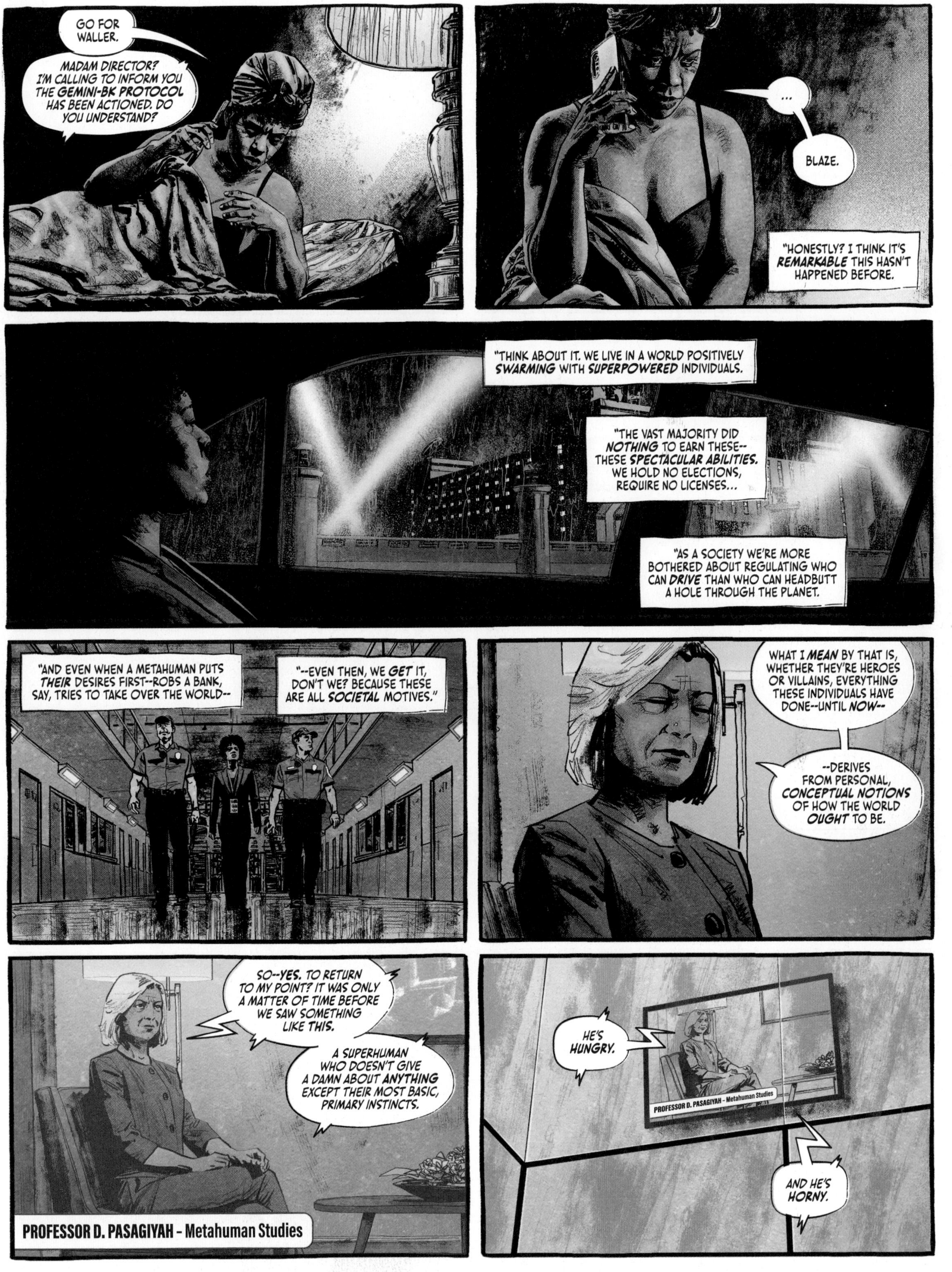
GO FOR WALLER.
MADAM DIRECTOR? I'M CALLING TO INFORM YOU THE GEMINI-BK PROTOCOL HAS BEEN ACTIONED. DO YOU UNDERSTAND?
...
BLAZE.
"HONESTLY? I THINK IT'S REMARKABLE THIS HASN'T HAPPENED BEFORE.
"THINK ABOUT IT. WE LIVE IN A WORLD POSITIVELY SWARMING WITH SUPERPOWERED INDIVIDUALS.
"THE VAST MAJORITY DID NOTHING TO EARN THESE-- THESE SPECTACULAR ABILITIES. WE HOLD NO ELECTIONS, REQUIRE NO LICENSES...
"AS A SOCIETY WE'RE MORE BOTHERED ABOUT REGULATING WHO CAN DRIVE THAN WHO CAN HEADBUTT A HOLE THROUGH THE PLANET.
"AND EVEN WHEN A METAHUMAN PUTS THEIR DESIRES FIRST--ROBS A BANK, SAY, TRIES TO TAKE OVER THE WORLD--
"--EVEN THEN, WE GET IT, DON'T WE? BECAUSE THESE ARE ALL SOCIETAL MOTIVES."
WHAT I MEAN BY THAT IS, WHETHER THEY'RE HEROES OR VILLAINS, EVERYTHING THESE INDIVIDUALS HAVE DONE--UNTIL NOW--
--DERIVES FROM PERSONAL, CONCEPTUAL NOTIONS OF HOW THE WORLD OUGHT TO BE.
SO--YES. TO RETURN TO MY POINT? IT WAS ONLY A MATTER OF TIME BEFORE WE SAW SOMETHING LIKE THIS.
A SUPERHUMAN WHO DOESN'T GIVE A DAMN ABOUT ANYTHING EXCEPT THEIR MOST BASIC, PRIMARY INSTINCTS.
PROFESSOR D. PASAGIYAH - Metahuman Studies
HE'S HUNGRY.
PROFESSOR D. PASAGIYAH - Metahuman Studies
AND HE'S HORNY.

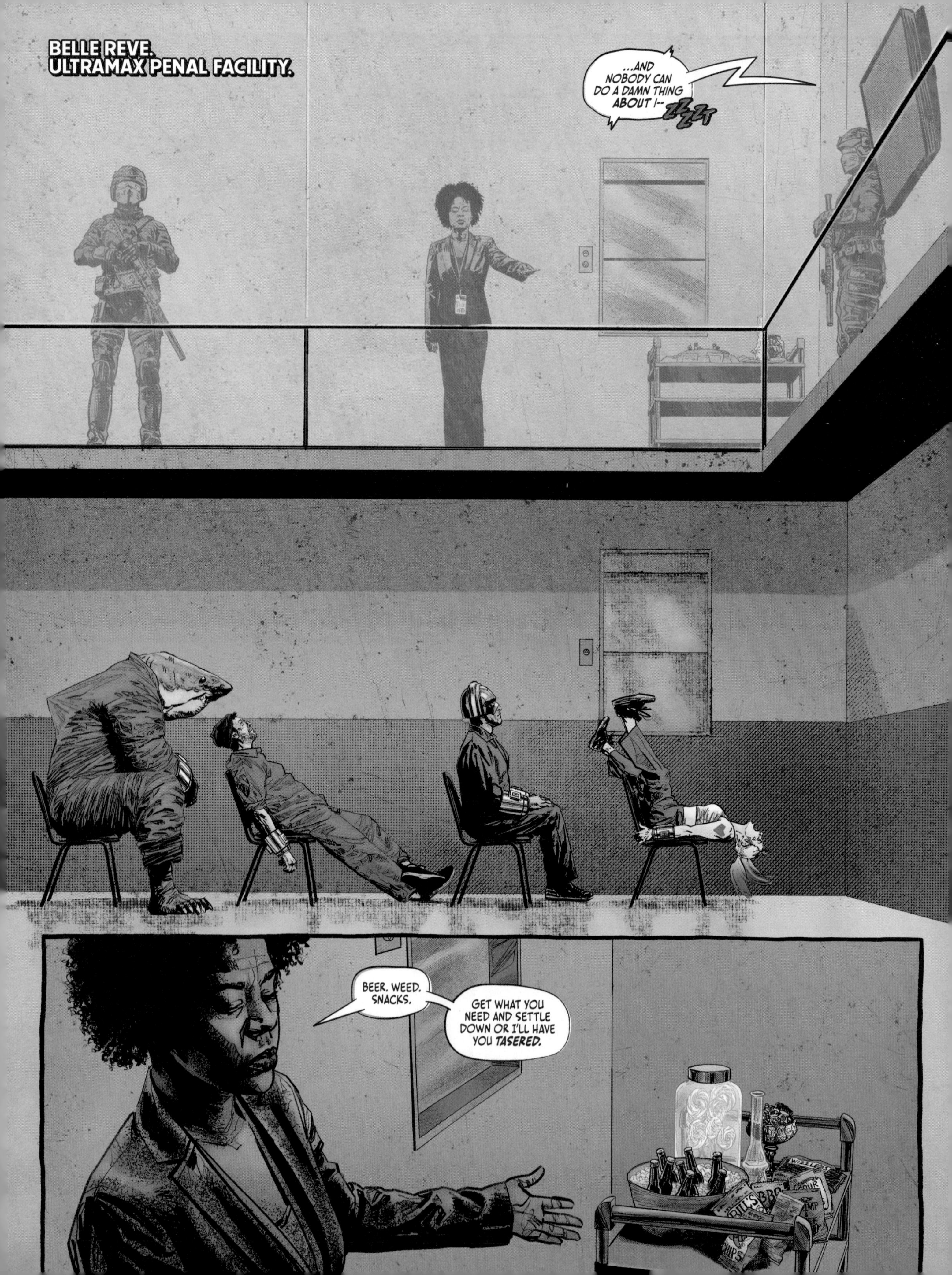
BELLE REVE.
ULTRAMAX PENAL FACILITY.
...AND NOBODY CAN DO A DAMN THING ABOUT I--
ZZZZT
BEER. WEED. SNACKS.
GET WHAT YOU NEED AND SETTLE DOWN OR I'LL HAVE YOU *TASERED.*

YOU'VE BEEN SELECTED FOR A SPECIAL TASK. I KNOW YOU'VE ALL SERVED ON *SUICIDE SQUADS* BEFORE, SO--

--SO YOU CAN SKIP THE *DETAILS,* BOSSLADY-- WE KNOW THE *SCORE.*

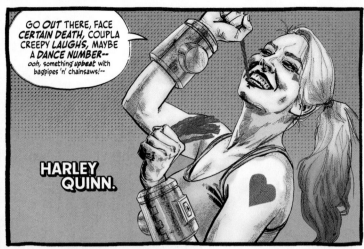

GO *OUT* THERE, FACE *CERTAIN DEATH,* COUPLA CREEPY *LAUGHS,* MAYBE A *DANCE NUMBER*-- *ooh, something upbeat* with bagpipes 'n' chainsaws!--

HARLEY QUINN.

--IN RETURN FOR WHICH STATE-SPONSORED *VIOLENCE* WE GAIN ACCESS TO CERTAIN *OFF-LIST* PRIVILEGES-- *chin-fuckin'-chin,* fellas--

--AND A BLOODY *MASSIVE* REDUCTION IN OUR SENTENCES.

CAPTAIN BOOMERANG.

I *don't* even *like* violence.

KING SHARK.

ONLY QUESTION IS, WHO D'YOU NEED US TO *SLAUGHTER* IN THE NAME OF *HARMONY* AND *PROGRESS?*

PEACEMAKER.

...

AS I WAS *ABOUT* TO SAY:

YOU'VE ALL SERVED ON SUICIDE SQUADS BEFORE, SO IT'S IMPORTANT YOU UNDERSTAND THIS IS *DIFFERENT.*

TODAY I AM *NOT* OFFERING YOU TIME OFF FOR GOOD BEHAVIOR.

TODAY I'M OFFERING *POWER.*

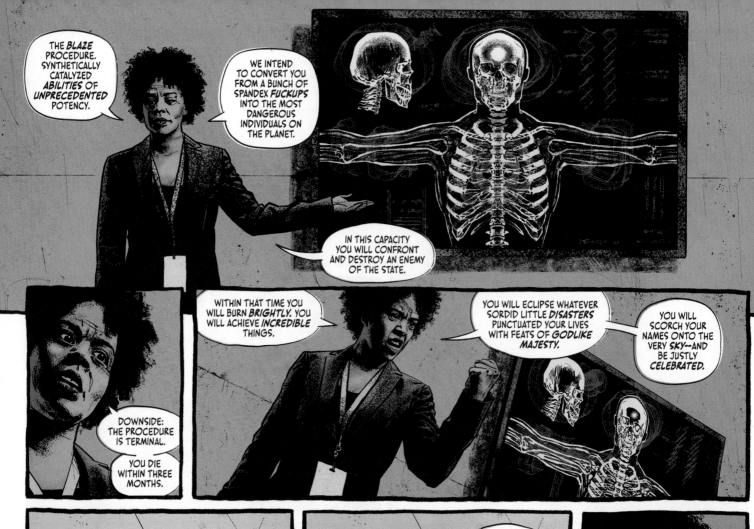

THE *BLAZE* PROCEDURE. SYNTHETICALLY CATALYZED *ABILITIES* OF *UNPRECEDENTED* POTENCY.

WE INTEND TO CONVERT YOU FROM A BUNCH OF SPANDEX *FUCKUPS* INTO THE MOST DANGEROUS INDIVIDUALS ON THE PLANET.

IN THIS CAPACITY YOU WILL CONFRONT AND DESTROY AN ENEMY OF THE STATE.

WITHIN THAT TIME YOU WILL BURN *BRIGHTLY.* YOU WILL ACHIEVE *INCREDIBLE* THINGS.

YOU WILL ECLIPSE WHATEVER SORDID LITTLE *DISASTERS* PUNCTUATED YOUR LIVES WITH FEATS OF *GODLIKE* MAJESTY.

YOU WILL SCORCH YOUR NAMES ONTO THE VERY *SKY*--AND BE JUSTLY *CELEBRATED.*

DOWNSIDE: THE PROCEDURE IS TERMINAL.

YOU DIE WITHIN THREE MONTHS.

YEAH, FUCK *THAT.*

I JUST WANNA CALL MY MOM. C-CAN I CALL MY MOM NOW?

NOT GONNA HAPPEN, LADY.

CLONK

FWEETIE, YOU'RE *CRAFEE*-- OO KNOW NAT?

PLAN B.

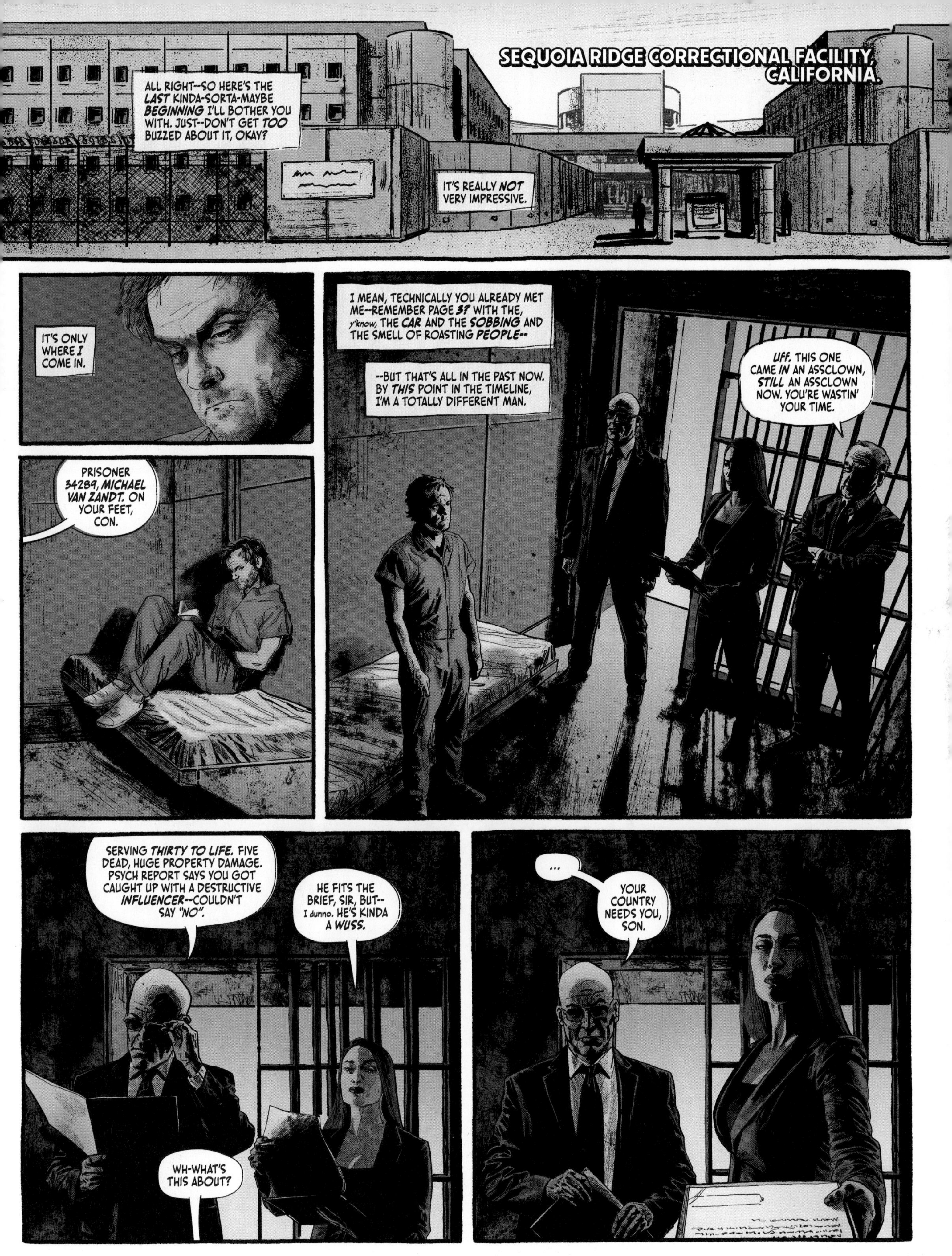
SEQUOIA RIDGE CORRECTIONAL FACILITY, CALIFORNIA.
ALL RIGHT--SO HERE'S THE LAST KINDA-SORTA-MAYBE BEGINNING I'LL BOTHER YOU WITH. JUST--DON'T GET TOO BUZZED ABOUT IT, OKAY?
IT'S REALLY NOT VERY IMPRESSIVE.
IT'S ONLY WHERE I COME IN.
PRISONER 34289, MICHAEL VAN ZANDT. ON YOUR FEET, CON.
I MEAN, TECHNICALLY YOU ALREADY MET ME--REMEMBER PAGE 3? WITH THE, y'know, THE CAR AND THE SOBBING AND THE SMELL OF ROASTING PEOPLE--
--BUT THAT'S ALL IN THE PAST NOW. BY THIS POINT IN THE TIMELINE, I'M A TOTALLY DIFFERENT MAN.
UFF. THIS ONE CAME IN AN ASSCLOWN, STILL AN ASSCLOWN NOW. YOU'RE WASTIN' YOUR TIME.
SERVING THIRTY TO LIFE. FIVE DEAD, HUGE PROPERTY DAMAGE. PSYCH REPORT SAYS YOU GOT CAUGHT UP WITH A DESTRUCTIVE INFLUENCER--COULDN'T SAY "NO".
HE FITS THE BRIEF, SIR, BUT-- I dunno. HE'S KINDA A WUSS.
WH-WHAT'S THIS ABOUT?
...
YOUR COUNTRY NEEDS YOU, SON.

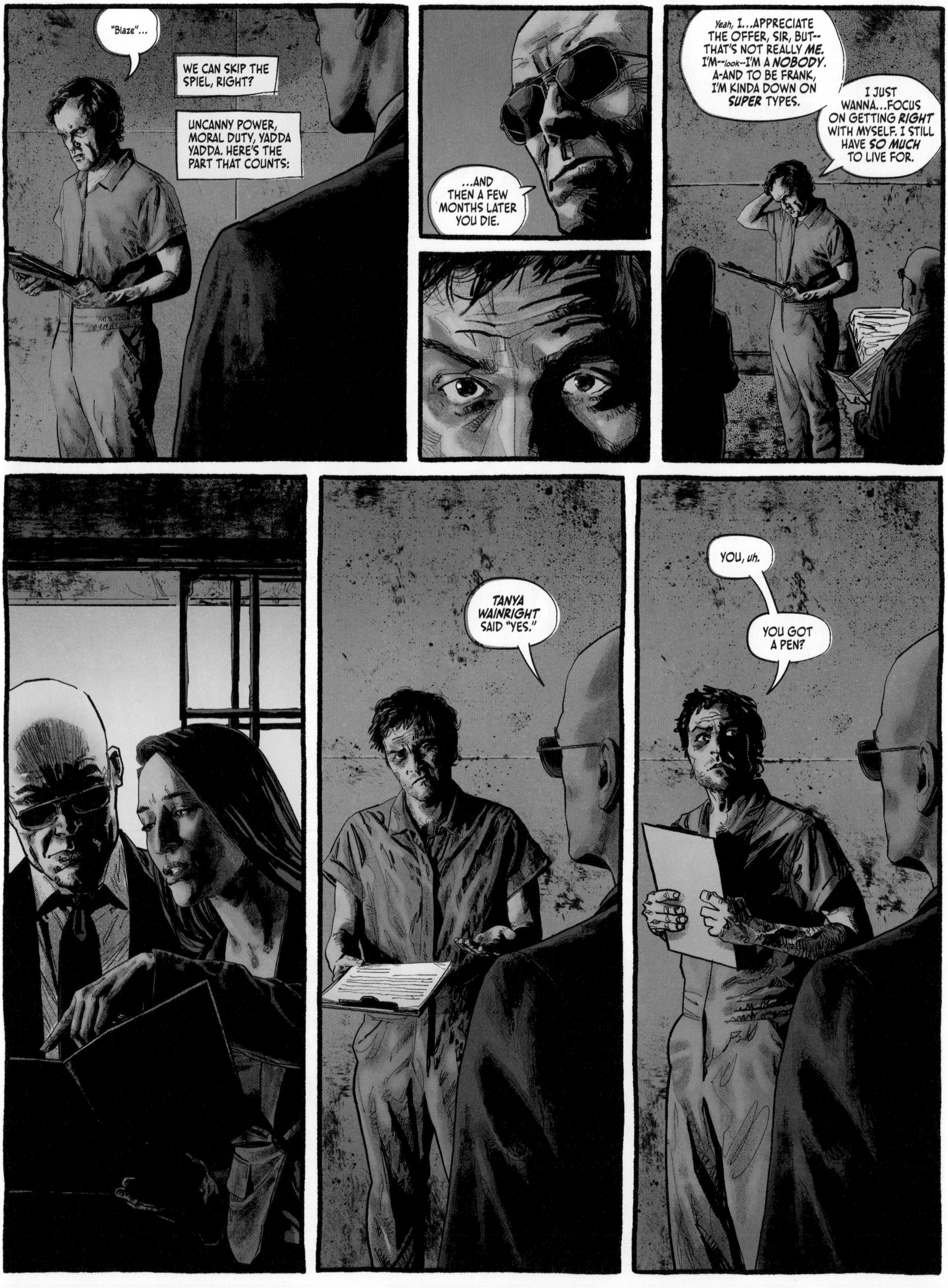
"Blaze"...
WE CAN SKIP THE SPIEL, RIGHT?
UNCANNY POWER, MORAL DUTY, YADDA YADDA. HERE'S THE PART THAT COUNTS:
...AND THEN A FEW MONTHS LATER YOU DIE.
Yeah, I...APPRECIATE THE OFFER, SIR, BUT--THAT'S NOT REALLY ME. I'M--look--I'M A NOBODY. A-AND TO BE FRANK, I'M KINDA DOWN ON SUPER TYPES.
I JUST WANNA...FOCUS ON GETTING RIGHT WITH MYSELF. I STILL HAVE SO MUCH TO LIVE FOR.
TANYA WAINRIGHT SAID "YES."
YOU, uh.
YOU GOT A PEN?

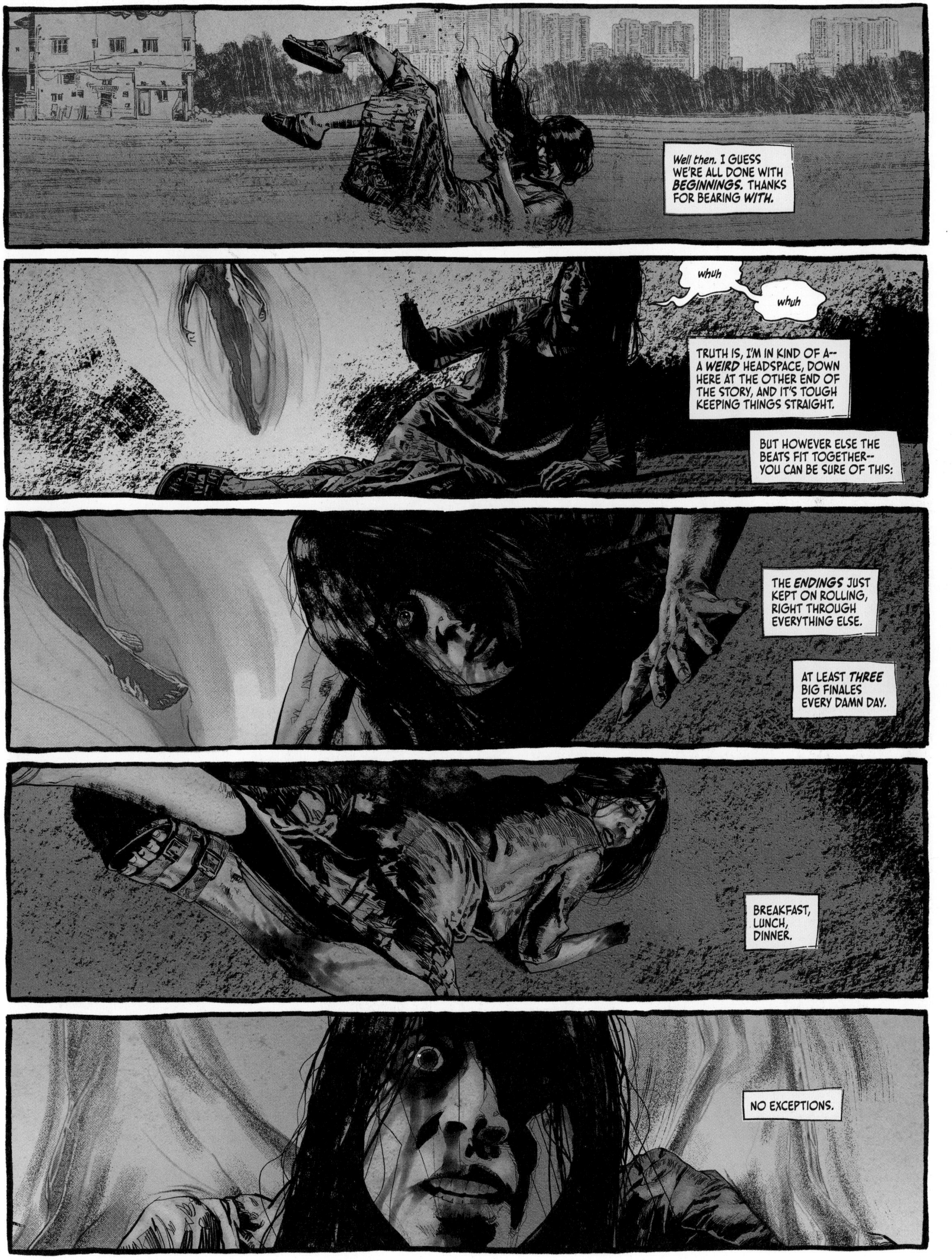
Well then. I GUESS WE'RE ALL DONE WITH BEGINNINGS. THANKS FOR BEARING WITH.
whuh
whuh
TRUTH IS, I'M IN KIND OF A-- A WEIRD HEADSPACE, DOWN HERE AT THE OTHER END OF THE STORY, AND IT'S TOUGH KEEPING THINGS STRAIGHT.
BUT HOWEVER ELSE THE BEATS FIT TOGETHER-- YOU CAN BE SURE OF THIS:
THE ENDINGS JUST KEPT ON ROLLING, RIGHT THROUGH EVERYTHING ELSE.
AT LEAST THREE BIG FINALES EVERY DAMN DAY.
BREAKFAST, LUNCH, DINNER.
NO EXCEPTIONS.

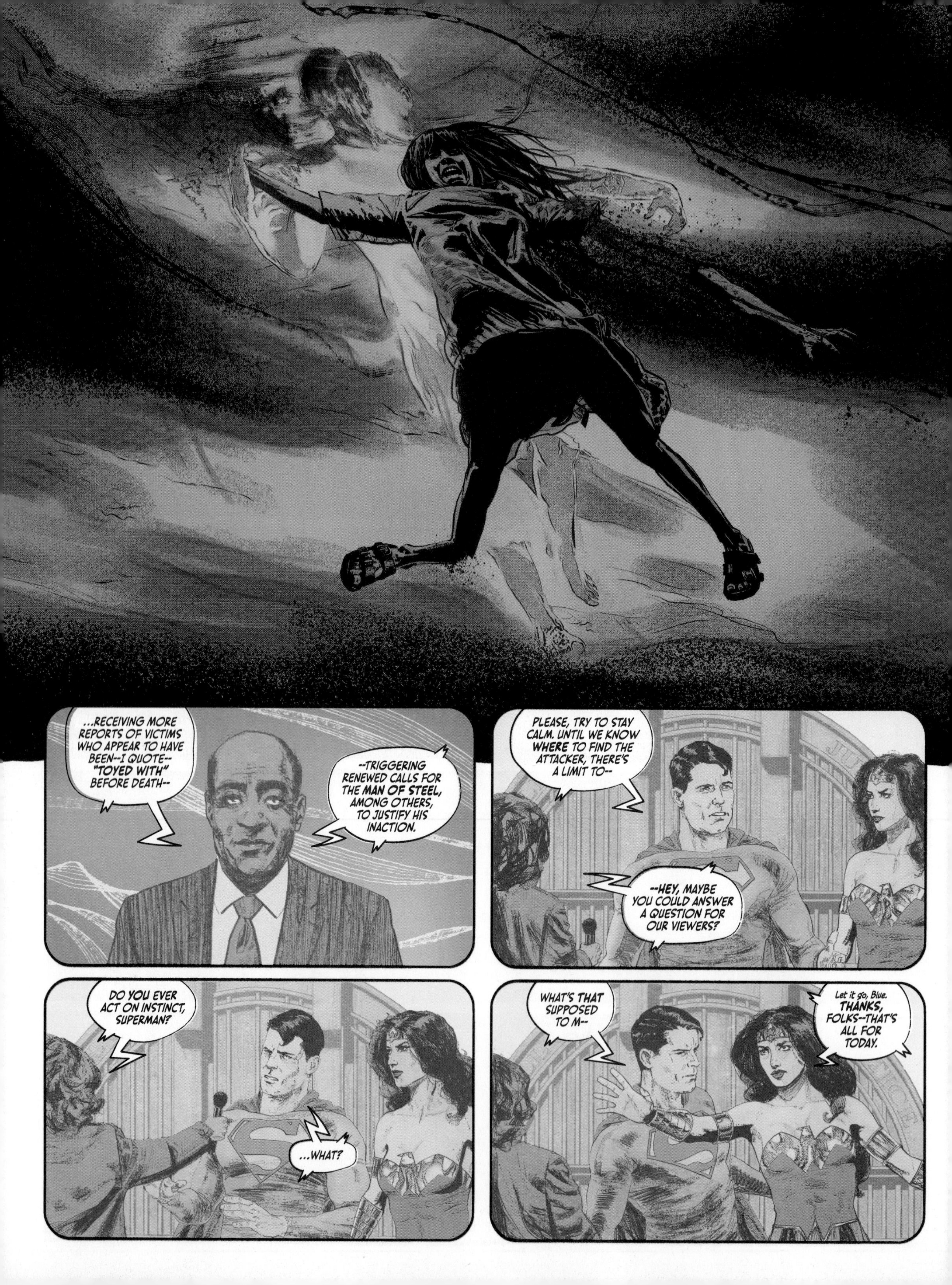
...RECEIVING MORE REPORTS OF VICTIMS WHO APPEAR TO HAVE BEEN--I QUOTE--"TOYED WITH" BEFORE DEATH--
--TRIGGERING RENEWED CALLS FOR THE MAN OF STEEL, AMONG OTHERS, TO JUSTIFY HIS INACTION.
PLEASE, TRY TO STAY CALM. UNTIL WE KNOW WHERE TO FIND THE ATTACKER, THERE'S A LIMIT TO--
--HEY, MAYBE YOU COULD ANSWER A QUESTION FOR OUR VIEWERS?
DO YOU EVER ACT ON INSTINCT, SUPERMAN?
...WHAT?
WHAT'S THAT SUPPOSED TO M--
Let it go, Blue. THANKS, FOLKS--THAT'S ALL FOR TODAY.

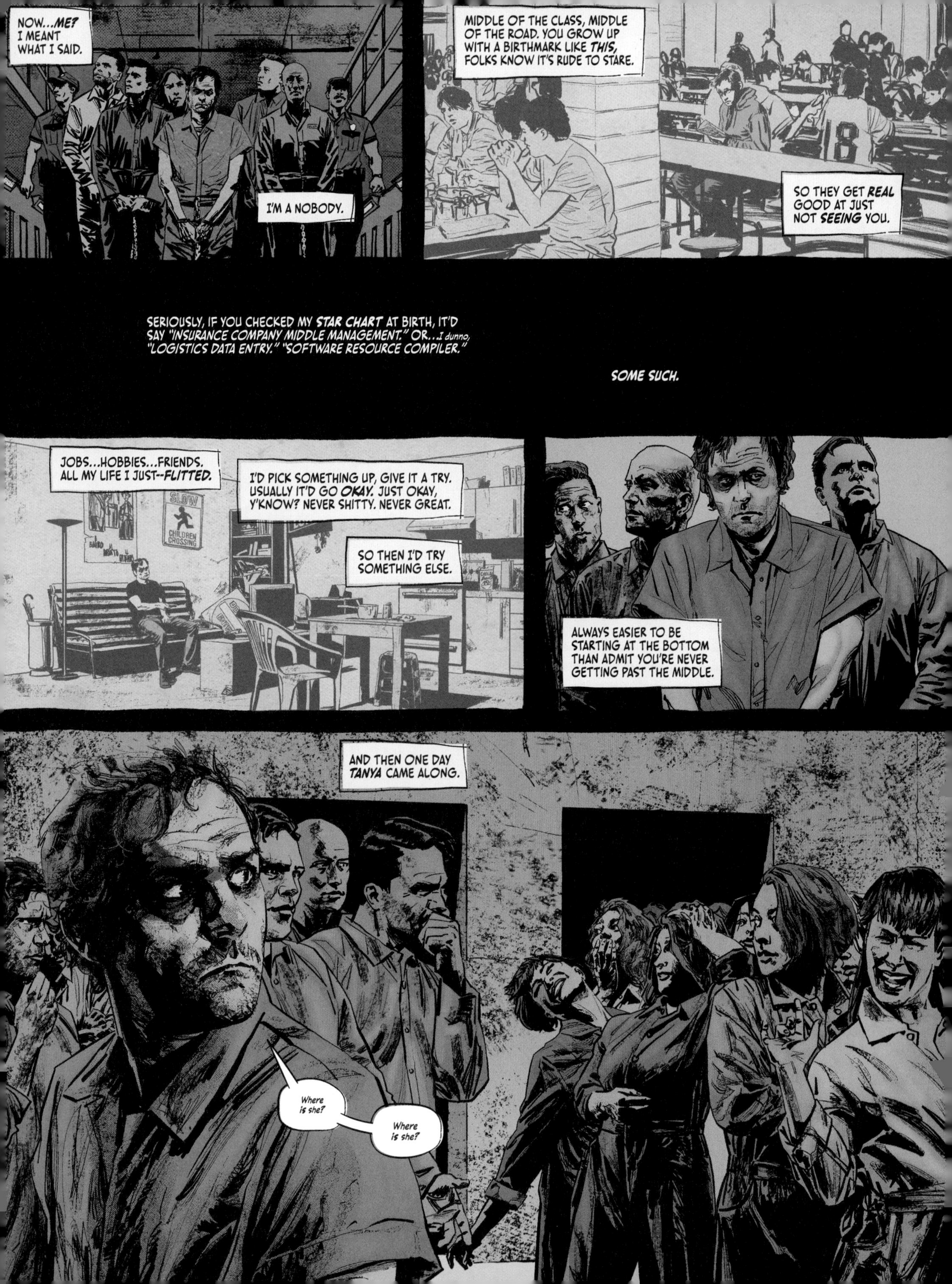
NOW...ME? I MEANT WHAT I SAID.
I'M A NOBODY.
MIDDLE OF THE CLASS, MIDDLE OF THE ROAD. YOU GROW UP WITH A BIRTHMARK LIKE THIS, FOLKS KNOW IT'S RUDE TO STARE.
SO THEY GET REAL GOOD AT JUST NOT SEEING YOU.
SERIOUSLY, IF YOU CHECKED MY STAR CHART AT BIRTH, IT'D SAY "INSURANCE COMPANY MIDDLE MANAGEMENT." OR...I dunno, "LOGISTICS DATA ENTRY." "SOFTWARE RESOURCE COMPILER."
SOME SUCH.
JOBS...HOBBIES...FRIENDS. ALL MY LIFE I JUST--FLITTED.
I'D PICK SOMETHING UP, GIVE IT A TRY. USUALLY IT'D GO OKAY. JUST OKAY, Y'KNOW? NEVER SHITTY. NEVER GREAT.
SO THEN I'D TRY SOMETHING ELSE.
SLOW
CHILDREN CROSSING
ALWAYS EASIER TO BE STARTING AT THE BOTTOM THAN ADMIT YOU'RE NEVER GETTING PAST THE MIDDLE.
AND THEN ONE DAY TANYA CAME ALONG.
Where is she?
Where is she?

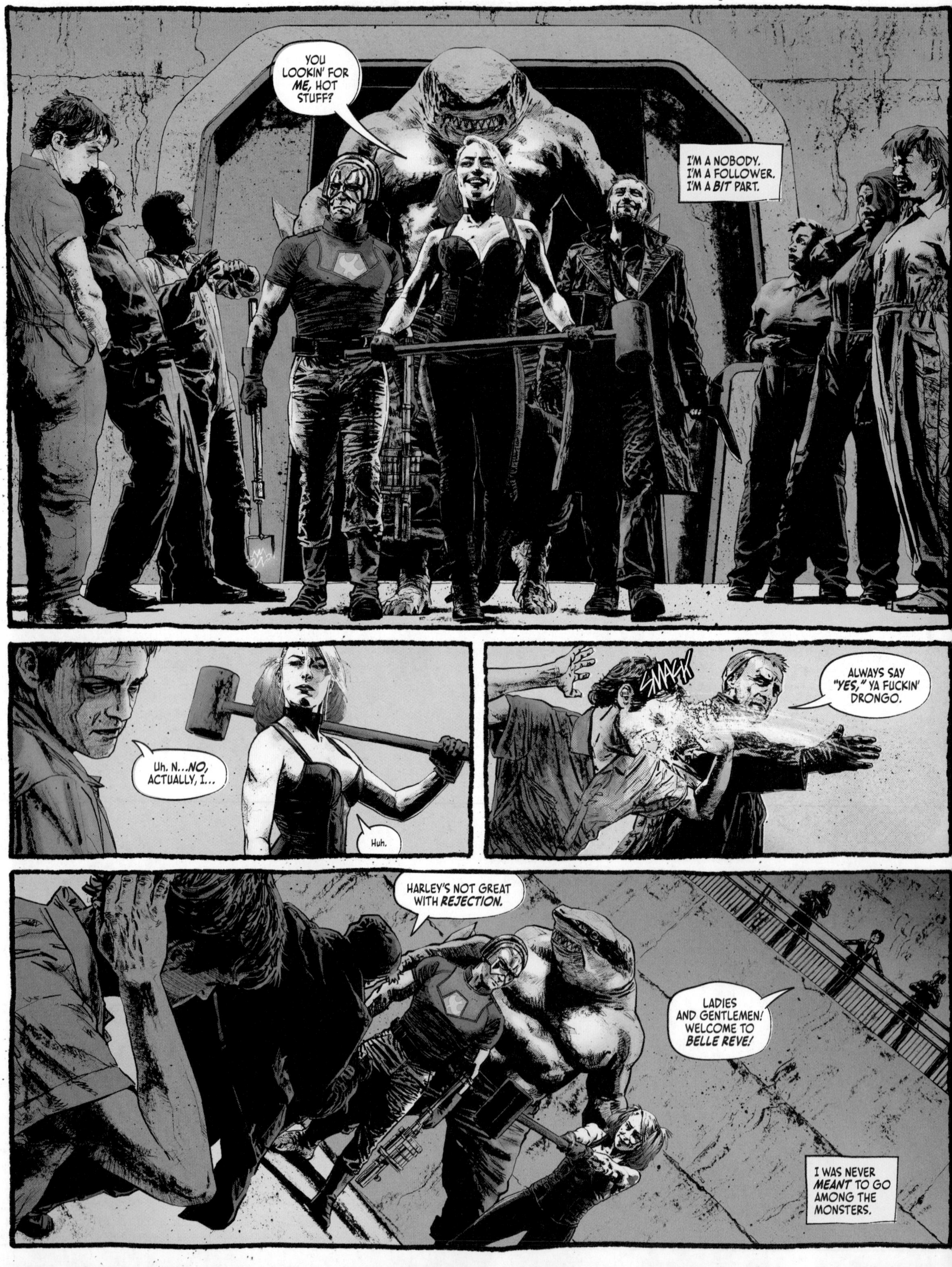
YOU LOOKIN' FOR ME, HOT STUFF?
I'M A NOBODY. I'M A FOLLOWER. I'M A BIT PART.
Uh. N...NO, ACTUALLY, I...
Huh.
SMACK
ALWAYS SAY "YES," YA FUCKIN' DRONGO.
HARLEY'S NOT GREAT WITH REJECTION.
LADIES AND GENTLEMEN! WELCOME TO BELLE REVE!
I WAS NEVER MEANT TO GO AMONG THE MONSTERS.

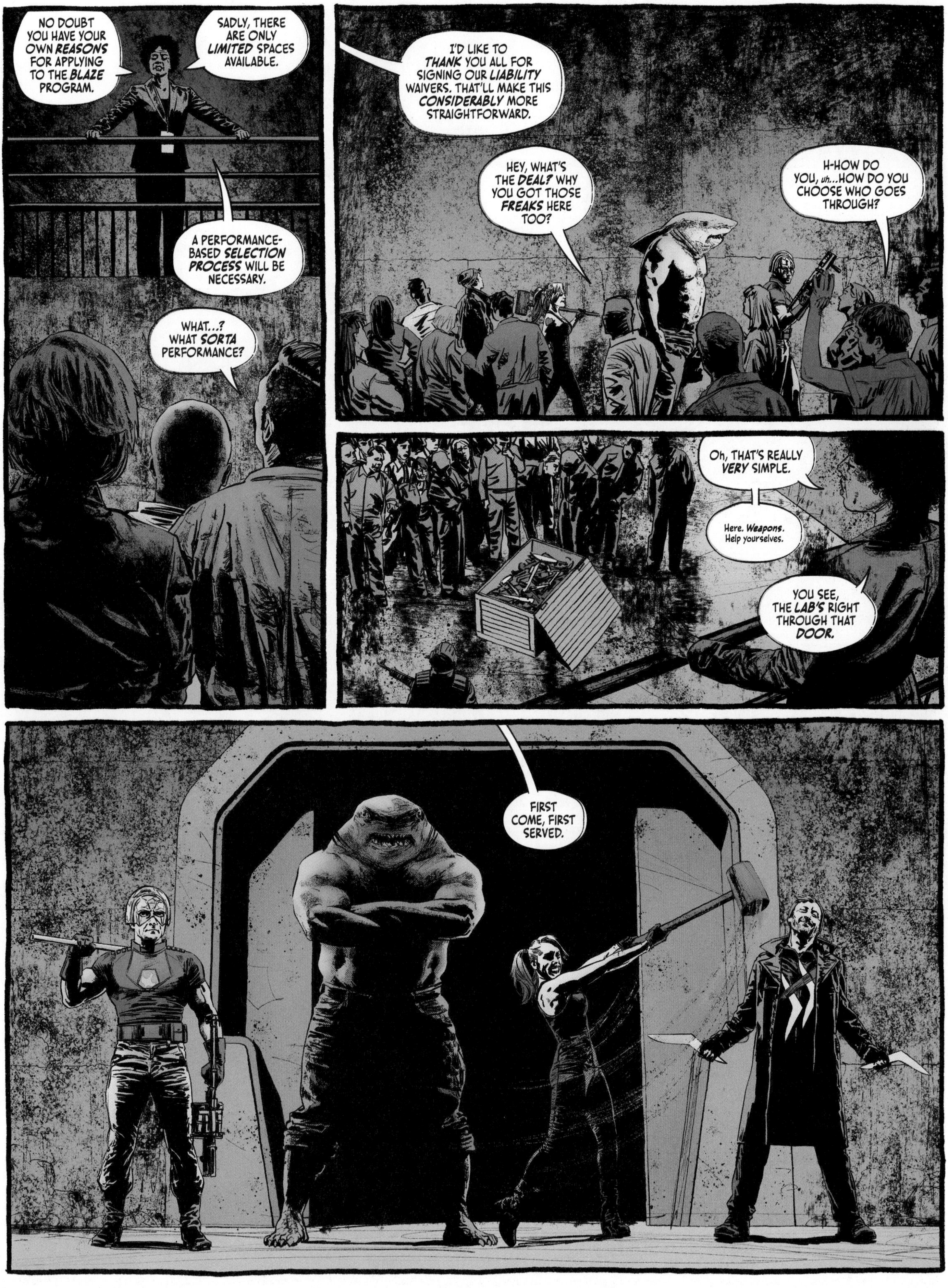
NO DOUBT YOU HAVE YOUR OWN REASONS FOR APPLYING TO THE BLAZE PROGRAM.
SADLY, THERE ARE ONLY LIMITED SPACES AVAILABLE.
A PERFORMANCE-BASED SELECTION PROCESS WILL BE NECESSARY.
WHAT...? WHAT SORTA PERFORMANCE?
I'D LIKE TO THANK YOU ALL FOR SIGNING OUR LIABILITY WAIVERS. THAT'LL MAKE THIS CONSIDERABLY MORE STRAIGHTFORWARD.
HEY, WHAT'S THE DEAL? WHY YOU GOT THOSE FREAKS HERE TOO?
H-HOW DO YOU, uh...HOW DO YOU CHOOSE WHO GOES THROUGH?
Oh, THAT'S REALLY VERY SIMPLE.
Here. Weapons. Help yourselves.
YOU SEE, THE LAB'S RIGHT THROUGH THAT DOOR.
FIRST COME, FIRST SERVED.

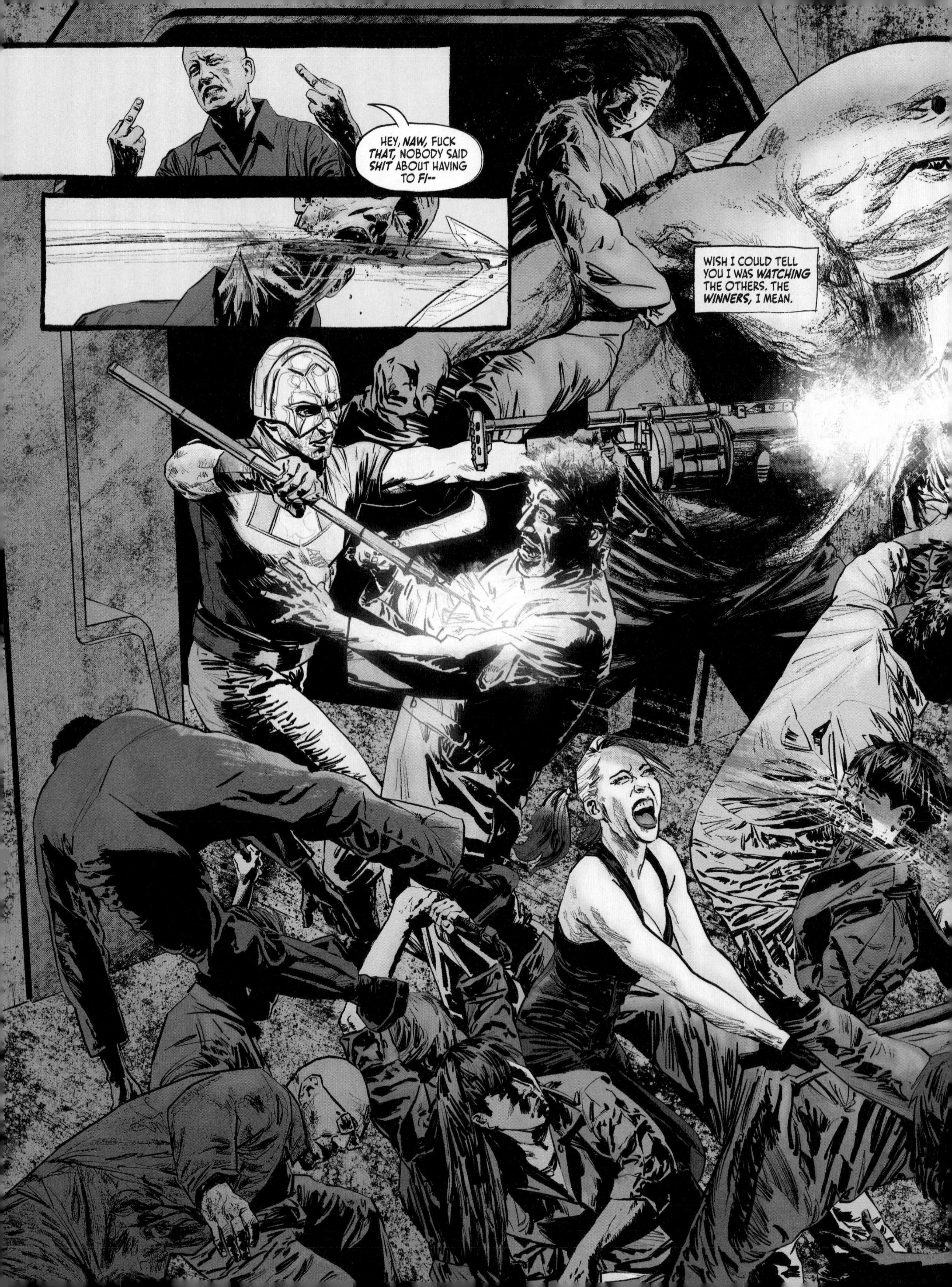
HEY, NAW, FUCK THAT, NOBODY SAID SHIT ABOUT HAVING TO FI--
WISH I COULD TELL YOU I WAS WATCHING THE OTHERS. THE WINNERS, I MEAN.

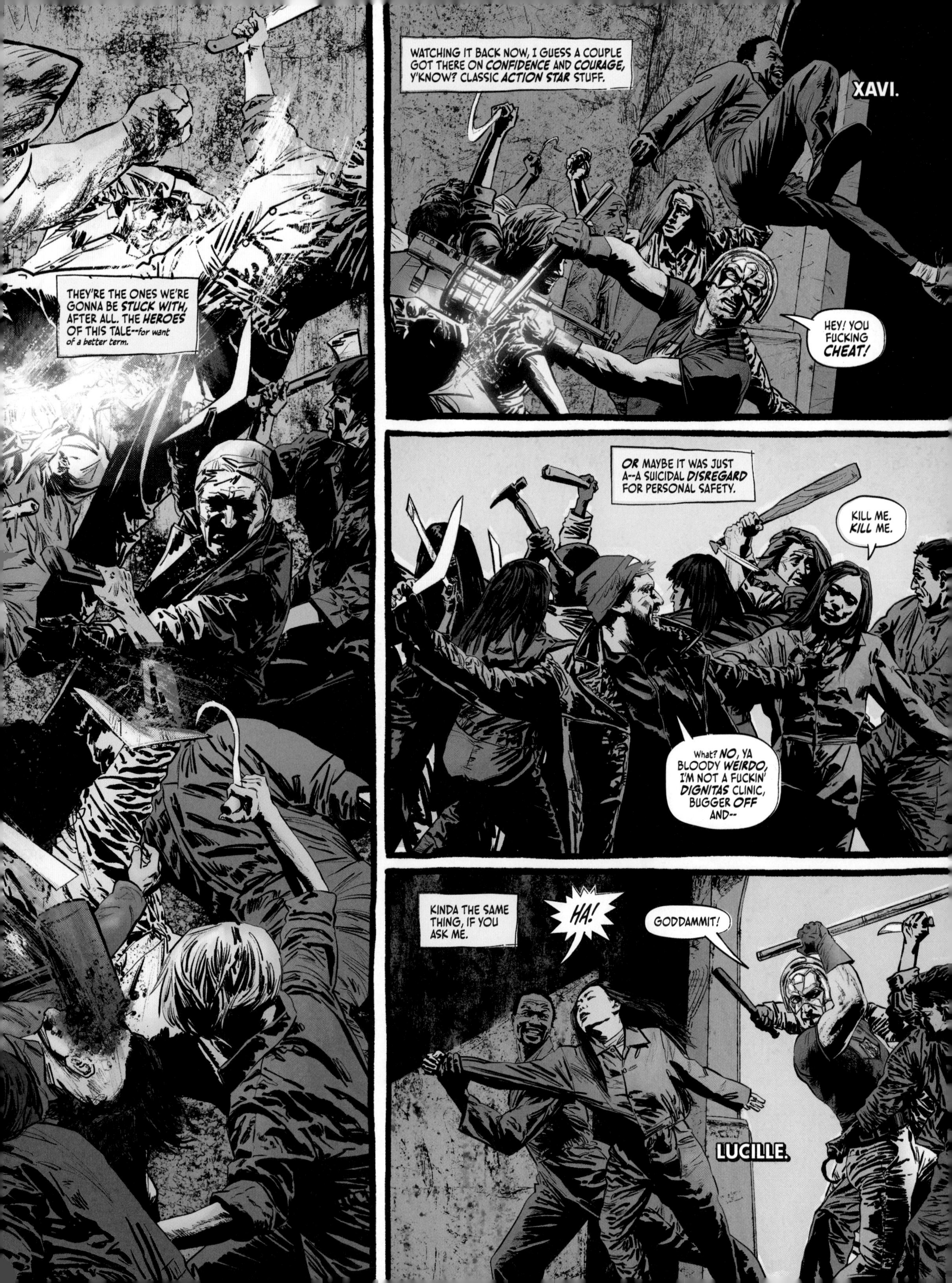
THEY'RE THE ONES WE'RE GONNA BE STUCK WITH, AFTER ALL. THE HEROES OF THIS TALE--for want of a better term.
WATCHING IT BACK NOW, I GUESS A COUPLE GOT THERE ON CONFIDENCE AND COURAGE, Y'KNOW? CLASSIC ACTION STAR STUFF.
XAVI.
HEY! YOU FUCKING CHEAT!
OR MAYBE IT WAS JUST A--A SUICIDAL DISREGARD FOR PERSONAL SAFETY.
KILL ME. KILL ME.
What? NO, YA BLOODY WEIRDO, I'M NOT A FUCKIN' DIGNITAS CLINIC, BUGGER OFF AND--
KINDA THE SAME THING, IF YOU ASK ME.
HA!
GODDAMMIT!
LUCILLE.

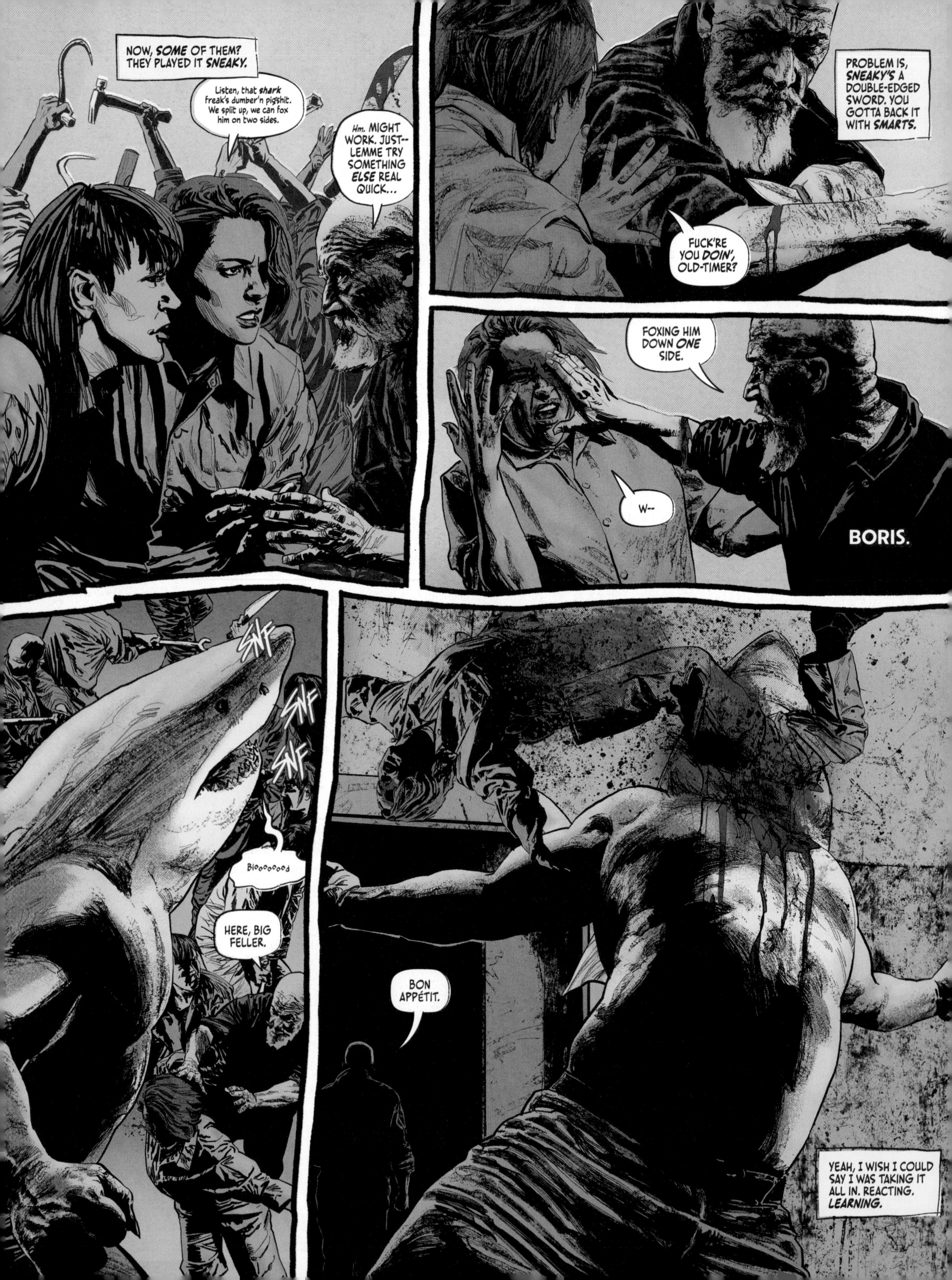
NOW, *SOME* OF THEM? THEY PLAYED IT *SNEAKY.*
Listen, that *shark* freak's dumber'n pigshit. We split up, we can fox him on two sides.
Hm. MIGHT WORK. JUST-- LEMME TRY SOMETHING *ELSE* REAL QUICK...
PROBLEM IS, *SNEAKY'S* A DOUBLE-EDGED SWORD. YOU GOTTA BACK IT WITH *SMARTS.*
FUCK'RE YOU *DOIN'*, OLD-TIMER?
FOXING HIM DOWN *ONE* SIDE.
W--
BORIS.
SNF
SNF
SNF
Blooooood
HERE, BIG FELLER.
BON APPÉTIT.
YEAH, I WISH I COULD SAY I WAS TAKING IT ALL IN. REACTING. *LEARNING.*

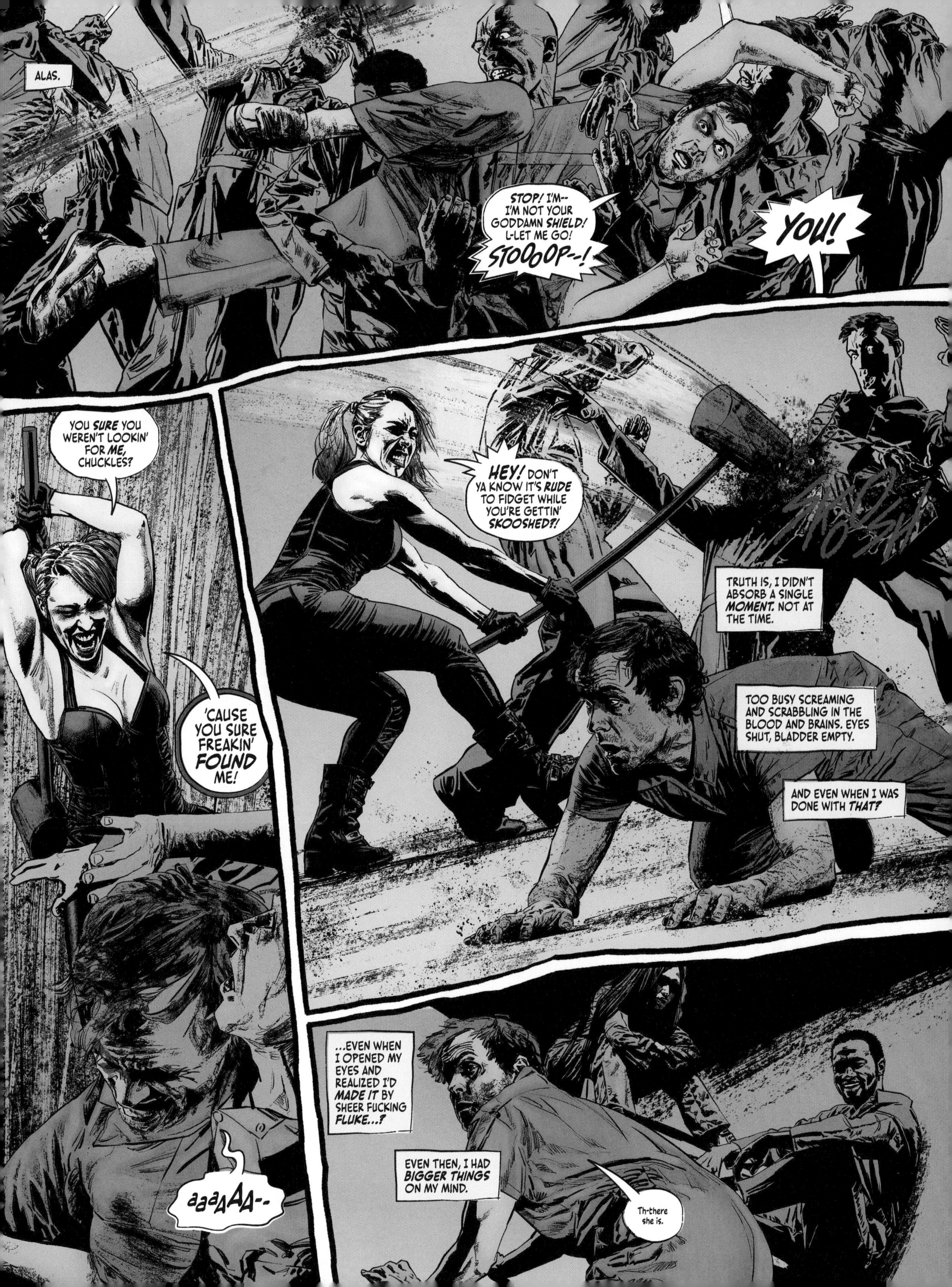

ALAS.
STOP! I'M-- I'M NOT YOUR GODDAMN SHIELD! L-LET ME GO! STOOOOP--!
YOU!
YOU SURE YOU WEREN'T LOOKIN' FOR ME, CHUCKLES?
'CAUSE YOU SURE FREAKIN' FOUND ME!
aaaAAA--
HEY! DON'T YA KNOW IT'S RUDE TO FIDGET WHILE YOU'RE GETTIN' SKOOSHED?!
TRUTH IS, I DIDN'T ABSORB A SINGLE MOMENT. NOT AT THE TIME.
TOO BUSY SCREAMING AND SCRABBLING IN THE BLOOD AND BRAINS. EYES SHUT, BLADDER EMPTY.
AND EVEN WHEN I WAS DONE WITH THAT?
...EVEN WHEN I OPENED MY EYES AND REALIZED I'D MADE IT BY SHEER FUCKING FLUKE...?
EVEN THEN, I HAD BIGGER THINGS ON MY MIND.
Th-there she is.

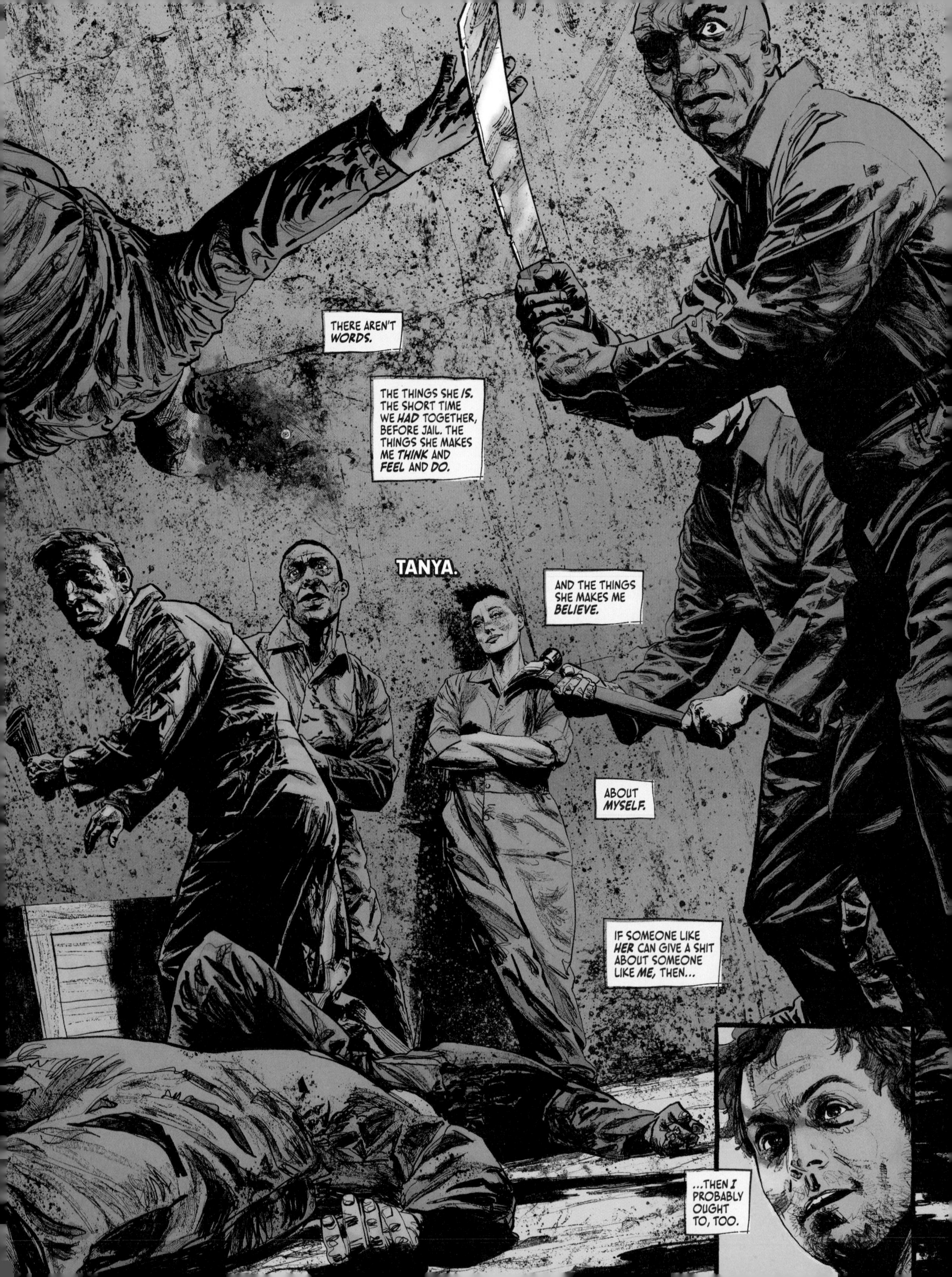
THERE AREN'T WORDS.
THE THINGS SHE IS. THE SHORT TIME WE HAD TOGETHER, BEFORE JAIL. THE THINGS SHE MAKES ME THINK AND FEEL AND DO.
TANYA.
AND THE THINGS SHE MAKES ME BELIEVE.
ABOUT MYSELF.
IF SOMEONE LIKE HER CAN GIVE A SHIT ABOUT SOMEONE LIKE ME, THEN...
...THEN I PROBABLY OUGHT TO, TOO.

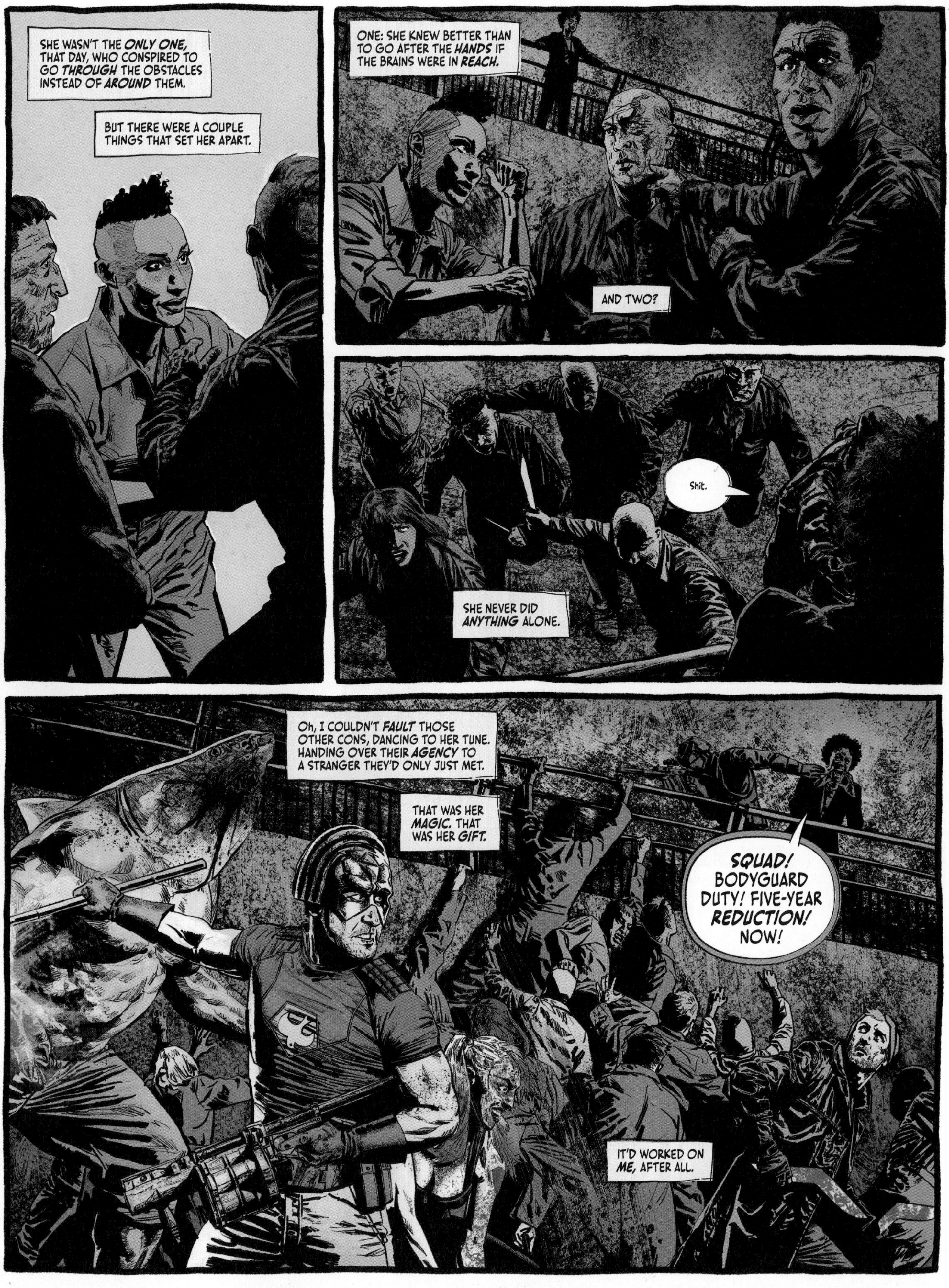

SHE WASN'T THE *ONLY ONE,* THAT DAY, WHO CONSPIRED TO GO *THROUGH* THE OBSTACLES INSTEAD OF *AROUND* THEM.
BUT THERE WERE A COUPLE THINGS THAT SET HER APART.
ONE: SHE KNEW BETTER THAN TO GO AFTER THE *HANDS* IF THE BRAINS WERE IN *REACH.*
AND TWO?
Shit.
SHE NEVER DID *ANYTHING* ALONE.
Oh, I COULDN'T *FAULT* THOSE OTHER CONS, DANCING TO HER TUNE. HANDING OVER THEIR *AGENCY* TO A STRANGER THEY'D ONLY JUST MET.
THAT WAS HER *MAGIC.* THAT WAS HER *GIFT.*
SQUAD! BODYGUARD DUTY! FIVE-YEAR *REDUCTION!* NOW!
IT'D WORKED ON *ME,* AFTER ALL.

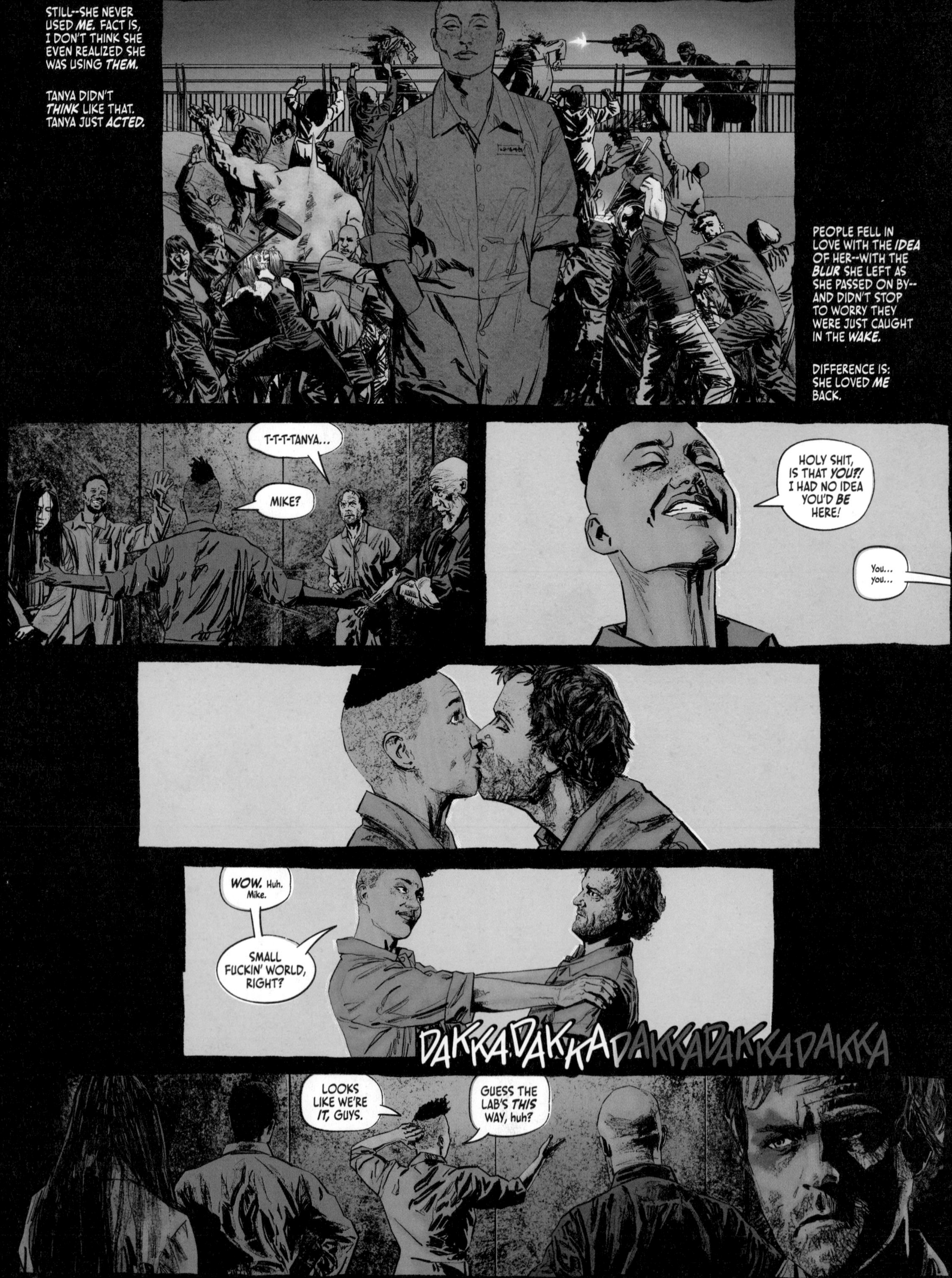
STILL--SHE NEVER USED ME. FACT IS, I DON'T THINK SHE EVEN REALIZED SHE WAS USING THEM.
TANYA DIDN'T THINK LIKE THAT. TANYA JUST ACTED.
PEOPLE FELL IN LOVE WITH THE IDEA OF HER--WITH THE BLUR SHE LEFT AS SHE PASSED ON BY--AND DIDN'T STOP TO WORRY THEY WERE JUST CAUGHT IN THE WAKE.
DIFFERENCE IS: SHE LOVED ME BACK.
T-T-T-TANYA...
MIKE?
HOLY SHIT, IS THAT YOU?! I HAD NO IDEA YOU'D BE HERE!
You... you...
WOW. Huh. Mike.
SMALL FUCKIN' WORLD, RIGHT?
DAKKADAKKADAKKADAKKADAKKA
LOOKS LIKE WE'RE IT, GUYS.
GUESS THE LAB'S THIS WAY, huh?

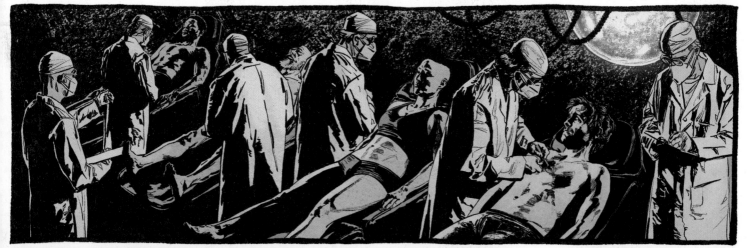

Nnf. *UH.* HEY. WHAT, uh. WHAT KIND OF...y'know...

SUPERPOWER?

YEAH. WH-WHAT WILL WE *GET?*

LITTLE LATE TO START WONDERING *NOW, eh,* AMIGO?

IT DOESN'T MATTER.

I'M AFRAID THERE'S NO GOOD ANSWER TO THAT QUESTION ANYWAY.

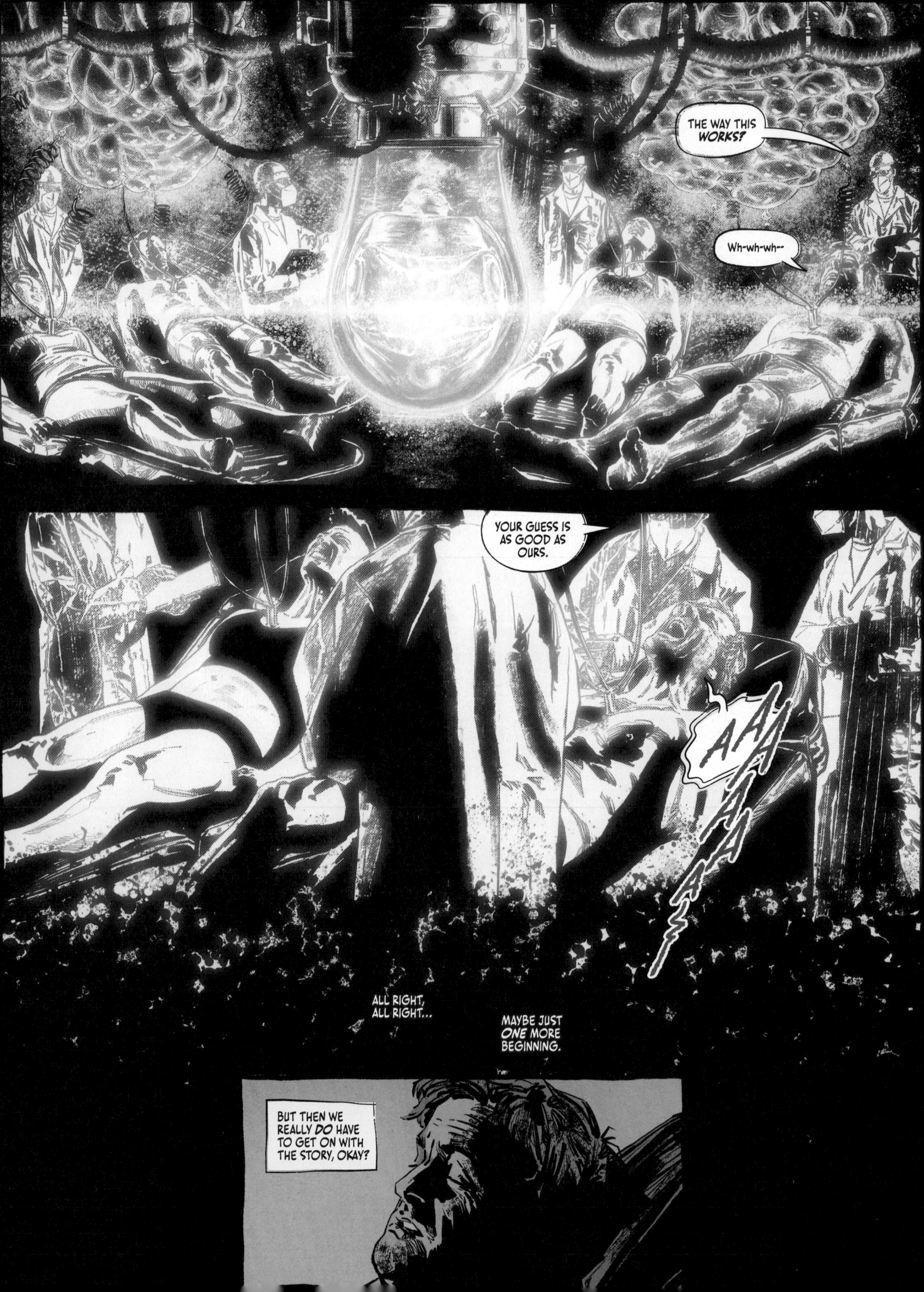
THE WAY THIS WORKS?
Wh-wh-wh--
YOUR GUESS IS AS GOOD AS OURS.
AAAAAAAAAAA!
ALL RIGHT, ALL RIGHT...
MAYBE JUST ONE MORE BEGINNING.
BUT THEN WE REALLY DO HAVE TO GET ON WITH THE STORY, OKAY?

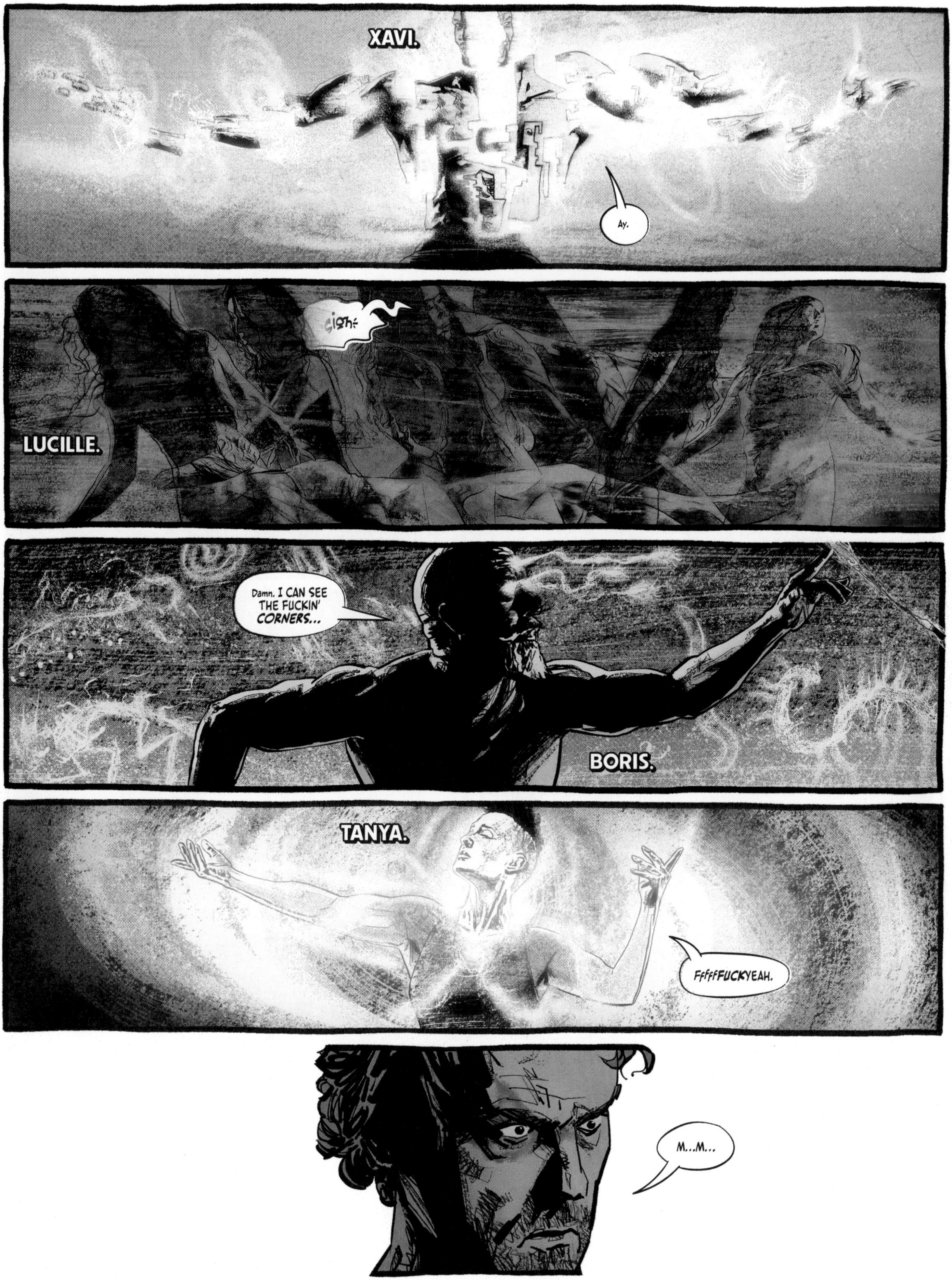
XAVI.
Ay.
sigh
LUCILLE.
Damn. I CAN SEE THE FUCKIN' CORNERS...
BORIS.
TANYA.
FfffFUCKYEAH.
M...M...

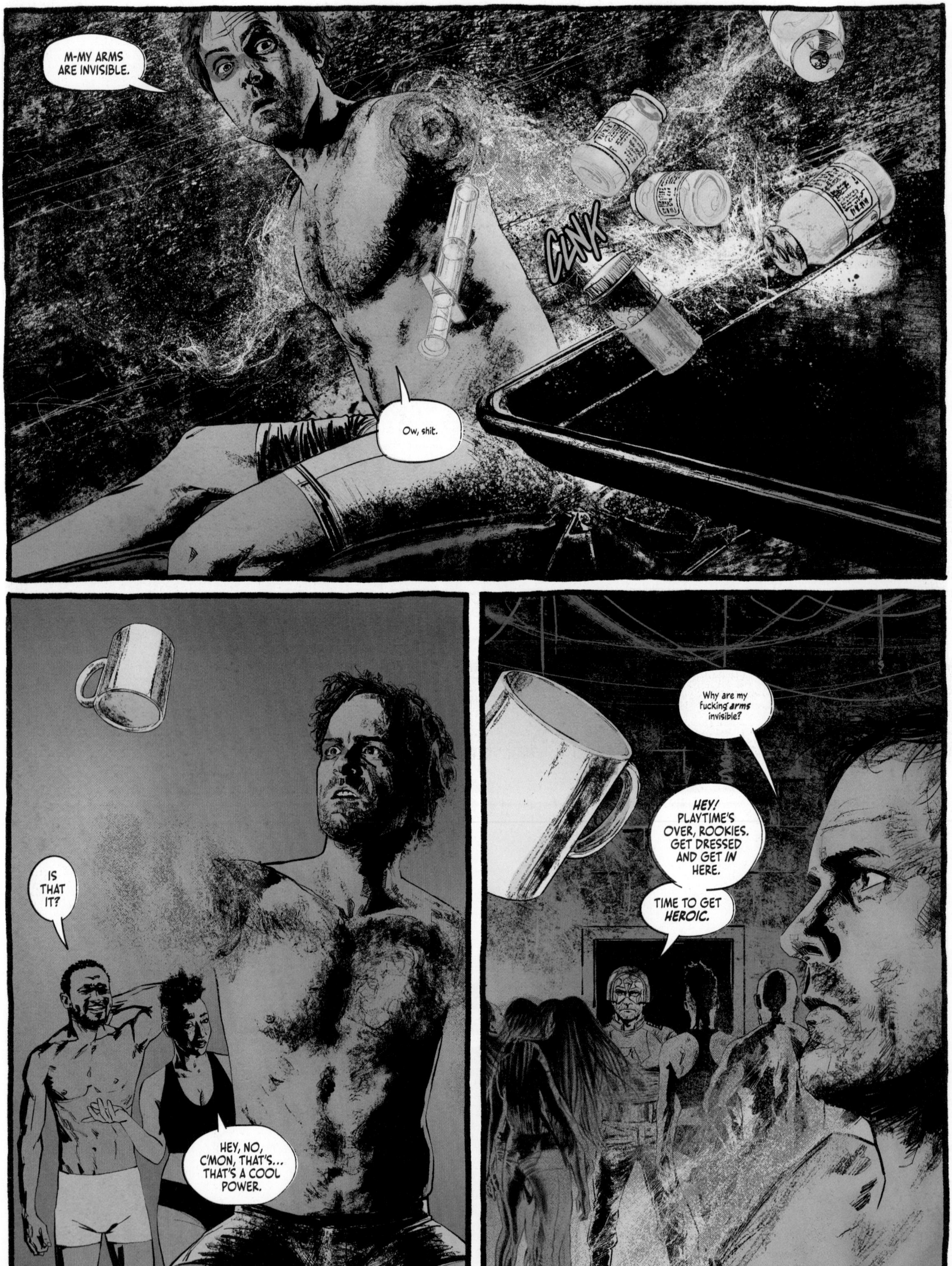
M-MY ARMS ARE INVISIBLE.
CLNK
Ow, shit.
IS THAT IT?
HEY, NO, C'MON, THAT'S... THAT'S A COOL POWER.
Why are my fucking *arms* invisible?
HEY! PLAYTIME'S OVER, ROOKIES. GET DRESSED AND GET *IN* HERE.
TIME TO GET *HEROIC.*

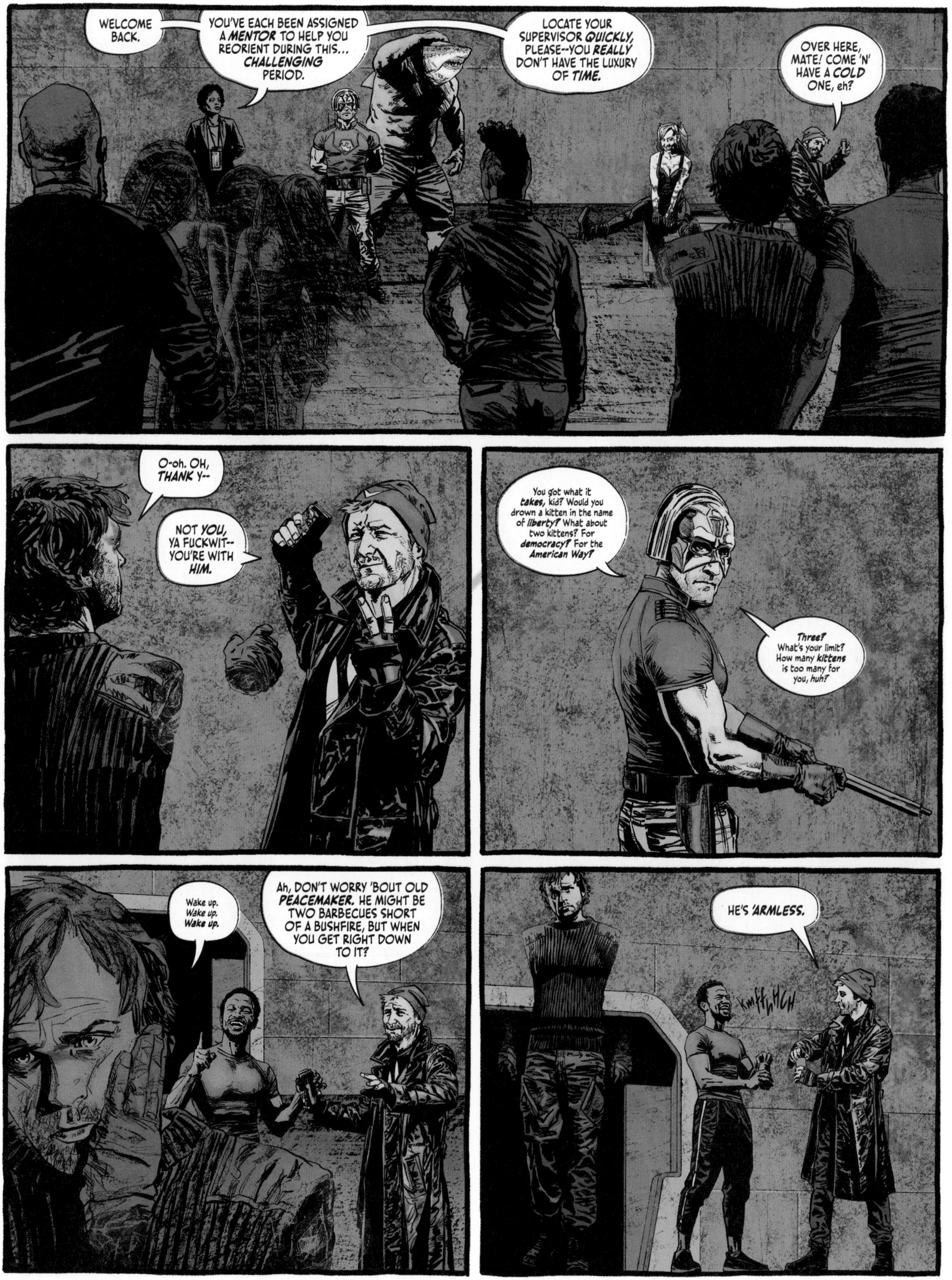
WELCOME BACK.
YOU'VE EACH BEEN ASSIGNED A MENTOR TO HELP YOU REORIENT DURING THIS... CHALLENGING PERIOD.
LOCATE YOUR SUPERVISOR QUICKLY, PLEASE--YOU REALLY DON'T HAVE THE LUXURY OF TIME.
OVER HERE, MATE! COME 'N' HAVE A COLD ONE, eh?
O-oh. OH, THANK Y--
NOT YOU, YA FUCKWIT-- YOU'RE WITH HIM.
You got what it takes, kid? Would you drown a kitten in the name of liberty? What about two kittens? For democracy? For the American Way?
Three? What's your limit? How many kittens is too many for you, huh?
Wake up. Wake up. Wake up.
Ah, DON'T WORRY 'BOUT OLD PEACEMAKER. HE MIGHT BE TWO BARBECUES SHORT OF A BUSHFIRE, BUT WHEN YOU GET RIGHT DOWN TO IT?
HE'S 'ARMLESS.
KMFFLHCH

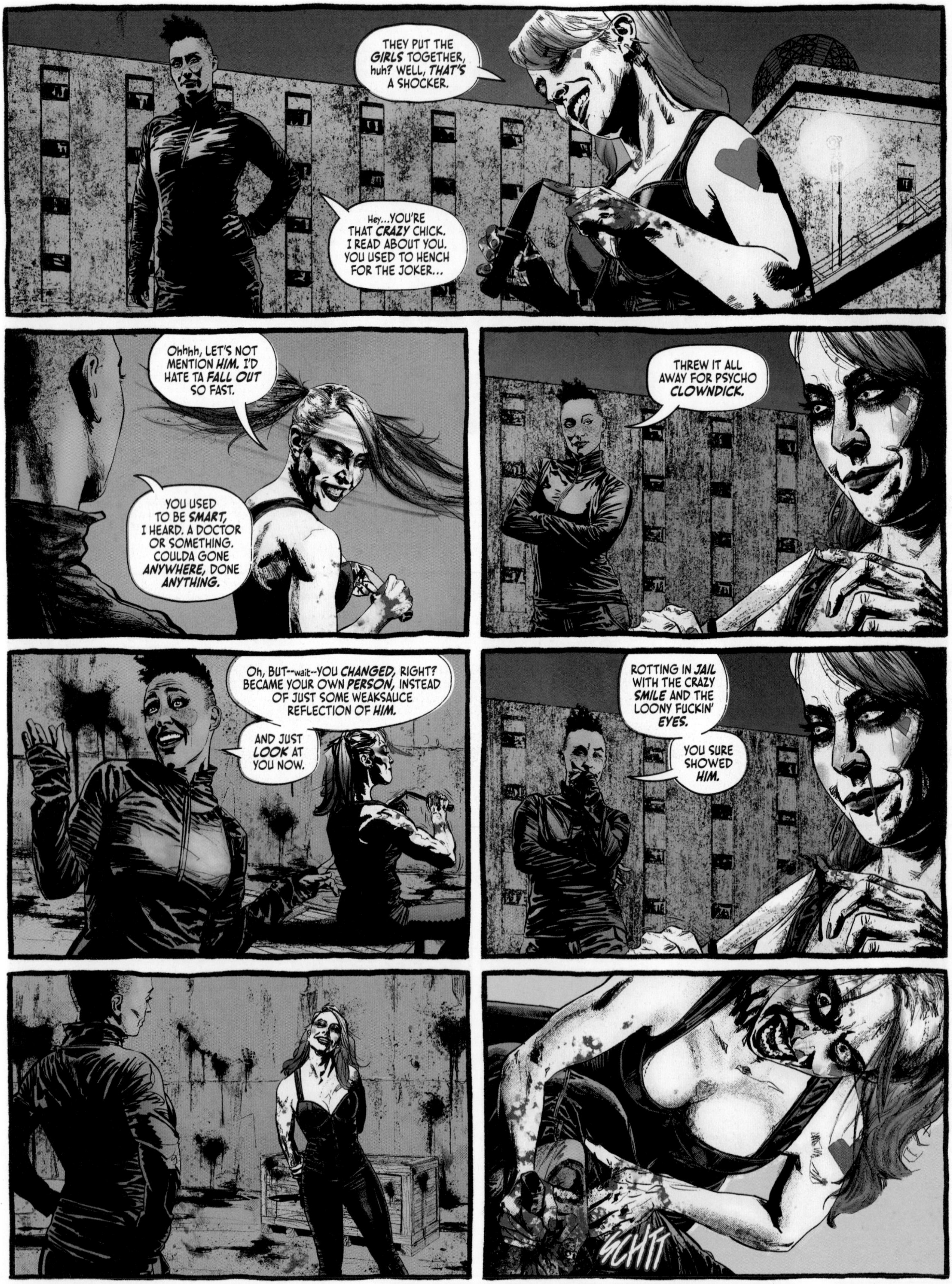
THEY PUT THE GIRLS TOGETHER, huh? WELL, THAT'S A SHOCKER.
Hey...YOU'RE THAT CRAZY CHICK. I READ ABOUT YOU. YOU USED TO HENCH FOR THE JOKER...
Ohhhh, LET'S NOT MENTION HIM. I'D HATE TA FALL OUT SO FAST.
YOU USED TO BE SMART, I HEARD. A DOCTOR OR SOMETHING. COULDA GONE ANYWHERE, DONE ANYTHING.
THREW IT ALL AWAY FOR PSYCHO CLOWNDICK.
Oh, BUT--wait--YOU CHANGED, RIGHT? BECAME YOUR OWN PERSON, INSTEAD OF JUST SOME WEAKSAUCE REFLECTION OF HIM.
AND JUST LOOK AT YOU NOW.
ROTTING IN JAIL WITH THE CRAZY SMILE AND THE LOONY FUCKIN' EYES.
YOU SURE SHOWED HIM.
SCHTT

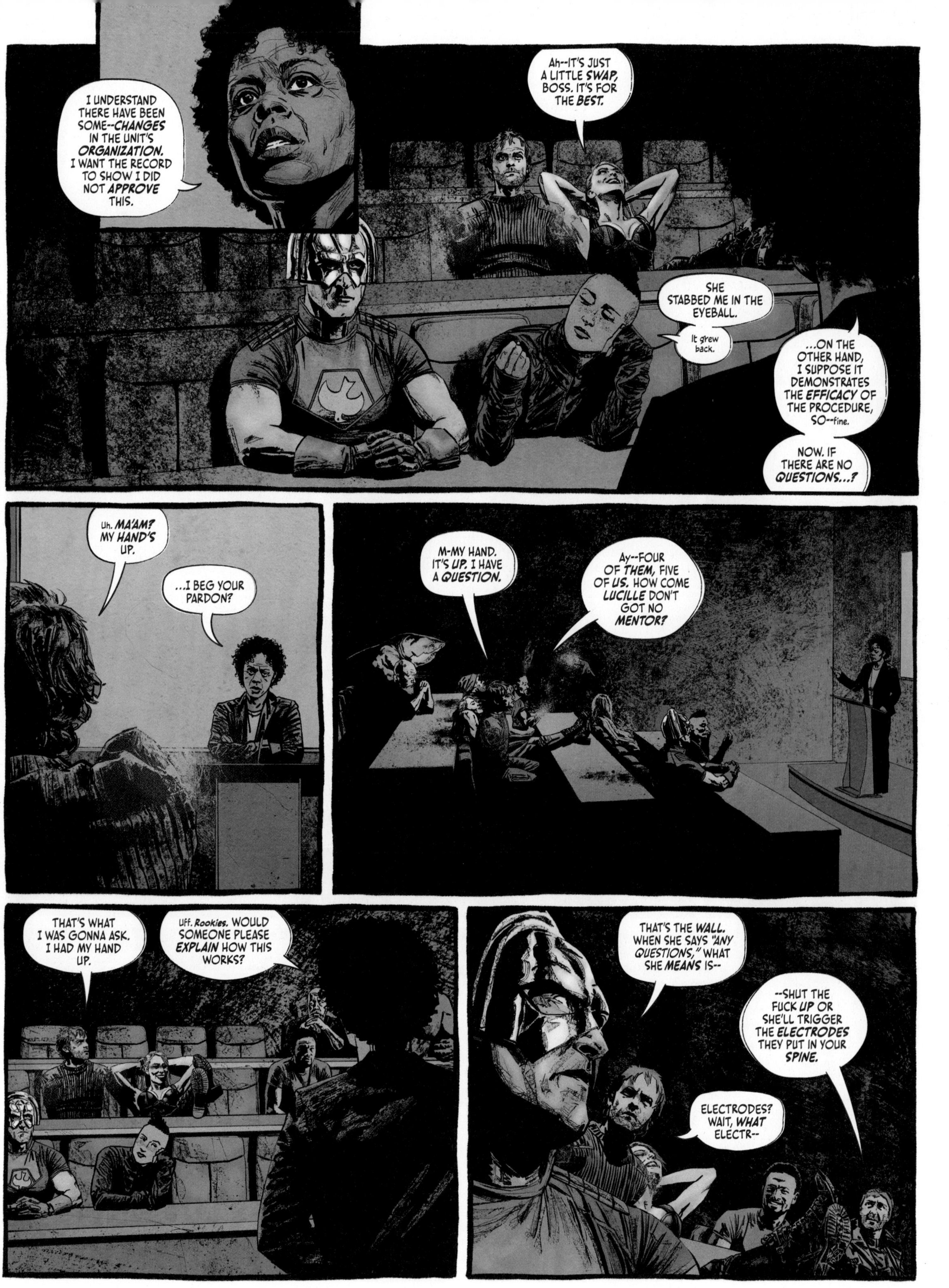
I UNDERSTAND THERE HAVE BEEN SOME--CHANGES IN THE UNIT'S ORGANIZATION. I WANT THE RECORD TO SHOW I DID NOT APPROVE THIS.
Ah--IT'S JUST A LITTLE SWAP, BOSS. IT'S FOR THE BEST.
SHE STABBED ME IN THE EYEBALL.
It grew back.
...ON THE OTHER HAND, I SUPPOSE IT DEMONSTRATES THE EFFICACY OF THE PROCEDURE, SO--fine.
NOW. IF THERE ARE NO QUESTIONS...?
Uh. MA'AM? MY HAND'S UP.
...I BEG YOUR PARDON?
M-MY HAND. IT'S UP. I HAVE A QUESTION.
Ay--FOUR OF THEM, FIVE OF US. HOW COME LUCILLE DON'T GOT NO MENTOR?
THAT'S WHAT I WAS GONNA ASK. I HAD MY HAND UP.
Uff. Rookies. WOULD SOMEONE PLEASE EXPLAIN HOW THIS WORKS?
THAT'S THE WALL. WHEN SHE SAYS "ANY QUESTIONS," WHAT SHE MEANS IS--
--SHUT THE FUCK UP OR SHE'LL TRIGGER THE ELECTRODES THEY PUT IN YOUR SPINE.
ELECTRODES? WAIT, WHAT ELECTR--

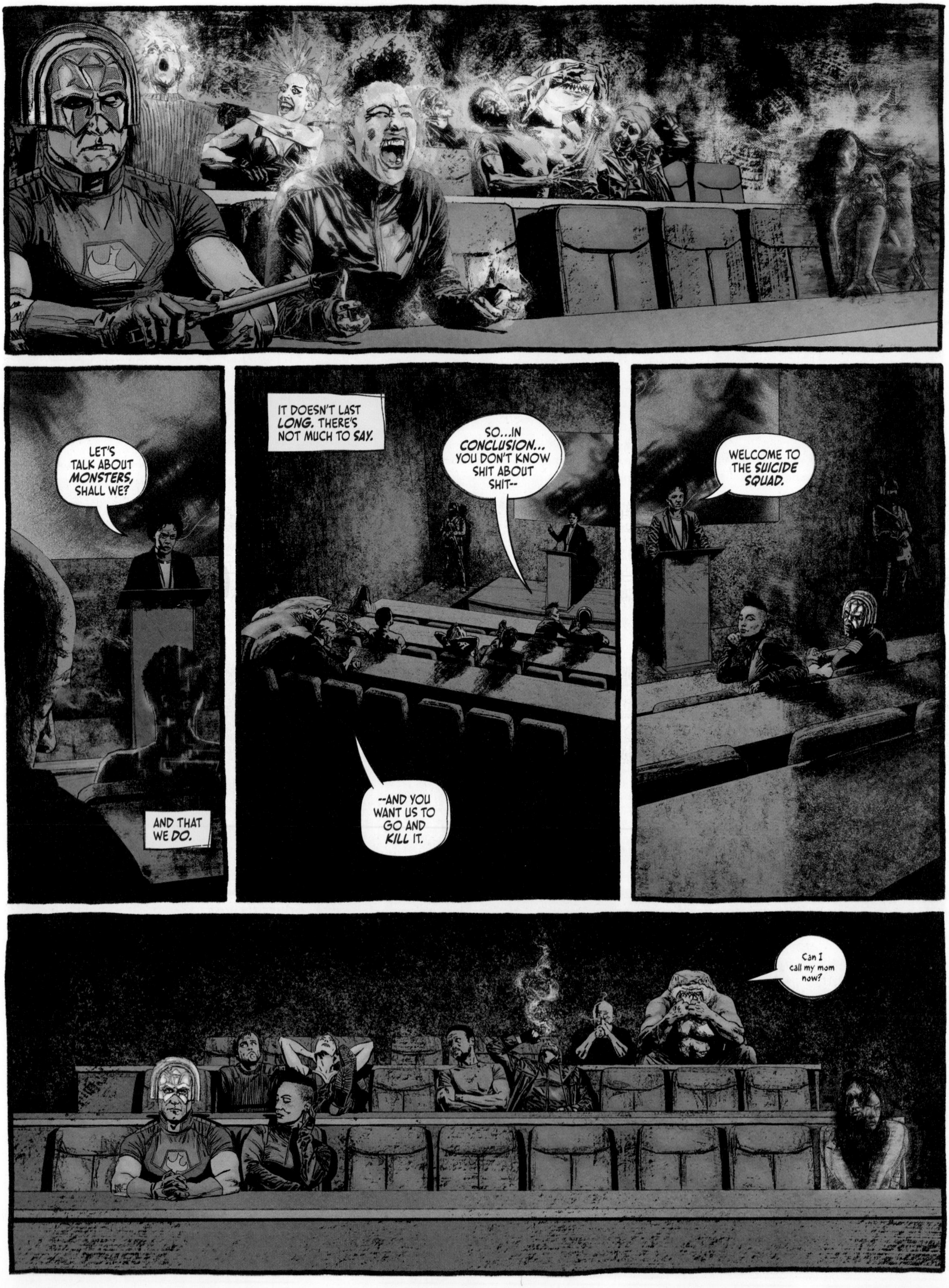
LET'S TALK ABOUT MONSTERS, SHALL WE?
AND THAT WE DO.
IT DOESN'T LAST LONG. THERE'S NOT MUCH TO SAY.
SO...IN CONCLUSION... YOU DON'T KNOW SHIT ABOUT SHIT--
--AND YOU WANT US TO GO AND KILL IT.
WELCOME TO THE SUICIDE SQUAD.
Can I call my mom now?

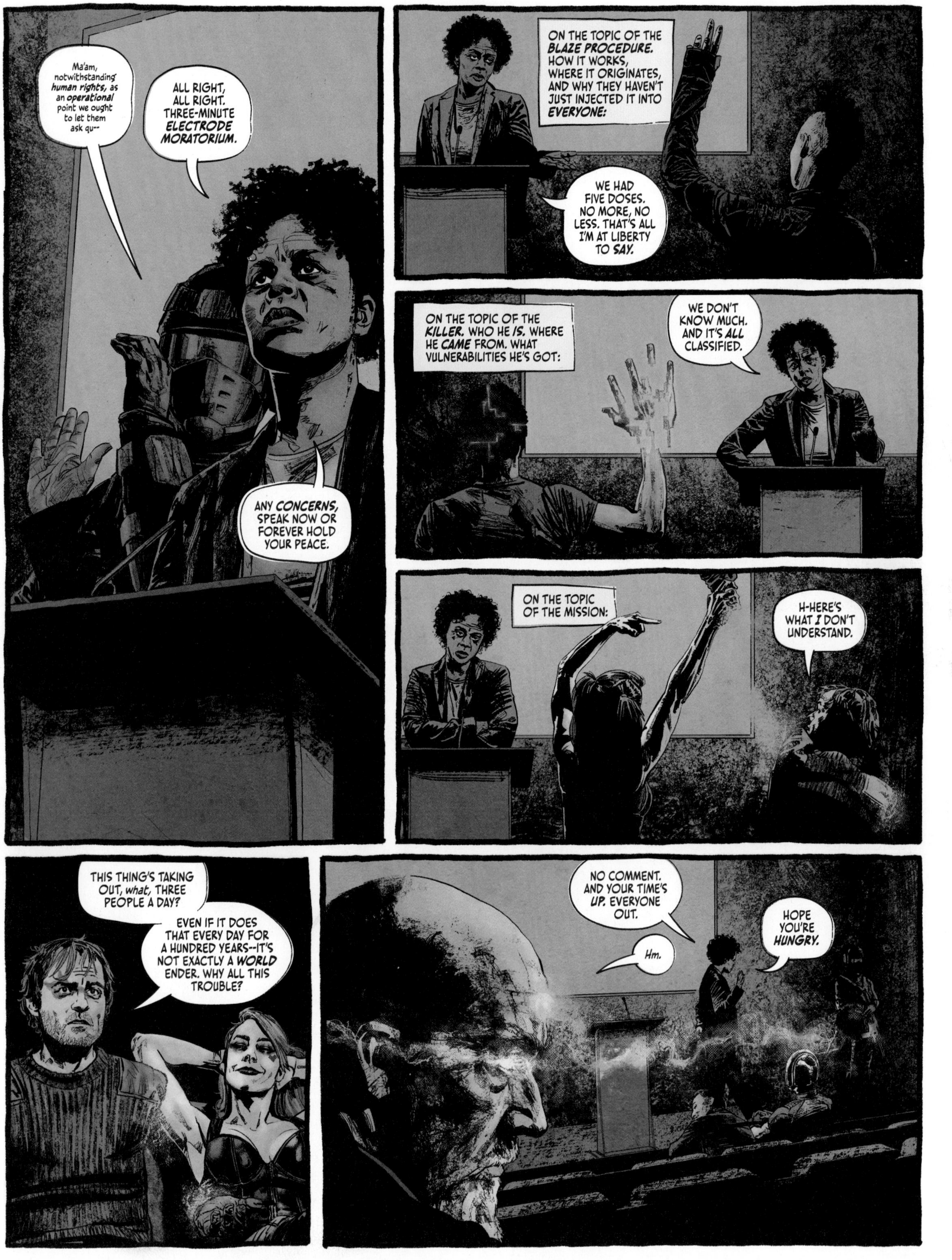

Ma'am, notwithstanding human rights, as an operational point we ought to let them ask qu--
ALL RIGHT, ALL RIGHT. THREE-MINUTE ELECTRODE MORATORIUM.
ANY CONCERNS, SPEAK NOW OR FOREVER HOLD YOUR PEACE.
ON THE TOPIC OF THE BLAZE PROCEDURE. HOW IT WORKS, WHERE IT ORIGINATES, AND WHY THEY HAVEN'T JUST INJECTED IT INTO EVERYONE:
WE HAD FIVE DOSES. NO MORE, NO LESS. THAT'S ALL I'M AT LIBERTY TO SAY.
ON THE TOPIC OF THE KILLER. WHO HE IS. WHERE HE CAME FROM. WHAT VULNERABILITIES HE'S GOT:
WE DON'T KNOW MUCH. AND IT'S ALL CLASSIFIED.
ON THE TOPIC OF THE MISSION:
H-HERE'S WHAT I DON'T UNDERSTAND.
THIS THING'S TAKING OUT, what, THREE PEOPLE A DAY?
EVEN IF IT DOES THAT EVERY DAY FOR A HUNDRED YEARS--IT'S NOT EXACTLY A WORLD ENDER. WHY ALL THIS TROUBLE?
NO COMMENT. AND YOUR TIME'S UP. EVERYONE OUT.
Hm.
HOPE YOU'RE HUNGRY.

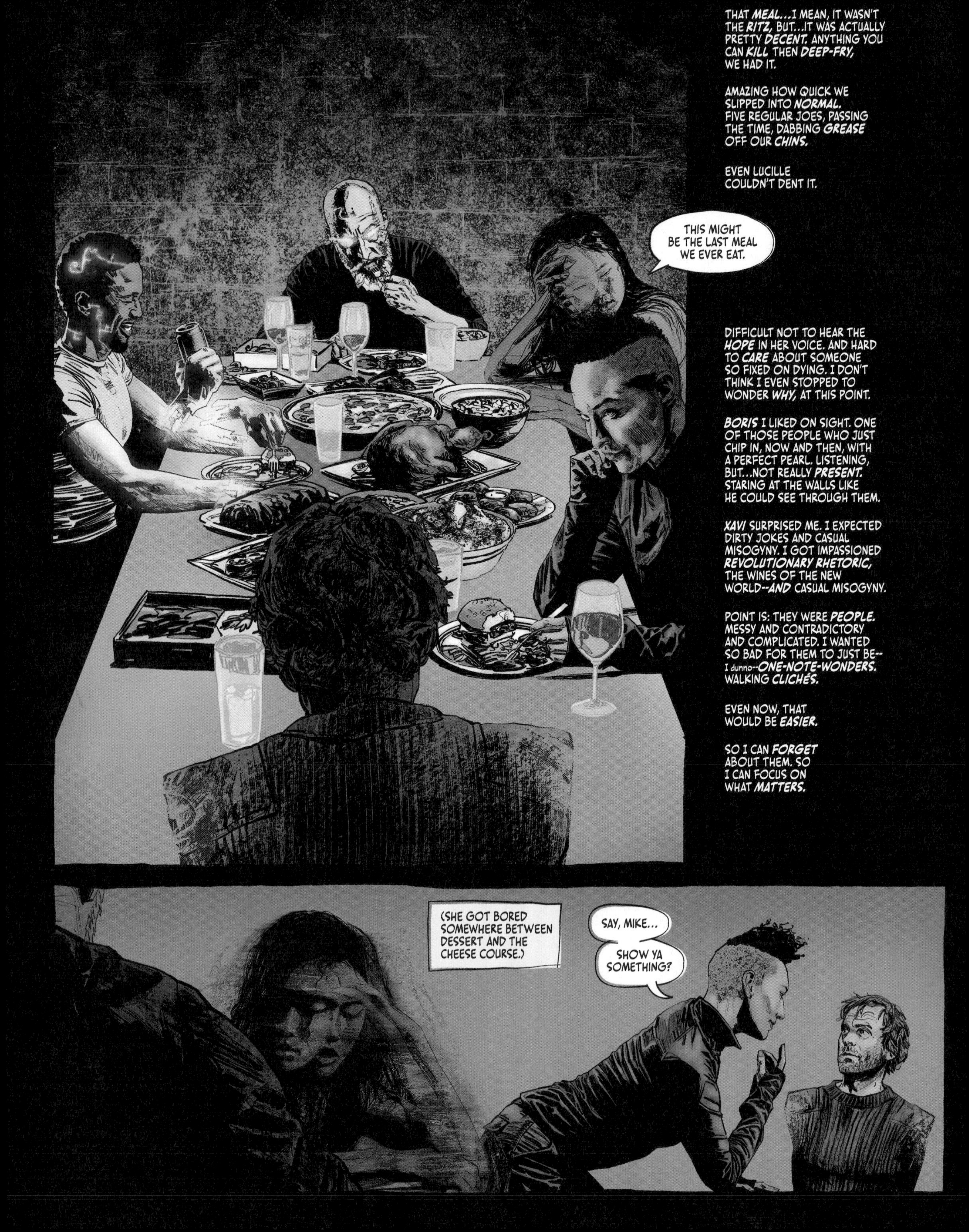
THAT MEAL...I MEAN, IT WASN'T THE RITZ, BUT...IT WAS ACTUALLY PRETTY DECENT. ANYTHING YOU CAN KILL THEN DEEP-FRY, WE HAD IT.
AMAZING HOW QUICK WE SLIPPED INTO NORMAL. FIVE REGULAR JOES, PASSING THE TIME, DABBING GREASE OFF OUR CHINS.
EVEN LUCILLE COULDN'T DENT IT.
THIS MIGHT BE THE LAST MEAL WE EVER EAT.
DIFFICULT NOT TO HEAR THE HOPE IN HER VOICE. AND HARD TO CARE ABOUT SOMEONE SO FIXED ON DYING. I DON'T THINK I EVEN STOPPED TO WONDER WHY, AT THIS POINT.
BORIS I LIKED ON SIGHT. ONE OF THOSE PEOPLE WHO JUST CHIP IN, NOW AND THEN, WITH A PERFECT PEARL. LISTENING, BUT...NOT REALLY PRESENT. STARING AT THE WALLS LIKE HE COULD SEE THROUGH THEM.
XAVI SURPRISED ME. I EXPECTED DIRTY JOKES AND CASUAL MISOGYNY. I GOT IMPASSIONED REVOLUTIONARY RHETORIC, THE WINES OF THE NEW WORLD--AND CASUAL MISOGYNY.
POINT IS: THEY WERE PEOPLE. MESSY AND CONTRADICTORY AND COMPLICATED. I WANTED SO BAD FOR THEM TO JUST BE-- I dunno--ONE-NOTE-WONDERS. WALKING CLICHÉS.
EVEN NOW, THAT WOULD BE EASIER.
SO I CAN FORGET ABOUT THEM. SO I CAN FOCUS ON WHAT MATTERS.
(SHE GOT BORED SOMEWHERE BETWEEN DESSERT AND THE CHEESE COURSE.)
SAY, MIKE...
SHOW YA SOMETHING?

TWO YEARS APART.

TWO YEARS, LONGING. TWO YEARS FEELING LIKE A PIECE OF ME GOT CUT OUT.

SURPRISE ME WITH THAT *HAND.*

SURPRISE ME WITH THAT *HAND.*

SURPRISE ME WITH THAT *HHHHHAAAAHH...*

TWO YEARS DREAMING OF THE ADVENTURES. OF THE GROANS AND SWEAT-SMELL AND SKIN. TWO YEARS PICTURING--*THIS.*

IT SHOULD'VE BEEN *PERFECT.* IT SHOULD'VE BEEN THE FUCK TO END ALL FUCKS.

Mmmm.

INSTEAD... well...

THAT WAS *NICE.*

THANKS, MIKE.

Uh.

LISTEN, I'M GONNA GO PRACTICE WITH THESE POWERS, OKAY?

WE SHOULD DO THIS *AGAIN.*

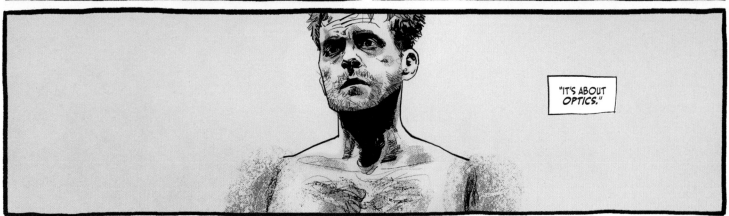

"IT'S ABOUT *OPTICS.*"

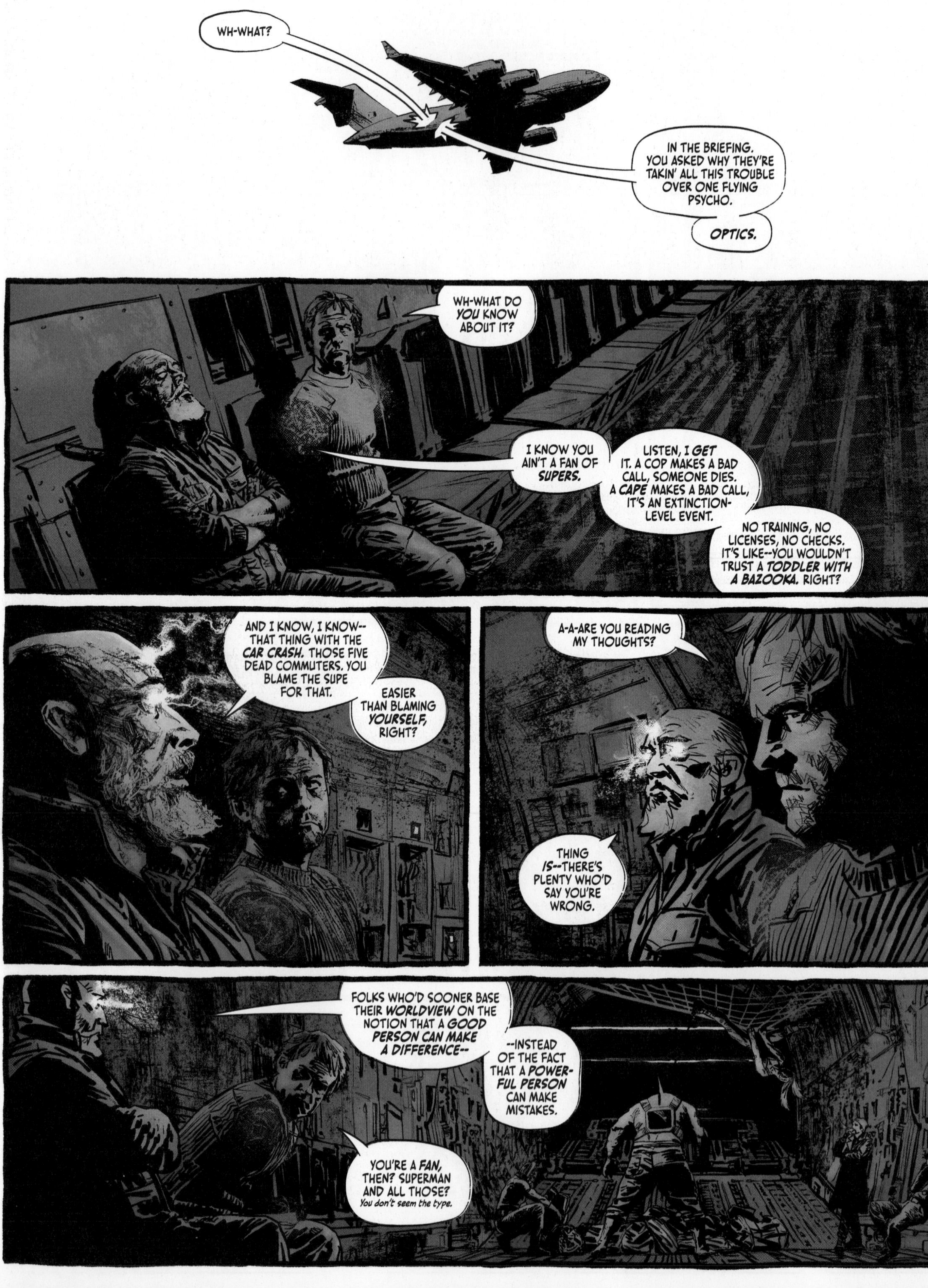
WH-WHAT?
IN THE BRIEFING. YOU ASKED WHY THEY'RE TAKIN' ALL THIS TROUBLE OVER ONE FLYING PSYCHO.
OPTICS.
WH-WHAT DO YOU KNOW ABOUT IT?
I KNOW YOU AIN'T A FAN OF SUPERS.
LISTEN, I GET IT. A COP MAKES A BAD CALL, SOMEONE DIES. A CAPE MAKES A BAD CALL, IT'S AN EXTINCTION-LEVEL EVENT.
NO TRAINING, NO LICENSES, NO CHECKS. IT'S LIKE--YOU WOULDN'T TRUST A TODDLER WITH A BAZOOKA. RIGHT?
AND I KNOW, I KNOW-- THAT THING WITH THE CAR CRASH. THOSE FIVE DEAD COMMUTERS. YOU BLAME THE SUPE FOR THAT.
EASIER THAN BLAMING YOURSELF, RIGHT?
A-A-ARE YOU READING MY THOUGHTS?
THING IS--THERE'S PLENTY WHO'D SAY YOU'RE WRONG.
FOLKS WHO'D SOONER BASE THEIR WORLDVIEW ON THE NOTION THAT A GOOD PERSON CAN MAKE A DIFFERENCE--
--INSTEAD OF THE FACT THAT A POWERFUL PERSON CAN MAKE MISTAKES.
YOU'RE A FAN, THEN? SUPERMAN AND ALL THOSE?
You don't seem the type.

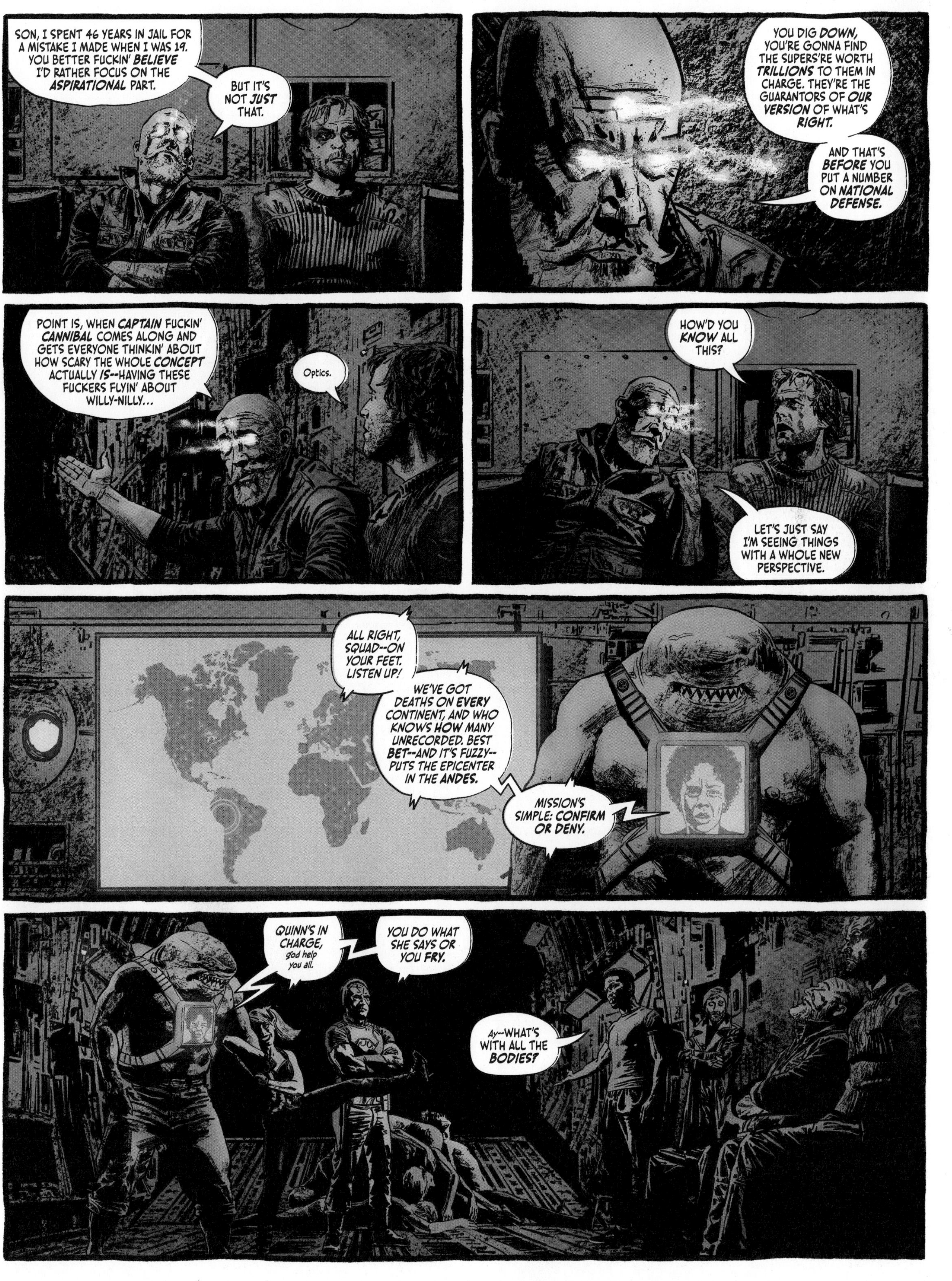
SON, I SPENT 46 YEARS IN JAIL FOR A MISTAKE I MADE WHEN I WAS 19. YOU BETTER FUCKIN' BELIEVE I'D RATHER FOCUS ON THE ASPIRATIONAL PART.
BUT IT'S NOT JUST THAT.
YOU DIG DOWN, YOU'RE GONNA FIND THE SUPERS'RE WORTH TRILLIONS TO THEM IN CHARGE. THEY'RE THE GUARANTORS OF OUR VERSION OF WHAT'S RIGHT.
AND THAT'S BEFORE YOU PUT A NUMBER ON NATIONAL DEFENSE.
POINT IS, WHEN CAPTAIN FUCKIN' CANNIBAL COMES ALONG AND GETS EVERYONE THINKIN' ABOUT HOW SCARY THE WHOLE CONCEPT ACTUALLY IS--HAVING THESE FUCKERS FLYIN' ABOUT WILLY-NILLY...
Optics.
HOW'D YOU KNOW ALL THIS?
LET'S JUST SAY I'M SEEING THINGS WITH A WHOLE NEW PERSPECTIVE.
ALL RIGHT, SQUAD--ON YOUR FEET. LISTEN UP!
WE'VE GOT DEATHS ON EVERY CONTINENT, AND WHO KNOWS HOW MANY UNRECORDED. BEST BET--AND IT'S FUZZY--PUTS THE EPICENTER IN THE ANDES.
MISSION'S SIMPLE: CONFIRM OR DENY.
QUINN'S IN CHARGE, god help you all.
YOU DO WHAT SHE SAYS OR YOU FRY.
Ay--WHAT'S WITH ALL THE BODIES?

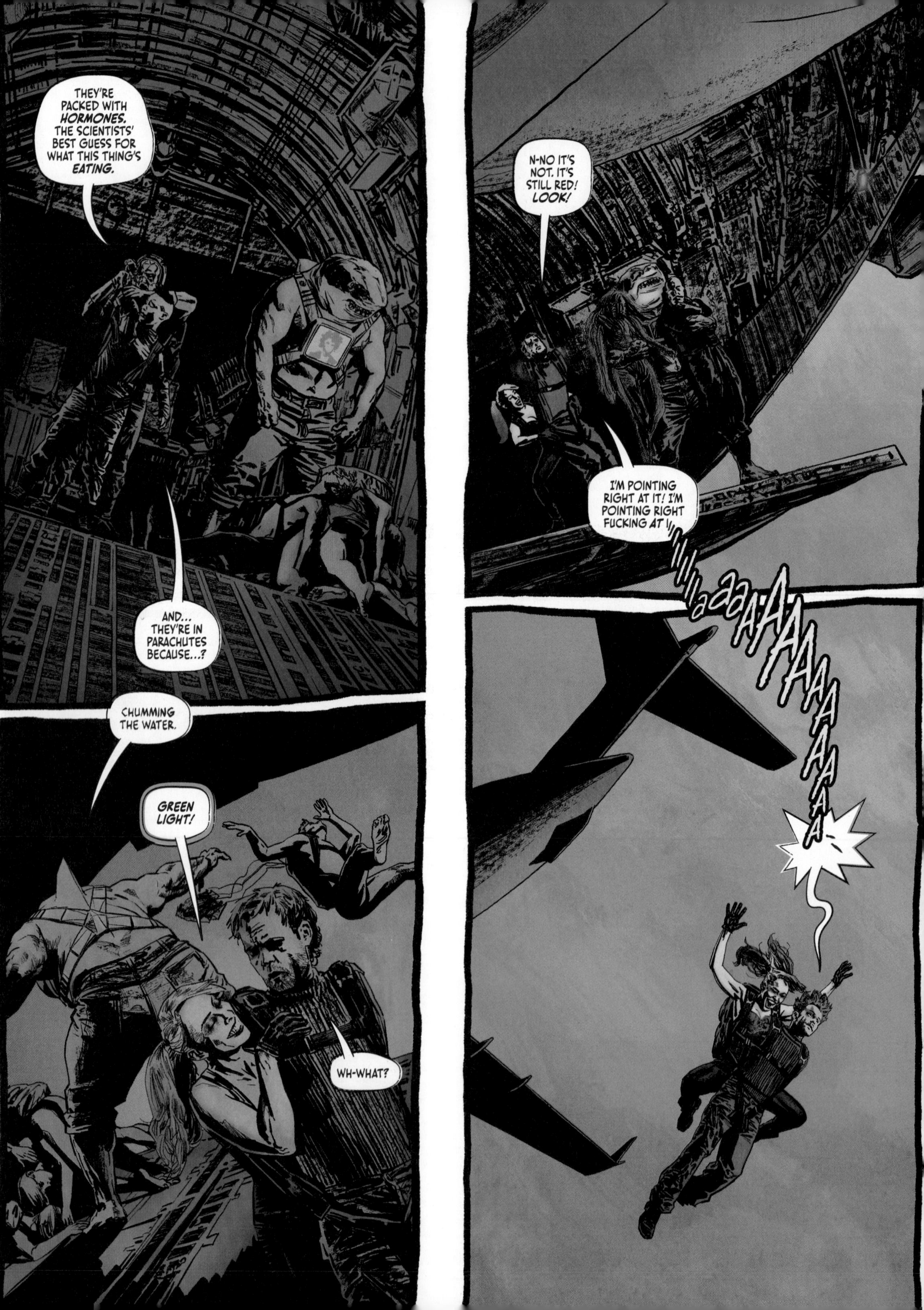
THEY'RE PACKED WITH HORMONES. THE SCIENTISTS' BEST GUESS FOR WHAT THIS THING'S EATING.
AND... THEY'RE IN PARACHUTES BECAUSE...?
CHUMMING THE WATER.
GREEN LIGHT!
WH-WHAT?
N-NO IT'S NOT. IT'S STILL RED! LOOK!
I'M POINTING RIGHT AT IT! I'M POINTING RIGHT FUCKING AT I
IIIIaaaAAAAAAAAAAAAAA-

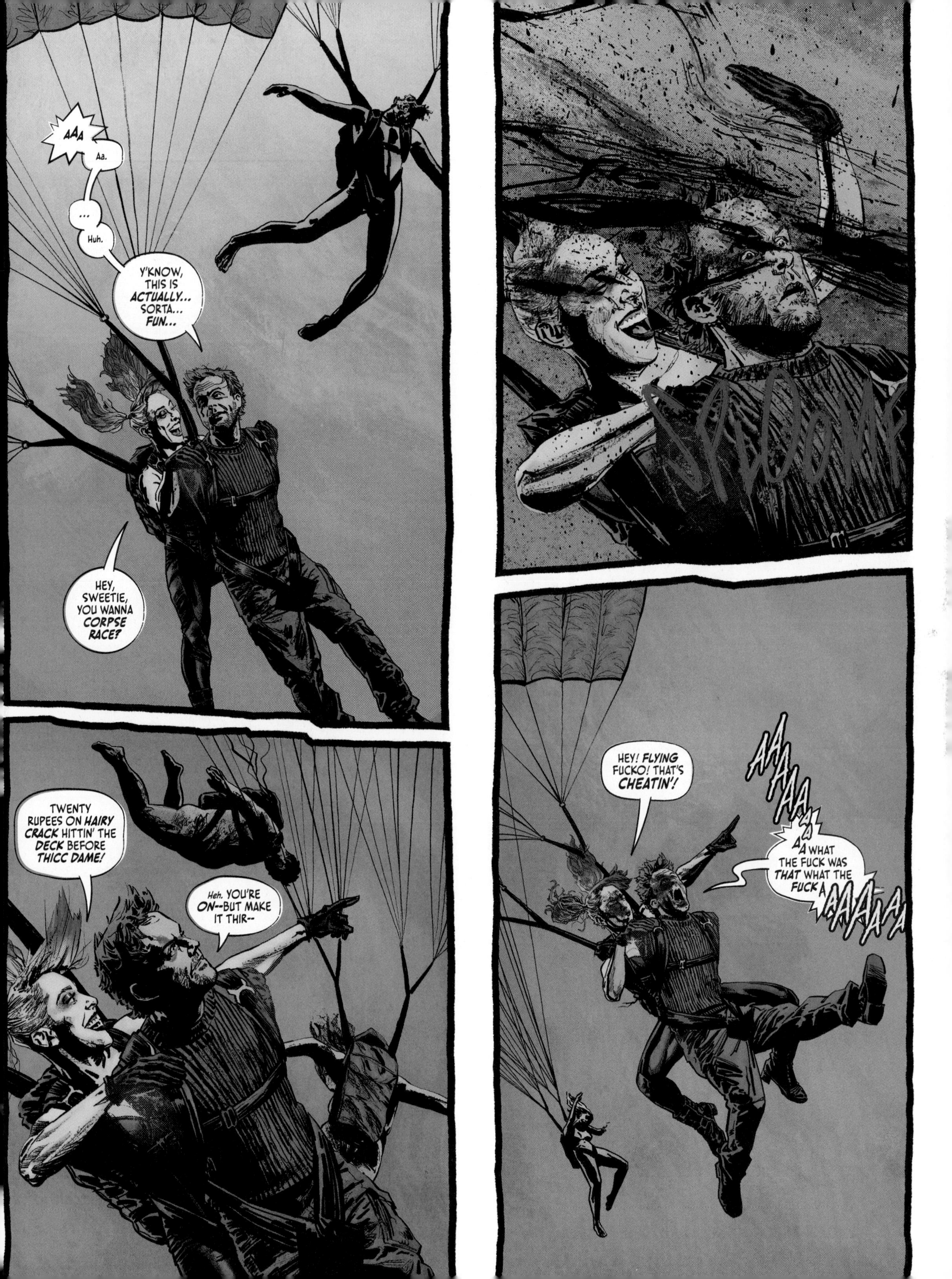
AAA
Aa.
...
Huh.
Y'KNOW, THIS IS ACTUALLY... SORTA... FUN...
HEY, SWEETIE, YOU WANNA CORPSE RACE?
TWENTY RUPEES ON HAIRY CRACK HITTIN' THE DECK BEFORE THICC DAME!
Heh. YOU'RE ON--BUT MAKE IT THIR--
HEY! FLYING FUCKO! THAT'S CHEATIN'!
A WHAT THE FUCK WAS THAT WHAT THE FUCK A

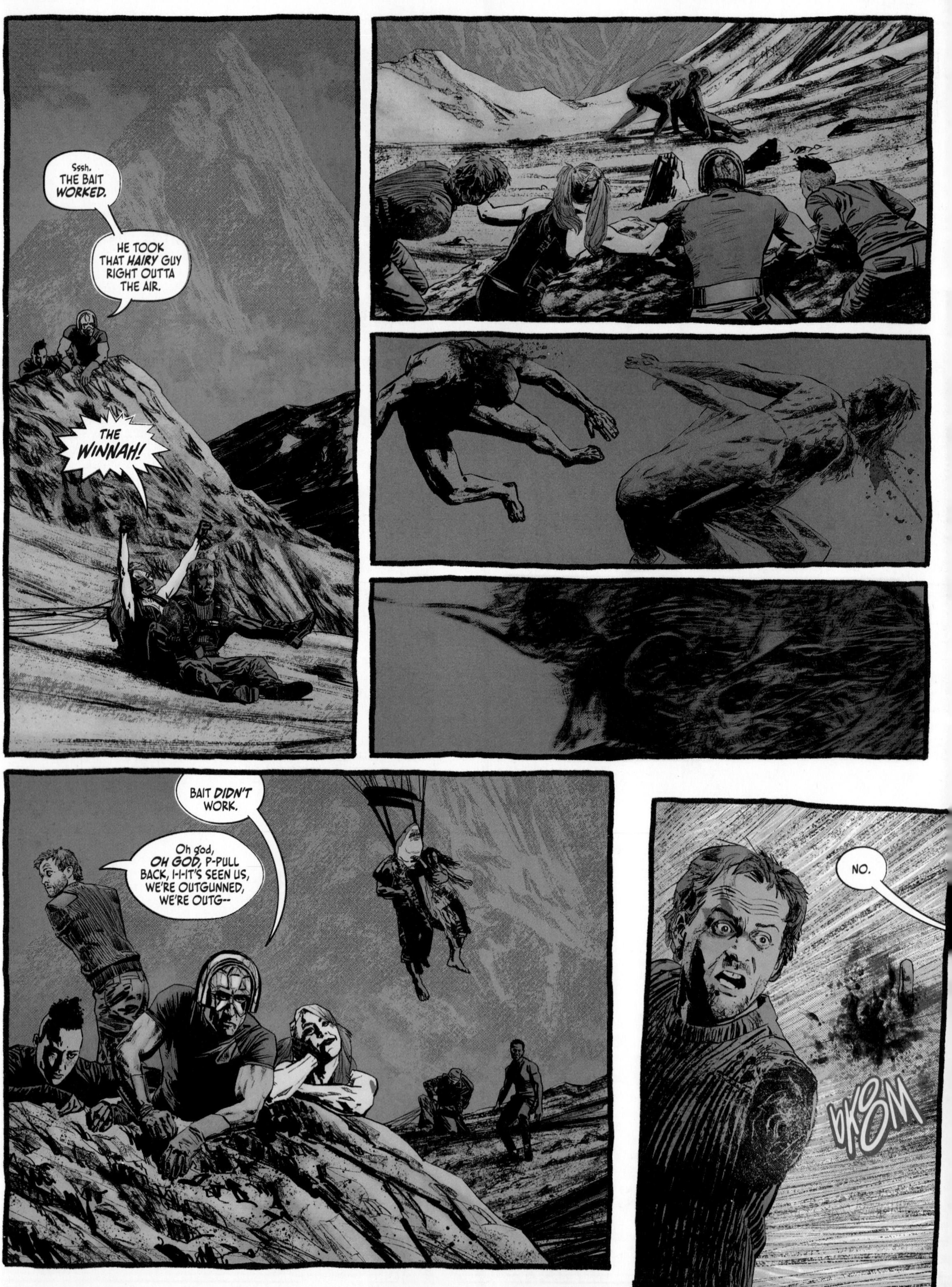
Sssh. THE BAIT WORKED.
HE TOOK THAT HAIRY GUY RIGHT OUTTA THE AIR.
THE WINNAH!
BAIT DIDN'T WORK.
Oh god, OH GOD, P-PULL BACK, I-I-IT'S SEEN US, WE'RE OUTGUNNED, WE'RE OUTG--
NO.
bKOOM

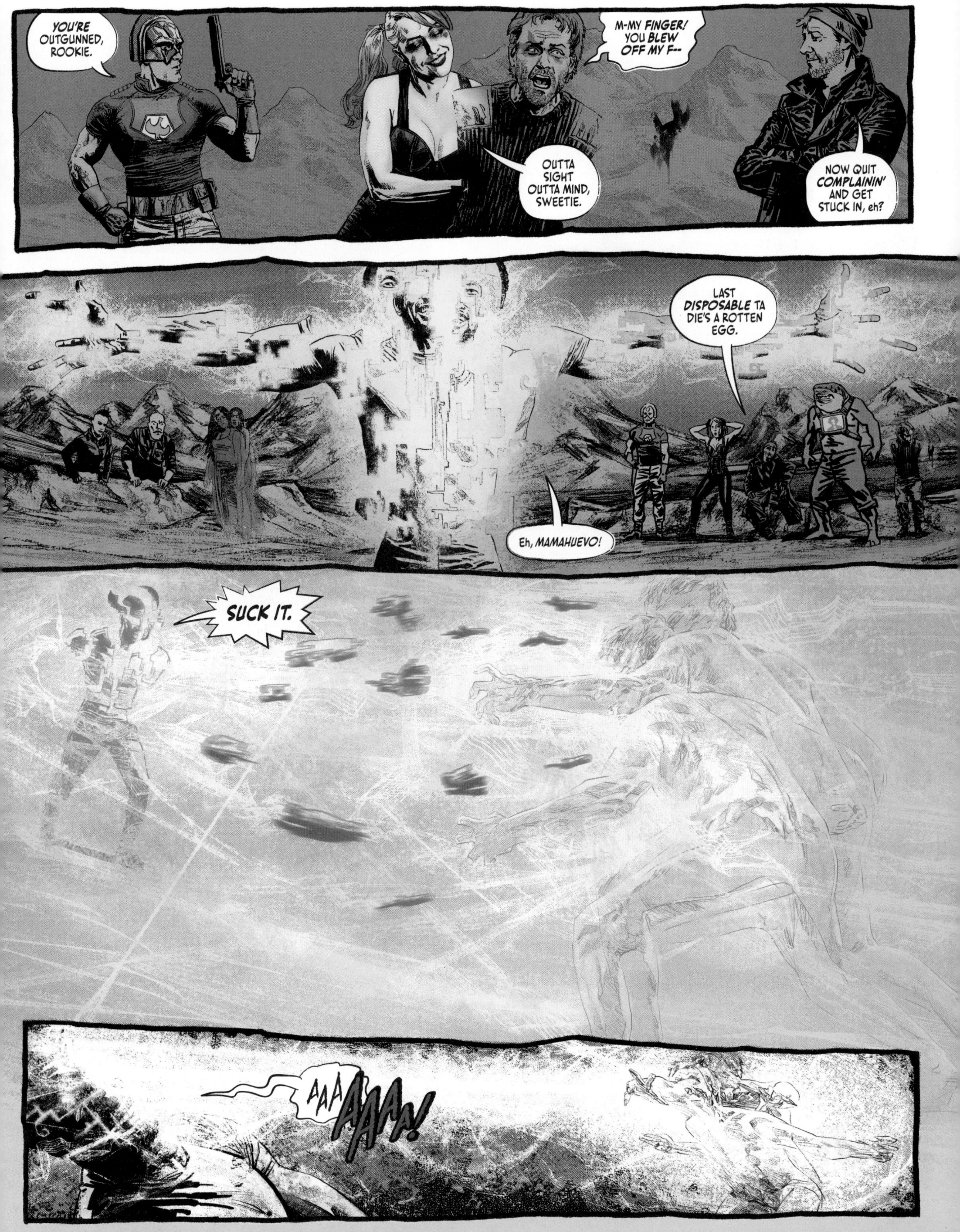
YOU'RE OUTGUNNED, ROOKIE.
M-MY FINGER! YOU BLEW OFF MY F--
OUTTA SIGHT OUTTA MIND, SWEETIE.
NOW QUIT COMPLAININ' AND GET STUCK IN, eh?
LAST DISPOSABLE TA DIE'S A ROTTEN EGG.
Eh, MAMAHUEVO!
SUCK IT.
AAAAAAA!

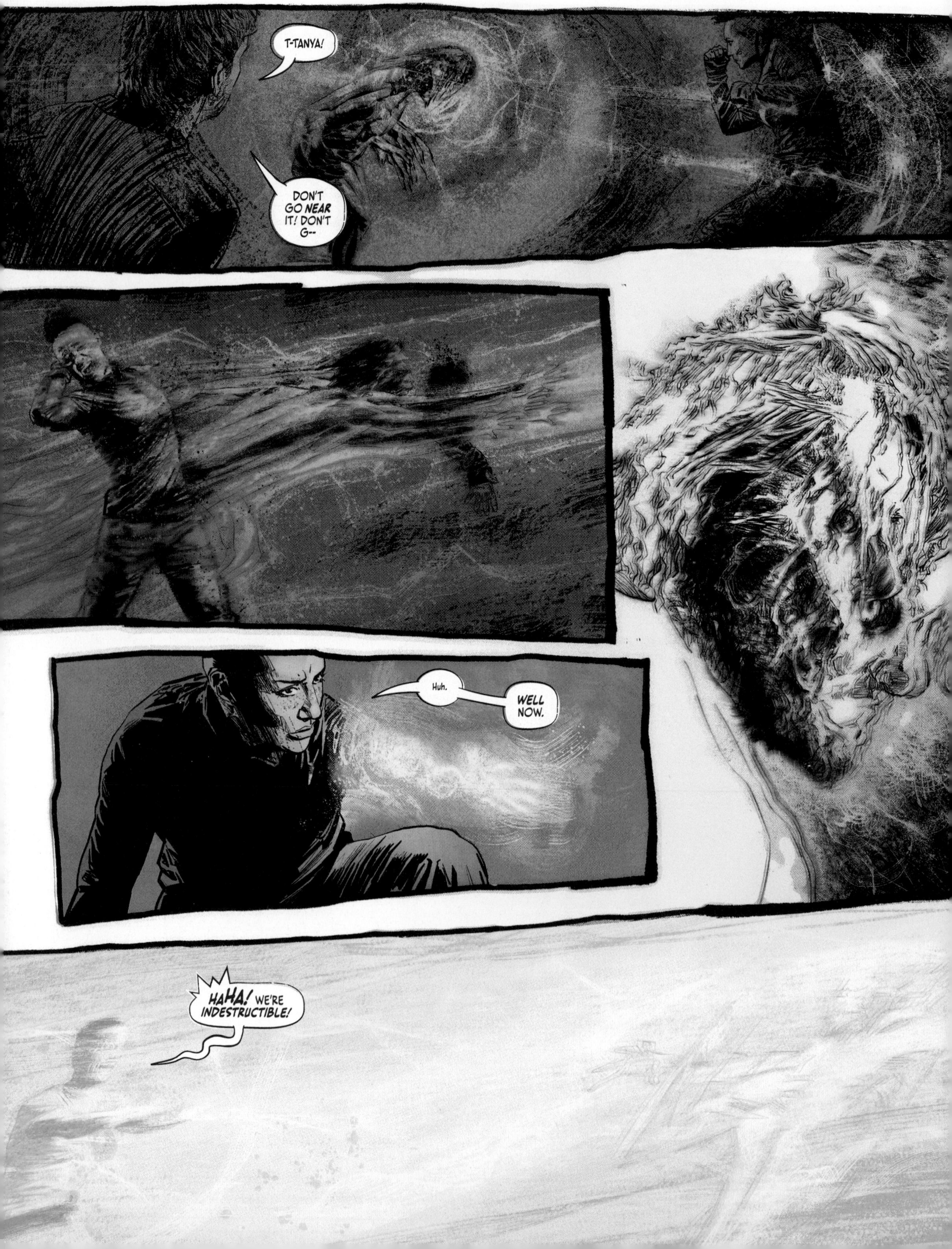
T-TANYA!
DON'T GO NEAR IT! DON'T G--
Huh.
WELL NOW.
HAHA! WE'RE INDESTRUCTIBLE!

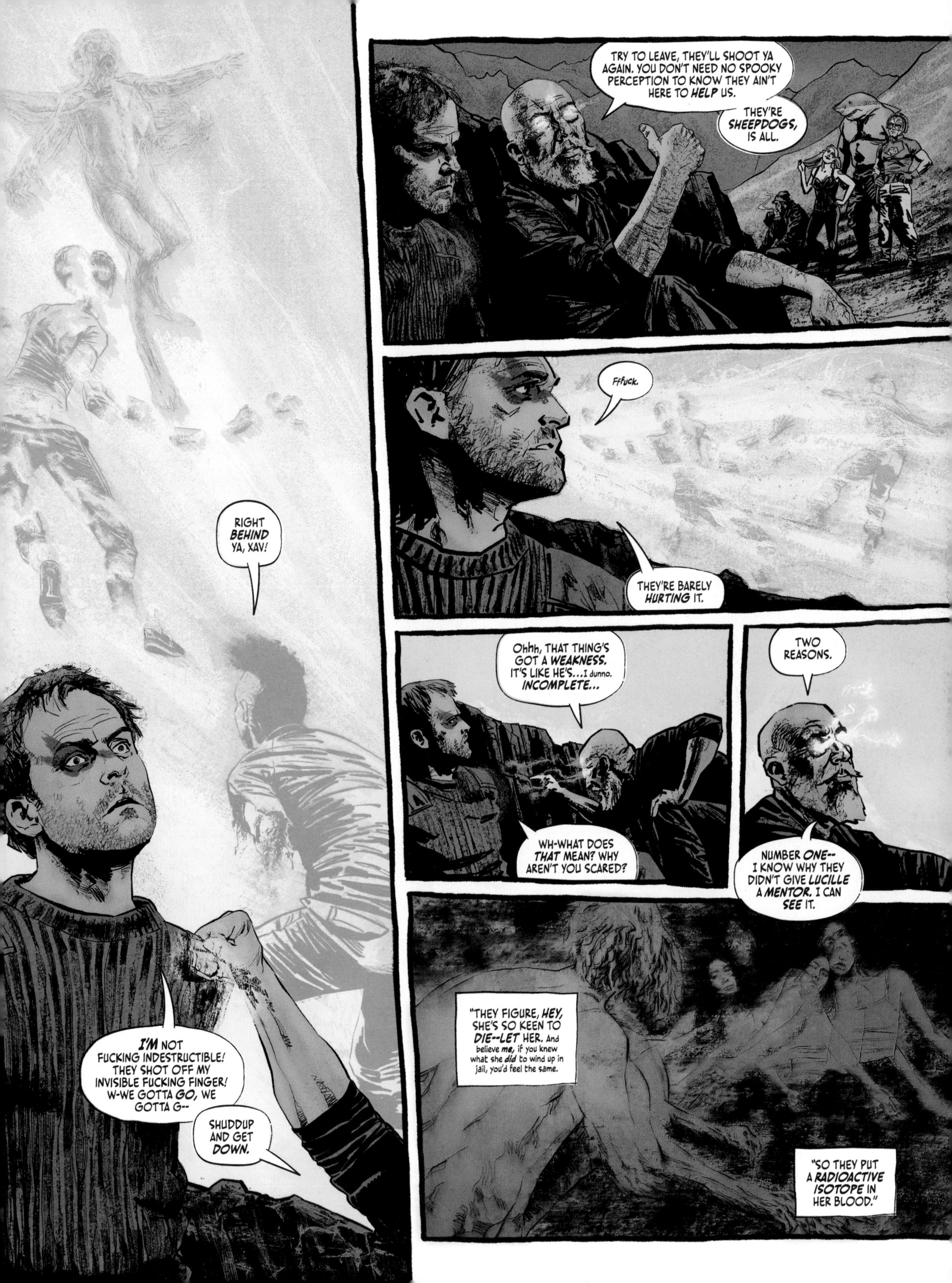
RIGHT BEHIND YA, XAV!
I'M NOT FUCKING INDESTRUCTIBLE! THEY SHOT OFF MY INVISIBLE FUCKING FINGER! W-WE GOTTA GO, WE GOTTA G--
SHUDDUP AND GET DOWN.
TRY TO LEAVE, THEY'LL SHOOT YA AGAIN. YOU DON'T NEED NO SPOOKY PERCEPTION TO KNOW THEY AIN'T HERE TO HELP US.
THEY'RE SHEEPDOGS, IS ALL.
Ffffuck.
THEY'RE BARELY HURTING IT.
Ohhh, THAT THING'S GOT A WEAKNESS. IT'S LIKE HE'S...I dunno. INCOMPLETE...
WH-WHAT DOES THAT MEAN? WHY AREN'T YOU SCARED?
TWO REASONS.
NUMBER ONE-- I KNOW WHY THEY DIDN'T GIVE LUCILLE A MENTOR. I CAN SEE IT.
"THEY FIGURE, HEY, SHE'S SO KEEN TO DIE--LET HER. And believe me, if you knew what she did to wind up in jail, you'd feel the same.
"SO THEY PUT A RADIOACTIVE ISOTOPE IN HER BLOOD."

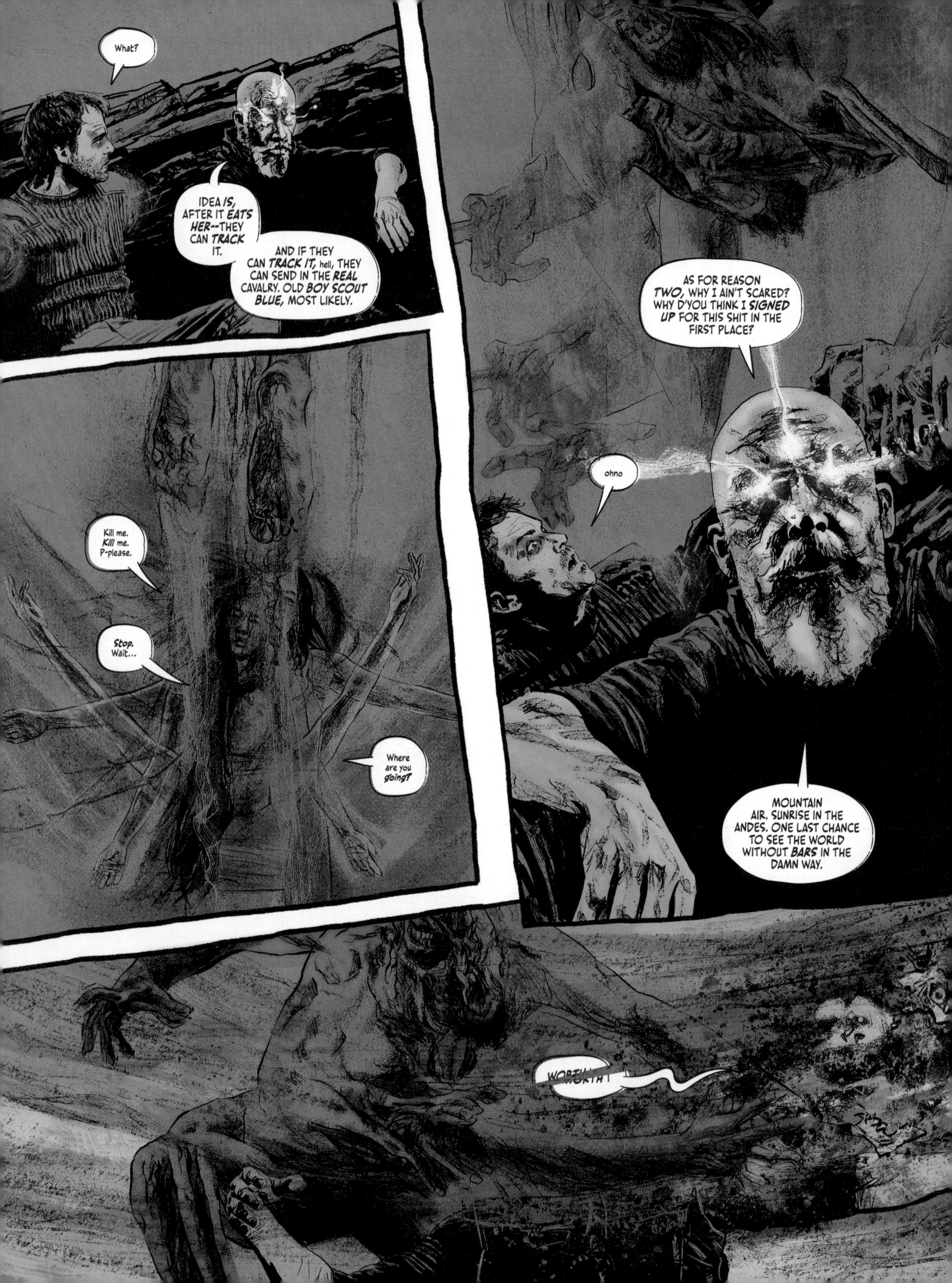
What?
IDEA IS, AFTER IT EATS HER--THEY CAN TRACK IT.
AND IF THEY CAN TRACK IT, hell, THEY CAN SEND IN THE REAL CAVALRY. OLD BOY SCOUT BLUE, MOST LIKELY.
Kill me. Kill me. P-please.
Stop. Wait...
Where are you going?
AS FOR REASON TWO, WHY I AIN'T SCARED? WHY D'YOU THINK I SIGNED UP FOR THIS SHIT IN THE FIRST PLACE?
ohno
MOUNTAIN AIR. SUNRISE IN THE ANDES. ONE LAST CHANCE TO SEE THE WORLD WITHOUT BARS IN THE DAMN WAY.
WORTH

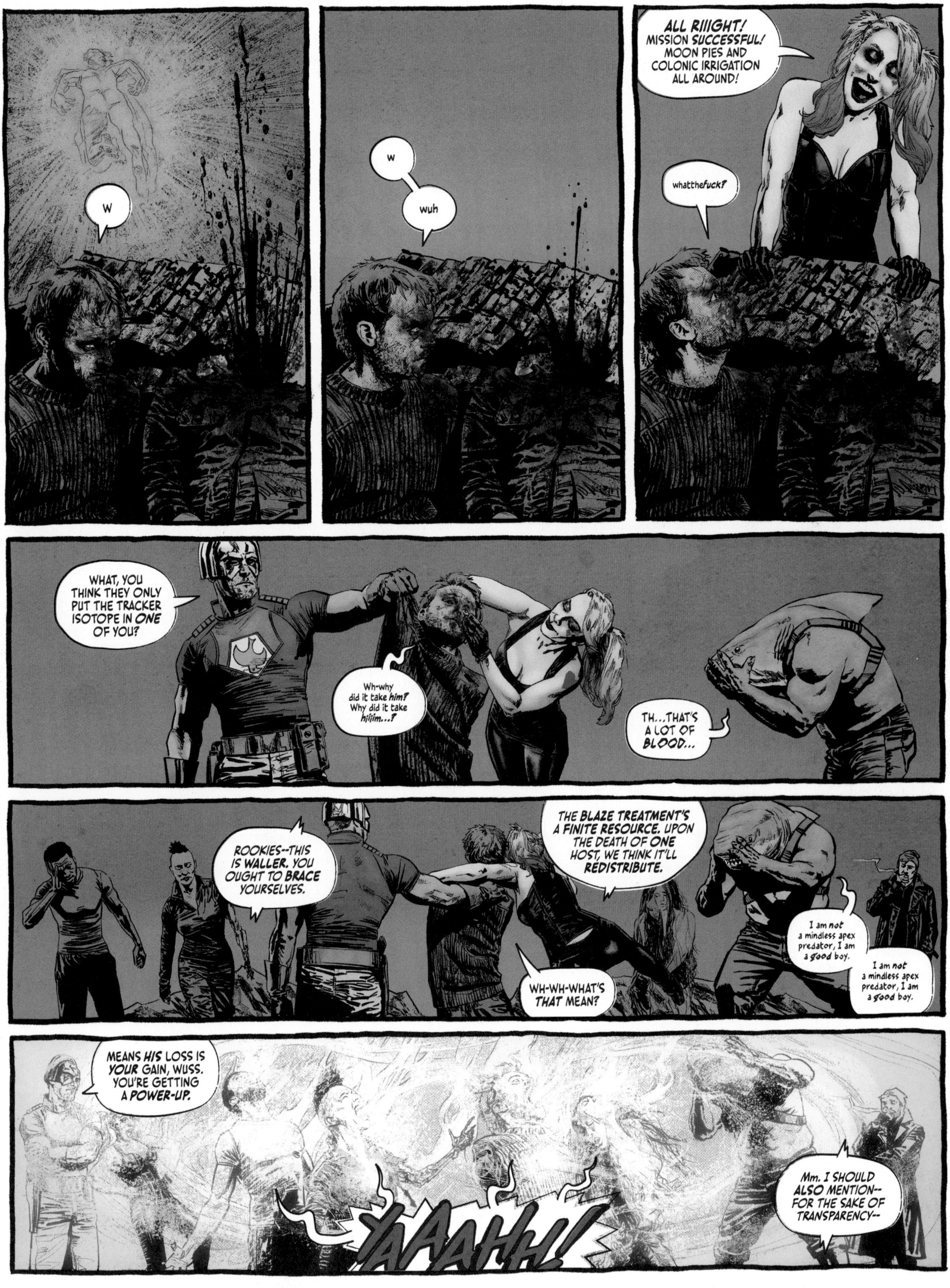
W
w
wuh
ALL RIIIGHT! MISSION SUCCESSFUL! MOON PIES AND COLONIC IRRIGATION ALL AROUND!
whatthefuck?
WHAT, YOU THINK THEY ONLY PUT THE TRACKER ISOTOPE IN ONE OF YOU?
Wh-why did it take him? Why did it take hiiiim...?
TH...THAT'S A LOT OF BLOOD...
ROOKIES--THIS IS WALLER. YOU OUGHT TO BRACE YOURSELVES.
THE BLAZE TREATMENT'S A FINITE RESOURCE. UPON THE DEATH OF ONE HOST, WE THINK IT'LL REDISTRIBUTE.
WH-WH-WHAT'S THAT MEAN?
I am not a mindless apex predator, I am a good boy.
I am not a mindless apex predator, I am a good boy.
MEANS HIS LOSS IS YOUR GAIN, WUSS. YOU'RE GETTING A POWER-UP.
YAAAHH!
Mm. I SHOULD ALSO MENTION-- FOR THE SAKE OF TRANSPARENCY--

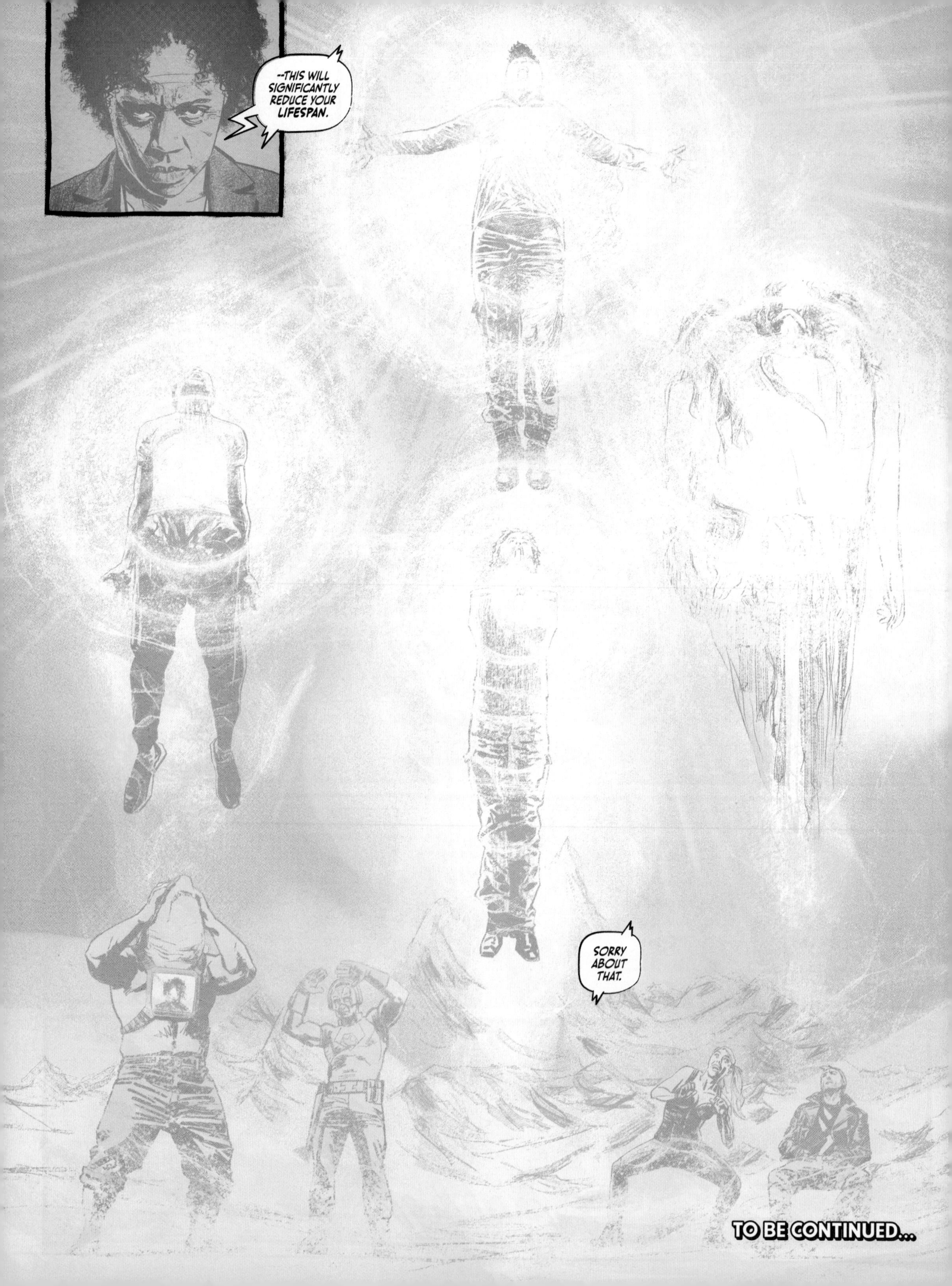
--THIS WILL SIGNIFICANTLY REDUCE YOUR LIFESPAN.
SORRY ABOUT THAT.
TO BE CONTINUED...

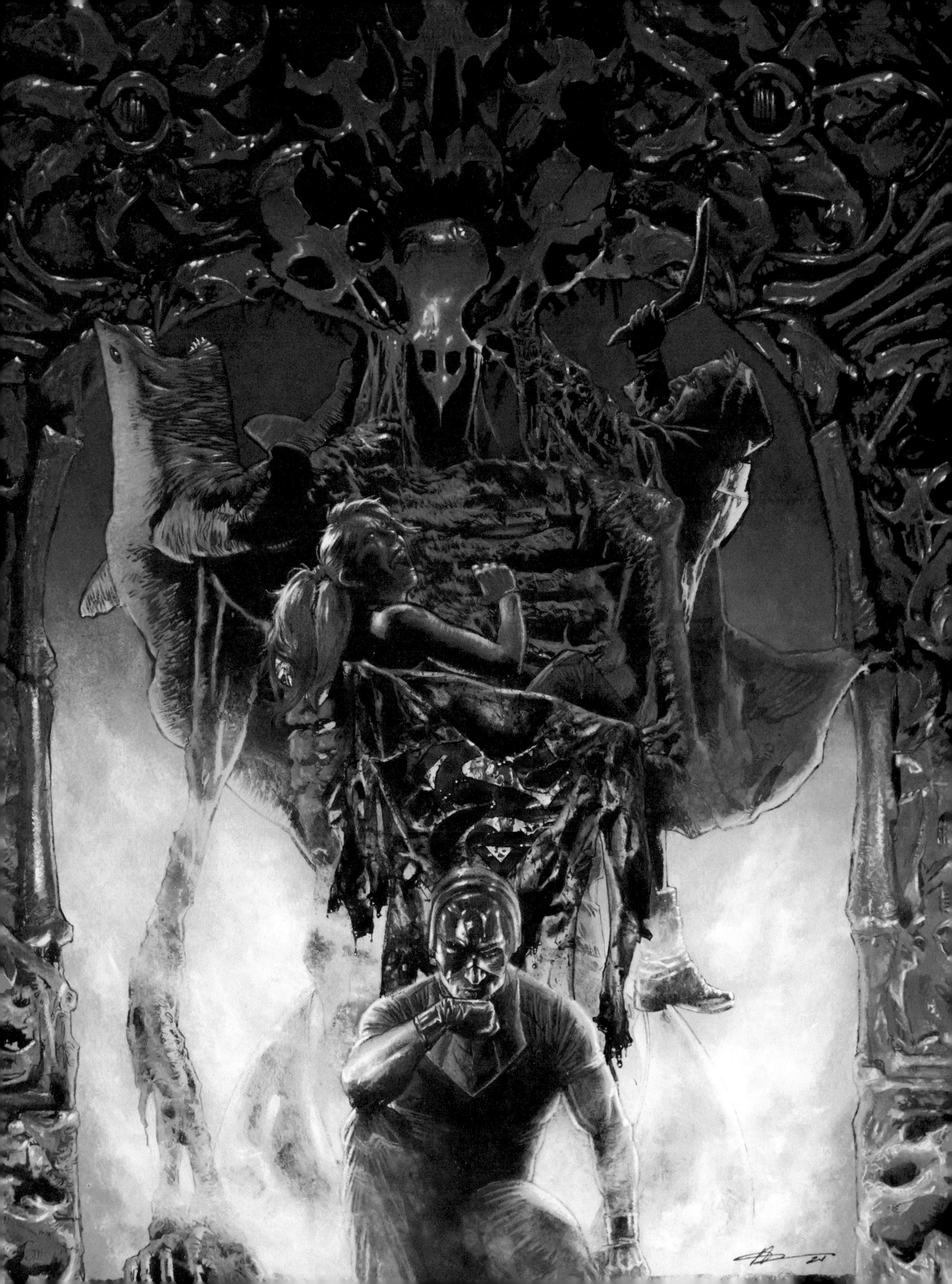

Suicide Squad: Blaze #2
variant cover by QISTINA KHALIDAH

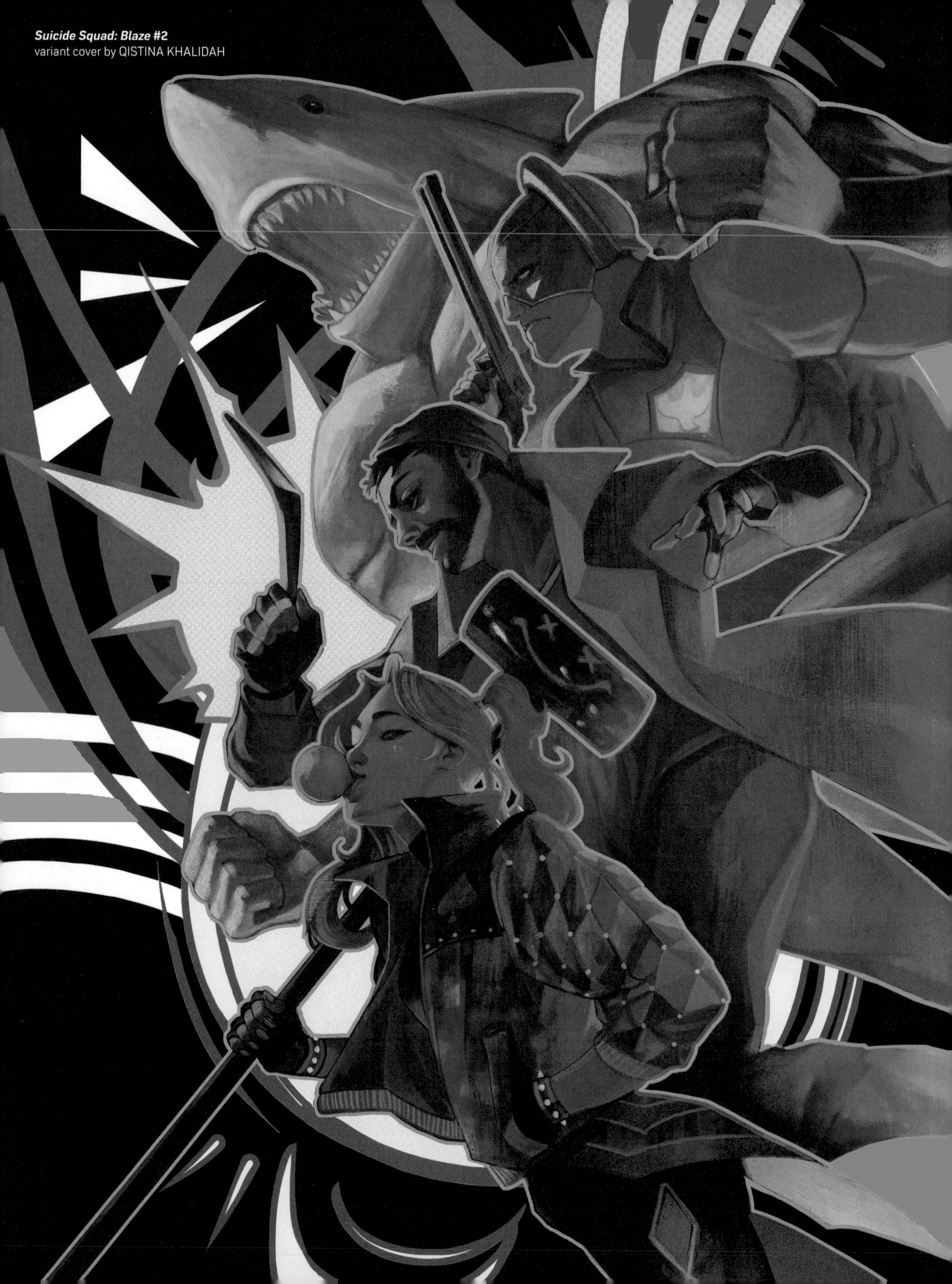

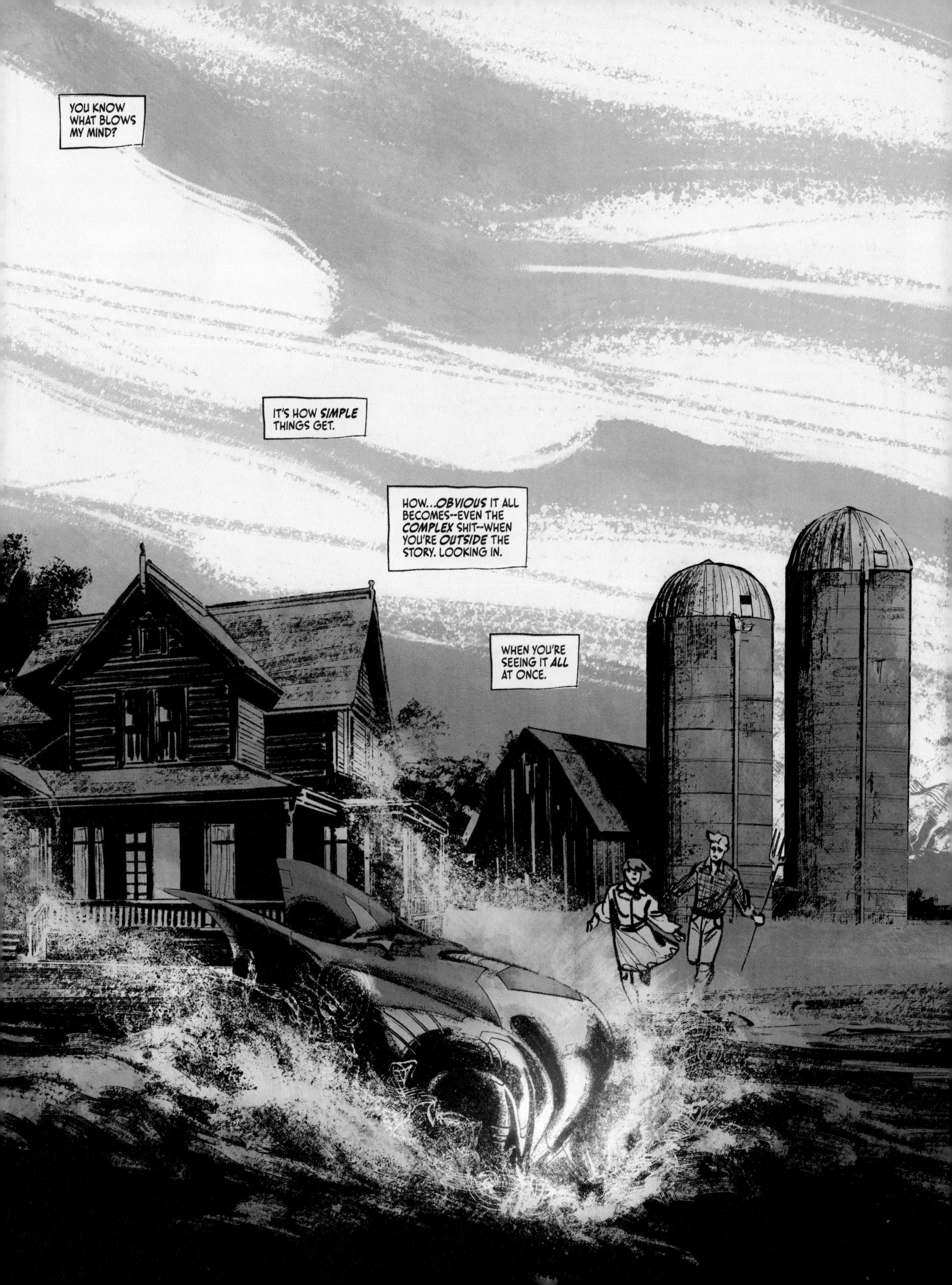
YOU KNOW WHAT BLOWS MY MIND?
IT'S HOW *SIMPLE* THINGS GET.
HOW...*OBVIOUS* IT ALL BECOMES--EVEN THE *COMPLEX* SHIT--WHEN YOU'RE *OUTSIDE* THE STORY. LOOKING IN.
WHEN YOU'RE SEEING IT *ALL* AT ONCE.

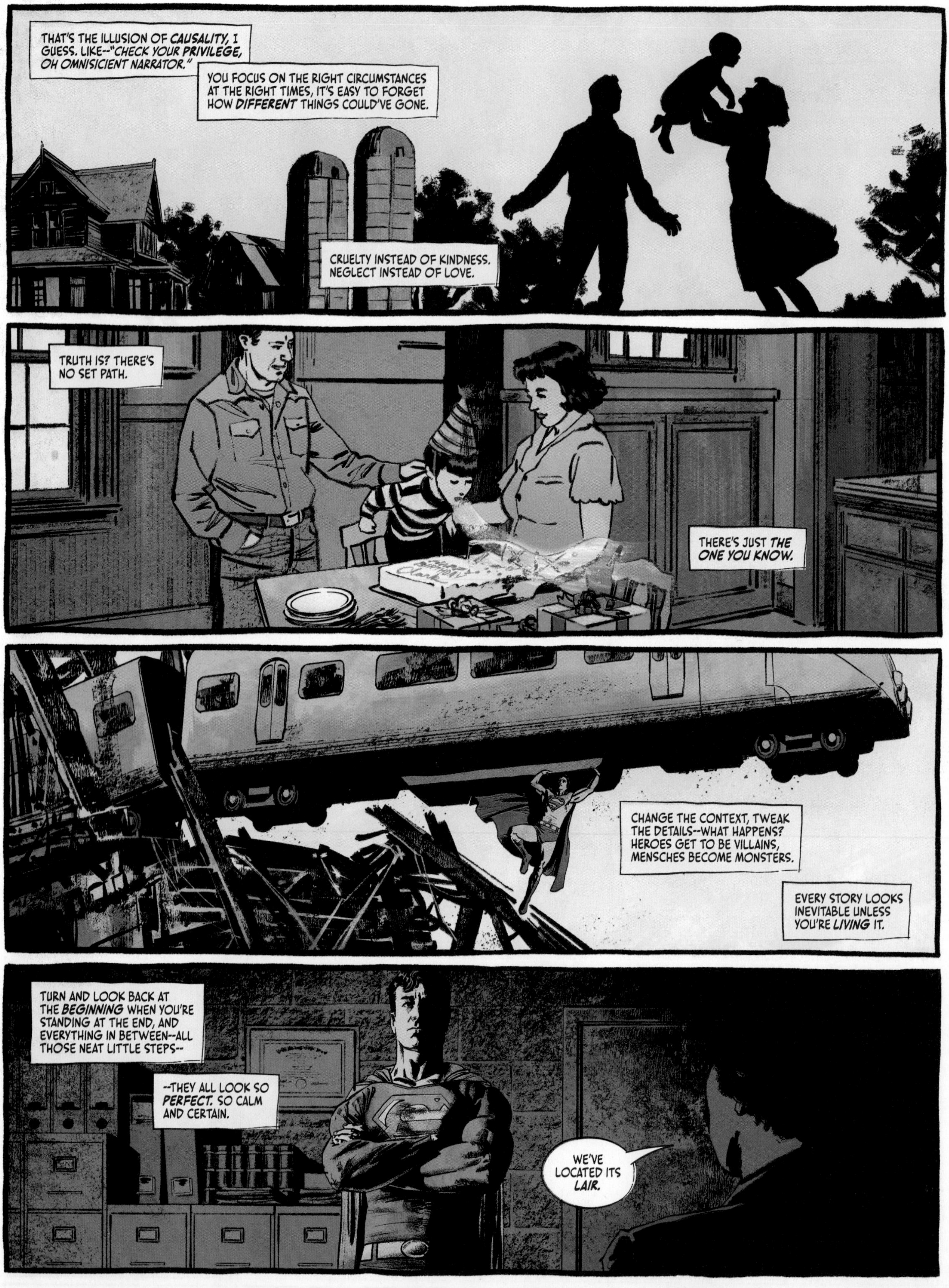
THAT'S THE ILLUSION OF *CAUSALITY,* I GUESS. LIKE--*"CHECK YOUR PRIVILEGE, OH OMNISICIENT NARRATOR."*
YOU FOCUS ON THE RIGHT CIRCUMSTANCES AT THE RIGHT TIMES, IT'S EASY TO FORGET HOW *DIFFERENT* THINGS COULD'VE GONE.
CRUELTY INSTEAD OF KINDNESS. NEGLECT INSTEAD OF LOVE.
TRUTH IS? THERE'S NO SET PATH.
THERE'S JUST *THE ONE YOU KNOW.*
CHANGE THE CONTEXT, TWEAK THE DETAILS--WHAT HAPPENS? HEROES GET TO BE VILLAINS, MENSCHES BECOME MONSTERS.
EVERY STORY LOOKS INEVITABLE UNLESS YOU'RE *LIVING* IT.
TURN AND LOOK BACK AT THE *BEGINNING* WHEN YOU'RE STANDING AT THE END, AND EVERYTHING IN BETWEEN--ALL THOSE NEAT LITTLE STEPS--
--THEY ALL LOOK SO *PERFECT.* SO CALM AND CERTAIN.
WE'VE LOCATED ITS *LAIR.*

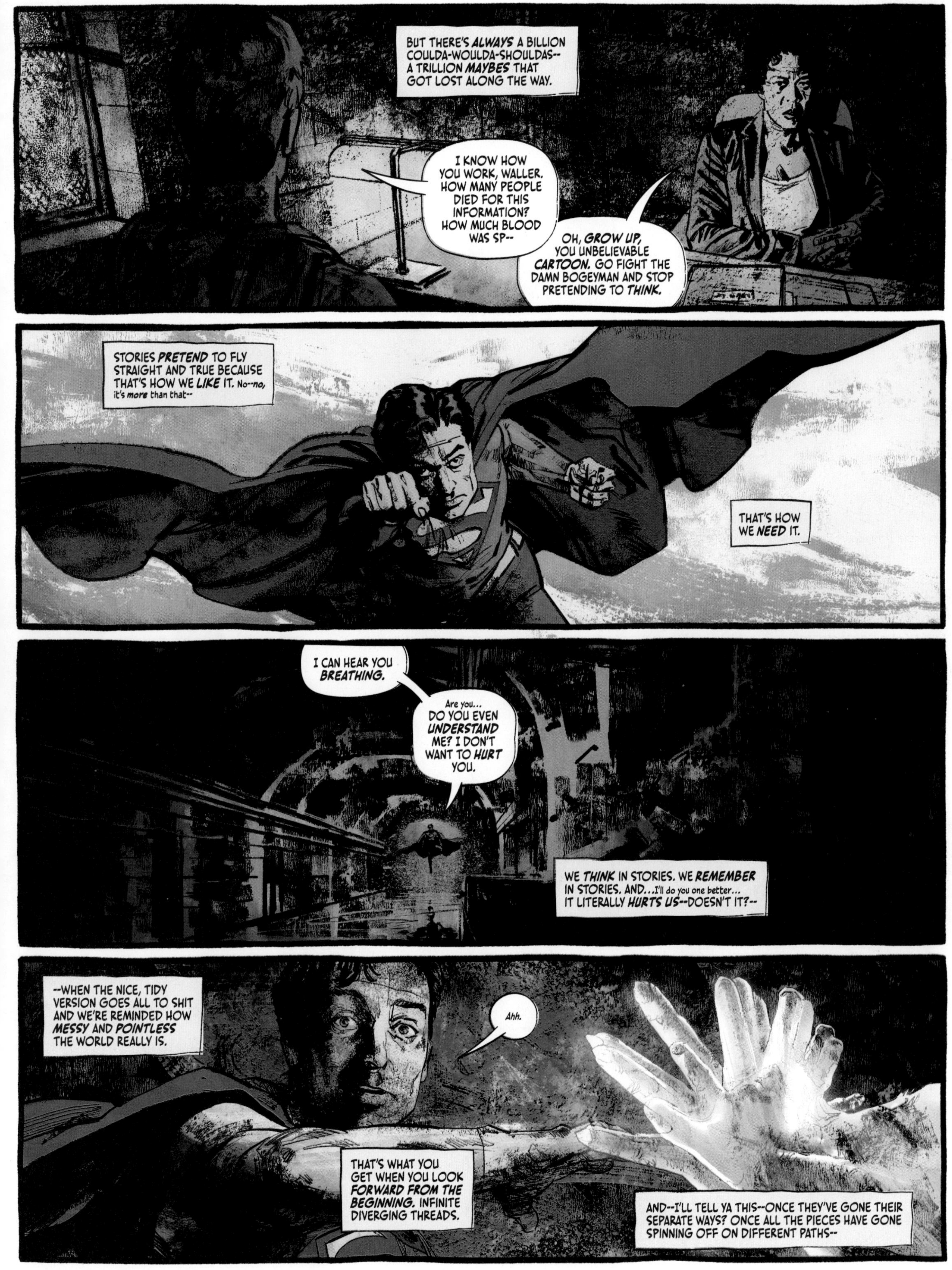
BUT THERE'S ALWAYS A BILLION COULDA-WOULDA-SHOULDAS-- A TRILLION MAYBES THAT GOT LOST ALONG THE WAY.
I KNOW HOW YOU WORK, WALLER. HOW MANY PEOPLE DIED FOR THIS INFORMATION? HOW MUCH BLOOD WAS SP--
OH, GROW UP, YOU UNBELIEVABLE CARTOON. GO FIGHT THE DAMN BOGEYMAN AND STOP PRETENDING TO THINK.
STORIES PRETEND TO FLY STRAIGHT AND TRUE BECAUSE THAT'S HOW WE LIKE IT. No--no, it's more than that--
THAT'S HOW WE NEED IT.
I CAN HEAR YOU BREATHING.
Are you... DO YOU EVEN UNDERSTAND ME? I DON'T WANT TO HURT YOU.
WE THINK IN STORIES. WE REMEMBER IN STORIES. AND...I'll do you one better... IT LITERALLY HURTS US--DOESN'T IT?--
--WHEN THE NICE, TIDY VERSION GOES ALL TO SHIT AND WE'RE REMINDED HOW MESSY AND POINTLESS THE WORLD REALLY IS.
Ahh.
THAT'S WHAT YOU GET WHEN YOU LOOK FORWARD FROM THE BEGINNING. INFINITE DIVERGING THREADS.
AND--I'LL TELL YA THIS--ONCE THEY'VE GONE THEIR SEPARATE WAYS? ONCE ALL THE PIECES HAVE GONE SPINNING OFF ON DIFFERENT PATHS--

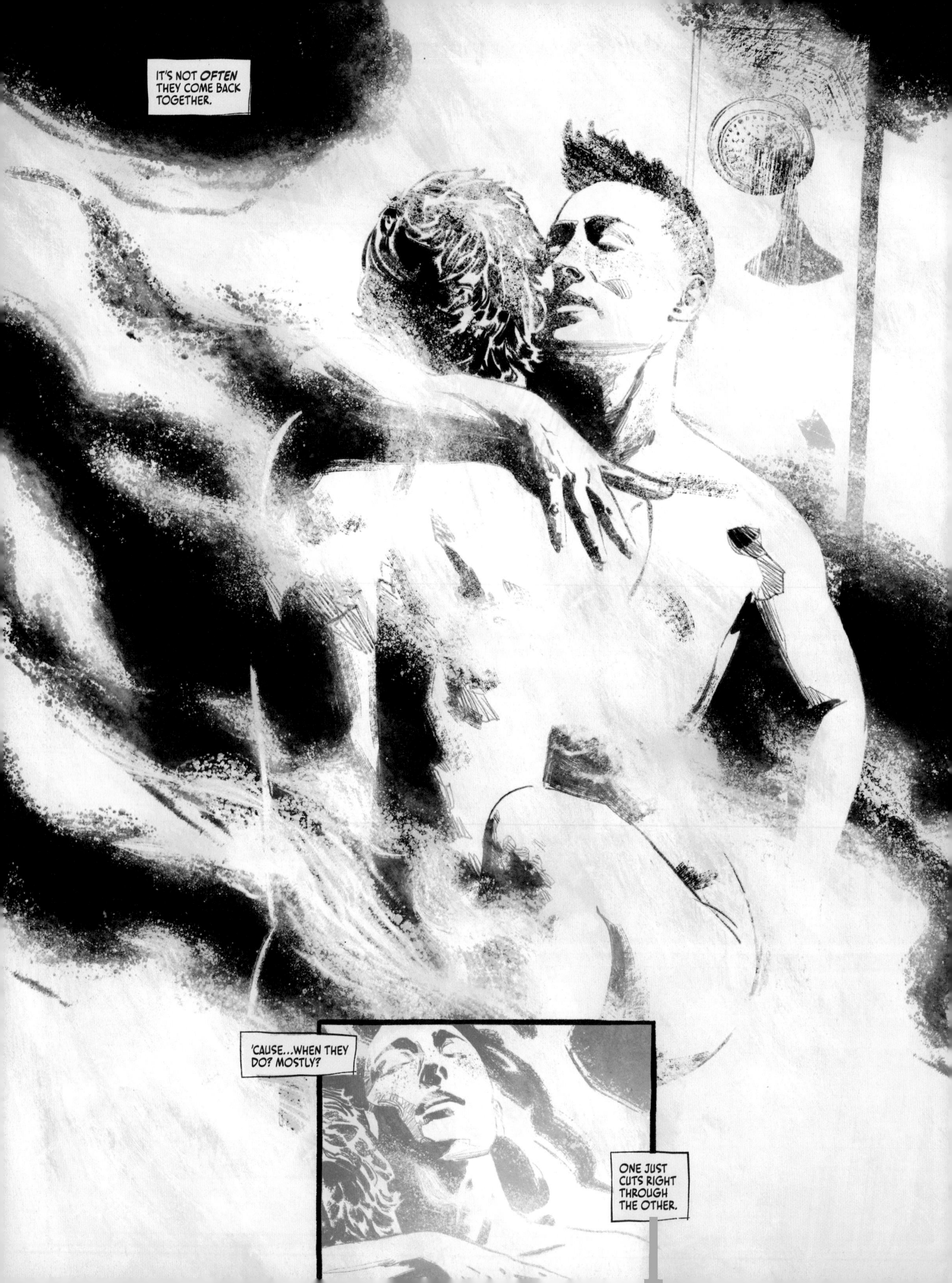
IT'S NOT *OFTEN* THEY COME BACK TOGETHER.
'CAUSE...WHEN THEY DO? MOSTLY?
ONE JUST CUTS RIGHT THROUGH THE OTHER.

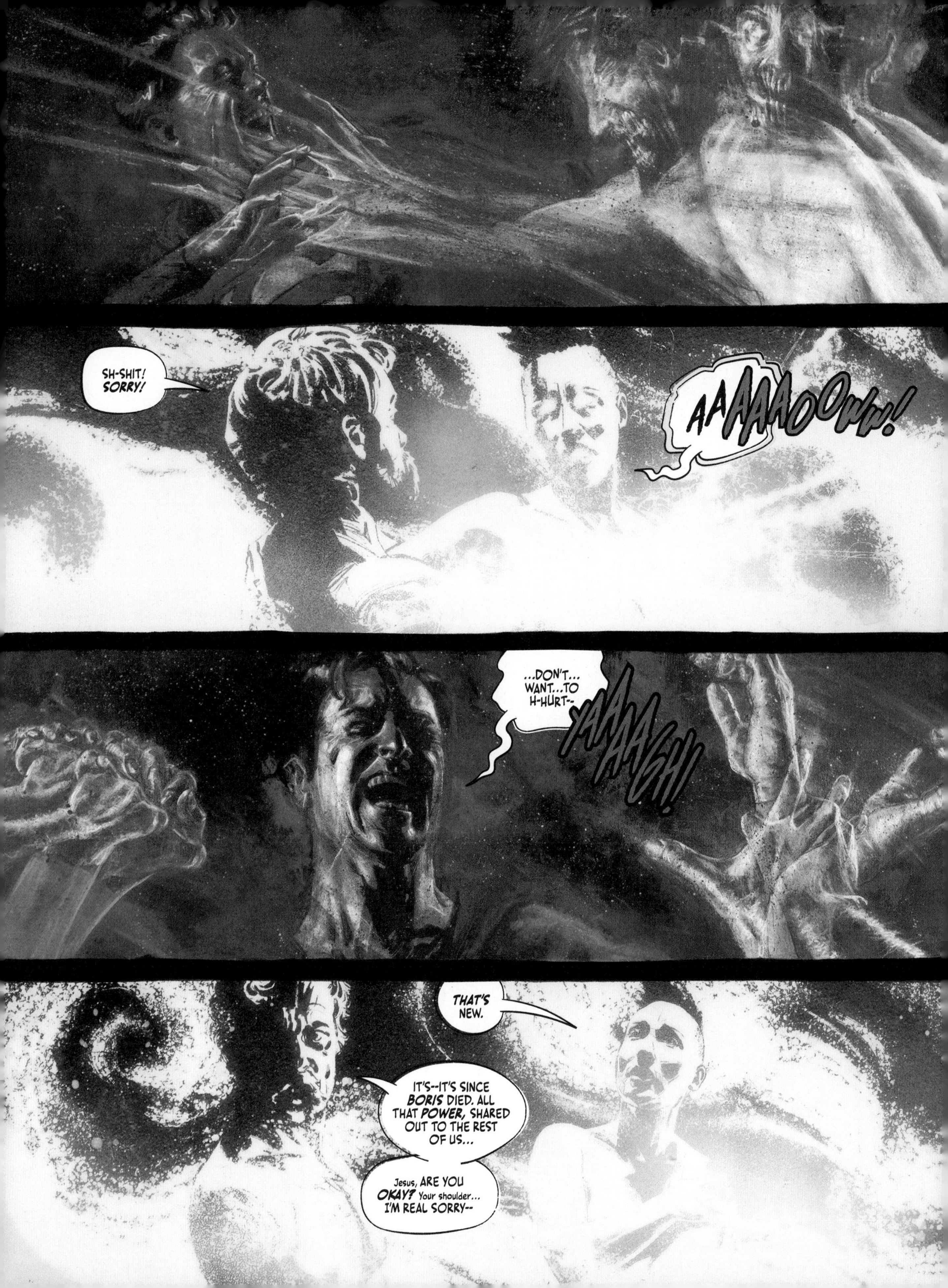
SH-SHIT! SORRY!
AAAAAAOOWW!
...DON'T... WANT...TO H-HURT--
YAAAAAGH!
THAT'S NEW.
IT'S--IT'S SINCE BORIS DIED. ALL THAT POWER, SHARED OUT TO THE REST OF US...
Jesus, ARE YOU OKAY? Your shoulder... I'M REAL SORRY--

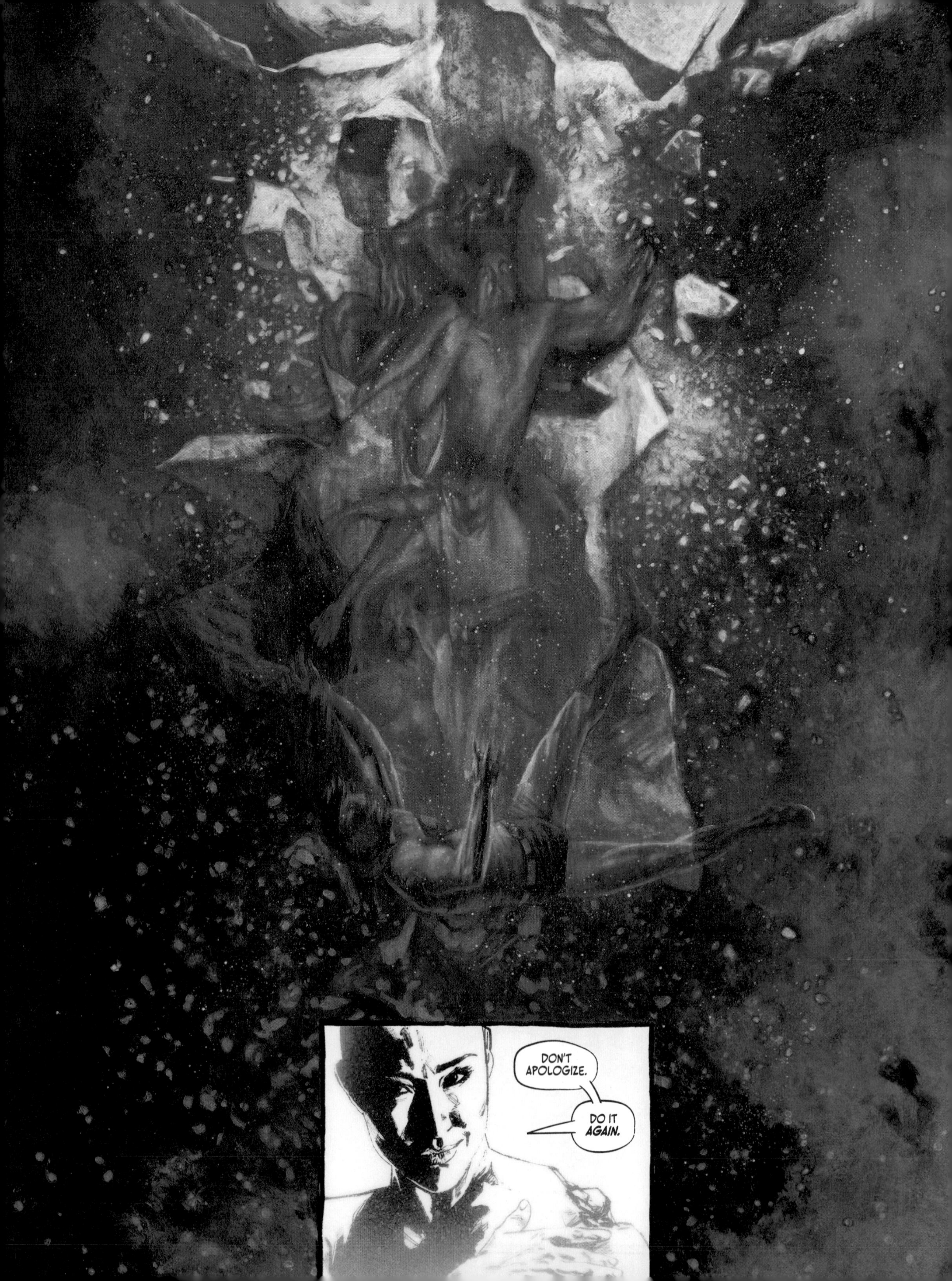
DON'T APOLOGIZE.
DO IT AGAIN.

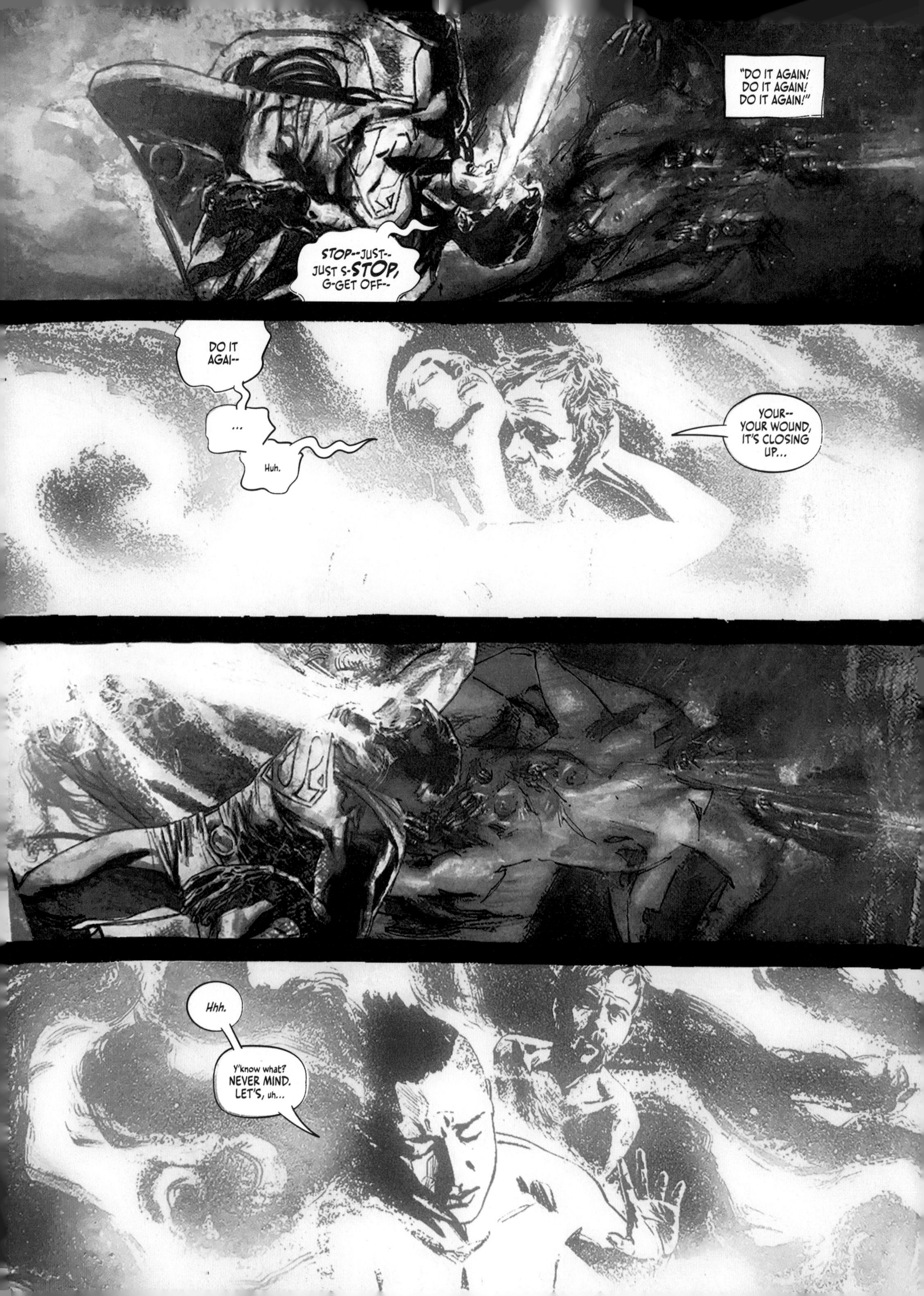
"DO IT AGAIN! DO IT AGAIN! DO IT AGAIN!"
STOP--JUST--JUST S-STOP, G-GET OFF--
DO IT AGAI--
...
Huh.
YOUR--YOUR WOUND, IT'S CLOSING UP...
Hhh.
Y'know what? NEVER MIND. LET'S, uh...

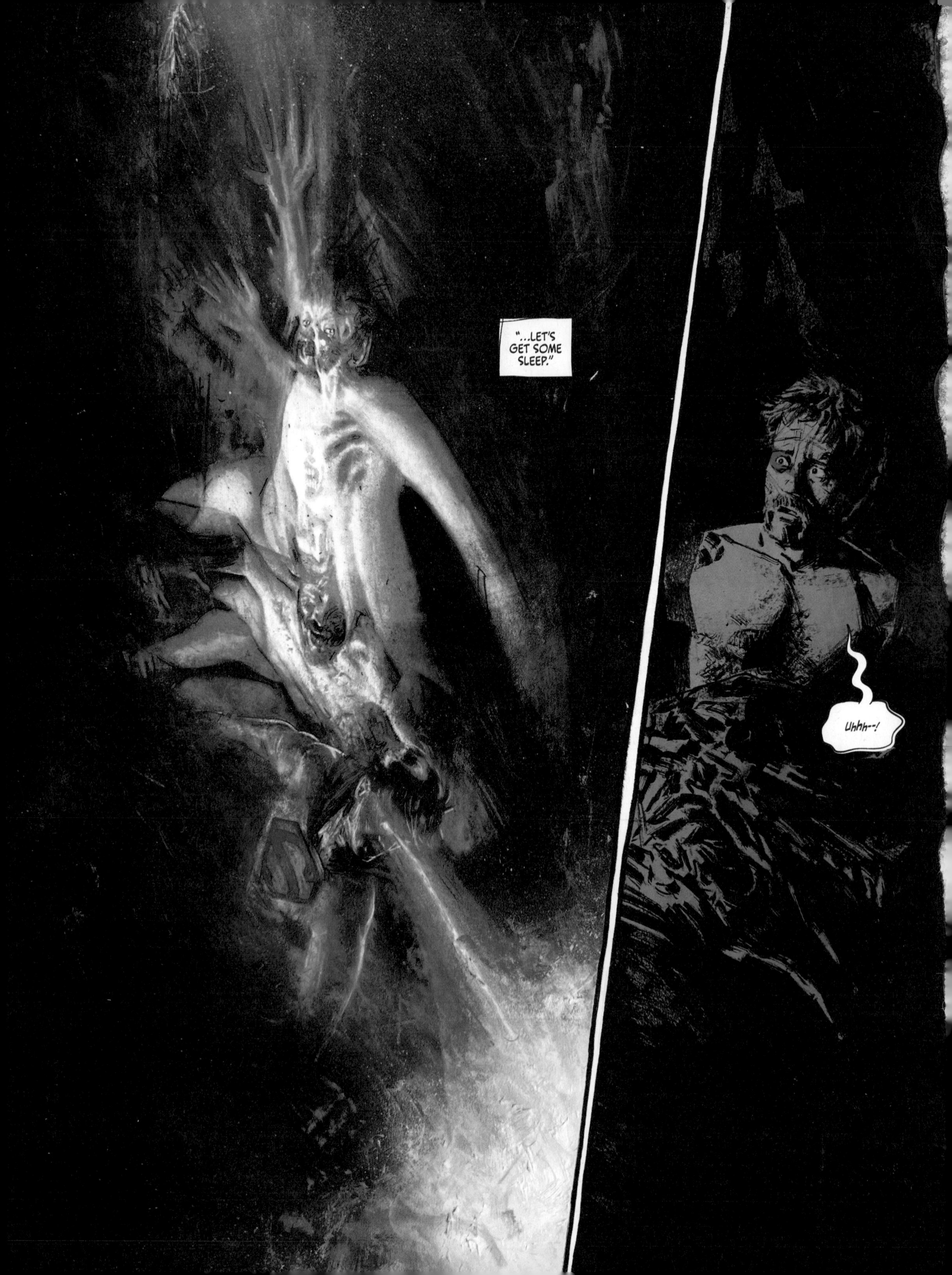
"...LET'S GET SOME SLEEP."
Uhhh--!

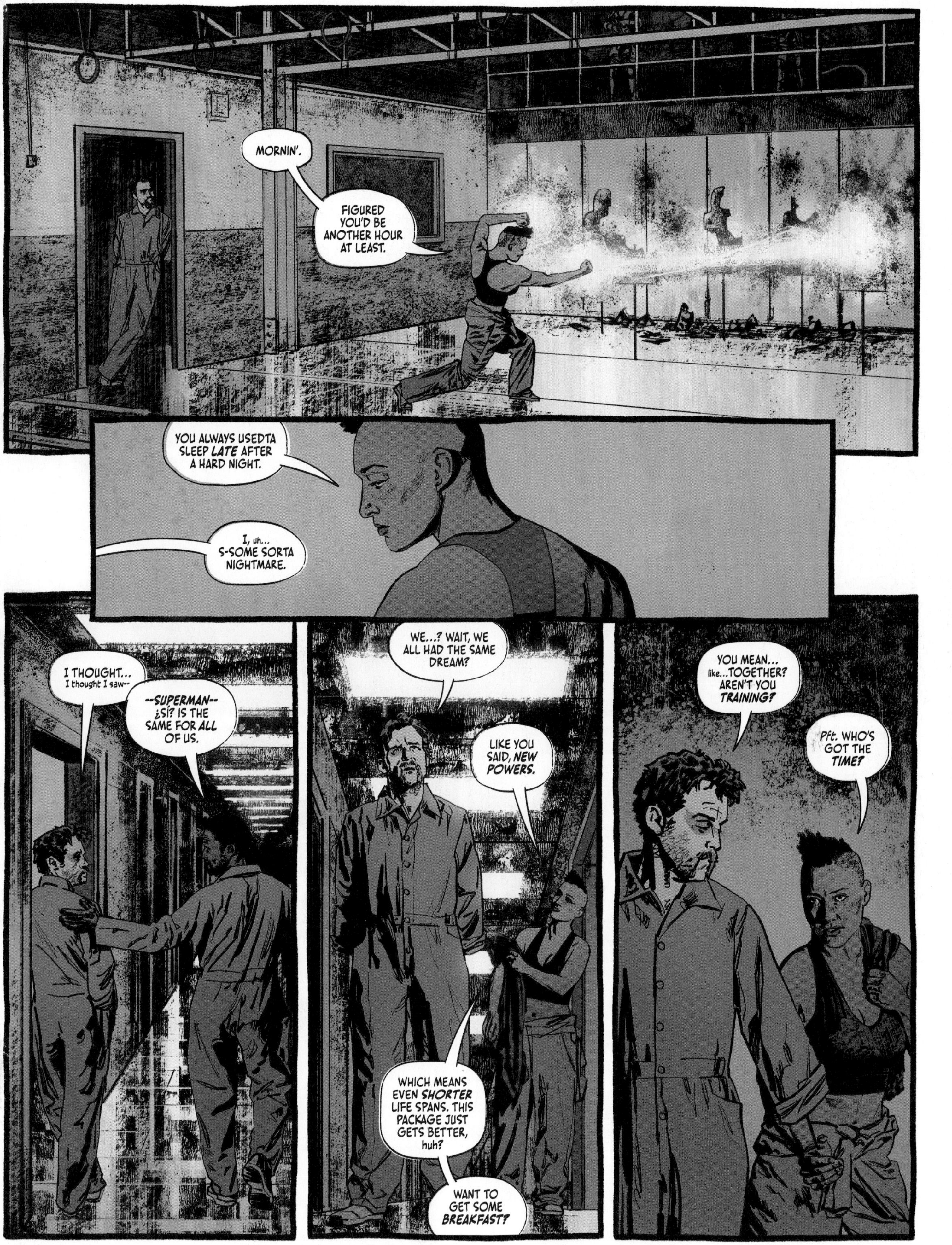
MORNIN'.
FIGURED YOU'D BE ANOTHER HOUR AT LEAST.
YOU ALWAYS USEDTA SLEEP *LATE* AFTER A HARD NIGHT.
I, uh... S-SOME SORTA NIGHTMARE.
I THOUGHT... I thought I saw--
--*SUPERMAN*-- ¿SÍ? IS THE SAME FOR *ALL* OF US.
WE...? WAIT, WE ALL HAD THE SAME DREAM?
LIKE YOU SAID, *NEW POWERS.*
WHICH MEANS EVEN *SHORTER* LIFE SPANS. THIS PACKAGE JUST GETS BETTER, huh?
WANT TO GET SOME *BREAKFAST?*
YOU MEAN... like...TOGETHER? AREN'T YOU *TRAINING?*
Pft. WHO'S GOT THE *TIME?*

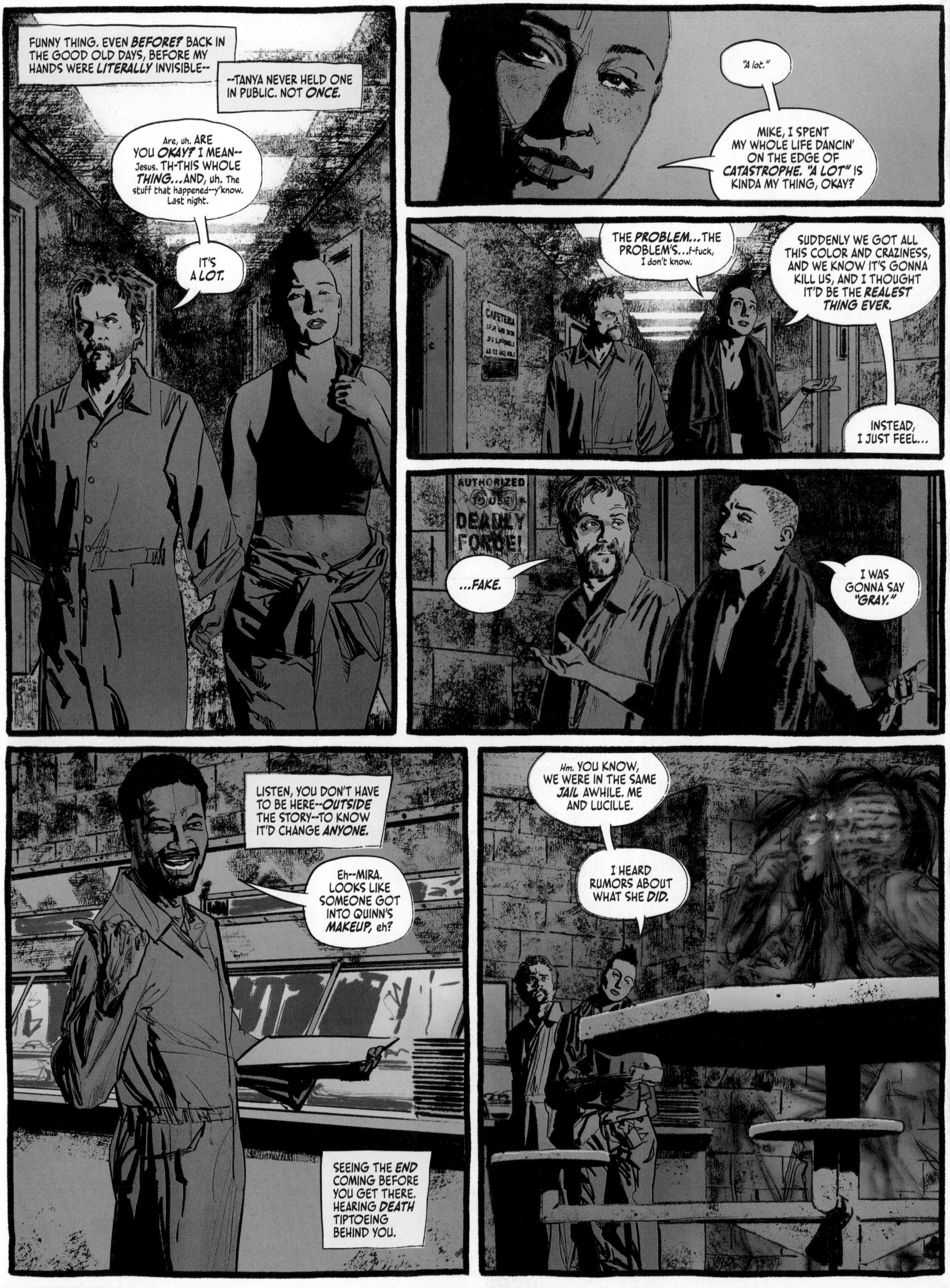
FUNNY THING. EVEN BEFORE? BACK IN THE GOOD OLD DAYS, BEFORE MY HANDS WERE LITERALLY INVISIBLE--
--TANYA NEVER HELD ONE IN PUBLIC. NOT ONCE.
Are, uh. ARE YOU OKAY? I MEAN-- Jesus. TH-THIS WHOLE THING...AND, uh. The stuff that happened--y'know. Last night.
IT'S A LOT.
"A lot."
MIKE, I SPENT MY WHOLE LIFE DANCIN' ON THE EDGE OF CATASTROPHE. "A LOT" IS KINDA MY THING, OKAY?
THE PROBLEM...THE PROBLEM'S...f-fuck, I don't know.
SUDDENLY WE GOT ALL THIS COLOR AND CRAZINESS, AND WE KNOW IT'S GONNA KILL US, AND I THOUGHT IT'D BE THE REALEST THING EVER.
INSTEAD, I JUST FEEL...
CAFETERIA
AUTHORIZED
DEADLY FORCE!
...FAKE.
I WAS GONNA SAY "GRAY."
LISTEN, YOU DON'T HAVE TO BE HERE--OUTSIDE THE STORY--TO KNOW IT'D CHANGE ANYONE.
Eh--MIRA. LOOKS LIKE SOMEONE GOT INTO QUINN'S MAKEUP, eh?
SEEING THE END COMING BEFORE YOU GET THERE. HEARING DEATH TIPTOEING BEHIND YOU.
Hm. YOU KNOW, WE WERE IN THE SAME JAIL AWHILE. ME AND LUCILLE.
I HEARD RUMORS ABOUT WHAT SHE DID.

THE WAY TANYA SAID IT,
LUCILLE WAS A *NANNY.*

JUST ONE MORE FOREIGN SUCKER, TAKING
HOME FUCK-ALL PAY FOR DOING THE KINDA
SHIT THAT FAT WHITE FOLKS WON'T.

FOR WHAT IT'S WORTH,
IT REALLY *WAS* THE DAY
FROM HELL. I'VE WATCHED
IT RIGHT THROUGH.

THE KID'S *PARENTS* CAME
IN DRUNK, GAVE HER SHIT...
THE *AGENCY* PEOPLE
WERE OUTRIGHT RACIST...
HER MOM WAS DYING
BACK IN MANILA, BUT
NOBODY WOULD LET
HER MAKE A *CALL...*

...AND THIS *BABY,* THIS
LITTLE CHUNK OF OVER-
FED *SKIN* AND *INSTINCT...*
IT *YELLED* FOR FOUR
HOURS SOLID.

THAT SPECIAL *RAW THROAT*
SCREAM THAT GOES RIGHT
TO YOUR *BACKBRAIN.*

THAT REACHES INTO YOUR
HEART AND *GRIPS.*

BUT HEY. I GET IT. THE
CIRCUMSTANCES DON'T
MATTER. WHY DEBATE
WHETHER SHE'S A GOOD
PERSON WHO *SNAPPED*
OR JUST PLAIN OLD *EVIL?*
THERE'S NO MITIGATING IT.

NO CONTEST
OF THE MURDER
CHARGE.
NO WORDS IN
DEFENSE. LUCILLE
WANTED NOTHING
MORE THAN TO
DIE FROM THE
SPLIT SECOND
THE BABY WENT
QUIET.

BUT--
SOMEBODY
SOUND THE
*RELIGION
ALARM--*
SUICIDE'S JUST
ANOTHER SIN.

THE BLAZE PROCEDURE...THE TICKING CLOCK...
DYING FOR SOMEONE ELSE'S CAUSE? THAT WAS
ALL JUST HER *WORKAROUND.*

BUT *THERE'S* THE IRONY, RIGHT? LUCILLE WAS HORNIER FOR
DEATH THAN ANY OF US, BUT ONE LITTLE DOSE OF POWER
AND--damn. FOR THE FIRST TIME SINCE SHE GRIPPED THOSE
TINY SHOULDERS AND *SHOOK* AND *SHOOK* AND *SHOOK--*

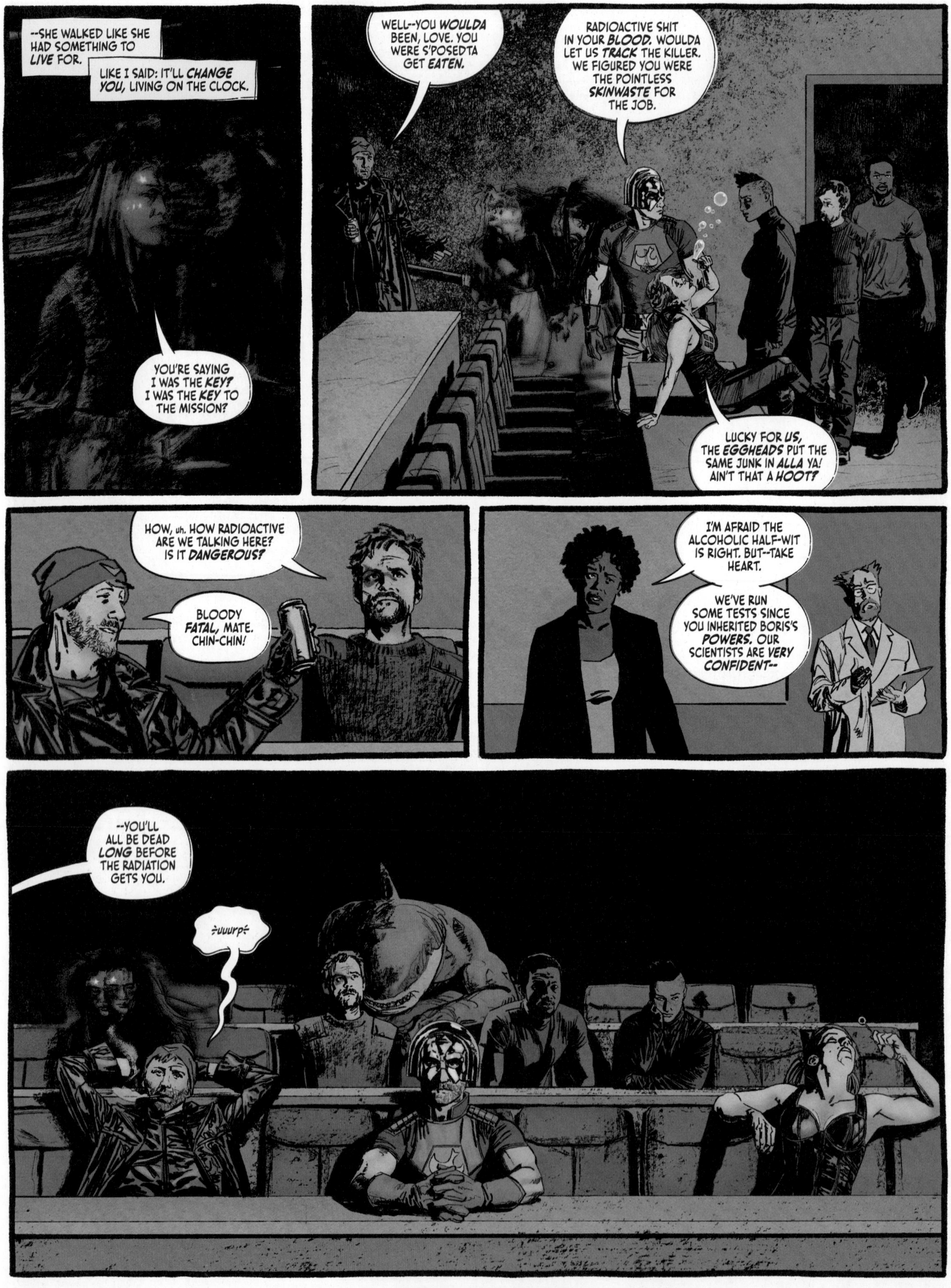
--SHE WALKED LIKE SHE HAD SOMETHING TO LIVE FOR.
LIKE I SAID: IT'LL CHANGE YOU, LIVING ON THE CLOCK.
YOU'RE SAYING I WAS THE KEY? I WAS THE KEY TO THE MISSION?
WELL--YOU WOULDA BEEN, LOVE. YOU WERE S'POSEDTA GET EATEN.
RADIOACTIVE SHIT IN YOUR BLOOD. WOULDA LET US TRACK THE KILLER. WE FIGURED YOU WERE THE POINTLESS SKINWASTE FOR THE JOB.
LUCKY FOR US, THE EGGHEADS PUT THE SAME JUNK IN ALLA YA! AIN'T THAT A HOOT?
HOW, uh, HOW RADIOACTIVE ARE WE TALKING HERE? IS IT DANGEROUS?
BLOODY FATAL, MATE. CHIN-CHIN!
I'M AFRAID THE ALCOHOLIC HALF-WIT IS RIGHT. BUT--TAKE HEART.
WE'VE RUN SOME TESTS SINCE YOU INHERITED BORIS'S POWERS. OUR SCIENTISTS ARE VERY CONFIDENT--
--YOU'LL ALL BE DEAD LONG BEFORE THE RADIATION GETS YOU.
uuurp

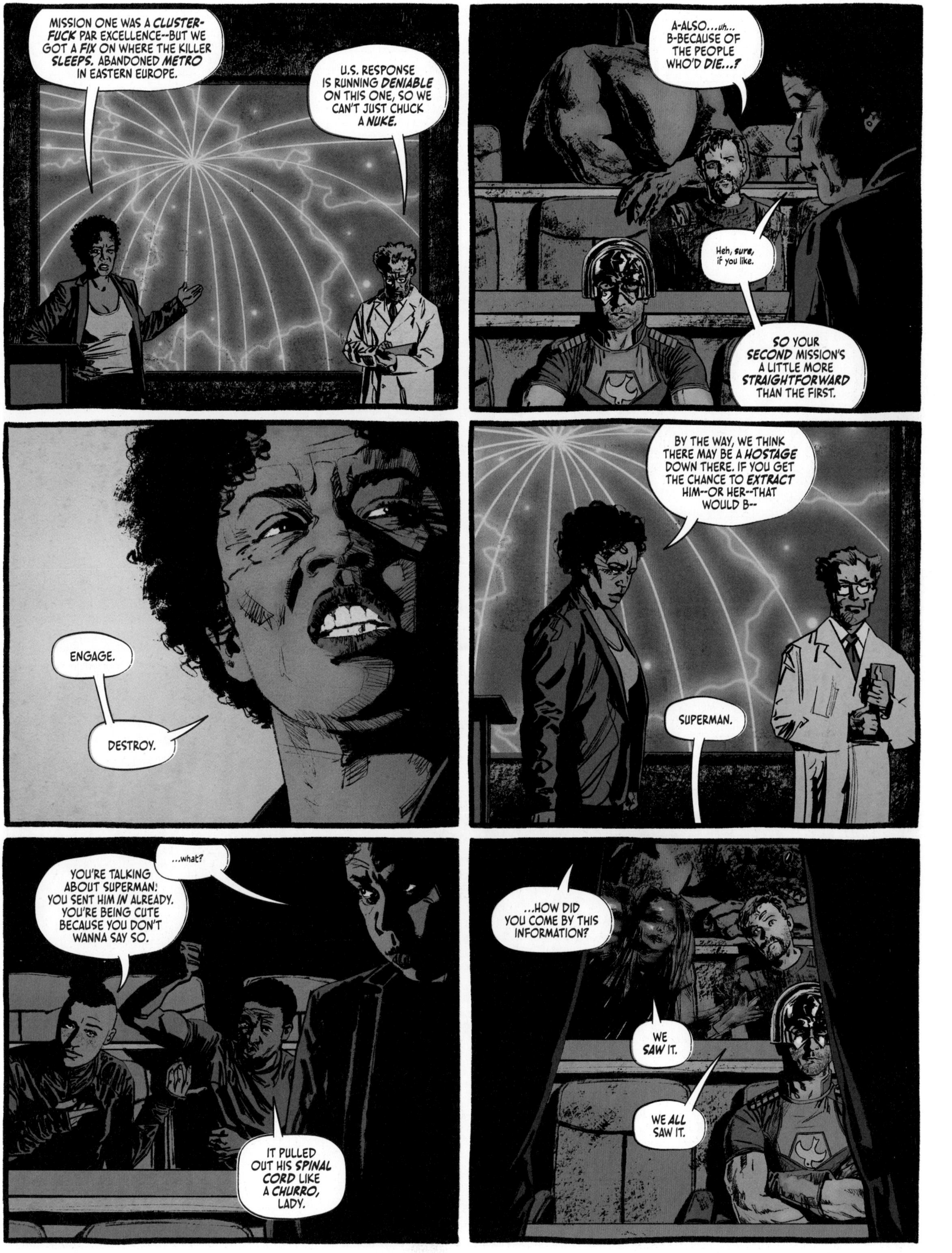
MISSION ONE WAS A CLUSTER-FUCK PAR EXCELLENCE--BUT WE GOT A FIX ON WHERE THE KILLER SLEEPS. ABANDONED METRO IN EASTERN EUROPE.
U.S. RESPONSE IS RUNNING DENIABLE ON THIS ONE, SO WE CAN'T JUST CHUCK A NUKE.
A-ALSO...uh... B-BECAUSE OF THE PEOPLE WHO'D DIE...?
Heh, sure, if you like.
SO YOUR SECOND MISSION'S A LITTLE MORE STRAIGHTFORWARD THAN THE FIRST.
ENGAGE.
DESTROY.
BY THE WAY, WE THINK THERE MAY BE A HOSTAGE DOWN THERE. IF YOU GET THE CHANCE TO EXTRACT HIM--OR HER--THAT WOULD B--
SUPERMAN.
YOU'RE TALKING ABOUT SUPERMAN: YOU SENT HIM IN ALREADY. YOU'RE BEING CUTE BECAUSE YOU DON'T WANNA SAY SO.
...what?
IT PULLED OUT HIS SPINAL CORD LIKE A CHURRO, LADY.
...HOW DID YOU COME BY THIS INFORMATION?
WE SAW IT.
WE ALL SAW IT.

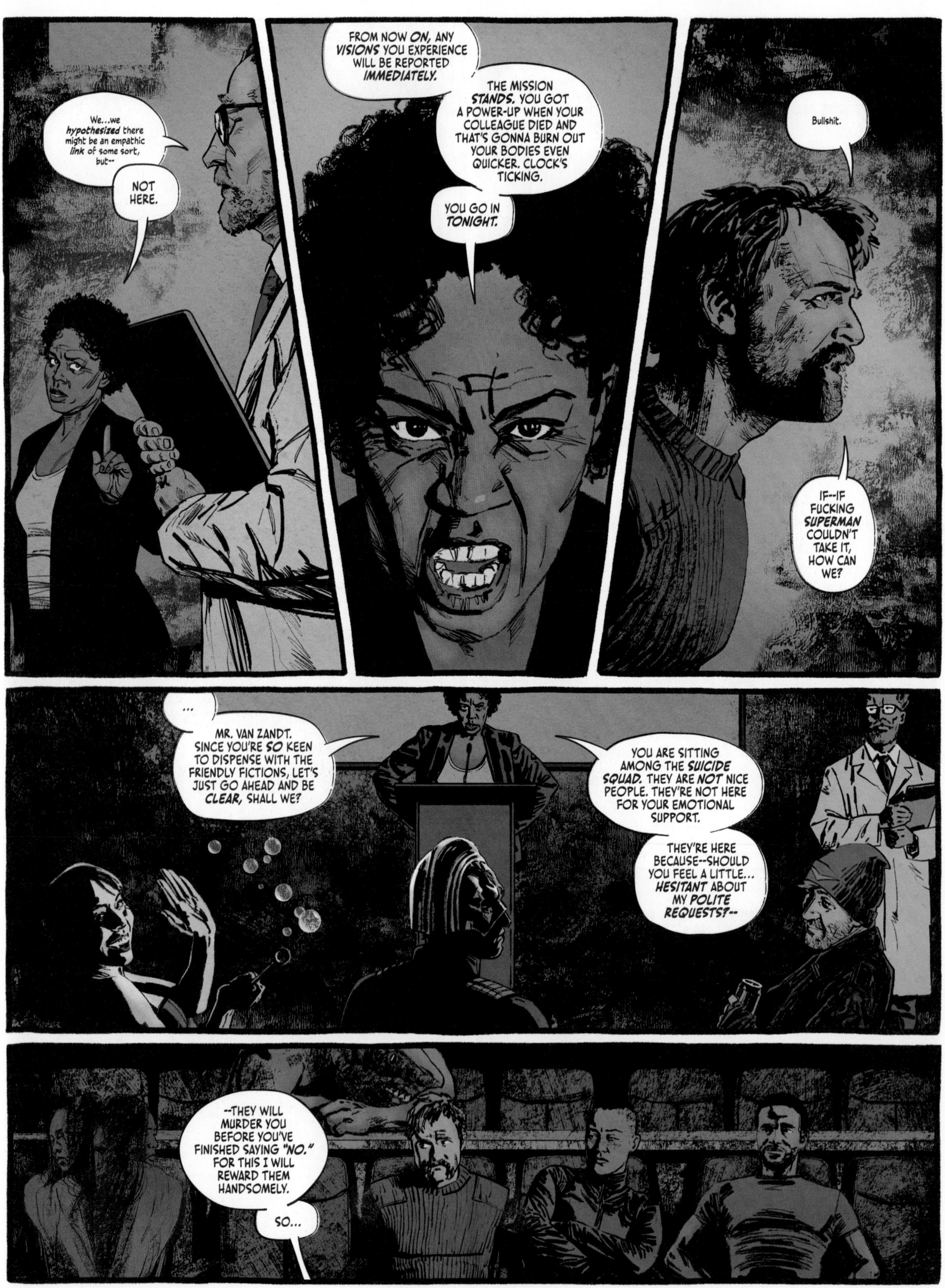
We...we hypothesized there might be an empathic link of some sort, but--
NOT HERE.
FROM NOW ON, ANY VISIONS YOU EXPERIENCE WILL BE REPORTED IMMEDIATELY.
THE MISSION STANDS. YOU GOT A POWER-UP WHEN YOUR COLLEAGUE DIED AND THAT'S GONNA BURN OUT YOUR BODIES EVEN QUICKER. CLOCK'S TICKING.
YOU GO IN TONIGHT.
Bullshit.
IF--IF FUCKING SUPERMAN COULDN'T TAKE IT, HOW CAN WE?
...
MR. VAN ZANDT. SINCE YOU'RE SO KEEN TO DISPENSE WITH THE FRIENDLY FICTIONS, LET'S JUST GO AHEAD AND BE CLEAR, SHALL WE?
YOU ARE SITTING AMONG THE SUICIDE SQUAD. THEY ARE NOT NICE PEOPLE. THEY'RE NOT HERE FOR YOUR EMOTIONAL SUPPORT.
THEY'RE HERE BECAUSE--SHOULD YOU FEEL A LITTLE... HESITANT ABOUT MY POLITE REQUESTS?--
--THEY WILL MURDER YOU BEFORE YOU'VE FINISHED SAYING "NO." FOR THIS I WILL REWARD THEM HANDSOMELY.
SO...

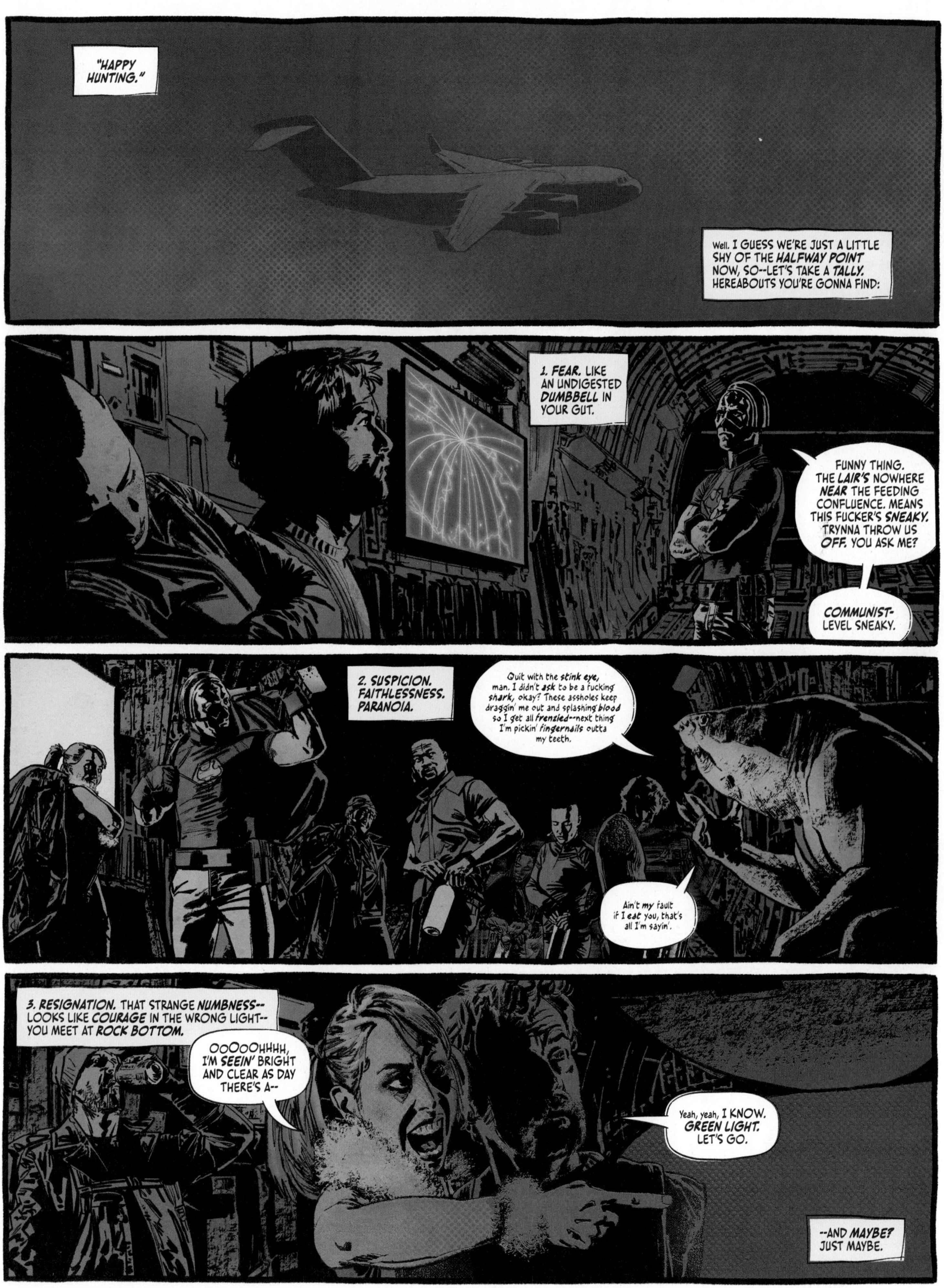
"HAPPY HUNTING."
Well. I GUESS WE'RE JUST A LITTLE SHY OF THE HALFWAY POINT NOW, SO--LET'S TAKE A TALLY. HEREABOUTS YOU'RE GONNA FIND:
1. FEAR. LIKE AN UNDIGESTED DUMBBELL IN YOUR GUT.
FUNNY THING. THE LAIR'S NOWHERE NEAR THE FEEDING CONFLUENCE. MEANS THIS FUCKER'S SNEAKY. TRYNNA THROW US OFF. YOU ASK ME?
COMMUNIST-LEVEL SNEAKY.
2. SUSPICION. FAITHLESSNESS. PARANOIA.
Quit with the stink eye, man. I didn't ask to be a fucking shark, okay? These assholes keep draggin' me out and splashing blood so I get all frenzied--next thing I'm pickin' fingernails outta my teeth.
Ain't my fault if I eat you, that's all I'm sayin'.
3. RESIGNATION. THAT STRANGE NUMBNESS--LOOKS LIKE COURAGE IN THE WRONG LIGHT--YOU MEET AT ROCK BOTTOM.
OOOOOHHHH, I'M SEEIN' BRIGHT AND CLEAR AS DAY THERE'S A--
Yeah, yeah, I KNOW. GREEN LIGHT. LET'S GO.
--AND MAYBE? JUST MAYBE.

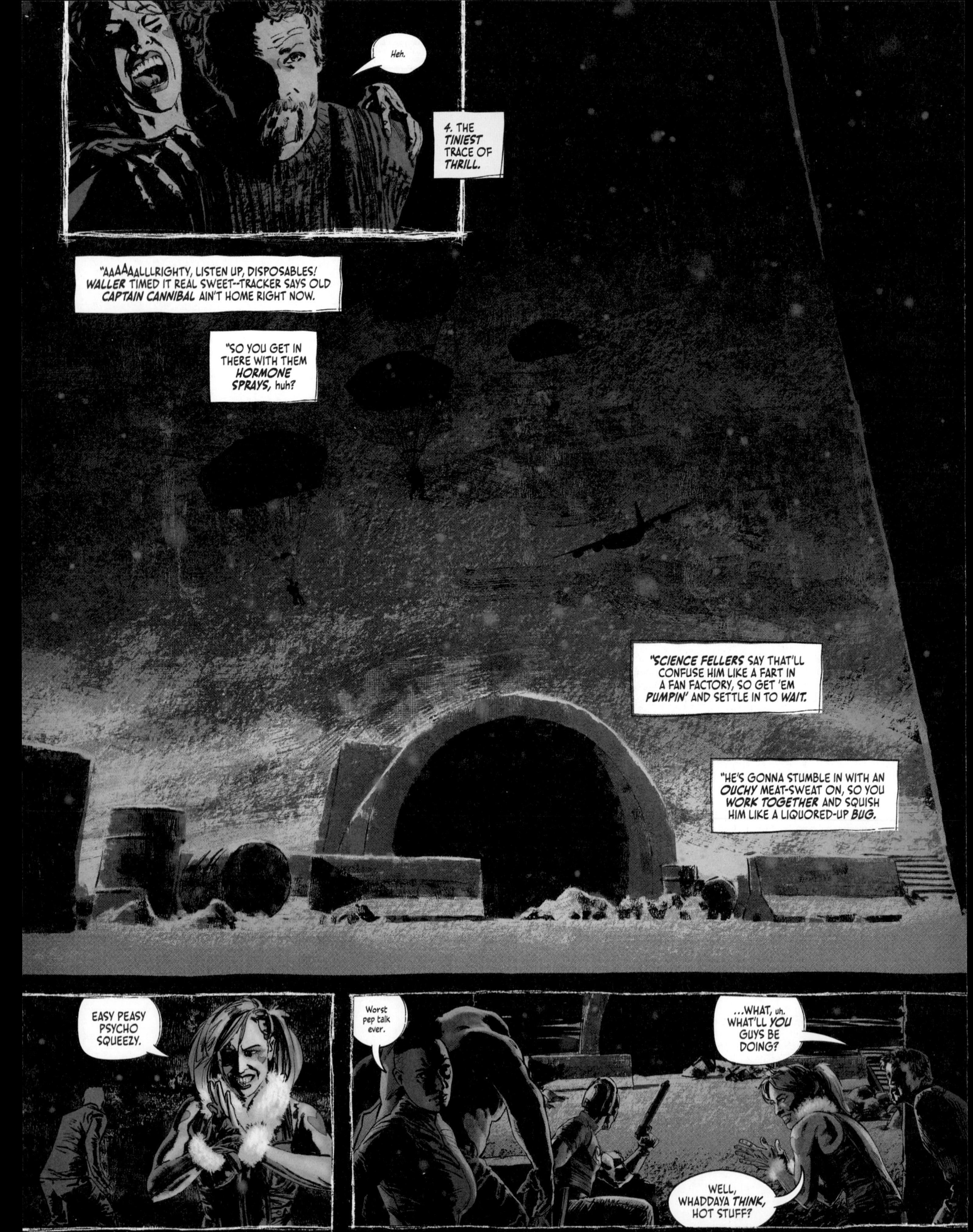

Heh.
4. THE TINIEST TRACE OF THRILL.
"AAAAAALLLRIGHTY, LISTEN UP, DISPOSABLES! WALLER TIMED IT REAL SWEET--TRACKER SAYS OLD CAPTAIN CANNIBAL AIN'T HOME RIGHT NOW.
"SO YOU GET IN THERE WITH THEM HORMONE SPRAYS, huh?
"SCIENCE FELLERS SAY THAT'LL CONFUSE HIM LIKE A FART IN A FAN FACTORY, SO GET 'EM PUMPIN' AND SETTLE IN TO WAIT.
"HE'S GONNA STUMBLE IN WITH AN OUCHY MEAT-SWEAT ON, SO YOU WORK TOGETHER AND SQUISH HIM LIKE A LIQUORED-UP BUG.
EASY PEASY PSYCHO SQUEEZY.
Worst pep talk ever.
...WHAT, uh. WHAT'LL YOU GUYS BE DOING?
WELL, WHADDAYA THINK, HOT STUFF?

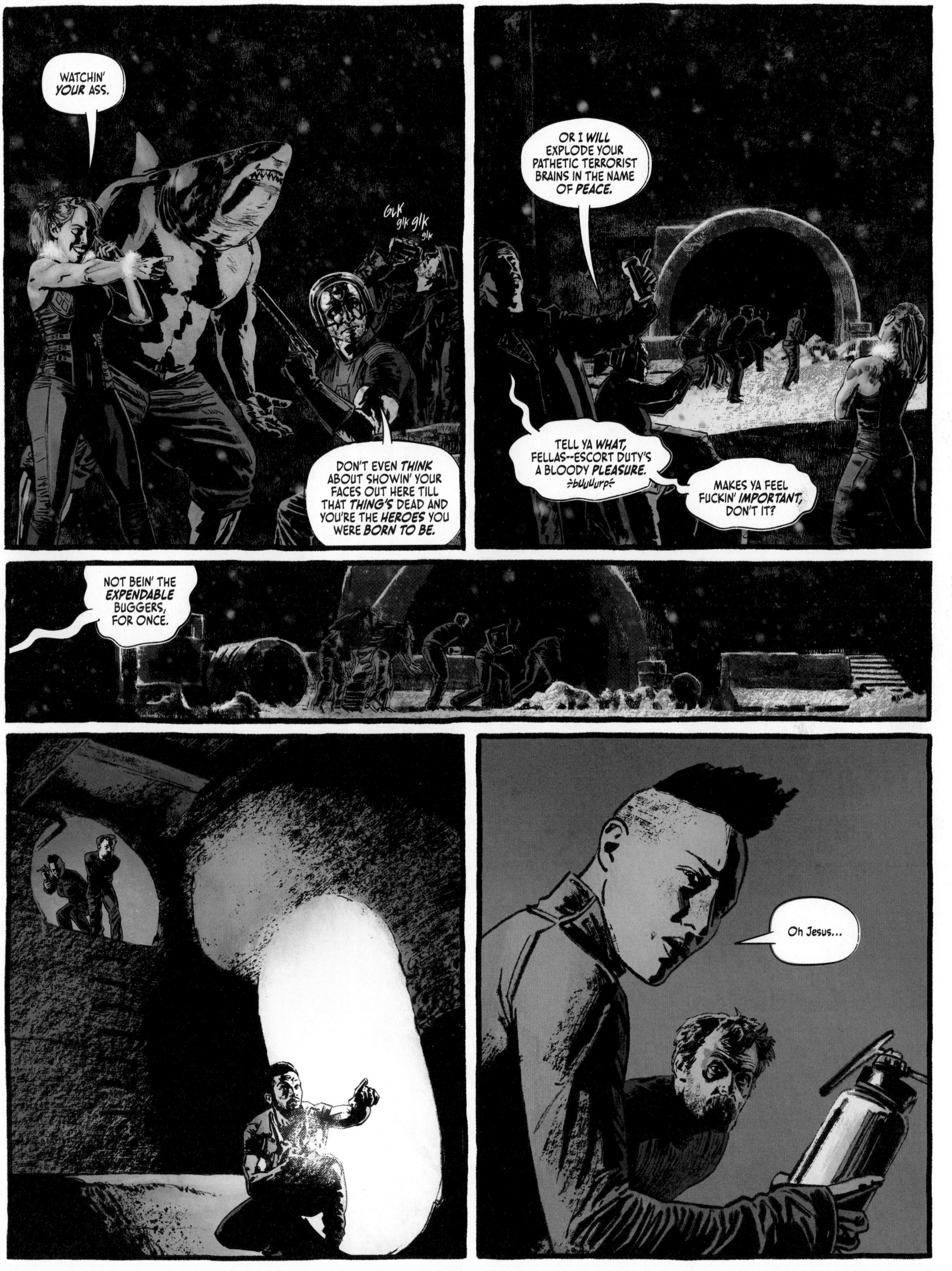
WATCHIN' YOUR ASS.
GLK glk glk glk
DON'T EVEN THINK ABOUT SHOWIN' YOUR FACES OUT HERE TILL THAT THING'S DEAD AND YOU'RE THE HEROES YOU WERE BORN TO BE.
OR I WILL EXPLODE YOUR PATHETIC TERRORIST BRAINS IN THE NAME OF PEACE.
TELL YA WHAT, FELLAS--ESCORT DUTY'S A BLOODY PLEASURE. ≠buuurp≠
MAKES YA FEEL FUCKIN' IMPORTANT, DON'T IT?
NOT BEIN' THE EXPENDABLE BUGGERS, FOR ONCE.
Oh Jesus...

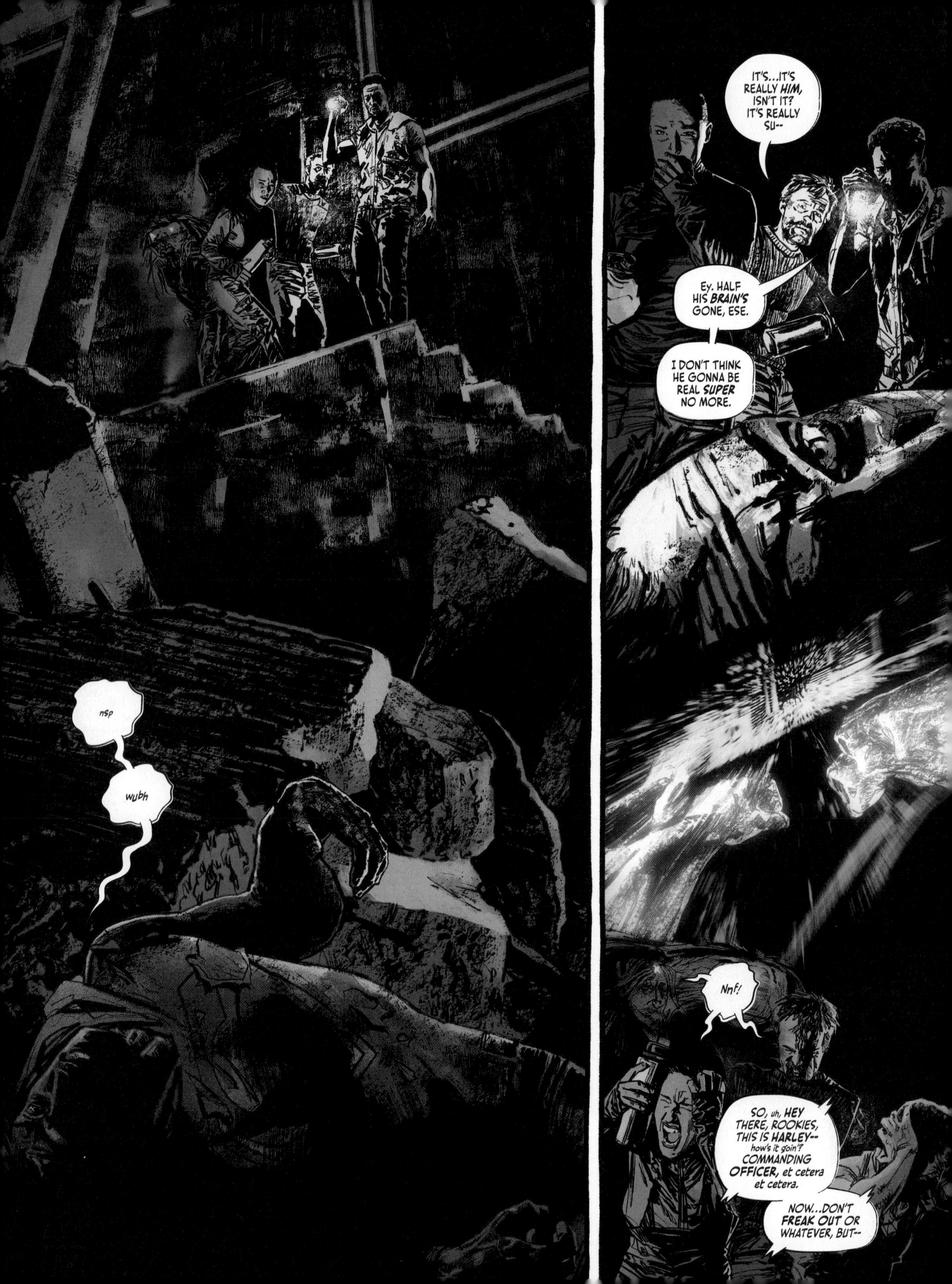
nsp
wubh
IT'S...IT'S REALLY HIM, ISN'T IT? IT'S REALLY SU--
Ey. HALF HIS BRAIN'S GONE, ESE.
I DON'T THINK HE GONNA BE REAL SUPER NO MORE.
Nnf!
SO, uh, HEY THERE, ROOKIES, THIS IS HARLEY-- how's it goin'? COMMANDING OFFICER, et cetera et cetera.
NOW...DON'T FREAK OUT OR WHATEVER, BUT--

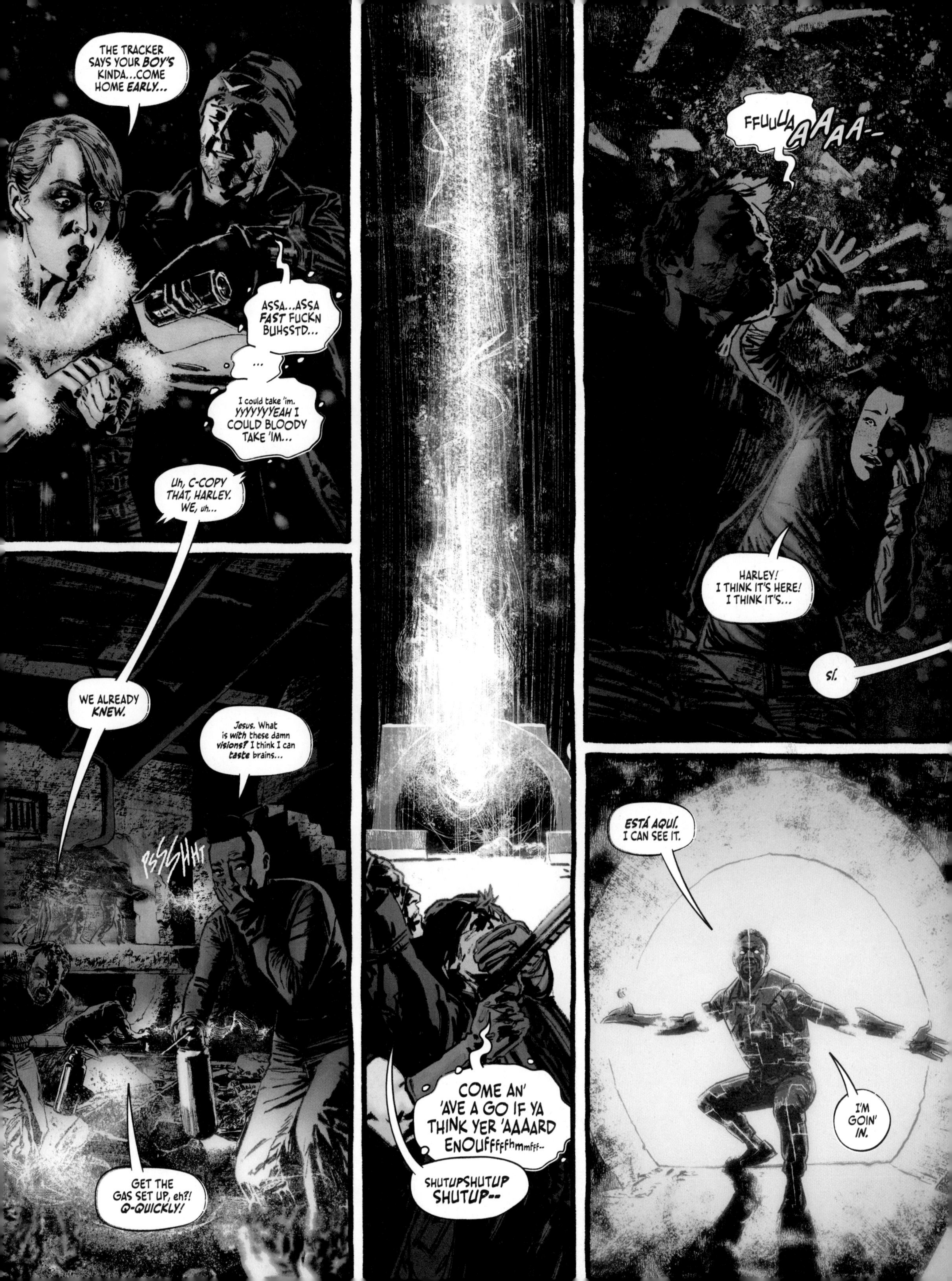
THE TRACKER SAYS YOUR BOY'S KINDA...COME HOME EARLY...
ASSA...ASSA FAST FUCKN BUHSSTD...
...
I could take 'im. YYYYYYYEAH I COULD BLOODY TAKE 'IM...
Uh, C-COPY THAT, HARLEY. WE, uh...
WE ALREADY KNEW.
Jesus. What is with these damn visions? I think I can taste brains...
PSSSHHT
GET THE GAS SET UP, eh?! Q-QUICKLY!
COME AN' 'AVE A GO IF YA THINK YER 'AAAARD ENOUFfffhmmfff--
SHUTUPSHUTUP SHUTUP--
FFUUUAAAAAA--
HARLEY! I THINK IT'S HERE! I THINK IT'S...
SÍ.
ESTÁ AQUÍ. I CAN SEE IT.
I'M GOIN' IN.

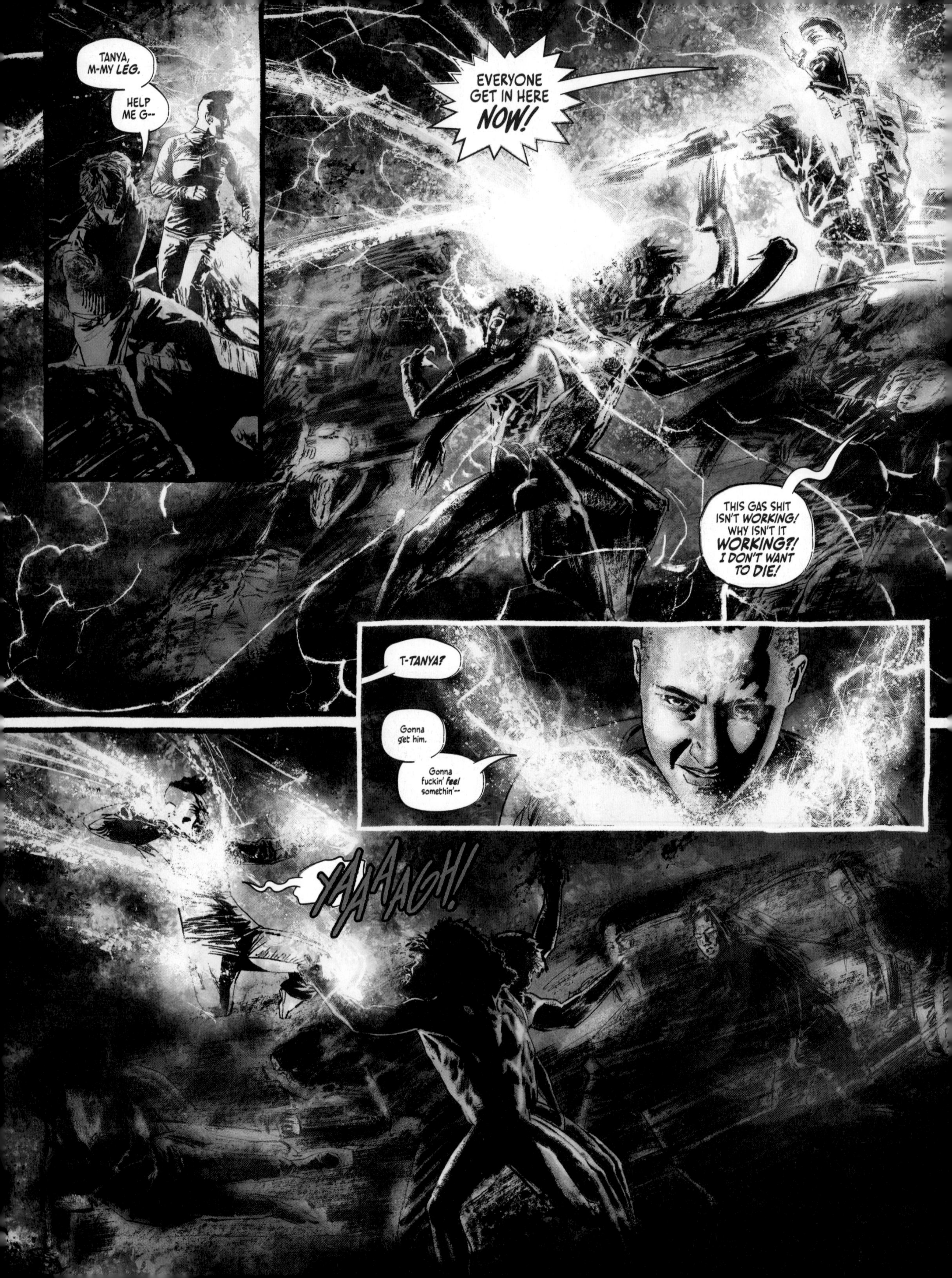
TANYA, M-MY *LEG.*
HELP ME G--
EVERYONE GET IN HERE *NOW!*
THIS GAS SHIT ISN'T *WORKING!* WHY ISN'T IT *WORKING?!* *I DON'T WANT TO DIE!*
T-*TANYA?*
Gonna get him.
Gonna fuckin' *feel* somethin'--
YAAAAGH!

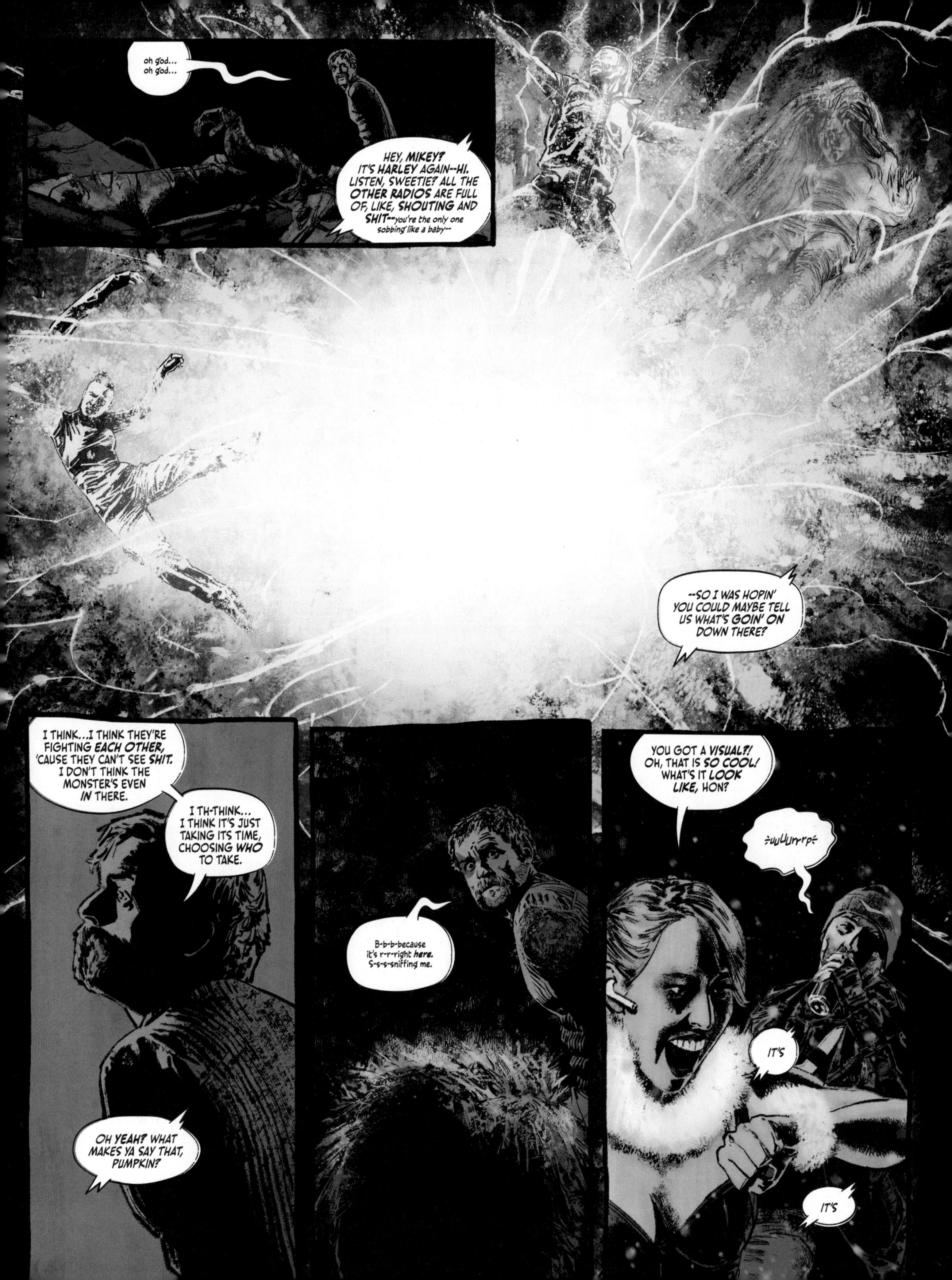

oh god... oh god...
HEY, MIKEY? IT'S HARLEY AGAIN--HI. LISTEN, SWEETIE? ALL THE OTHER RADIOS ARE FULL OF, LIKE, SHOUTING AND SHIT--you're the only one sobbing like a baby--
--SO I WAS HOPIN' YOU COULD MAYBE TELL US WHAT'S GOIN' ON DOWN THERE?
I THINK...I THINK THEY'RE FIGHTING EACH OTHER, 'CAUSE THEY CAN'T SEE SHIT. I DON'T THINK THE MONSTER'S EVEN IN THERE.
I TH-THINK... I THINK IT'S JUST TAKING ITS TIME, CHOOSING WHO TO TAKE.
OH YEAH? WHAT MAKES YA SAY THAT, PUMPKIN?
B-b-b-because it's r-r-right here. S-s-s-sniffing me.
YOU GOT A VISUAL?! OH, THAT IS SO COOL! WHAT'S IT LOOK LIKE, HON?
uuUUrr-rp
IT'S
IT'S

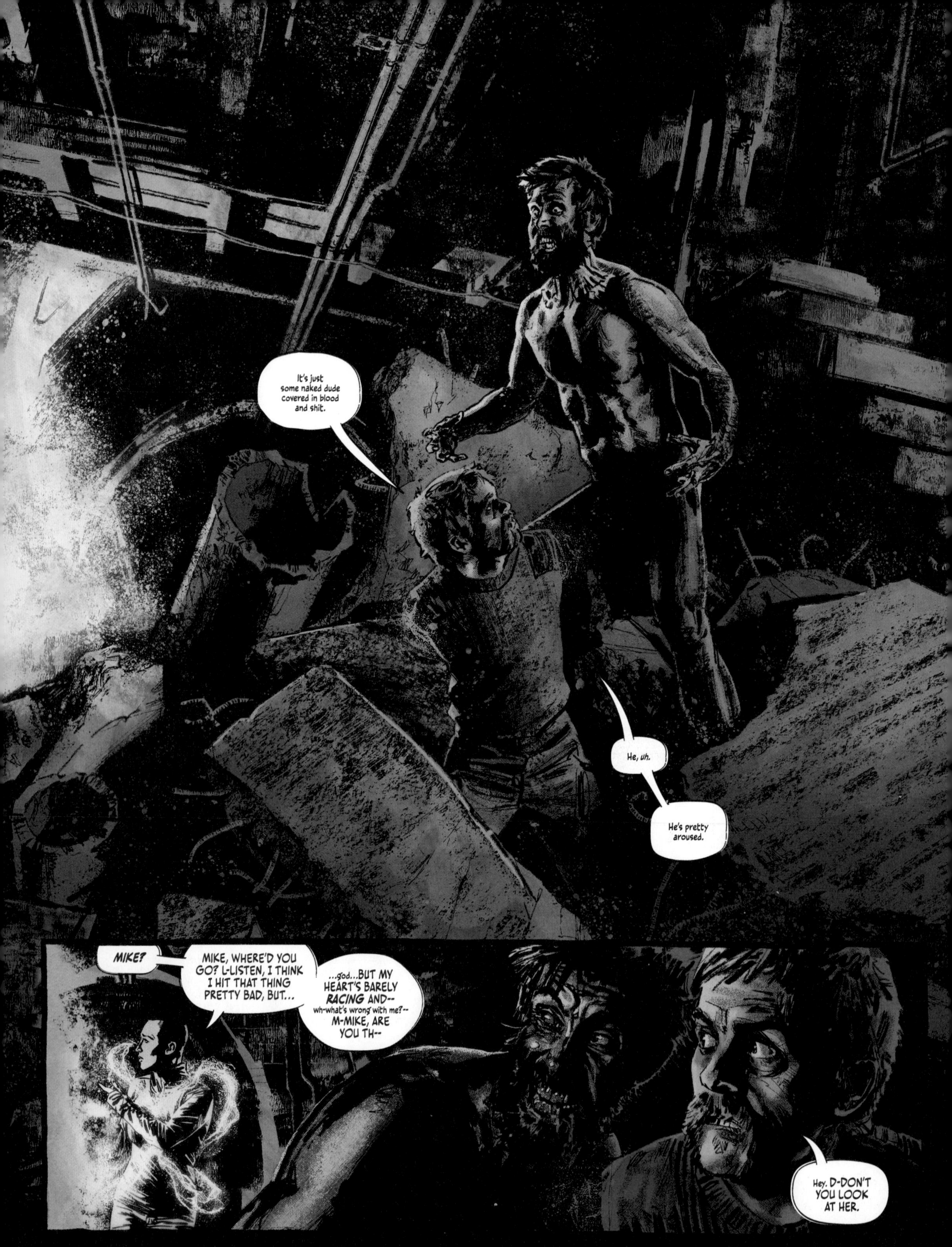
It's just some naked dude covered in blood and shit.
He, uh.
He's pretty aroused.
MIKE?
MIKE, WHERE'D YOU GO? L-LISTEN, I THINK I HIT THAT THING PRETTY BAD, BUT...
...god...BUT MY HEART'S BARELY RACING AND-- wh-what's wrong with me?-- M-MIKE, ARE YOU TH--
Hey. D-DON'T YOU LOOK AT HER.

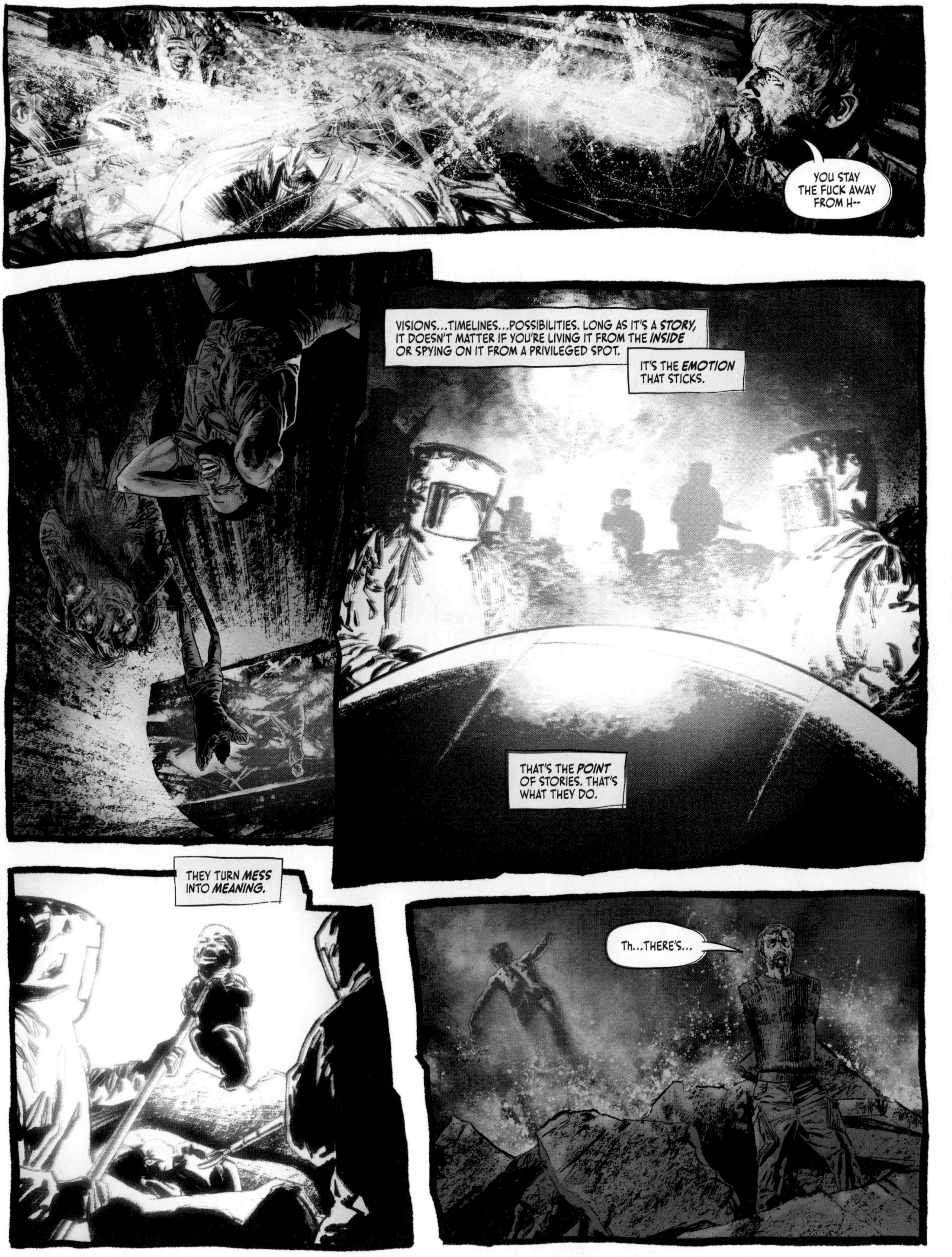
YOU STAY THE FUCK AWAY FROM H--
VISIONS...TIMELINES...POSSIBILITIES. LONG AS IT'S A *STORY,* IT DOESN'T MATTER IF YOU'RE LIVING IT FROM THE *INSIDE* OR SPYING ON IT FROM A PRIVILEGED SPOT.
IT'S THE *EMOTION* THAT STICKS.
THAT'S THE *POINT* OF STORIES. THAT'S WHAT THEY DO.
THEY TURN *MESS* INTO *MEANING.*
Th...THERE'S...

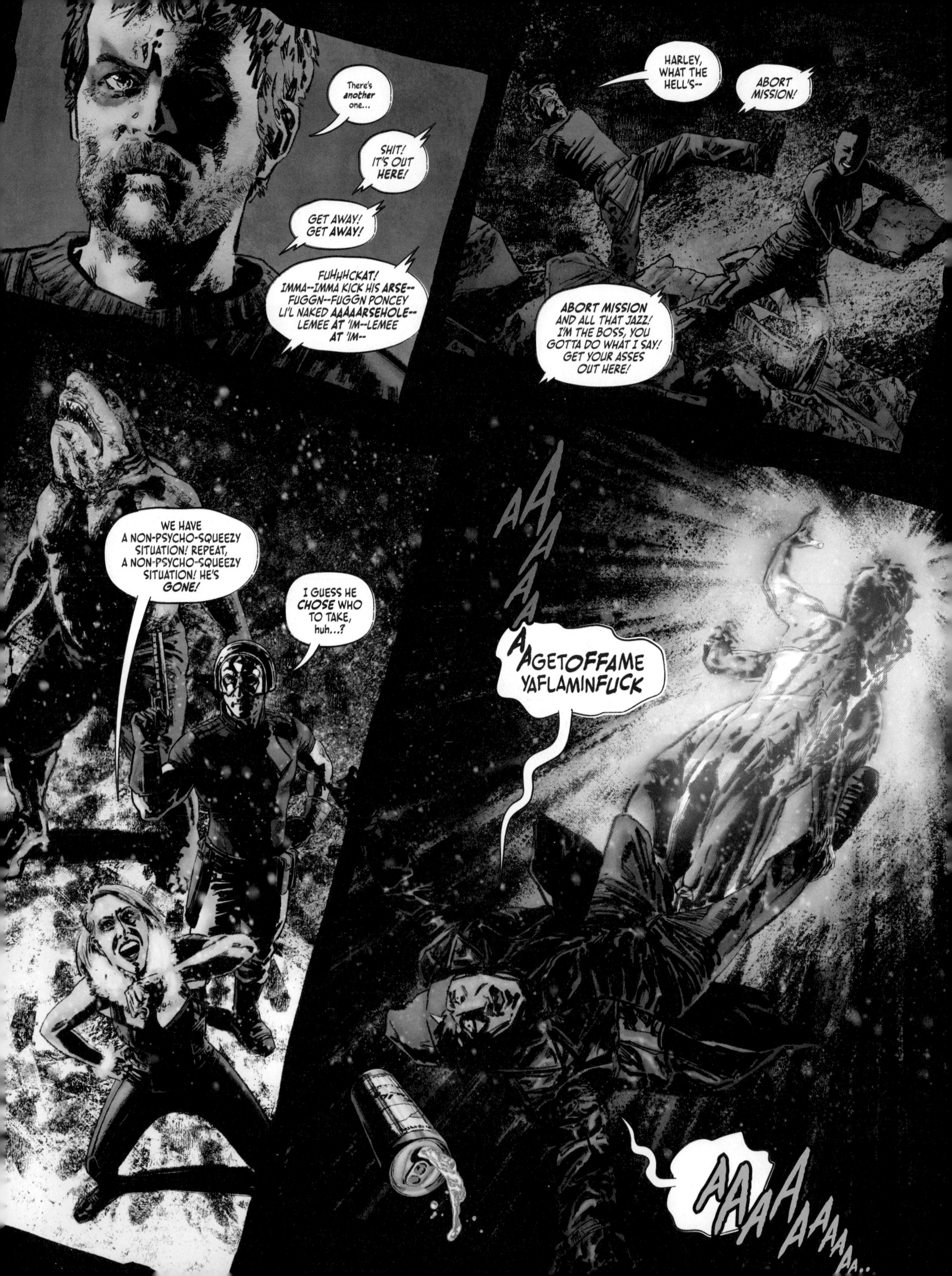
There's another one...
SHIT! IT'S OUT HERE!
GET AWAY! GET AWAY!
FUHHHCKAT! IMMA--IMMA KICK HIS ARSE-- FUGGN--FUGGN PONCEY LI'L NAKED AAAAARSEHOLE-- LEMEE AT 'IM--LEMEE AT 'IM--
HARLEY, WHAT THE HELL'S--
ABORT MISSION!
ABORT MISSION AND ALL THAT JAZZ! I'M THE BOSS, YOU GOTTA DO WHAT I SAY! GET YOUR ASSES OUT HERE!
WE HAVE A NON-PSYCHO-SQUEEZY SITUATION! REPEAT, A NON-PSYCHO-SQUEEZY SITUATION! HE'S GONE!
I GUESS HE CHOSE WHO TO TAKE, huh...?
AAAAAAAAAGETOFFAME YAFLAMINFUCK
AAAAAAAAA...

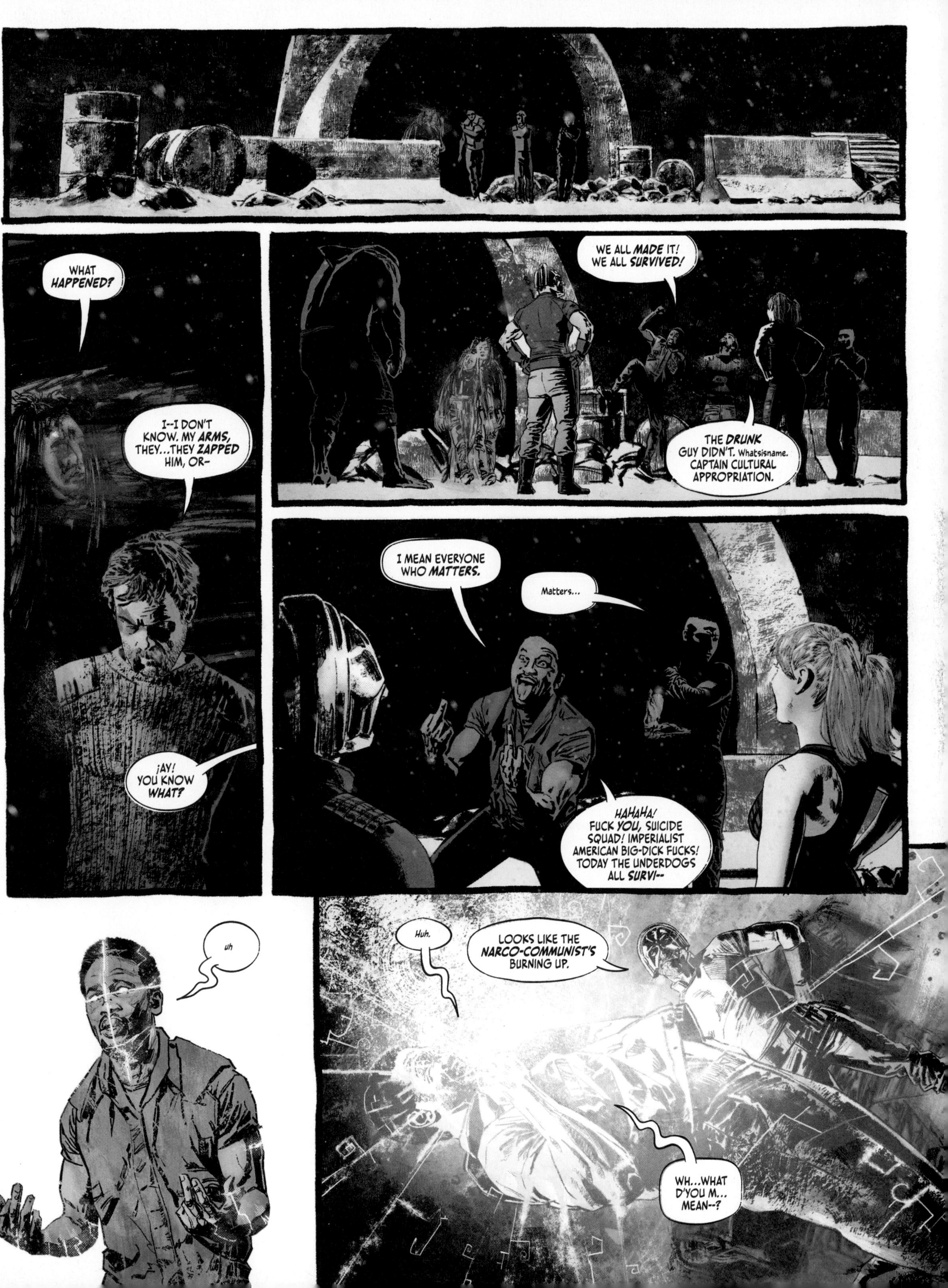
WHAT HAPPENED?
I--I DON'T KNOW. MY ARMS, THEY...THEY ZAPPED HIM, OR-
¡AY! YOU KNOW WHAT?
WE ALL MADE IT! WE ALL SURVIVED!
THE DRUNK GUY DIDN'T. Whatsisname. CAPTAIN CULTURAL APPROPRIATION.
I MEAN EVERYONE WHO MATTERS.
Matters...
HAHAHA! FUCK YOU, SUICIDE SQUAD! IMPERIALIST AMERICAN BIG-DICK FUCKS! TODAY THE UNDERDOGS ALL SURVI--
uh
Huh.
LOOKS LIKE THE NARCO-COMMUNIST'S BURNING UP.
WH...WHAT D'YOU M... MEAN--?

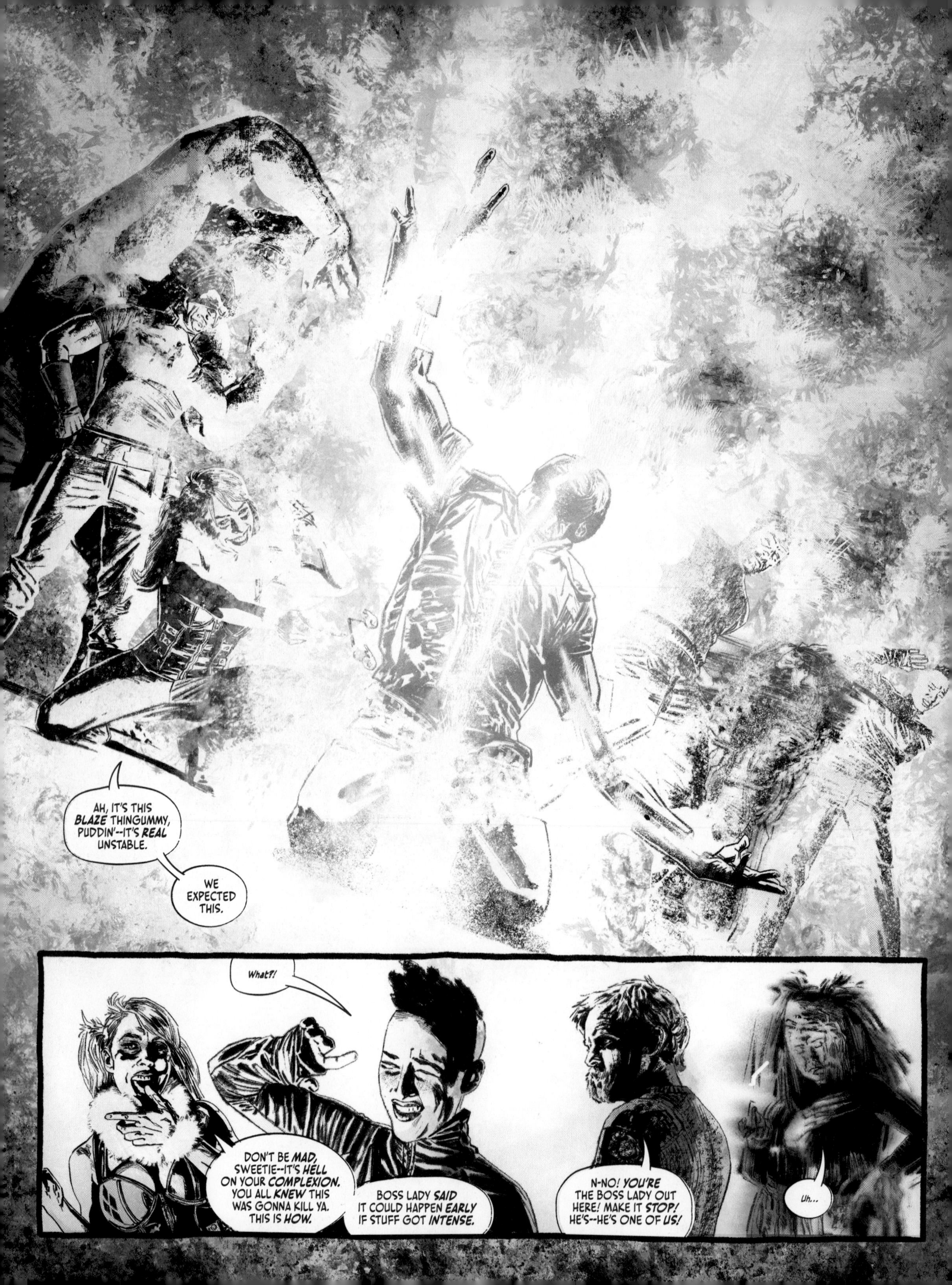

AH, IT'S THIS *BLAZE* THINGUMMY, PUDDIN'--IT'S *REAL* UNSTABLE.
WE EXPECTED THIS.
What?!
DON'T BE *MAD*, SWEETIE--IT'S *HELL* ON YOUR *COMPLEXION*. YOU ALL *KNEW* THIS WAS GONNA KILL YA. THIS IS *HOW*.
BOSS LADY *SAID* IT COULD HAPPEN *EARLY* IF STUFF GOT *INTENSE*.
N-NO! *YOU'RE* THE BOSS LADY OUT HERE! MAKE IT *STOP!* HE'S--HE'S ONE OF *US!*
Uh...

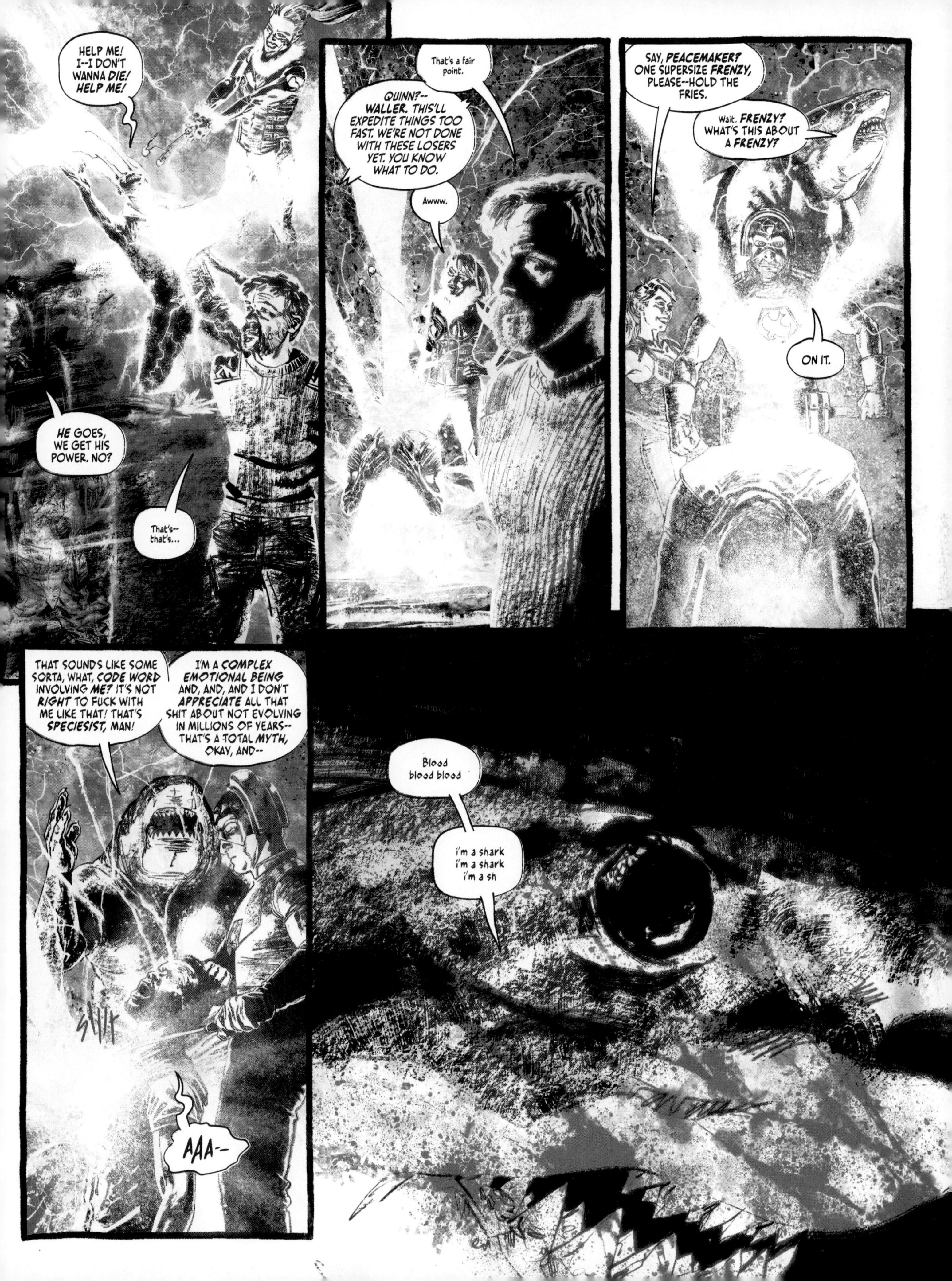
HELP ME! I--I DON'T WANNA DIE! HELP ME!
HE GOES, WE GET HIS POWER. NO?
That's-- that's...
That's a fair point.
QUINN?-- WALLER. THIS'LL EXPEDITE THINGS TOO FAST. WE'RE NOT DONE WITH THESE LOSERS YET. YOU KNOW WHAT TO DO.
Awww.
SAY, PEACEMAKER? ONE SUPERSIZE FRENZY, PLEASE--HOLD THE FRIES.
Wait. FRENZY? WHAT'S THIS ABOUT A FRENZY?
ON IT.
THAT SOUNDS LIKE SOME SORTA, WHAT, CODE WORD INVOLVING ME? IT'S NOT RIGHT TO FUCK WITH ME LIKE THAT! THAT'S SPECIESIST, MAN!
I'M A COMPLEX EMOTIONAL BEING AND, AND, AND I DON'T APPRECIATE ALL THAT SHIT ABOUT NOT EVOLVING IN MILLIONS OF YEARS-- THAT'S A TOTAL MYTH, OKAY, AND--
SHLT
AAA-
Blood blood blood
i'm a shark i'm a shark i'm a sh

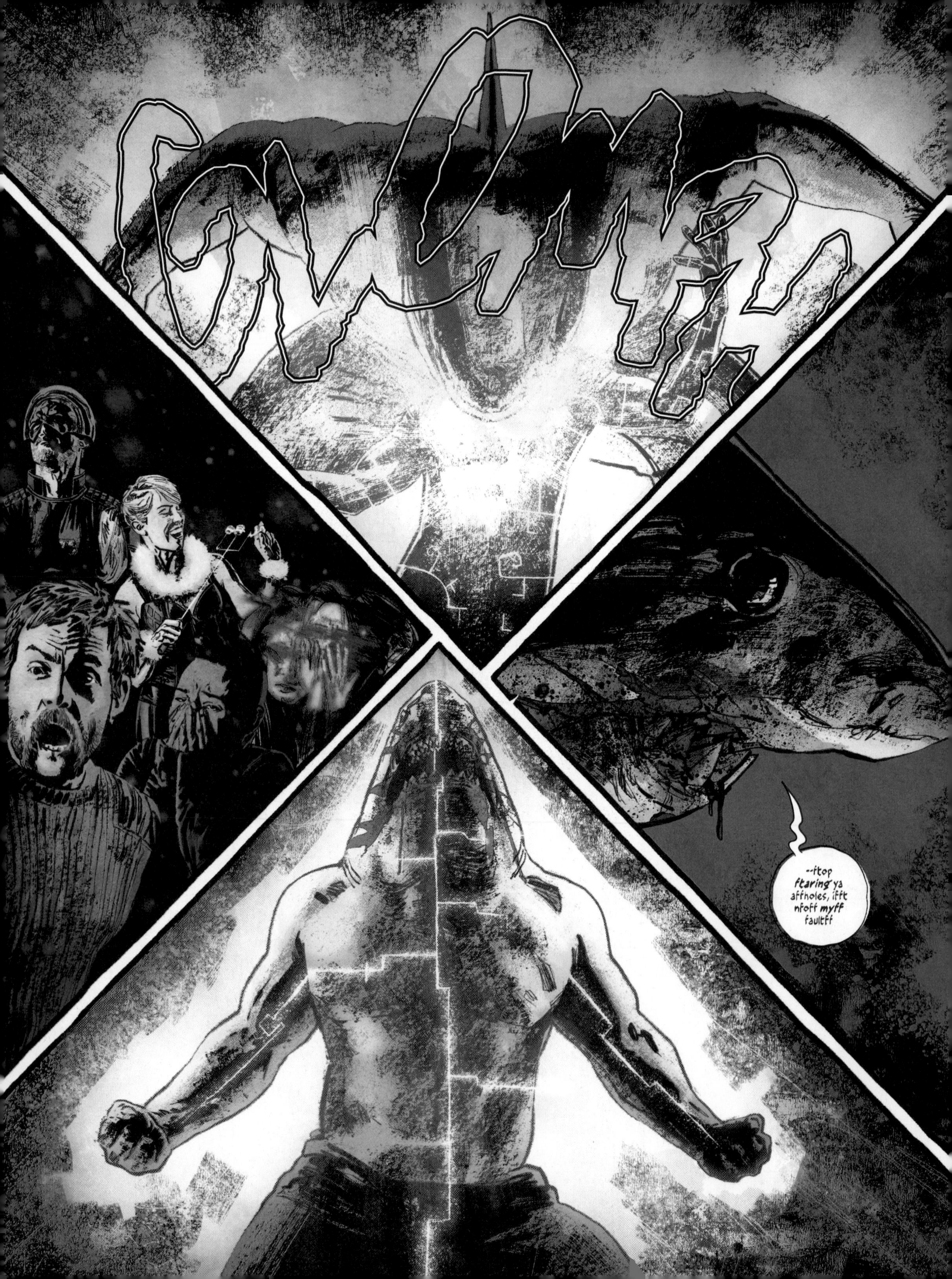
--ftop *ftaring* ya affholes, ifft nfoff *myff* faultff

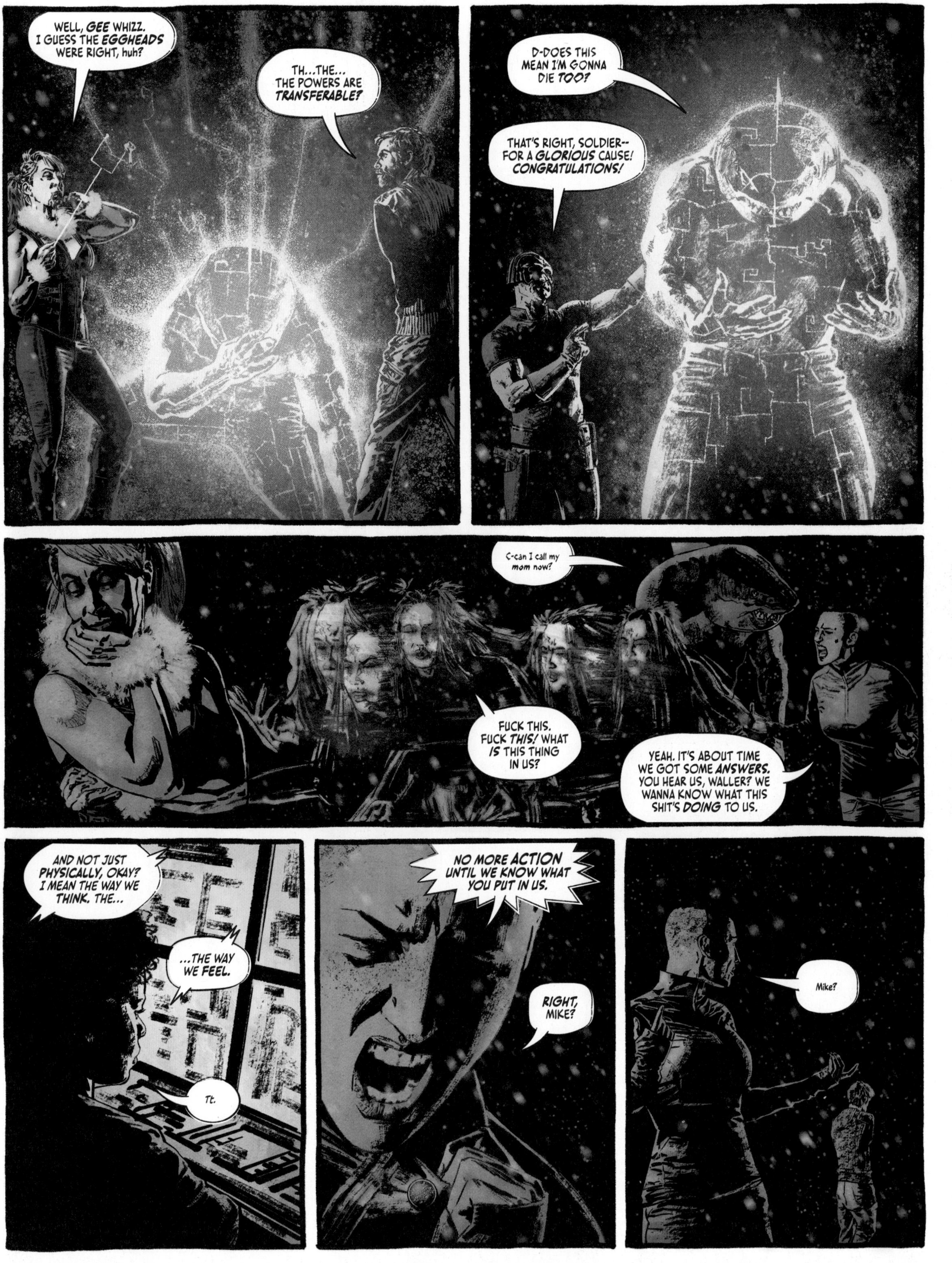

WELL, GEE WHIZZ. I GUESS THE EGGHEADS WERE RIGHT, huh?
TH...THE... THE POWERS ARE TRANSFERABLE?
D-DOES THIS MEAN I'M GONNA DIE TOO?
THAT'S RIGHT, SOLDIER-- FOR A GLORIOUS CAUSE! CONGRATULATIONS!
C-can I call my mom now?
FUCK THIS. FUCK THIS! WHAT IS THIS THING IN US?
YEAH. IT'S ABOUT TIME WE GOT SOME ANSWERS. YOU HEAR US, WALLER? WE WANNA KNOW WHAT THIS SHIT'S DOING TO US.
AND NOT JUST PHYSICALLY, OKAY? I MEAN THE WAY WE THINK. THE...
...THE WAY WE FEEL.
Tt.
NO MORE ACTION UNTIL WE KNOW WHAT YOU PUT IN US.
RIGHT, MIKE?
Mike?

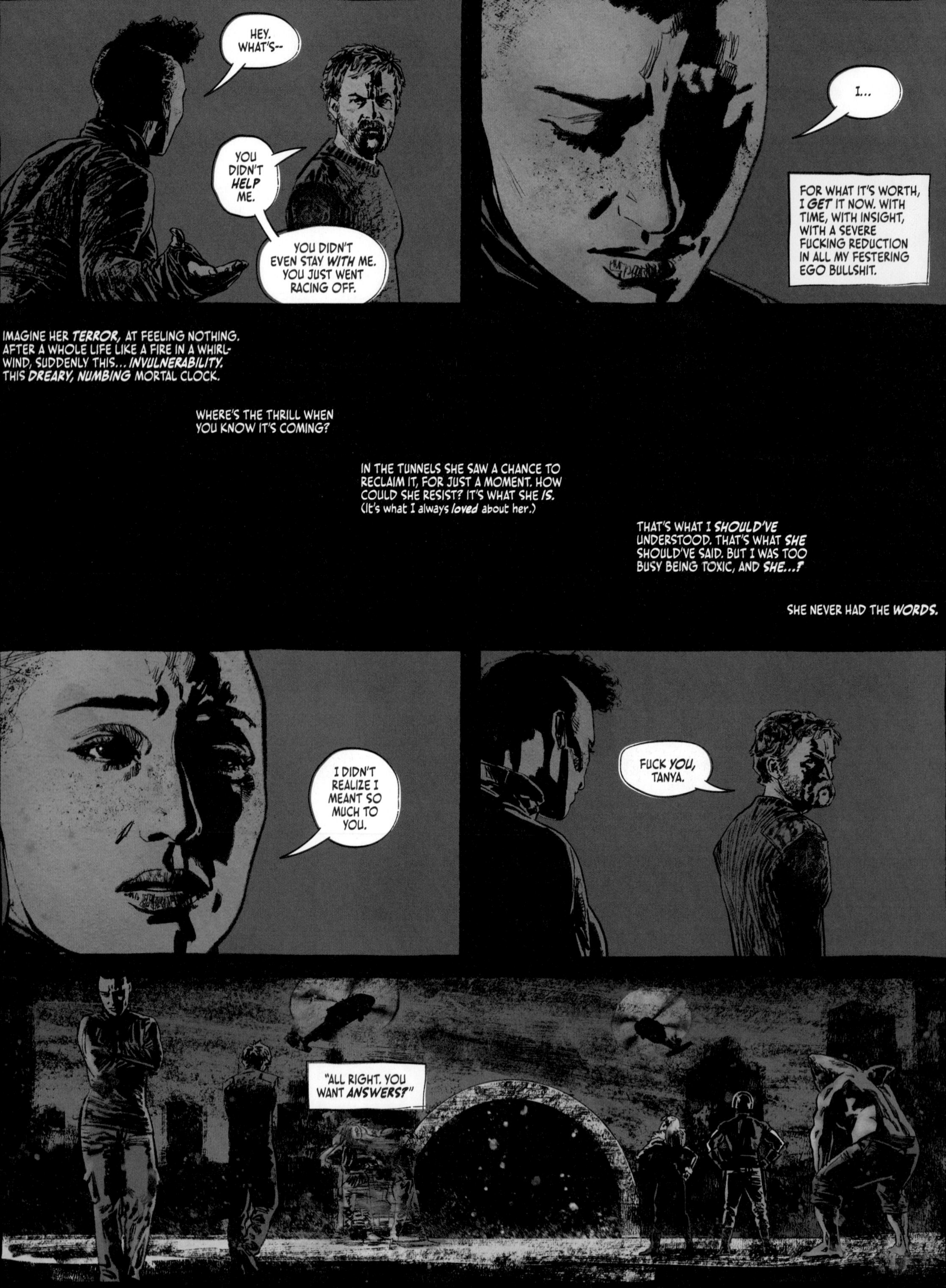
HEY. WHAT'S--
YOU DIDN'T HELP ME.
YOU DIDN'T EVEN STAY WITH ME. YOU JUST WENT RACING OFF.
I...
FOR WHAT IT'S WORTH, I GET IT NOW. WITH TIME, WITH INSIGHT, WITH A SEVERE FUCKING REDUCTION IN ALL MY FESTERING EGO BULLSHIT.
IMAGINE HER TERROR, AT FEELING NOTHING. AFTER A WHOLE LIFE LIKE A FIRE IN A WHIRLWIND, SUDDENLY THIS... INVULNERABILITY. THIS DREARY, NUMBING MORTAL CLOCK.
WHERE'S THE THRILL WHEN YOU KNOW IT'S COMING?
IN THE TUNNELS SHE SAW A CHANCE TO RECLAIM IT, FOR JUST A MOMENT. HOW COULD SHE RESIST? IT'S WHAT SHE IS. (It's what I always loved about her.)
THAT'S WHAT I SHOULD'VE UNDERSTOOD. THAT'S WHAT SHE SHOULD'VE SAID. BUT I WAS TOO BUSY BEING TOXIC, AND SHE...?
SHE NEVER HAD THE WORDS.
I DIDN'T REALIZE I MEANT SO MUCH TO YOU.
FUCK YOU, TANYA.
"ALL RIGHT. YOU WANT ANSWERS?"

I'LL GIVE YOU YOUR GODDAMN ANSWERS.

SHUT UP, FOLLOW ME, *LISTEN.*

BATMAN? *BATMAN!* NEWS 24. ANY COMMENT ON RUMORS THAT *SUPERMAN'S* STILL *MISSING* AFTER CONFRONTING TH--

SORRY, FOLKS, WE'RE NOT TAKING QUESTIONS TODAY.

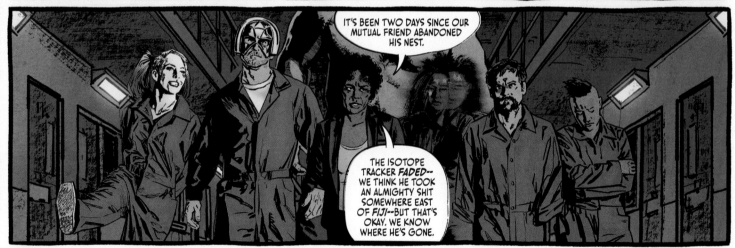

IT'S BEEN TWO DAYS SINCE OUR MUTUAL FRIEND ABANDONED HIS NEST.

THE ISOTOPE TRACKER *FADED*-- WE THINK HE TOOK AN ALMIGHTY SHIT SOMEWHERE EAST OF *FIJI*--BUT THAT'S OKAY. WE KNOW WHERE HE'S GONE.

SAY, *FLASH?* WORLDNET TV. DO YOU AGREE WITH THE *PRESIDENT* THAT WE SHOULDN'T THROW MORE *RESOURCES* AT THE KILLER NOW THAT IT'S SOME- ONE *ELSE'S* PROBLEM?

RESOURCES?

RESOURCES?

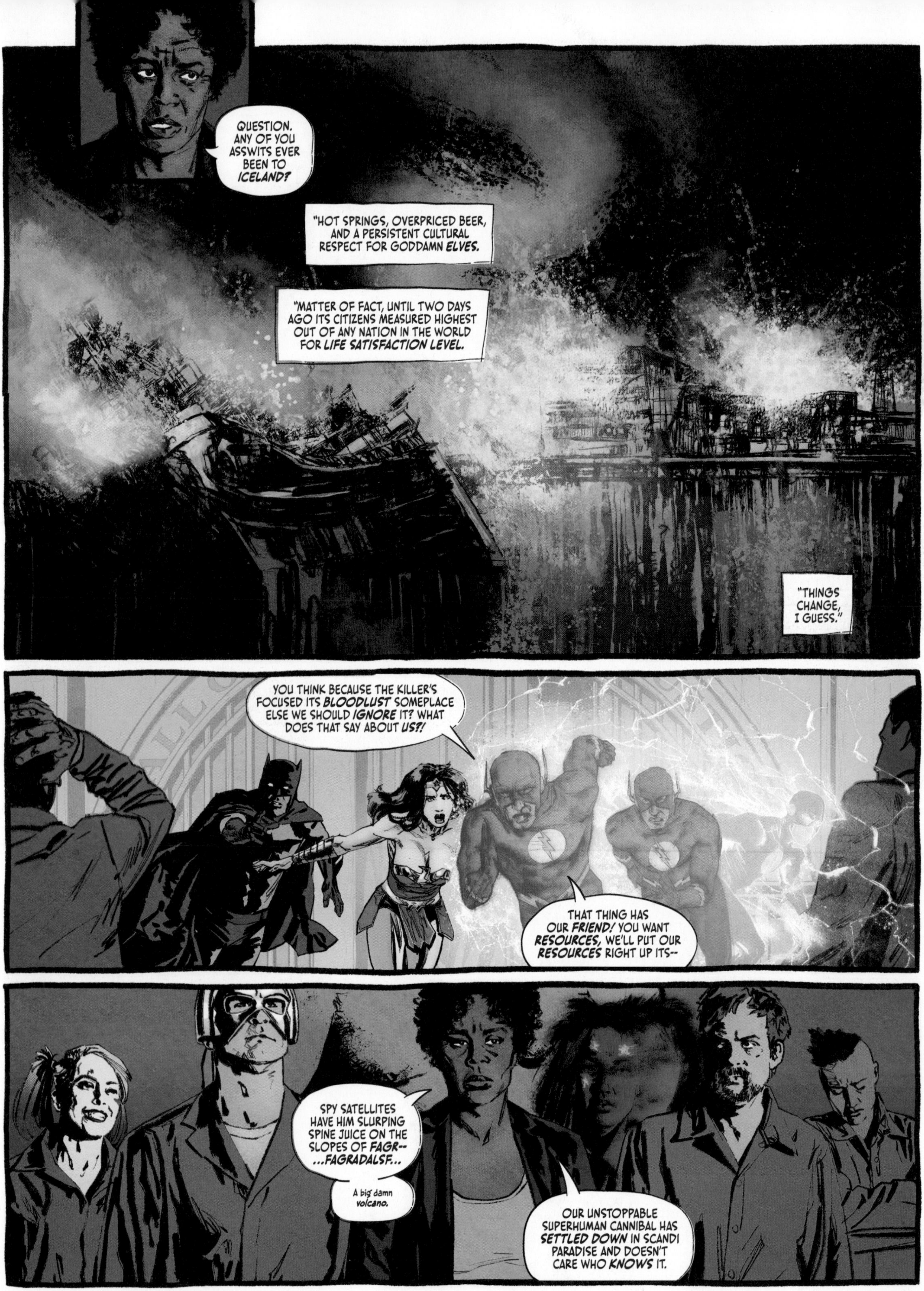
QUESTION. ANY OF YOU ASSWITS EVER BEEN TO *ICELAND?*
"HOT SPRINGS, OVERPRICED BEER, AND A PERSISTENT CULTURAL RESPECT FOR GODDAMN *ELVES.*
"MATTER OF FACT, UNTIL TWO DAYS AGO ITS CITIZENS MEASURED HIGHEST OUT OF ANY NATION IN THE WORLD FOR *LIFE SATISFACTION LEVEL.*
"THINGS CHANGE, I GUESS."
YOU THINK BECAUSE THE KILLER'S FOCUSED ITS *BLOODLUST* SOMEPLACE ELSE WE SHOULD *IGNORE* IT? WHAT DOES THAT SAY ABOUT *US?!*
THAT THING HAS OUR *FRIEND!* YOU WANT *RESOURCES,* WE'LL PUT OUR *RESOURCES* RIGHT UP ITS--
SPY SATELLITES HAVE HIM SLURPING SPINE JUICE ON THE SLOPES OF *FAGR-- ...FAGRADALSF...*
A big damn volcano.
OUR UNSTOPPABLE SUPERHUMAN CANNIBAL HAS *SETTLED DOWN* IN SCANDI PARADISE AND DOESN'T CARE WHO *KNOWS* IT.

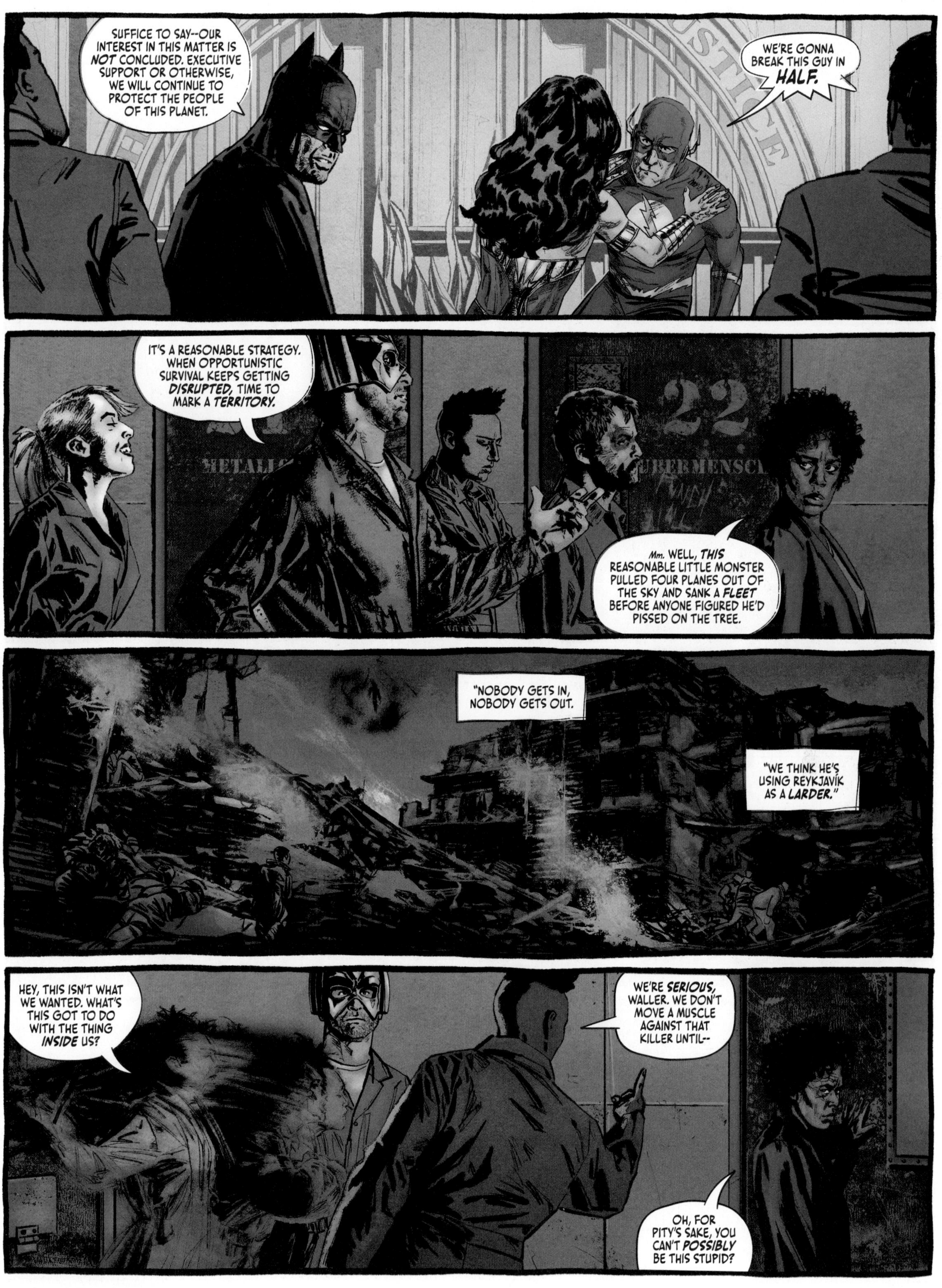

SUFFICE TO SAY--OUR INTEREST IN THIS MATTER IS NOT CONCLUDED. EXECUTIVE SUPPORT OR OTHERWISE, WE WILL CONTINUE TO PROTECT THE PEOPLE OF THIS PLANET.
WE'RE GONNA BREAK THIS GUY IN HALF.
IT'S A REASONABLE STRATEGY. WHEN OPPORTUNISTIC SURVIVAL KEEPS GETTING DISRUPTED, TIME TO MARK A TERRITORY.
Mm. WELL, THIS REASONABLE LITTLE MONSTER PULLED FOUR PLANES OUT OF THE SKY AND SANK A FLEET BEFORE ANYONE FIGURED HE'D PISSED ON THE TREE.
"NOBODY GETS IN, NOBODY GETS OUT.
"WE THINK HE'S USING REYKJAVÍK AS A LARDER."
HEY, THIS ISN'T WHAT WE WANTED. WHAT'S THIS GOT TO DO WITH THE THING INSIDE US?
WE'RE SERIOUS, WALLER. WE DON'T MOVE A MUSCLE AGAINST THAT KILLER UNTIL--
OH, FOR PITY'S SAKE, YOU CAN'T POSSIBLY BE THIS STUPID?

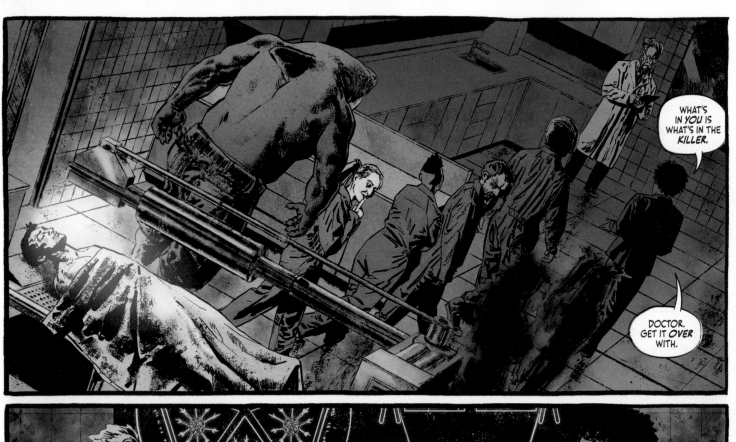

WHAT'S *IN YOU* IS WHAT'S IN THE *KILLER.*

DOCTOR. GET IT *OVER* WITH.

THE, *uh.* THE *BLAZE* ORGANISM. A *HIGHER-PLANE* ENTITY.

IT'S A--A *PARASITE,* OF SORTS. WE DON'T KNOW *EXACTLY* WHAT IT DRAINS FROM ITS HOST, BUT...BEST GUESS?

RELATIVISTIC IMPLOSIONS. IT FEEDS ON THE COLLAPSE OF PROBABILITY WAVEFORMS CAUSED BY YOUR *CHOICES*--IT'S ALL QUITE *HEISENBERGIAN,* OF COURSE--SO--

DOCTOR. CONVICTS AND LUNATICS. TELL THEM IT'S *MAGIC,* MOVE ON.

WELL, *uh.* WH-*WHATEVER* IT IS, IT CONSUMES ITS HOST RATHER *FAST.* Sorry. BUT HERE'S THE *COOL* PART:

AS IT *FEEDS,* IT EXCRETES THE MOST EXTRAORDINARY *DISRUPTIONS* TO REALITY.

HE MEANS YOUR *UNCANNY* ABILITIES.

YOUR *SUPER-POWERS* ARE THE *COSMIC SHIT* OF AN *EXTRADIMENSIONAL TAPEWORM.*

CONGRATULATIONS.

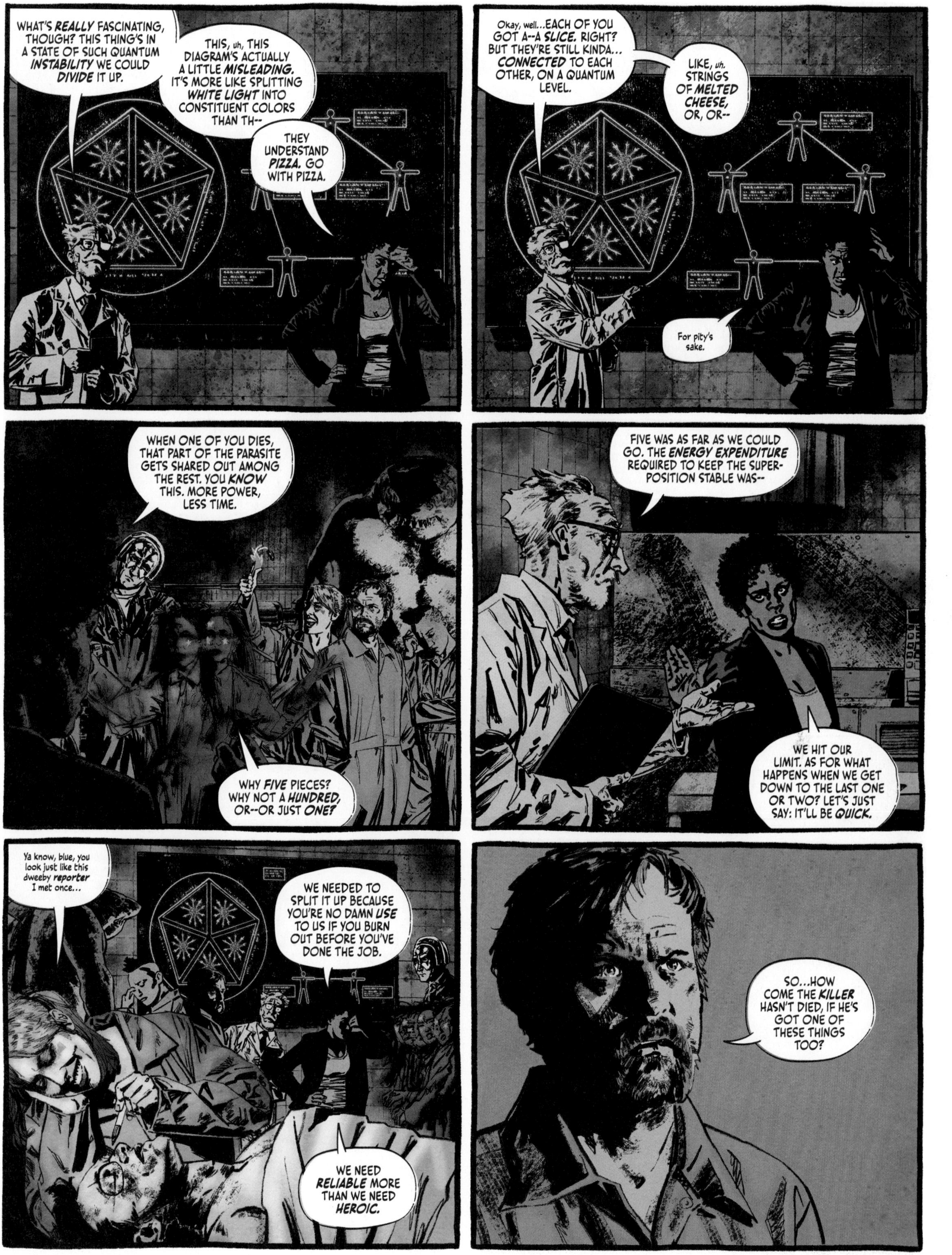
WHAT'S REALLY FASCINATING, THOUGH? THIS THING'S IN A STATE OF SUCH QUANTUM INSTABILITY WE COULD DIVIDE IT UP.
THIS, uh, THIS DIAGRAM'S ACTUALLY A LITTLE MISLEADING. IT'S MORE LIKE SPLITTING WHITE LIGHT INTO CONSTITUENT COLORS THAN TH--
THEY UNDERSTAND PIZZA. GO WITH PIZZA.
Okay, well...EACH OF YOU GOT A--A SLICE. RIGHT? BUT THEY'RE STILL KINDA... CONNECTED TO EACH OTHER, ON A QUANTUM LEVEL.
LIKE, uh, STRINGS OF MELTED CHEESE, OR, OR--
For pity's sake.
WHEN ONE OF YOU DIES, THAT PART OF THE PARASITE GETS SHARED OUT AMONG THE REST. YOU KNOW THIS. MORE POWER, LESS TIME.
WHY FIVE PIECES? WHY NOT A HUNDRED, OR--OR JUST ONE?
FIVE WAS AS FAR AS WE COULD GO. THE ENERGY EXPENDITURE REQUIRED TO KEEP THE SUPER-POSITION STABLE WAS--
WE HIT OUR LIMIT. AS FOR WHAT HAPPENS WHEN WE GET DOWN TO THE LAST ONE OR TWO? LET'S JUST SAY: IT'LL BE QUICK.
Ya know, blue, you look just like this dweeby reporter I met once...
WE NEEDED TO SPLIT IT UP BECAUSE YOU'RE NO DAMN USE TO US IF YOU BURN OUT BEFORE YOU'VE DONE THE JOB.
WE NEED RELIABLE MORE THAN WE NEED HEROIC.
SO...HOW COME THE KILLER HASN'T DIED, IF HE'S GOT ONE OF THESE THINGS TOO?

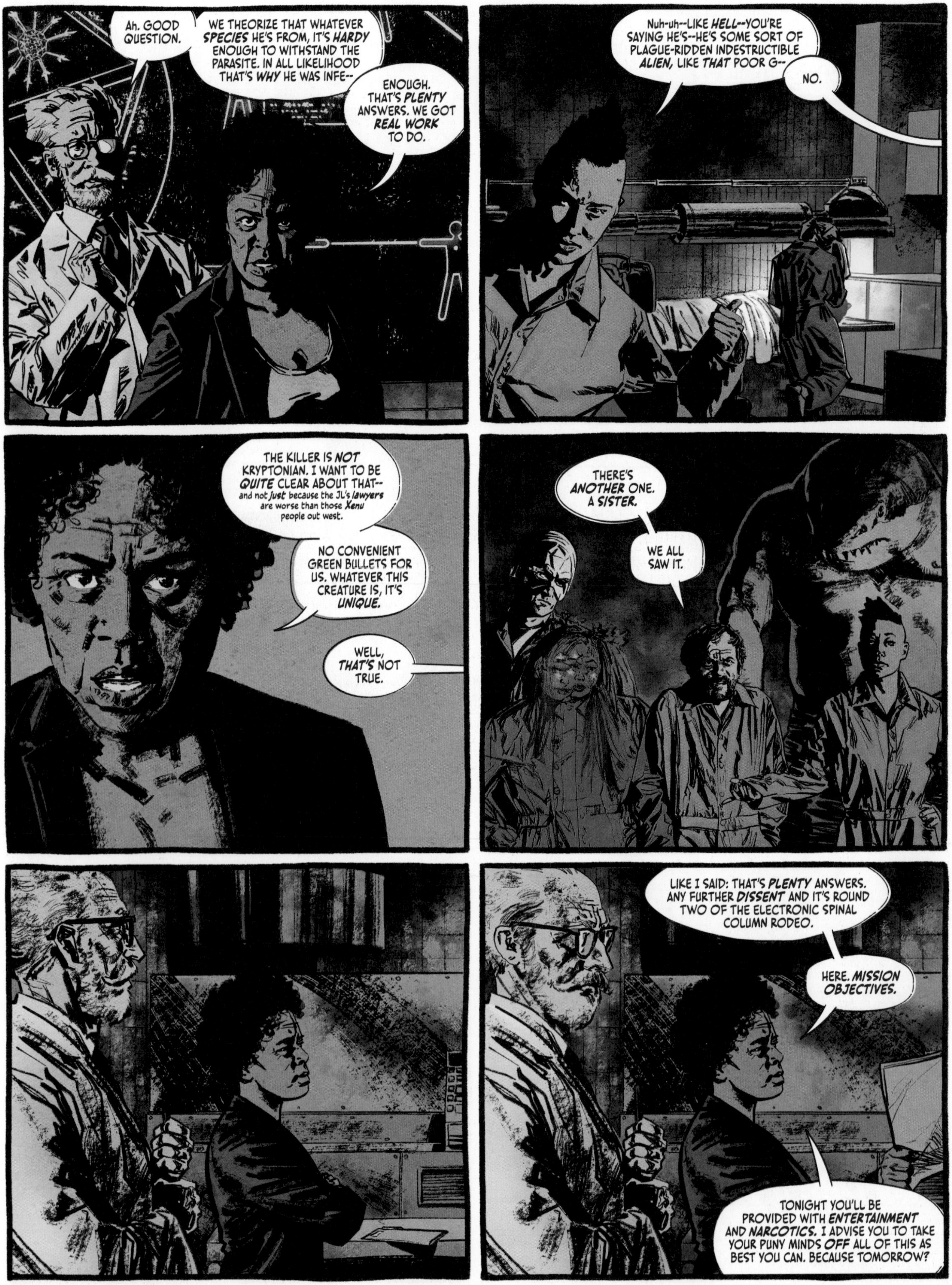
Ah. GOOD QUESTION.
WE THEORIZE THAT WHATEVER SPECIES HE'S FROM, IT'S HARDY ENOUGH TO WITHSTAND THE PARASITE. IN ALL LIKELIHOOD THAT'S WHY HE WAS INFE--
ENOUGH. THAT'S PLENTY ANSWERS. WE GOT REAL WORK TO DO.
Nuh-uh--LIKE HELL--YOU'RE SAYING HE'S--HE'S SOME SORT OF PLAGUE-RIDDEN INDESTRUCTIBLE ALIEN, LIKE THAT POOR G--
NO.
THE KILLER IS NOT KRYPTONIAN. I WANT TO BE QUITE CLEAR ABOUT THAT-- and not just because the JL's lawyers are worse than those Xenu people out west.
NO CONVENIENT GREEN BULLETS FOR US. WHATEVER THIS CREATURE IS, IT'S UNIQUE.
WELL, THAT'S NOT TRUE.
THERE'S ANOTHER ONE. A SISTER.
WE ALL SAW IT.
LIKE I SAID: THAT'S PLENTY ANSWERS. ANY FURTHER DISSENT AND IT'S ROUND TWO OF THE ELECTRONIC SPINAL COLUMN RODEO.
HERE. MISSION OBJECTIVES.
TONIGHT YOU'LL BE PROVIDED WITH ENTERTAINMENT AND NARCOTICS. I ADVISE YOU TO TAKE YOUR PUNY MINDS OFF ALL OF THIS AS BEST YOU CAN. BECAUSE TOMORROW?

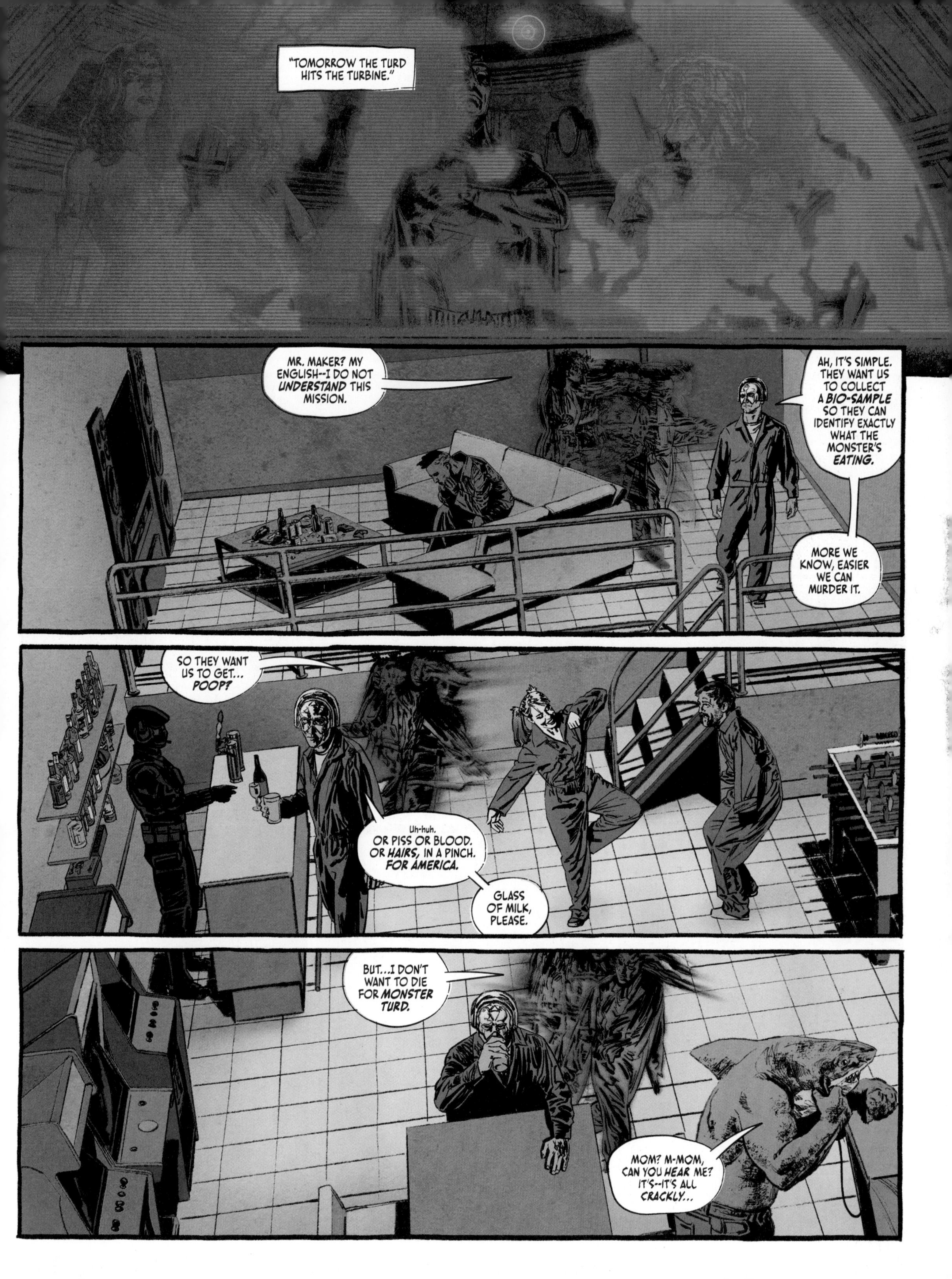
"TOMORROW THE TURD HITS THE TURBINE."
MR. MAKER? MY ENGLISH--I DO NOT UNDERSTAND THIS MISSION.
AH, IT'S SIMPLE. THEY WANT US TO COLLECT A BIO-SAMPLE SO THEY CAN IDENTIFY EXACTLY WHAT THE MONSTER'S EATING.
MORE WE KNOW, EASIER WE CAN MURDER IT.
SO THEY WANT US TO GET... POOP?
Uh-huh.
OR PISS OR BLOOD. OR HAIRS, IN A PINCH. FOR AMERICA.
GLASS OF MILK, PLEASE.
BUT...I DON'T WANT TO DIE FOR MONSTER TURD.
MOM? M-MOM, CAN YOU HEAR ME? IT'S--IT'S ALL CRACKLY...

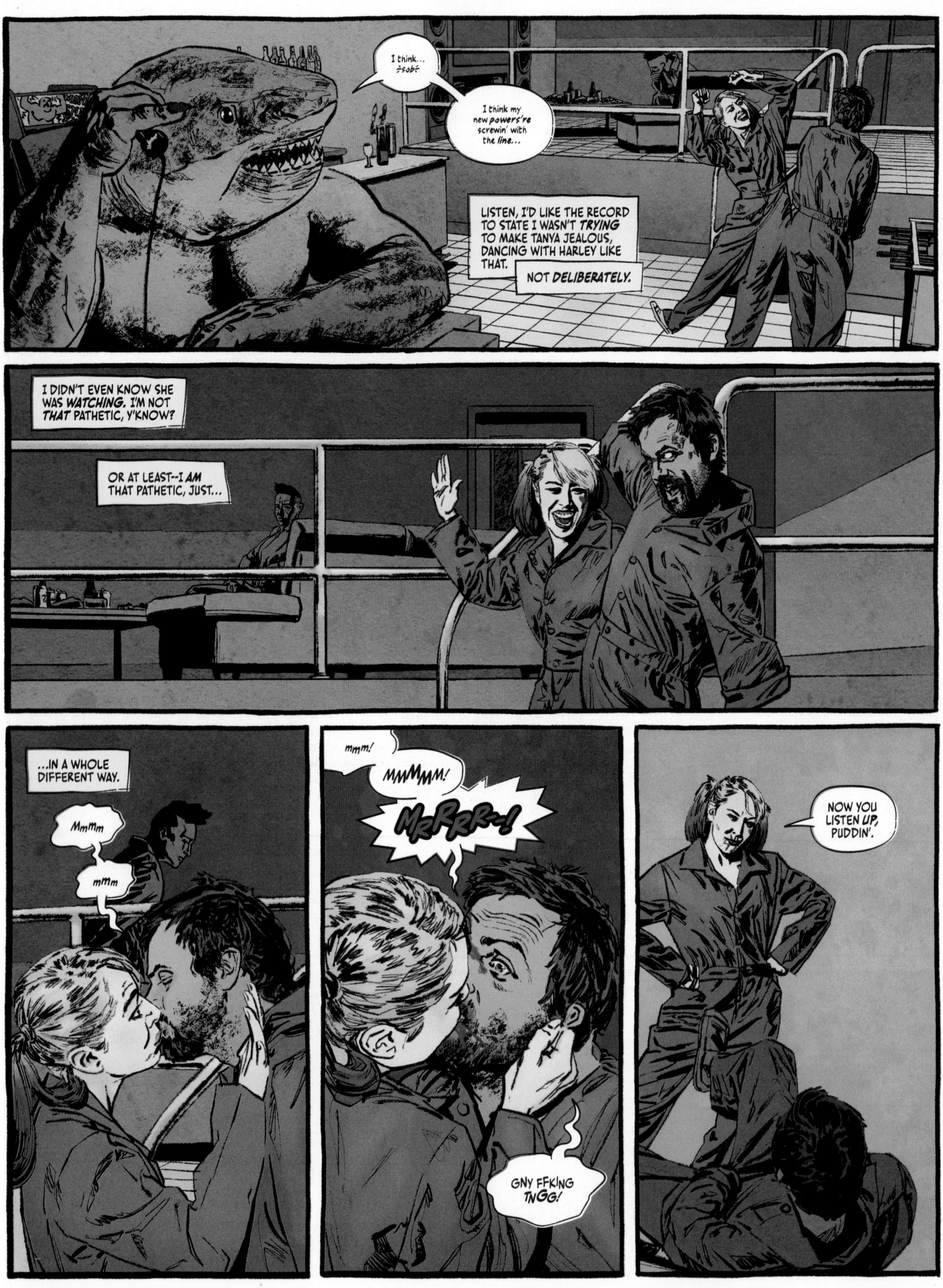
I think... ≠sob≠
I think my new powers're screwin' with the line...
LISTEN, I'D LIKE THE RECORD TO STATE I WASN'T TRYING TO MAKE TANYA JEALOUS, DANCING WITH HARLEY LIKE THAT.
NOT DELIBERATELY.
I DIDN'T EVEN KNOW SHE WAS WATCHING. I'M NOT THAT PATHETIC, Y'KNOW?
OR AT LEAST--I AM THAT PATHETIC, JUST...
...IN A WHOLE DIFFERENT WAY.
Mmmm
mmm
mmm!
MMMMM!
MRRRR--!
GNY FFKING TNGG!
NOW YOU LISTEN UP, PUDDIN'.

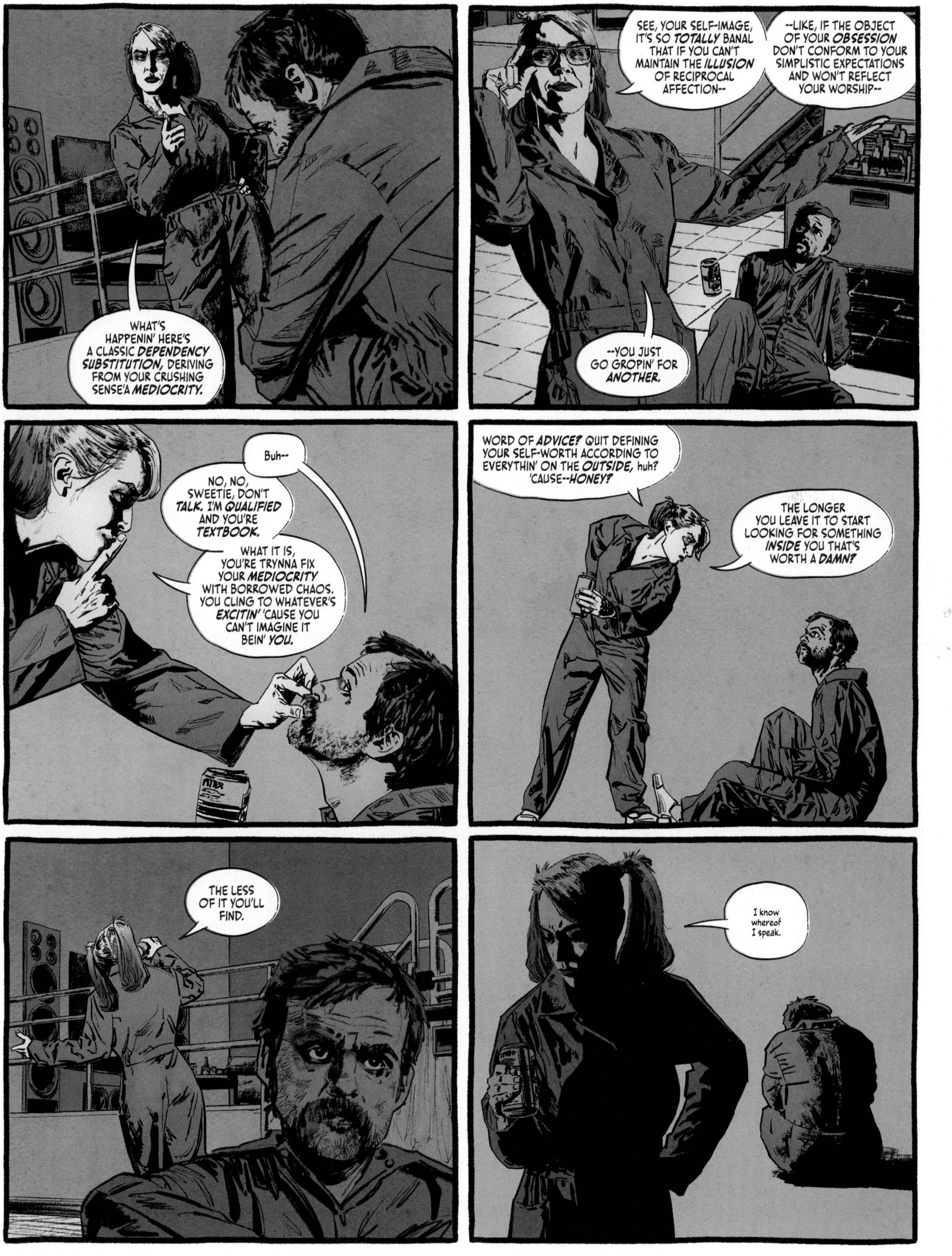
WHAT'S HAPPENIN' HERE'S A CLASSIC DEPENDENCY SUBSTITUTION, DERIVING FROM YOUR CRUSHING SENSE'A MEDIOCRITY.
SEE, YOUR SELF-IMAGE, IT'S SO TOTALLY BANAL THAT IF YOU CAN'T MAINTAIN THE ILLUSION OF RECIPROCAL AFFECTION--
--LIKE, IF THE OBJECT OF YOUR OBSESSION DON'T CONFORM TO YOUR SIMPLISTIC EXPECTATIONS AND WON'T REFLECT YOUR WORSHIP--
--YOU JUST GO GROPIN' FOR ANOTHER.
Buh--
NO, NO, SWEETIE, DON'T TALK. I'M QUALIFIED AND YOU'RE TEXTBOOK.
WHAT IT IS, YOU'RE TRYNNA FIX YOUR MEDIOCRITY WITH BORROWED CHAOS. YOU CLING TO WHATEVER'S EXCITIN' 'CAUSE YOU CAN'T IMAGINE IT BEIN' YOU.
WORD OF ADVICE? QUIT DEFINING YOUR SELF-WORTH ACCORDING TO EVERYTHIN' ON THE OUTSIDE, huh? 'CAUSE--HONEY?
THE LONGER YOU LEAVE IT TO START LOOKING FOR SOMETHING INSIDE YOU THAT'S WORTH A DAMN?
THE LESS OF IT YOU'LL FIND.
I know whereof I speak.

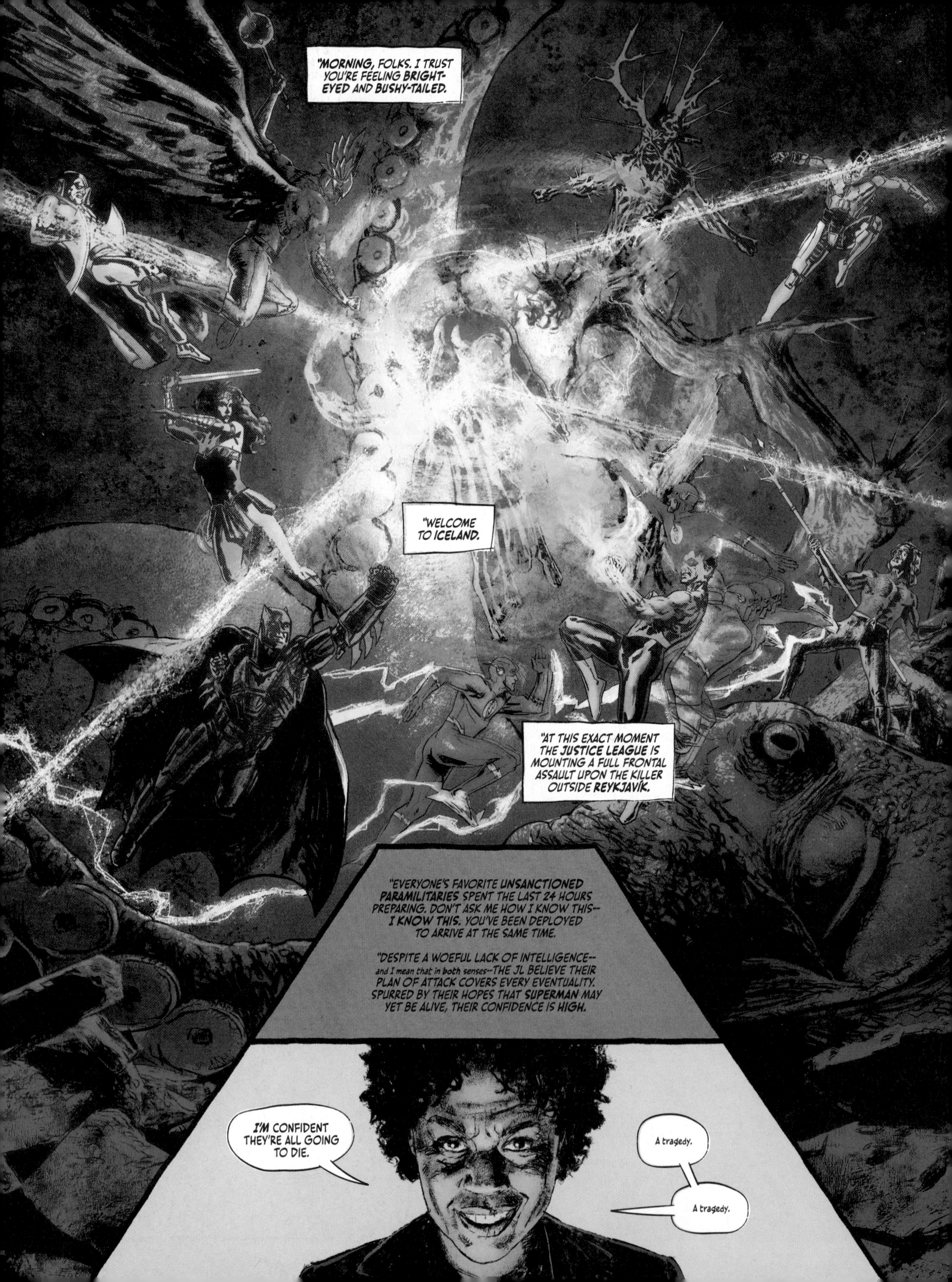
"MORNING, FOLKS. I TRUST YOU'RE FEELING BRIGHT-EYED AND BUSHY-TAILED.
"WELCOME TO ICELAND.
"AT THIS EXACT MOMENT THE JUSTICE LEAGUE IS MOUNTING A FULL FRONTAL ASSAULT UPON THE KILLER OUTSIDE REYKJAVÍK.
"EVERYONE'S FAVORITE UNSANCTIONED PARAMILITARIES SPENT THE LAST 24 HOURS PREPARING. DON'T ASK ME HOW I KNOW THIS--I KNOW THIS. YOU'VE BEEN DEPLOYED TO ARRIVE AT THE SAME TIME.
"DESPITE A WOEFUL LACK OF INTELLIGENCE--and I mean that in both senses--THE JL BELIEVE THEIR PLAN OF ATTACK COVERS EVERY EVENTUALITY. SPURRED BY THEIR HOPES THAT SUPERMAN MAY YET BE ALIVE, THEIR CONFIDENCE IS HIGH.
I'M CONFIDENT THEY'RE ALL GOING TO DIE.
A tragedy.
A tragedy.

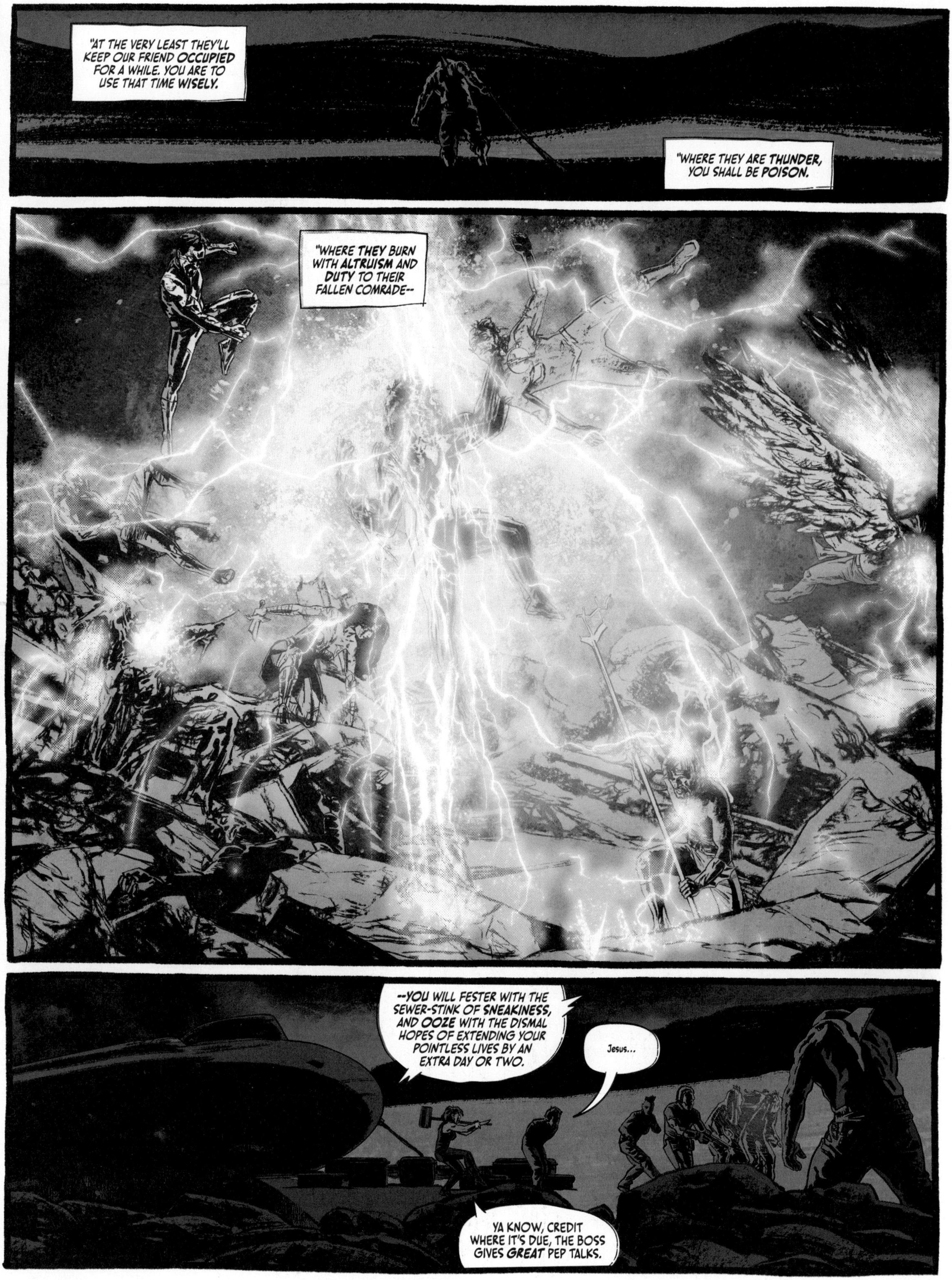
"AT THE VERY LEAST THEY'LL KEEP OUR FRIEND OCCUPIED FOR A WHILE. YOU ARE TO USE THAT TIME WISELY.
"WHERE THEY ARE THUNDER, YOU SHALL BE POISON.
"WHERE THEY BURN WITH ALTRUISM AND DUTY TO THEIR FALLEN COMRADE--
--YOU WILL FESTER WITH THE SEWER-STINK OF SNEAKINESS, AND OOZE WITH THE DISMAL HOPES OF EXTENDING YOUR POINTLESS LIVES BY AN EXTRA DAY OR TWO.
Jesus...
YA KNOW, CREDIT WHERE IT'S DUE, THE BOSS GIVES GREAT PEP TALKS.

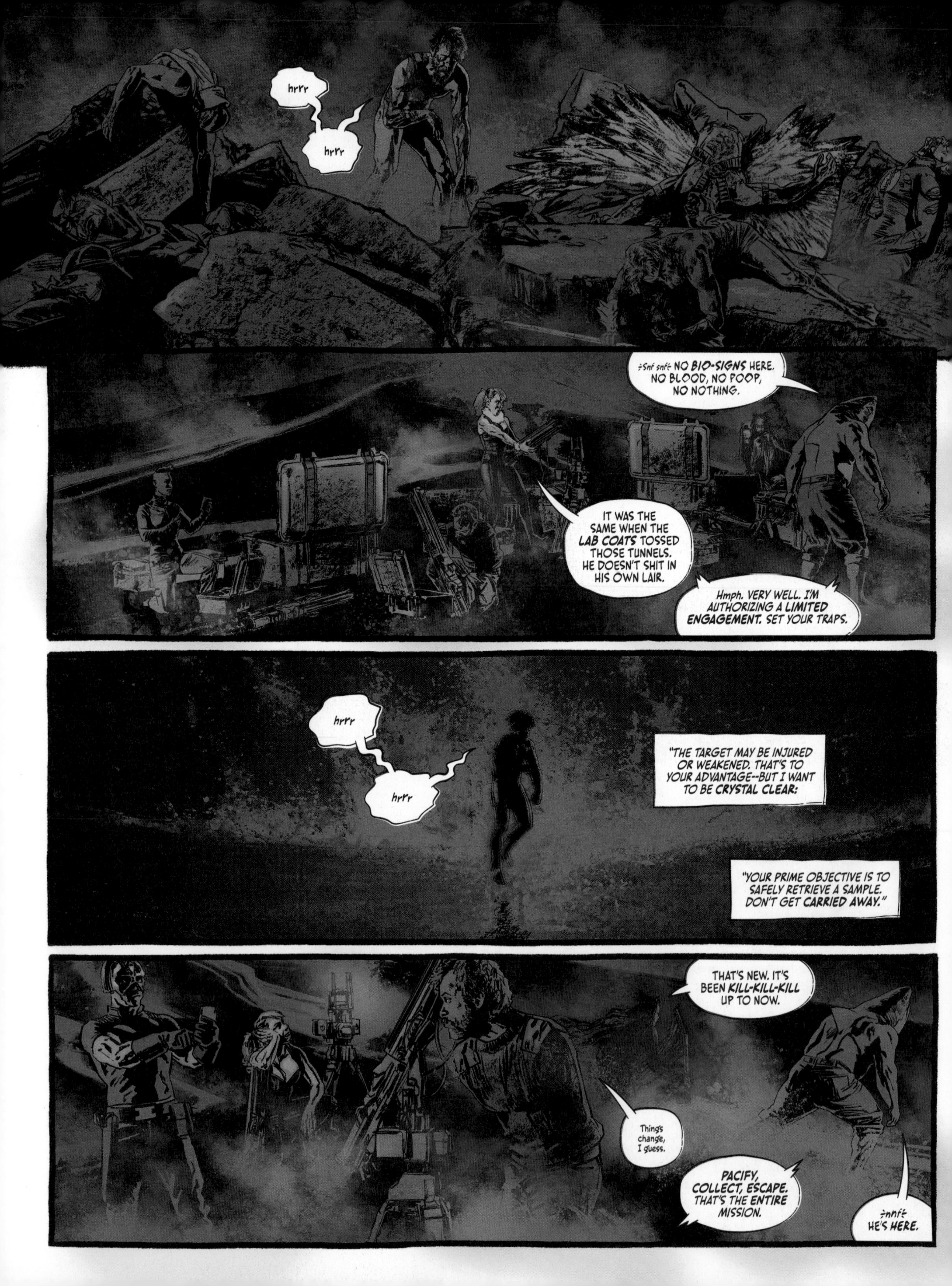
hrrr
hrrr
-Snf snf- NO BIO-SIGNS HERE. NO BLOOD, NO POOP, NO NOTHING.
IT WAS THE SAME WHEN THE LAB COATS TOSSED THOSE TUNNELS. HE DOESN'T SHIT IN HIS OWN LAIR.
Hmph. VERY WELL. I'M AUTHORIZING A LIMITED ENGAGEMENT. SET YOUR TRAPS.
hrrr
hrrr
"THE TARGET MAY BE INJURED OR WEAKENED. THAT'S TO YOUR ADVANTAGE--BUT I WANT TO BE CRYSTAL CLEAR:
"YOUR PRIME OBJECTIVE IS TO SAFELY RETRIEVE A SAMPLE. DON'T GET CARRIED AWAY."
THAT'S NEW. IT'S BEEN KILL-KILL-KILL UP TO NOW.
Things change, I guess.
PACIFY, COLLECT, ESCAPE. THAT'S THE ENTIRE MISSION.
-snf- HE'S HERE.

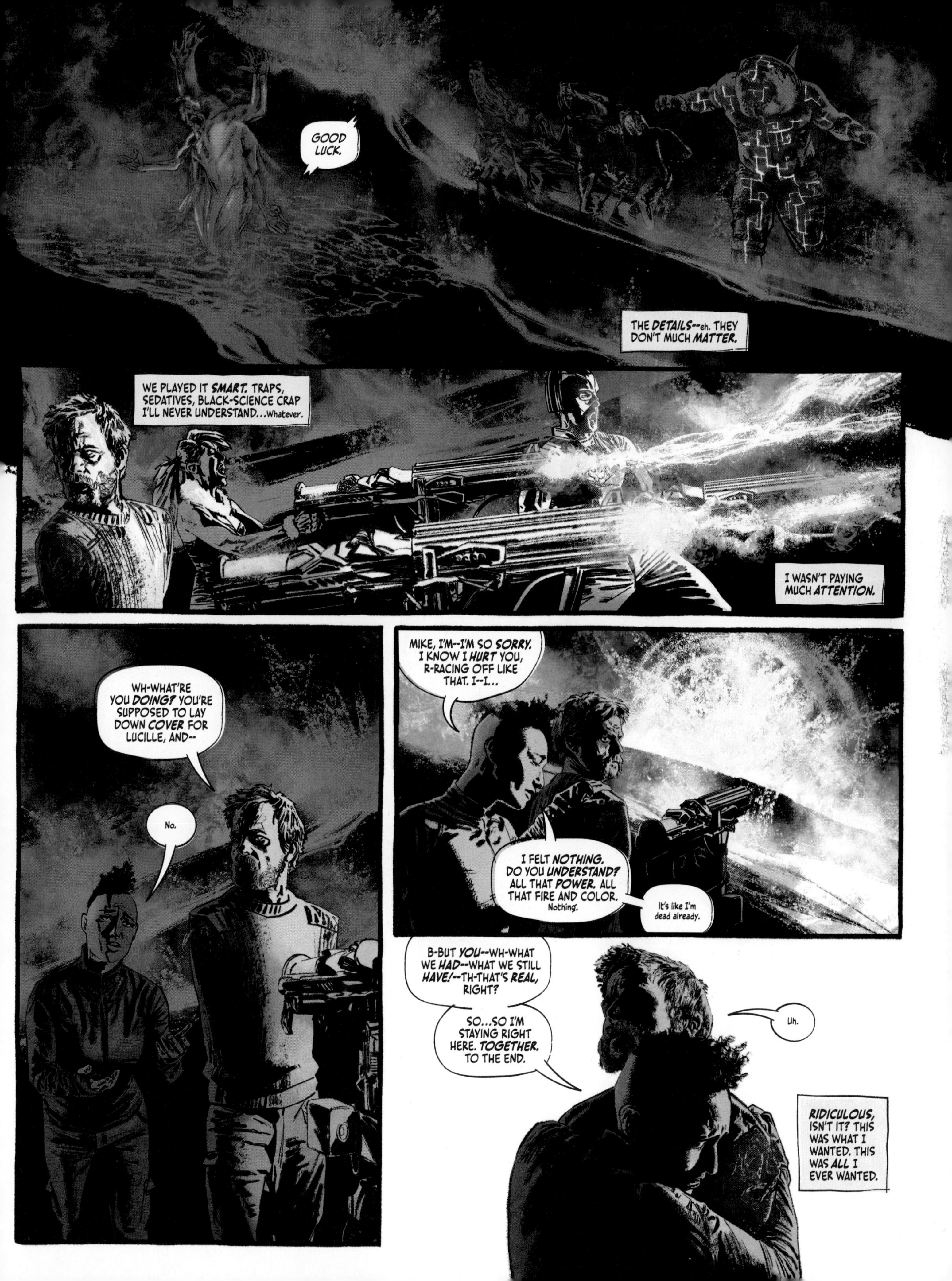

GOOD LUCK.
THE DETAILS--eh. THEY DON'T MUCH MATTER.
WE PLAYED IT SMART. TRAPS, SEDATIVES, BLACK-SCIENCE CRAP I'LL NEVER UNDERSTAND...Whatever.
I WASN'T PAYING MUCH ATTENTION.
WH-WHAT'RE YOU DOING? YOU'RE SUPPOSED TO LAY DOWN COVER FOR LUCILLE, AND--
No.
MIKE, I'M--I'M SO SORRY. I KNOW I HURT YOU, R-RACING OFF LIKE THAT. I--I...
I FELT NOTHING. DO YOU UNDERSTAND? ALL THAT POWER. ALL THAT FIRE AND COLOR. Nothing.
It's like I'm dead already.
B-BUT YOU--WH-WHAT WE HAD--WHAT WE STILL HAVE!--TH-THAT'S REAL, RIGHT?
SO...SO I'M STAYING RIGHT HERE. TOGETHER. TO THE END.
Uh.
RIDICULOUS, ISN'T IT? THIS WAS WHAT I WANTED. THIS WAS ALL I EVER WANTED.

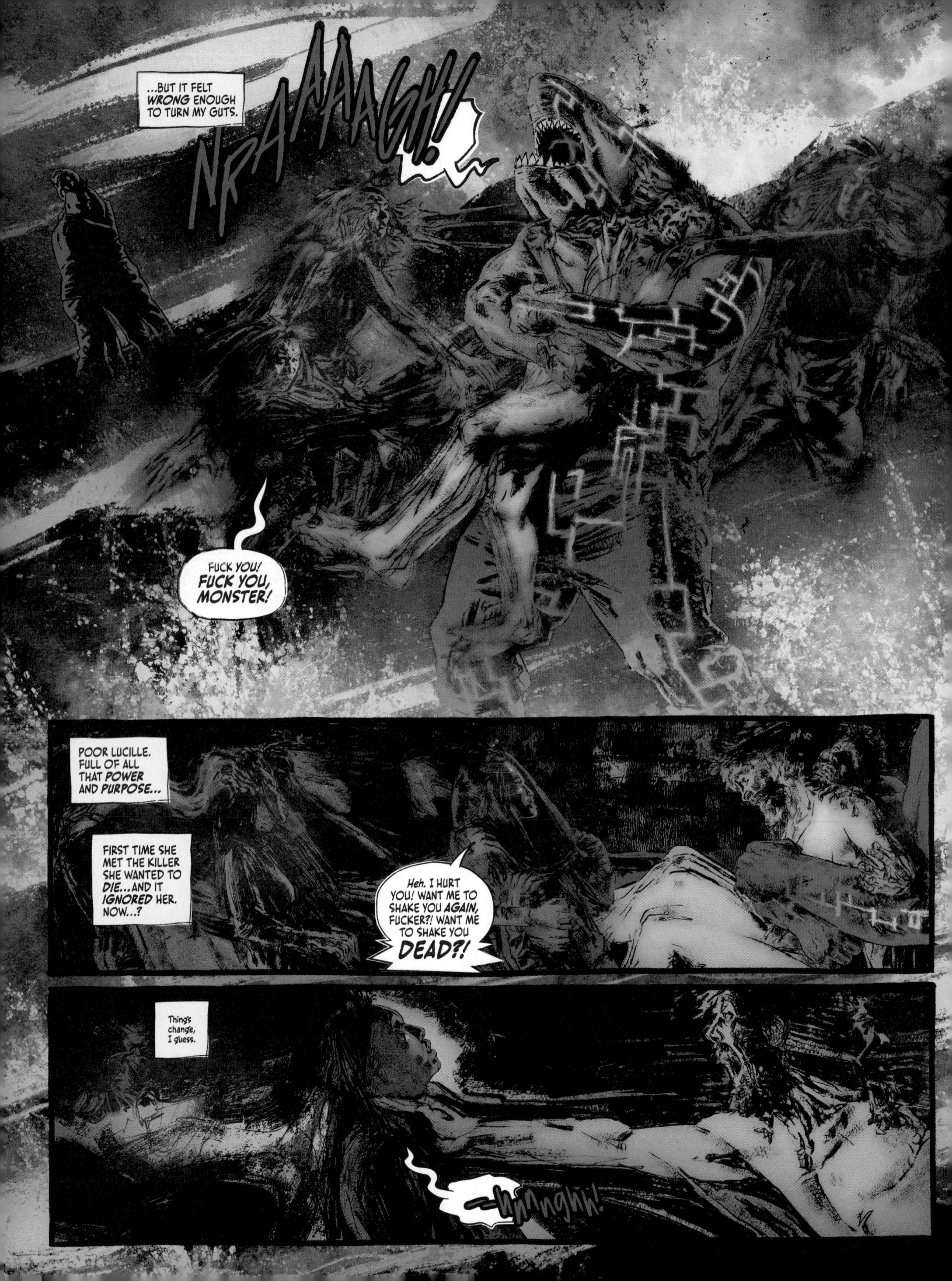
...BUT IT FELT WRONG ENOUGH TO TURN MY GUTS.
NRAAAAAGH!
FUCK YOU! FUCK YOU, MONSTER!
POOR LUCILLE. FULL OF ALL THAT POWER AND PURPOSE...
FIRST TIME SHE MET THE KILLER SHE WANTED TO DIE...AND IT IGNORED HER. NOW...?
Heh. I HURT YOU! WANT ME TO SHAKE YOU AGAIN, FUCKER?! WANT ME TO SHAKE YOU DEAD?!
Thing's change, I guess.
—hnnnghh!

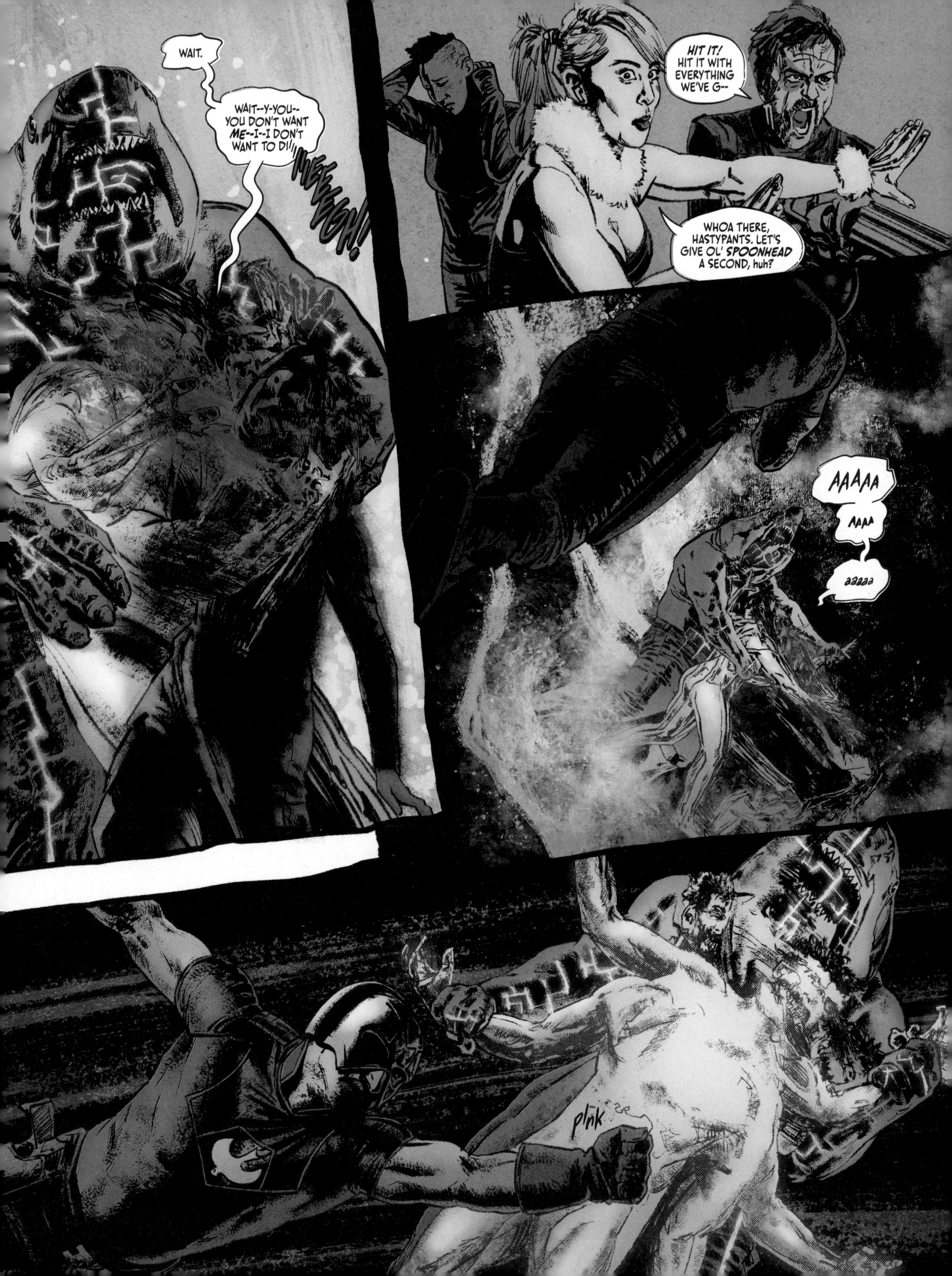
WAIT.
WAIT--Y-YOU--YOU DON'T WANT *ME*--I--I DON'T WANT TO DI//
MEEEOOH!
HIT IT! HIT IT WITH EVERYTHING WE'VE G--
WHOA THERE, HASTYPANTS. LET'S GIVE OL' *SPOONHEAD* A SECOND, huh?
AAAAA
AAAA
aaaaa
plink

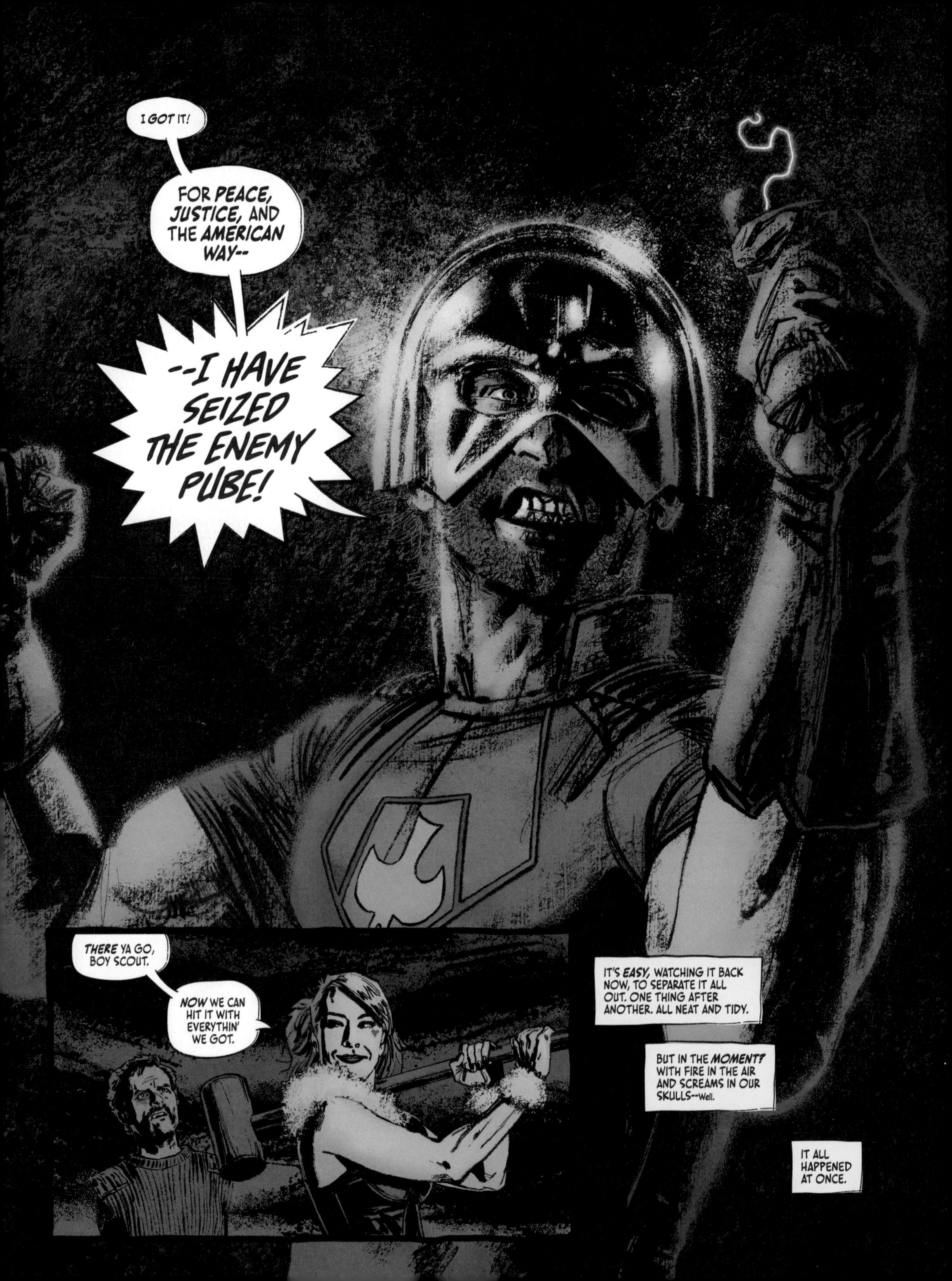
I GOT IT!
FOR PEACE, JUSTICE, AND THE AMERICAN WAY--
--I HAVE SEIZED THE ENEMY PUBE!
THERE YA GO, BOY SCOUT.
NOW WE CAN HIT IT WITH EVERYTHIN' WE GOT.
IT'S EASY, WATCHING IT BACK NOW, TO SEPARATE IT ALL OUT. ONE THING AFTER ANOTHER. ALL NEAT AND TIDY.
BUT IN THE MOMENT? WITH FIRE IN THE AIR AND SCREAMS IN OUR SKULLS--Well.
IT ALL HAPPENED AT ONCE.

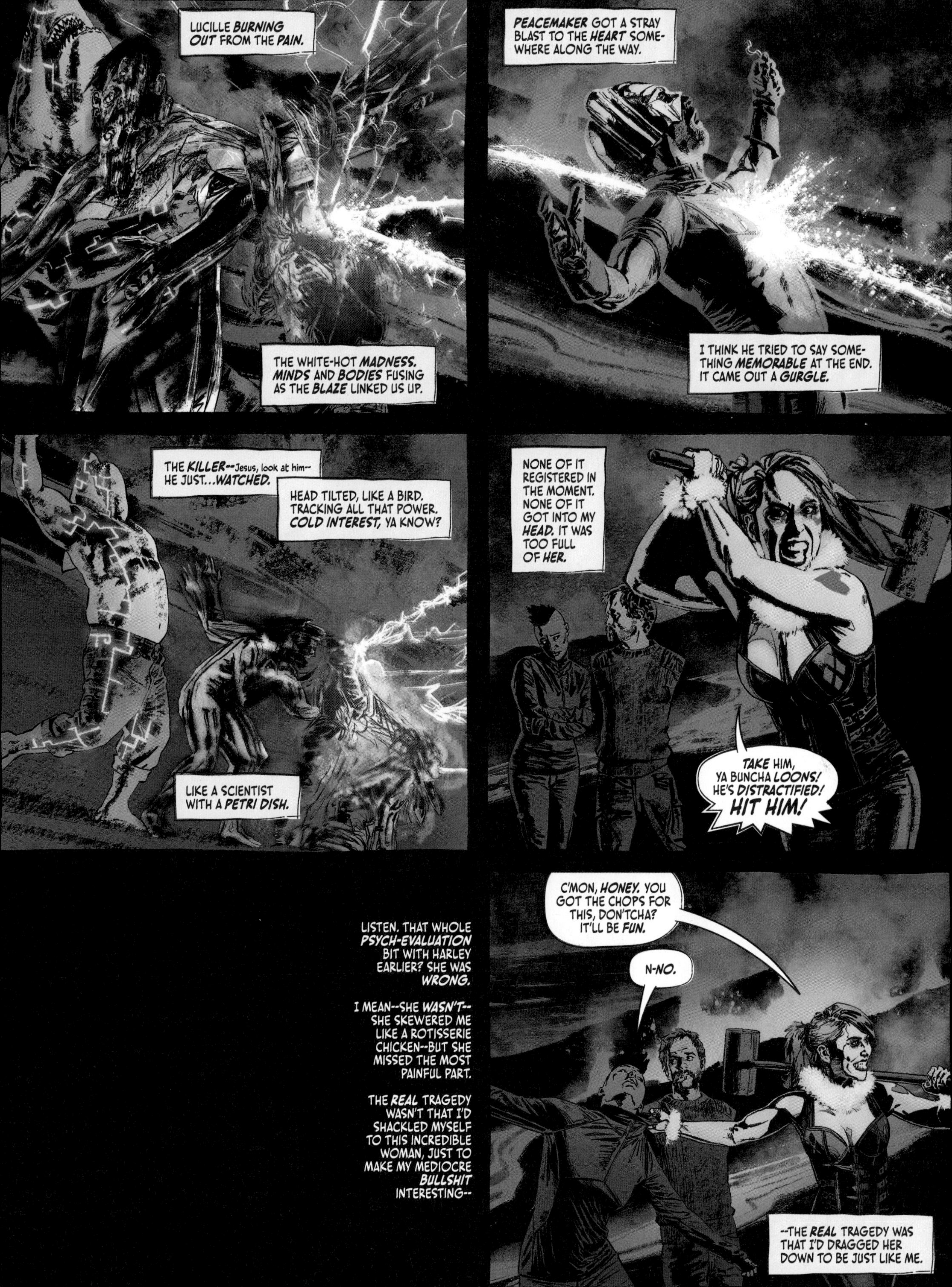
LUCILLE *BURNING OUT* FROM THE *PAIN.*
THE WHITE-HOT *MADNESS. MINDS* AND *BODIES* FUSING AS THE *BLAZE* LINKED US UP.
PEACEMAKER GOT A STRAY BLAST TO THE *HEART* SOMEWHERE ALONG THE WAY.
I THINK HE TRIED TO SAY SOMETHING *MEMORABLE* AT THE END. IT CAME OUT A *GURGLE.*
THE *KILLER*--Jesus, look at him--HE JUST...*WATCHED.*
HEAD TILTED, LIKE A BIRD. TRACKING ALL THAT POWER. *COLD INTEREST,* YA KNOW?
LIKE A SCIENTIST WITH A *PETRI DISH.*
NONE OF IT REGISTERED IN THE MOMENT. NONE OF IT GOT INTO MY *HEAD.* IT WAS TOO FULL OF *HER.*
TAKE HIM, YA BUNCHA *LOONS!* HE'S *DISTRACTIFIED!* **HIT HIM!**
LISTEN. THAT WHOLE *PSYCH-EVALUATION* BIT WITH HARLEY EARLIER? SHE WAS *WRONG.*
I MEAN--SHE *WASN'T*--SHE SKEWERED ME LIKE A ROTISSERIE CHICKEN--BUT SHE MISSED THE MOST PAINFUL PART.
THE *REAL* TRAGEDY WASN'T THAT I'D SHACKLED MYSELF TO THIS INCREDIBLE WOMAN, JUST TO MAKE MY MEDIOCRE *BULLSHIT* INTERESTING--
C'MON, *HONEY.* YOU GOT THE CHOPS FOR THIS, DON'TCHA? IT'LL BE *FUN.*
N-*NO.*
--THE *REAL* TRAGEDY WAS THAT I'D DRAGGED HER DOWN TO BE JUST LIKE ME.

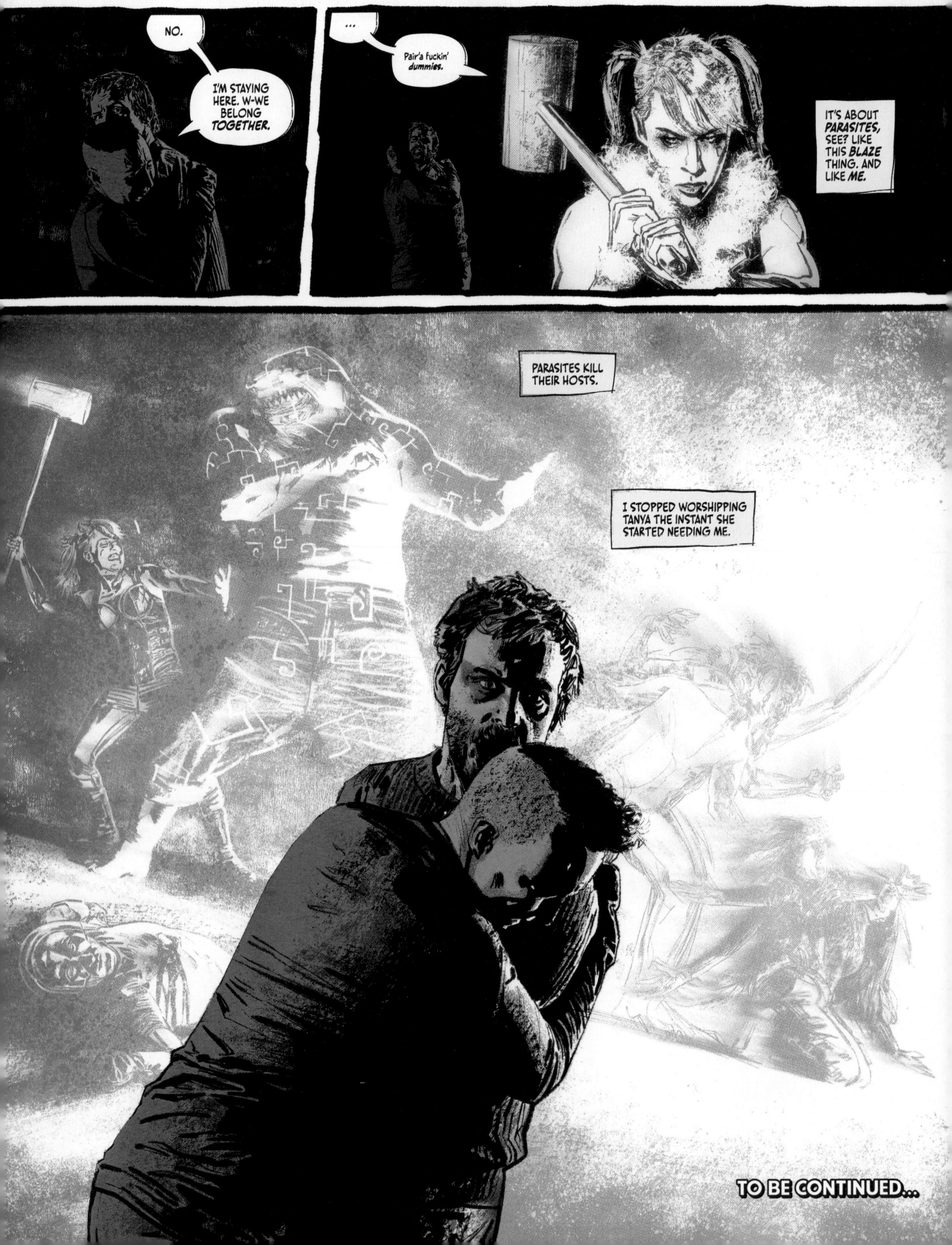
NO.
I'M STAYING HERE. W-WE BELONG TOGETHER.
...
Pair'a fuckin' dummies.
IT'S ABOUT PARASITES, SEE? LIKE THIS BLAZE THING. AND LIKE ME.
PARASITES KILL THEIR HOSTS.
I STOPPED WORSHIPPING TANYA THE INSTANT SHE STARTED NEEDING ME.
TO BE CONTINUED...

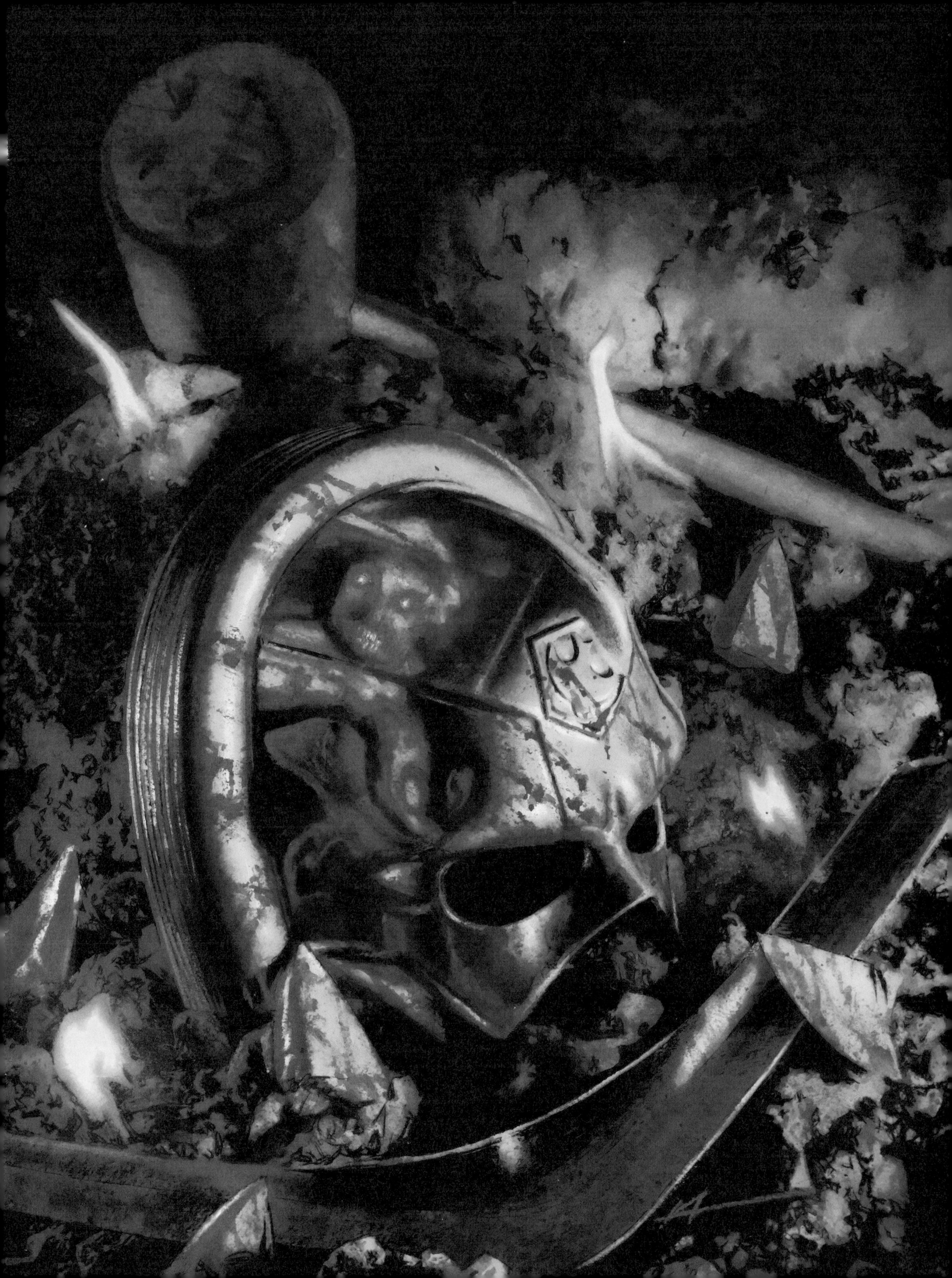

Suicide Squad: Blaze #3
variant cover by VALENTINE DE LANDRO

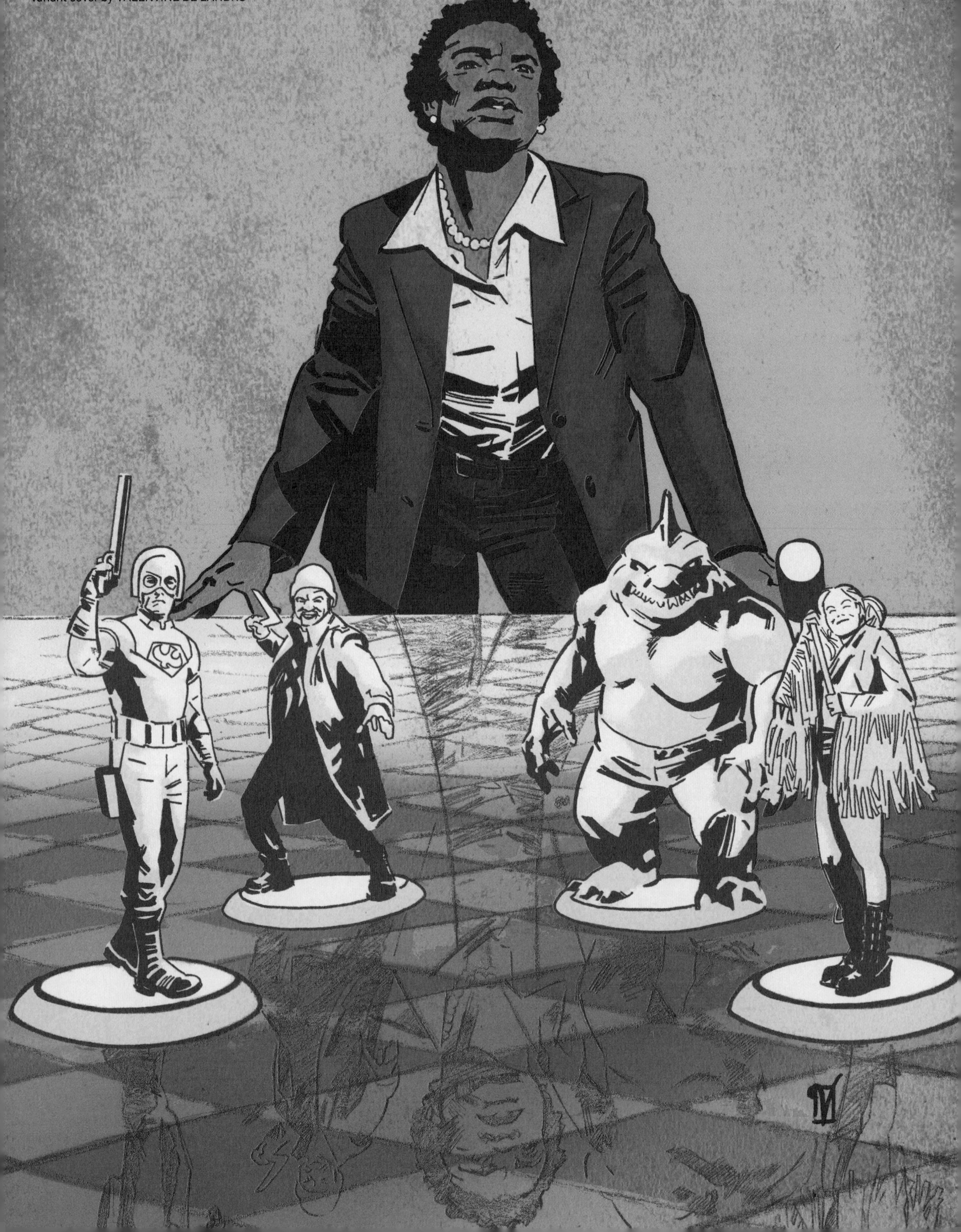

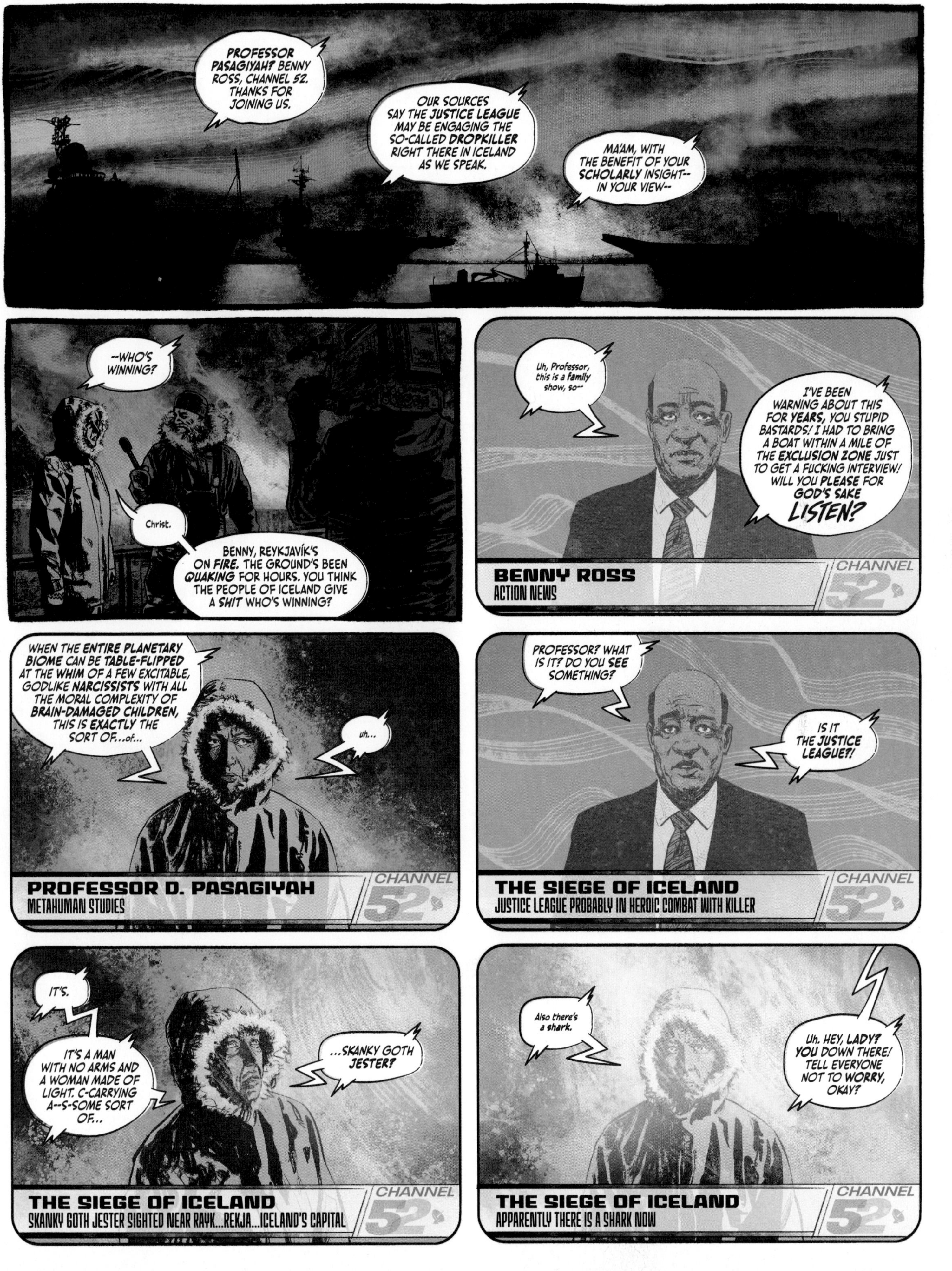
PROFESSOR PASAGIYAH? BENNY ROSS, CHANNEL 52. THANKS FOR JOINING US.
OUR SOURCES SAY THE JUSTICE LEAGUE MAY BE ENGAGING THE SO-CALLED DROPKILLER RIGHT THERE IN ICELAND AS WE SPEAK.
MA'AM, WITH THE BENEFIT OF YOUR SCHOLARLY INSIGHT-- IN YOUR VIEW--
--WHO'S WINNING?
Christ.
BENNY, REYKJAVÍK'S ON FIRE. THE GROUND'S BEEN QUAKING FOR HOURS. YOU THINK THE PEOPLE OF ICELAND GIVE A SHIT WHO'S WINNING?
Uh, Professor, this is a family show, so--
I'VE BEEN WARNING ABOUT THIS FOR YEARS, YOU STUPID BASTARDS! I HAD TO BRING A BOAT WITHIN A MILE OF THE EXCLUSION ZONE JUST TO GET A FUCKING INTERVIEW! WILL YOU PLEASE FOR GOD'S SAKE LISTEN?
BENNY ROSS
ACTION NEWS
CHANNEL 52
WHEN THE ENTIRE PLANETARY BIOME CAN BE TABLE-FLIPPED AT THE WHIM OF A FEW EXCITABLE, GODLIKE NARCISSISTS WITH ALL THE MORAL COMPLEXITY OF BRAIN-DAMAGED CHILDREN, THIS IS EXACTLY THE SORT OF...of...
uh...
PROFESSOR D. PASAGIYAH
METAHUMAN STUDIES
CHANNEL 52
PROFESSOR? WHAT IS IT? DO YOU SEE SOMETHING?
IS IT THE JUSTICE LEAGUE?!
THE SIEGE OF ICELAND
JUSTICE LEAGUE PROBABLY IN HEROIC COMBAT WITH KILLER
CHANNEL 52
IT'S.
IT'S A MAN WITH NO ARMS AND A WOMAN MADE OF LIGHT. C-CARRYING A--S-SOME SORT OF...
...SKANKY GOTH JESTER?
THE SIEGE OF ICELAND
SKANKY GOTH JESTER SIGHTED NEAR RAYK...REKJA...ICELAND'S CAPITAL
CHANNEL 52
Also there's a shark.
Uh. HEY, LADY? YOU DOWN THERE! TELL EVERYONE NOT TO WORRY, OKAY?
THE SIEGE OF ICELAND
APPARENTLY THERE IS A SHARK NOW
CHANNEL 52

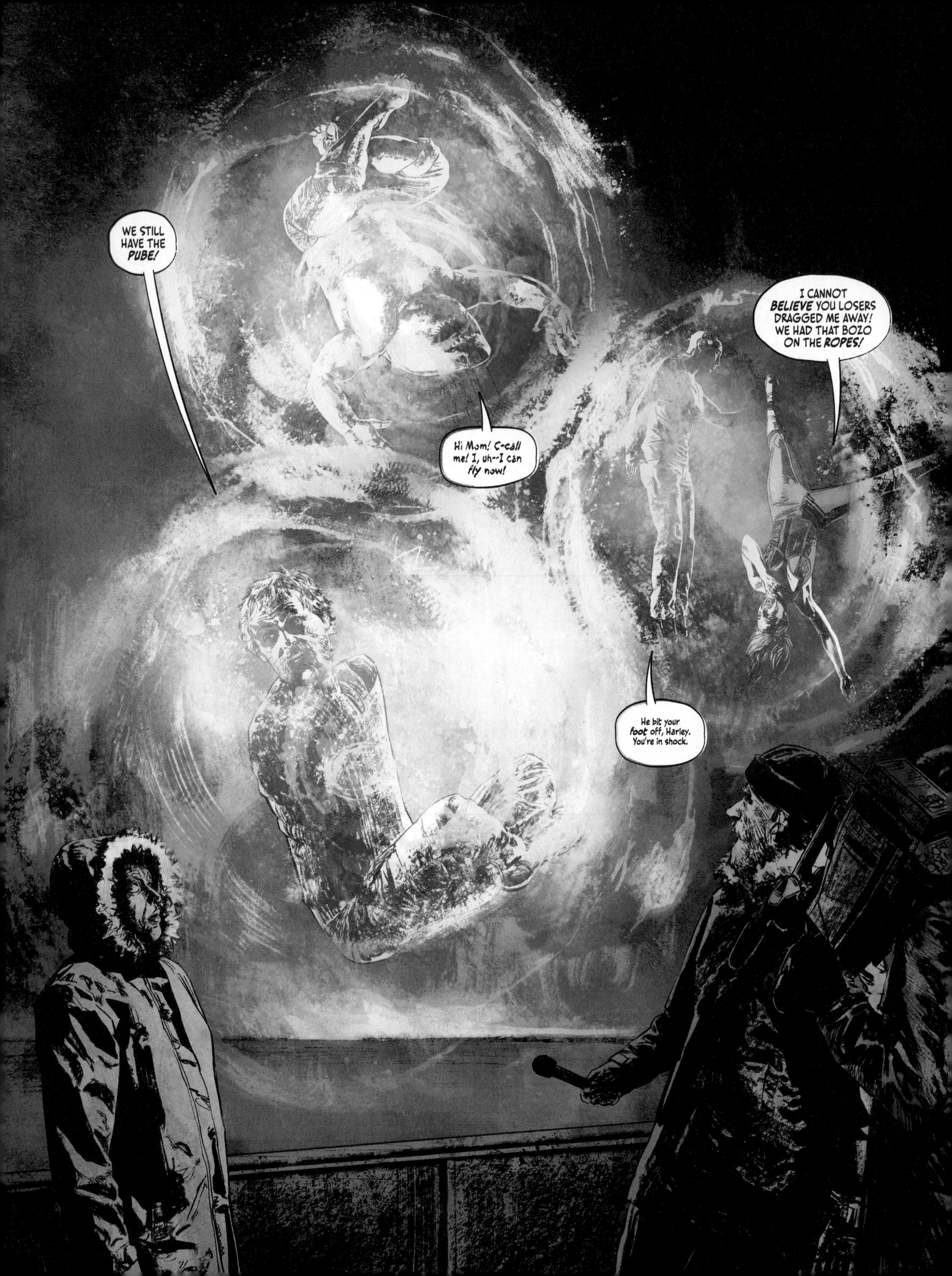
WE STILL HAVE THE PUBE!
Hi Mom! C-call me! I, uh--I can fly now!
I CANNOT BELIEVE YOU LOSERS DRAGGED ME AWAY! WE HAD THAT BOZO ON THE ROPES!
He bit your foot off, Harley. You're in shock.

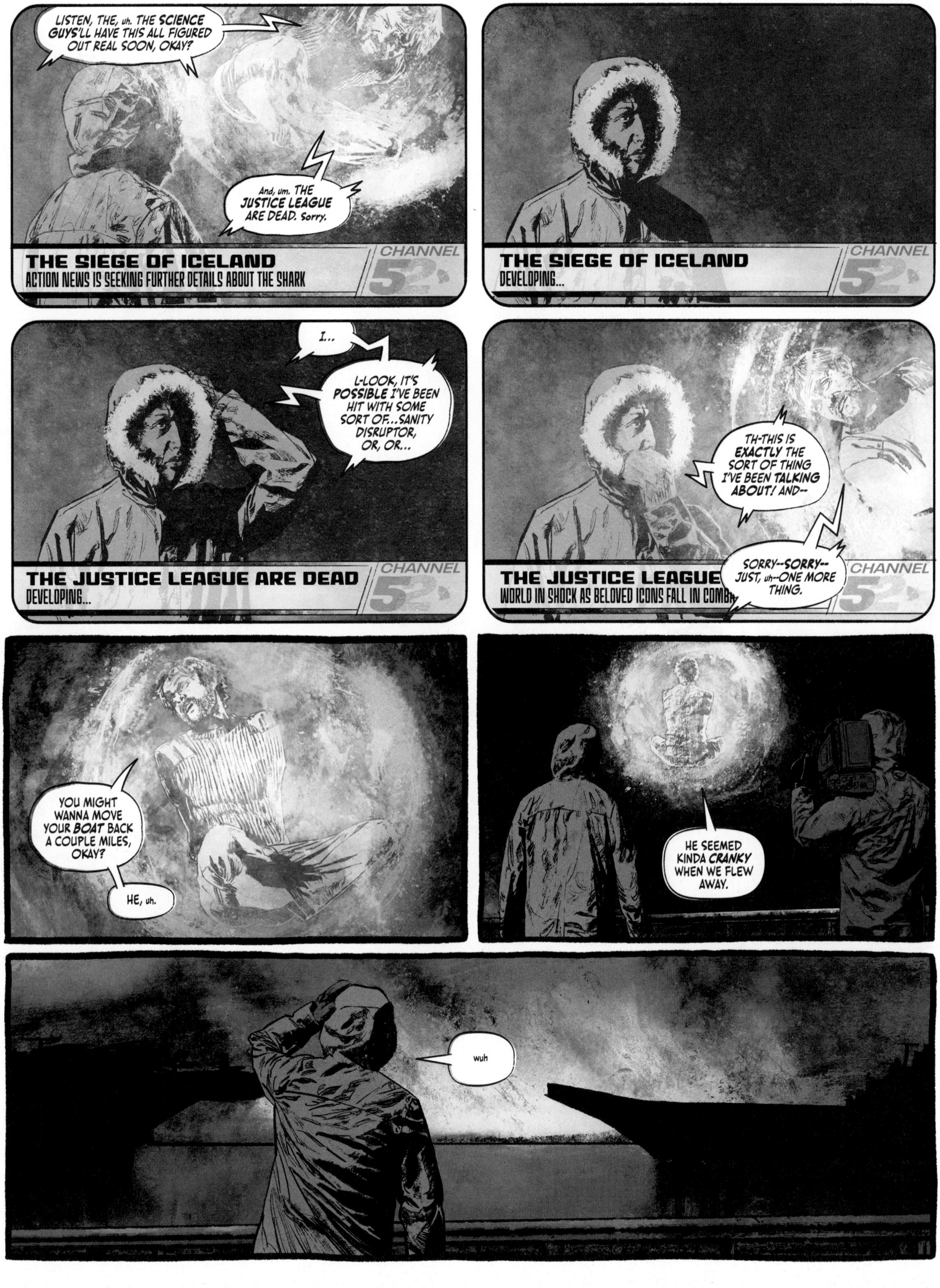
LISTEN, THE, uh. THE SCIENCE GUYS'LL HAVE THIS ALL FIGURED OUT REAL SOON, OKAY?
And, um. THE JUSTICE LEAGUE ARE DEAD. Sorry.
THE SIEGE OF ICELAND
ACTION NEWS IS SEEKING FURTHER DETAILS ABOUT THE SHARK
CHANNEL 52
THE SIEGE OF ICELAND
DEVELOPING...
CHANNEL 52
I...
L-LOOK, IT'S POSSIBLE I'VE BEEN HIT WITH SOME SORT OF...SANITY DISRUPTOR, OR, OR...
THE JUSTICE LEAGUE ARE DEAD
DEVELOPING...
CHANNEL 52
TH-THIS IS EXACTLY THE SORT OF THING I'VE BEEN TALKING ABOUT! AND--
SORRY--SORRY--JUST, uh--ONE MORE THING.
THE JUSTICE LEAGUE
WORLD IN SHOCK AS BELOVED ICONS FALL IN COMBA
CHANNEL 52
YOU MIGHT WANNA MOVE YOUR BOAT BACK A COUPLE MILES, OKAY?
HE, uh.
HE SEEMED KINDA CRANKY WHEN WE FLEW AWAY.
wuh

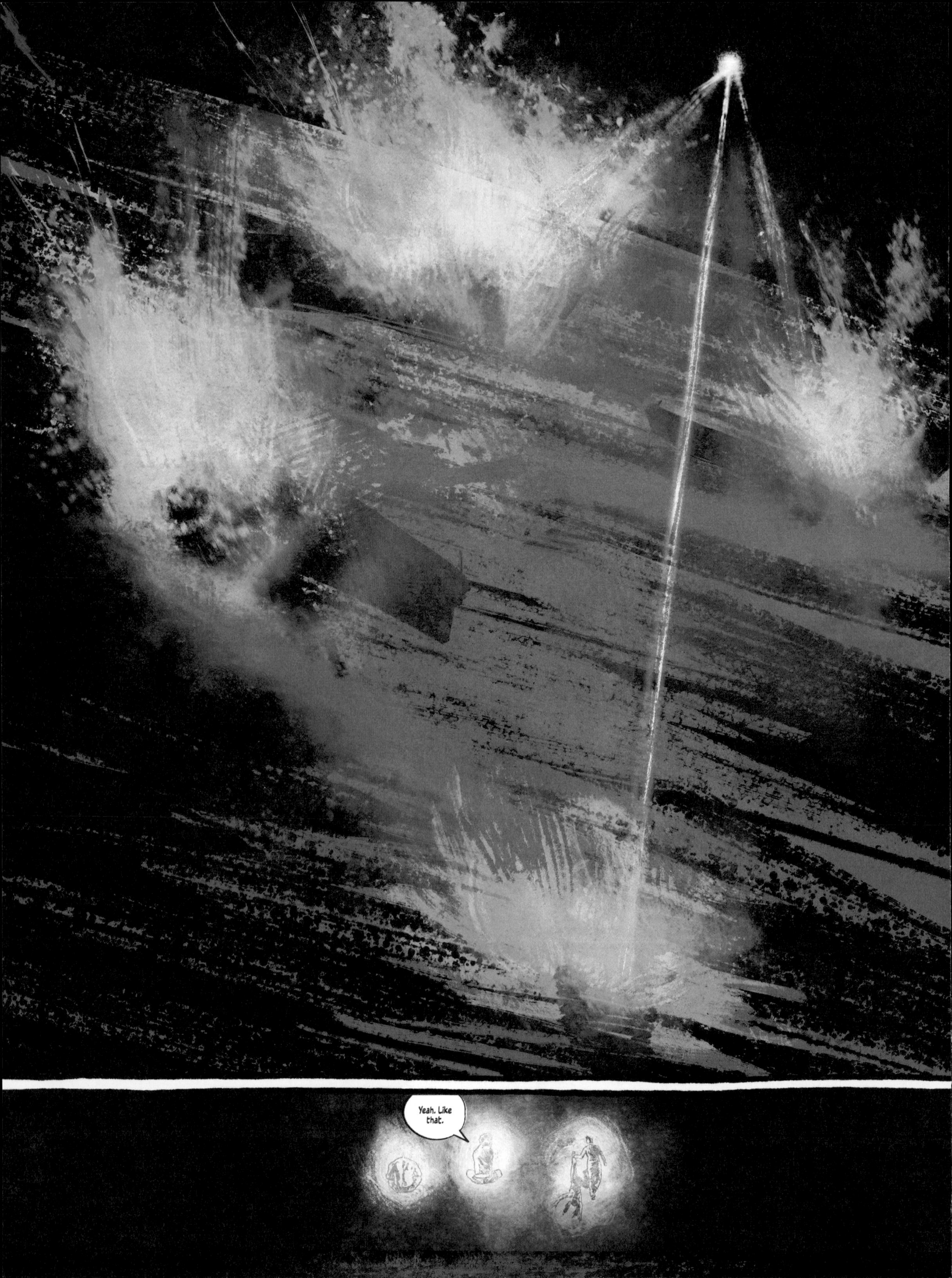
Yeah. Like that.

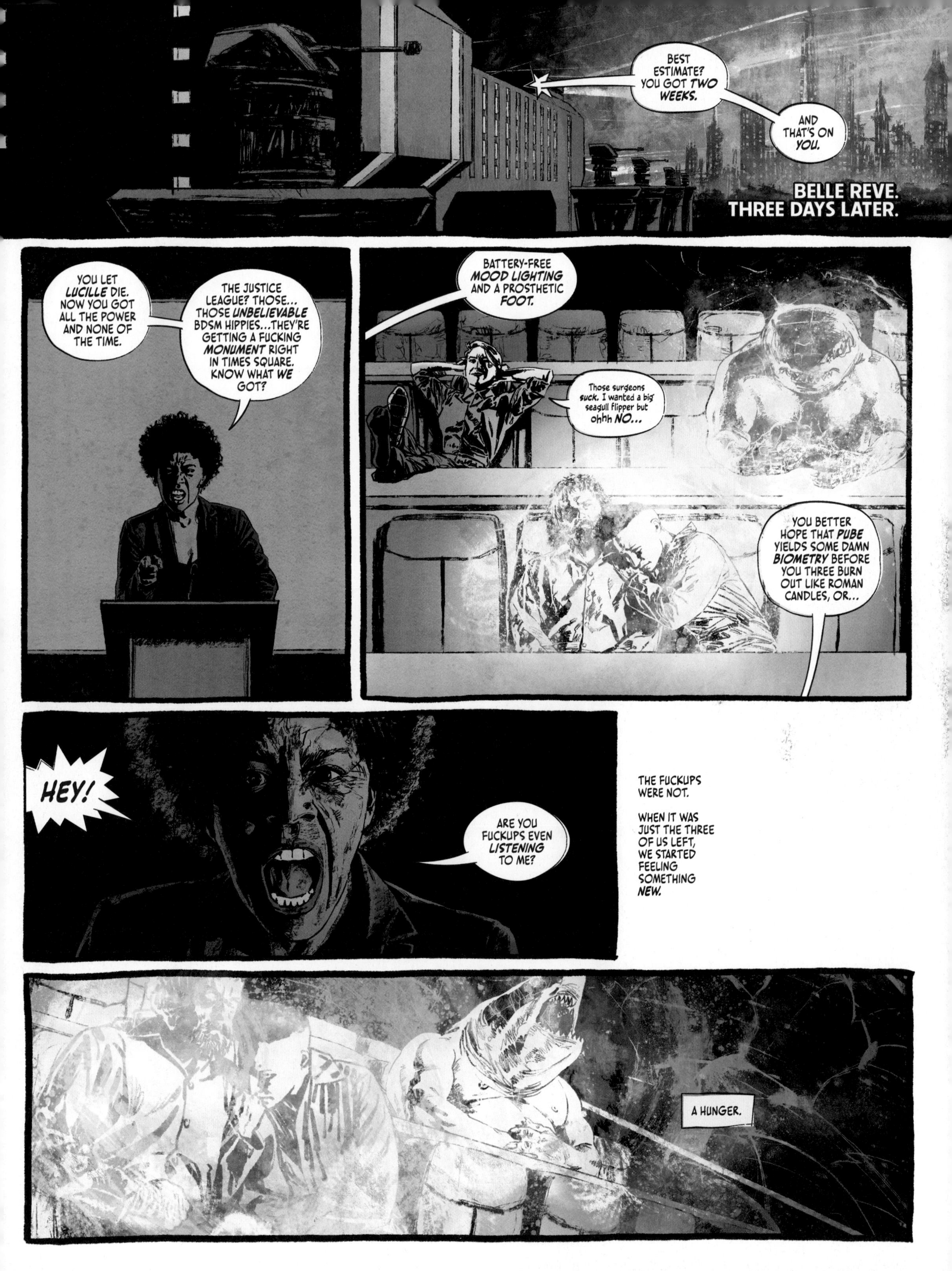
BEST ESTIMATE? YOU GOT TWO WEEKS.
AND THAT'S ON YOU.
BELLE REVE. THREE DAYS LATER.
YOU LET LUCILLE DIE. NOW YOU GOT ALL THE POWER AND NONE OF THE TIME.
THE JUSTICE LEAGUE? THOSE... THOSE UNBELIEVABLE BDSM HIPPIES...THEY'RE GETTING A FUCKING MONUMENT RIGHT IN TIMES SQUARE. KNOW WHAT WE GOT?
BATTERY-FREE MOOD LIGHTING AND A PROSTHETIC FOOT.
Those surgeons suck. I wanted a big seagull flipper but ohhh NO...
YOU BETTER HOPE THAT PUBE YIELDS SOME DAMN BIOMETRY BEFORE YOU THREE BURN OUT LIKE ROMAN CANDLES, OR...
HEY!
ARE YOU FUCKUPS EVEN LISTENING TO ME?
THE FUCKUPS WERE NOT.
WHEN IT WAS JUST THE THREE OF US LEFT, WE STARTED FEELING SOMETHING NEW.
A HUNGER.

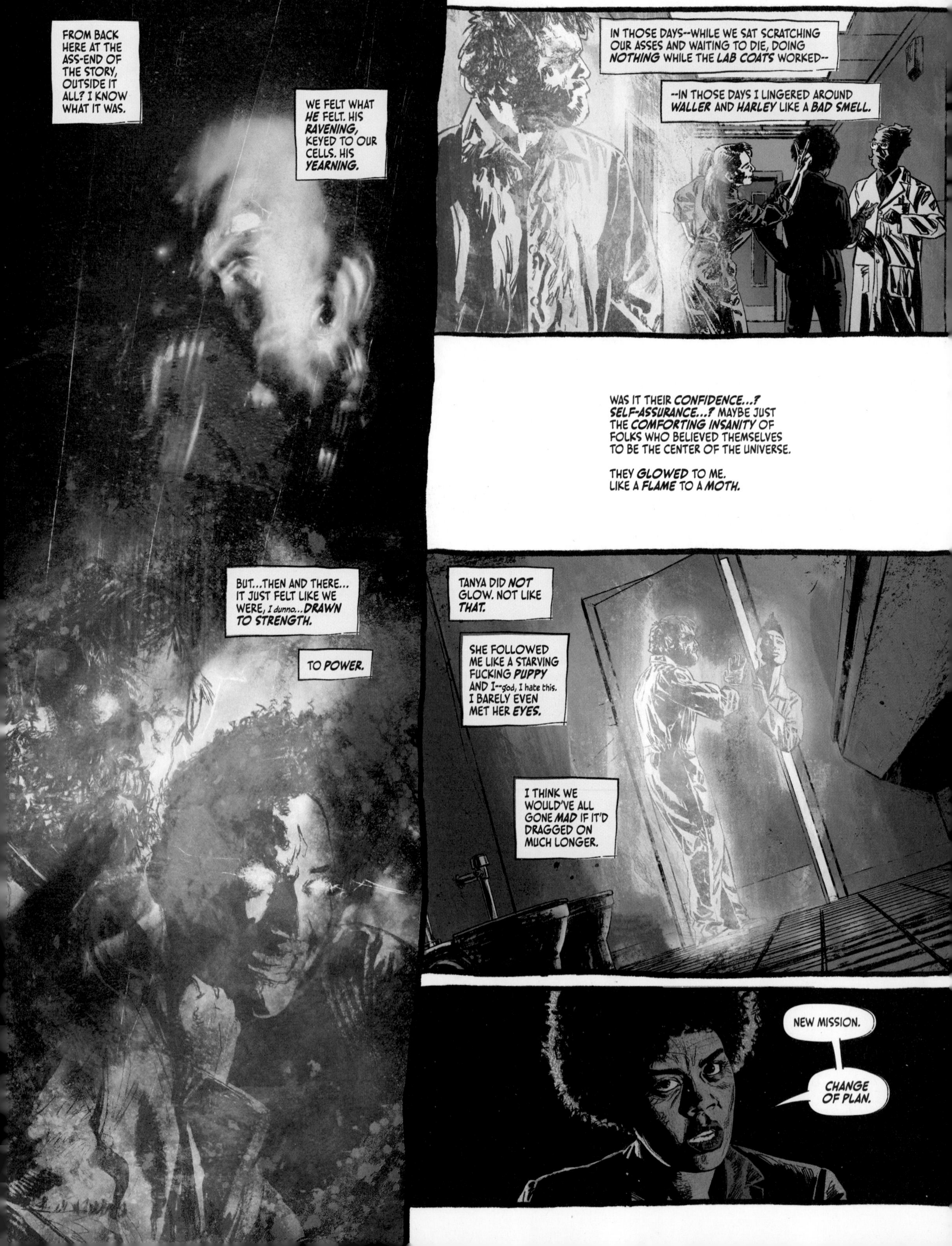
FROM BACK HERE AT THE ASS-END OF THE STORY, OUTSIDE IT ALL? I KNOW WHAT IT WAS.
WE FELT WHAT HE FELT. HIS RAVENING, KEYED TO OUR CELLS. HIS YEARNING.
BUT...THEN AND THERE... IT JUST FELT LIKE WE WERE, I dunno...DRAWN TO STRENGTH.
TO POWER.
IN THOSE DAYS--WHILE WE SAT SCRATCHING OUR ASSES AND WAITING TO DIE, DOING NOTHING WHILE THE LAB COATS WORKED--
--IN THOSE DAYS I LINGERED AROUND WALLER AND HARLEY LIKE A BAD SMELL.
WAS IT THEIR CONFIDENCE...? SELF-ASSURANCE...? MAYBE JUST THE COMFORTING INSANITY OF FOLKS WHO BELIEVED THEMSELVES TO BE THE CENTER OF THE UNIVERSE.
THEY GLOWED TO ME. LIKE A FLAME TO A MOTH.
TANYA DID NOT GLOW. NOT LIKE THAT.
SHE FOLLOWED ME LIKE A STARVING FUCKING PUPPY AND I--god, I hate this. I BARELY EVEN MET HER EYES.
I THINK WE WOULD'VE ALL GONE MAD IF IT'D DRAGGED ON MUCH LONGER.
NEW MISSION.
CHANGE OF PLAN.

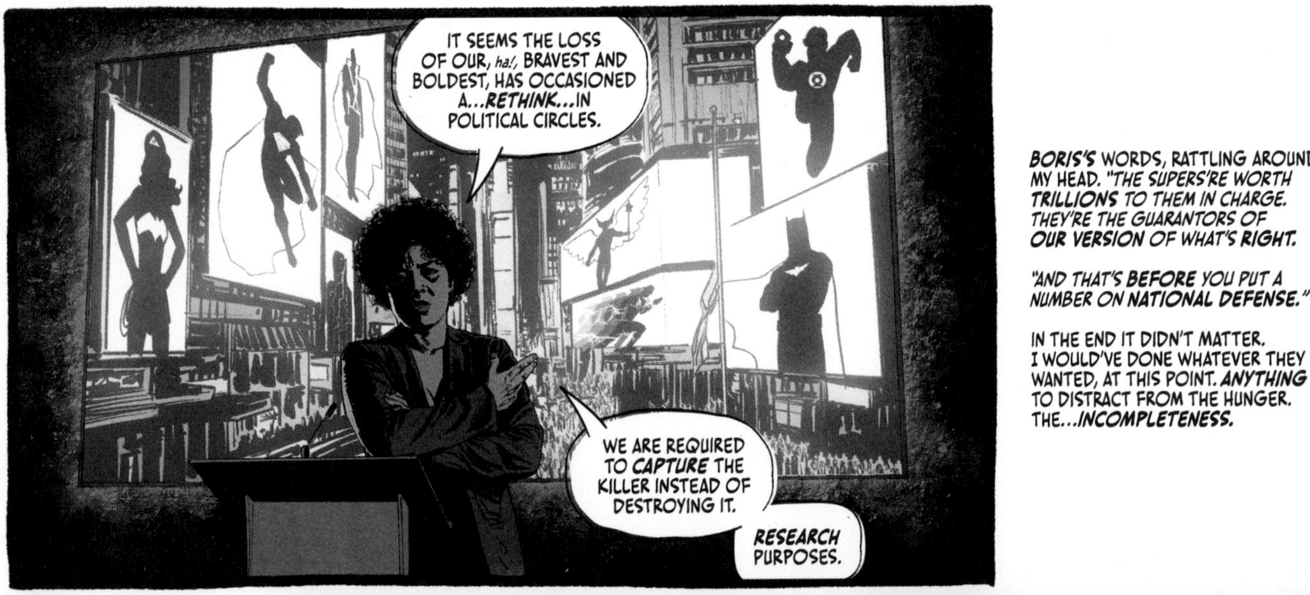
IT SEEMS THE LOSS OF OUR, *ha!,* BRAVEST AND BOLDEST, HAS OCCASIONED A...***RETHINK...*** IN POLITICAL CIRCLES.
WE ARE REQUIRED TO ***CAPTURE*** THE KILLER INSTEAD OF DESTROYING IT.
RESEARCH PURPOSES.

BORIS'S WORDS, RATTLING AROUND MY HEAD. *"THE SUPERS'RE WORTH* ***TRILLIONS*** *TO THEM IN CHARGE. THEY'RE THE GUARANTORS OF* ***OUR VERSION*** *OF WHAT'S* ***RIGHT.***

"AND THAT'S ***BEFORE*** *YOU PUT A NUMBER ON* ***NATIONAL DEFENSE."***

IN THE END IT DIDN'T MATTER. I WOULD'VE DONE WHATEVER THEY WANTED, AT THIS POINT. ***ANYTHING*** TO DISTRACT FROM THE HUNGER. THE...***INCOMPLETENESS.***

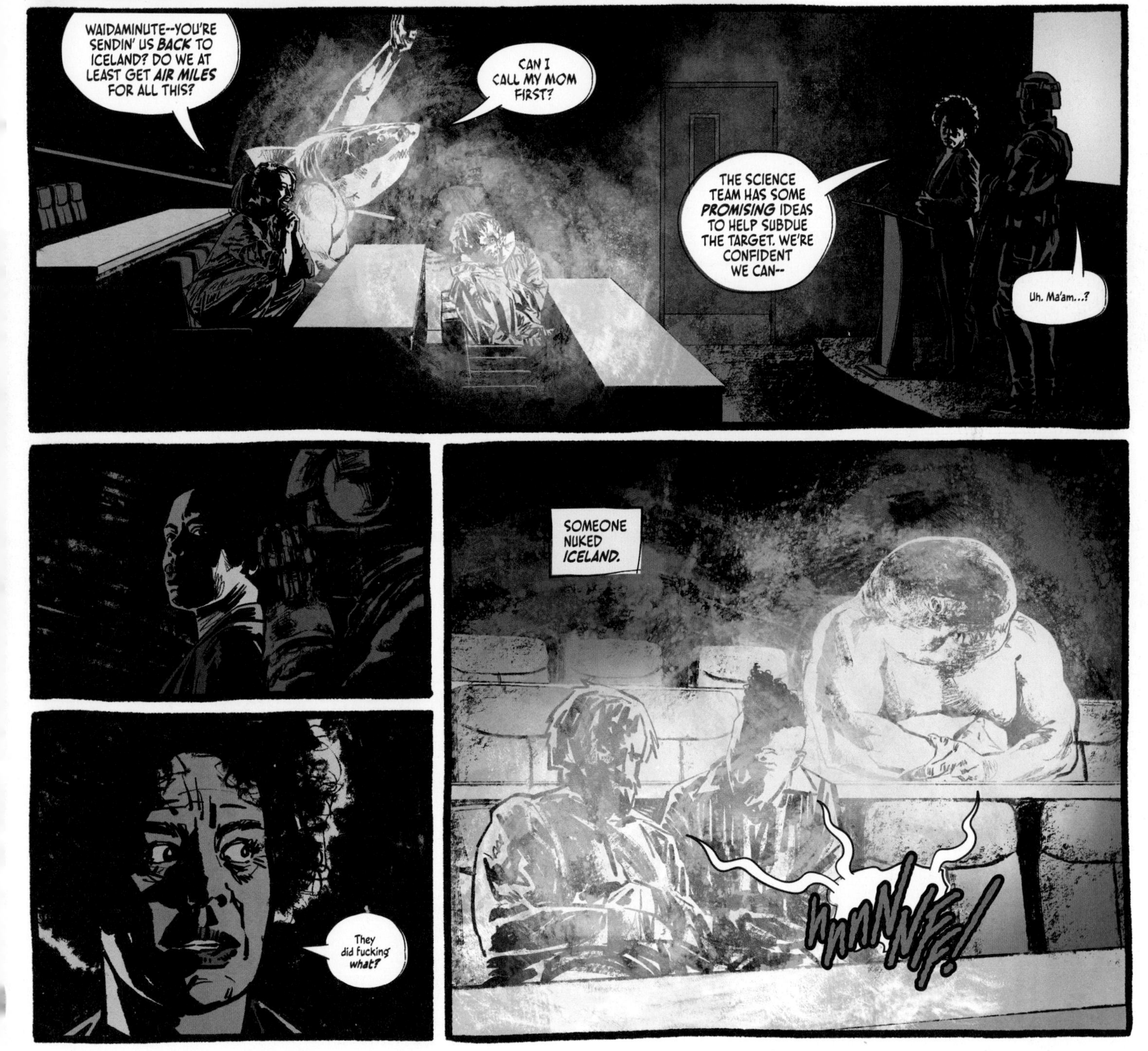
WAIDAMINUTE--YOU'RE SENDIN' US ***BACK*** TO ICELAND? DO WE AT LEAST GET ***AIR MILES*** FOR ALL THIS?
CAN I CALL MY MOM FIRST?
THE SCIENCE TEAM HAS SOME ***PROMISING*** IDEAS TO HELP SUBDUE THE TARGET. WE'RE CONFIDENT WE CAN--
Uh. Ma'am...?
SOMEONE NUKED ***ICELAND.***
They did fucking ***what?***
NNNNNF!

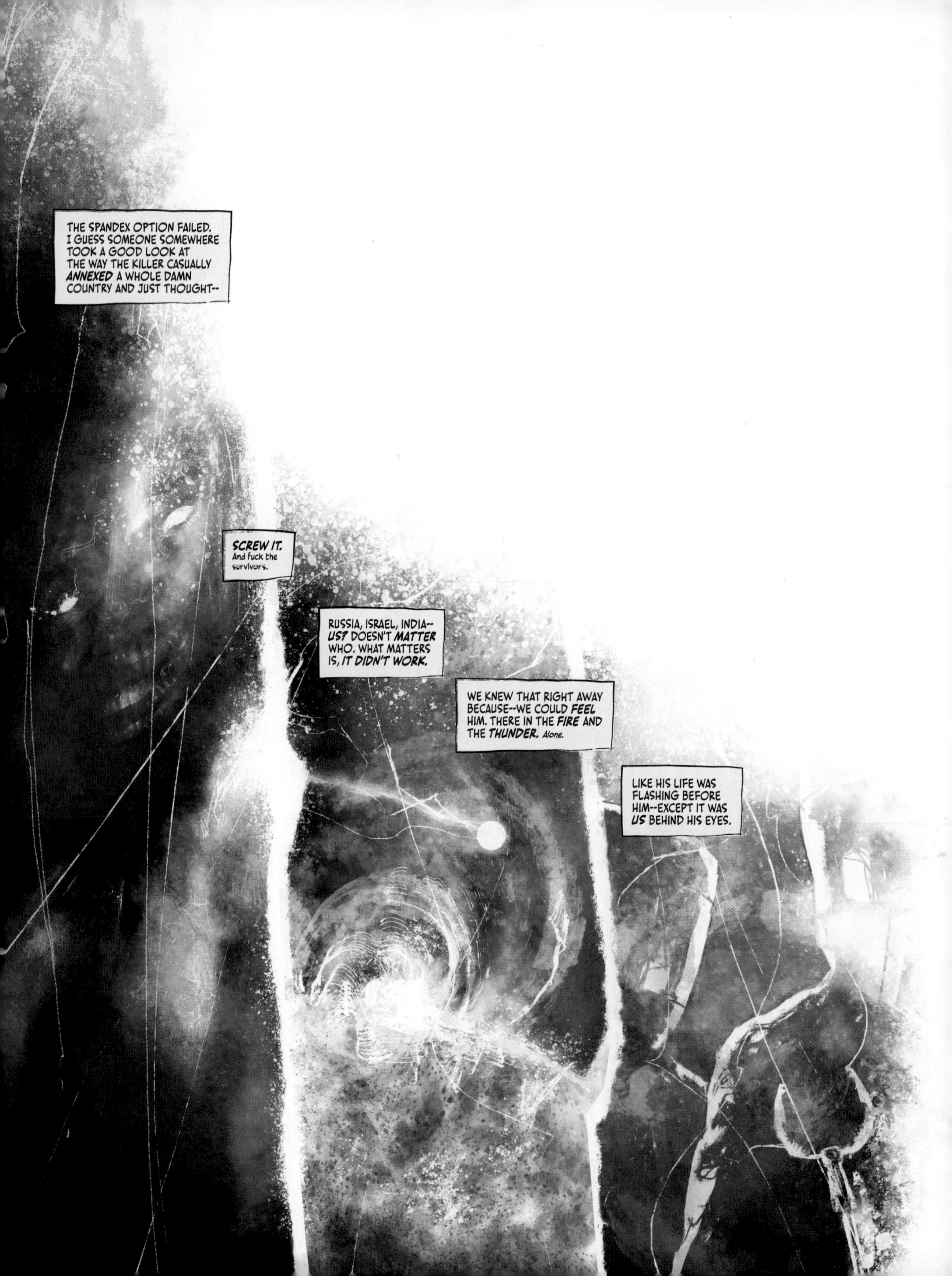
THE SPANDEX OPTION FAILED. I GUESS SOMEONE SOMEWHERE TOOK A GOOD LOOK AT THE WAY THE KILLER CASUALLY ANNEXED A WHOLE DAMN COUNTRY AND JUST THOUGHT--
SCREW IT. And fuck the survivors.
RUSSIA, ISRAEL, INDIA-- US? DOESN'T MATTER WHO. WHAT MATTERS IS, IT DIDN'T WORK.
WE KNEW THAT RIGHT AWAY BECAUSE--WE COULD FEEL HIM. THERE IN THE FIRE AND THE THUNDER. Alone.
LIKE HIS LIFE WAS FLASHING BEFORE HIM--EXCEPT IT WAS US BEHIND HIS EYES.

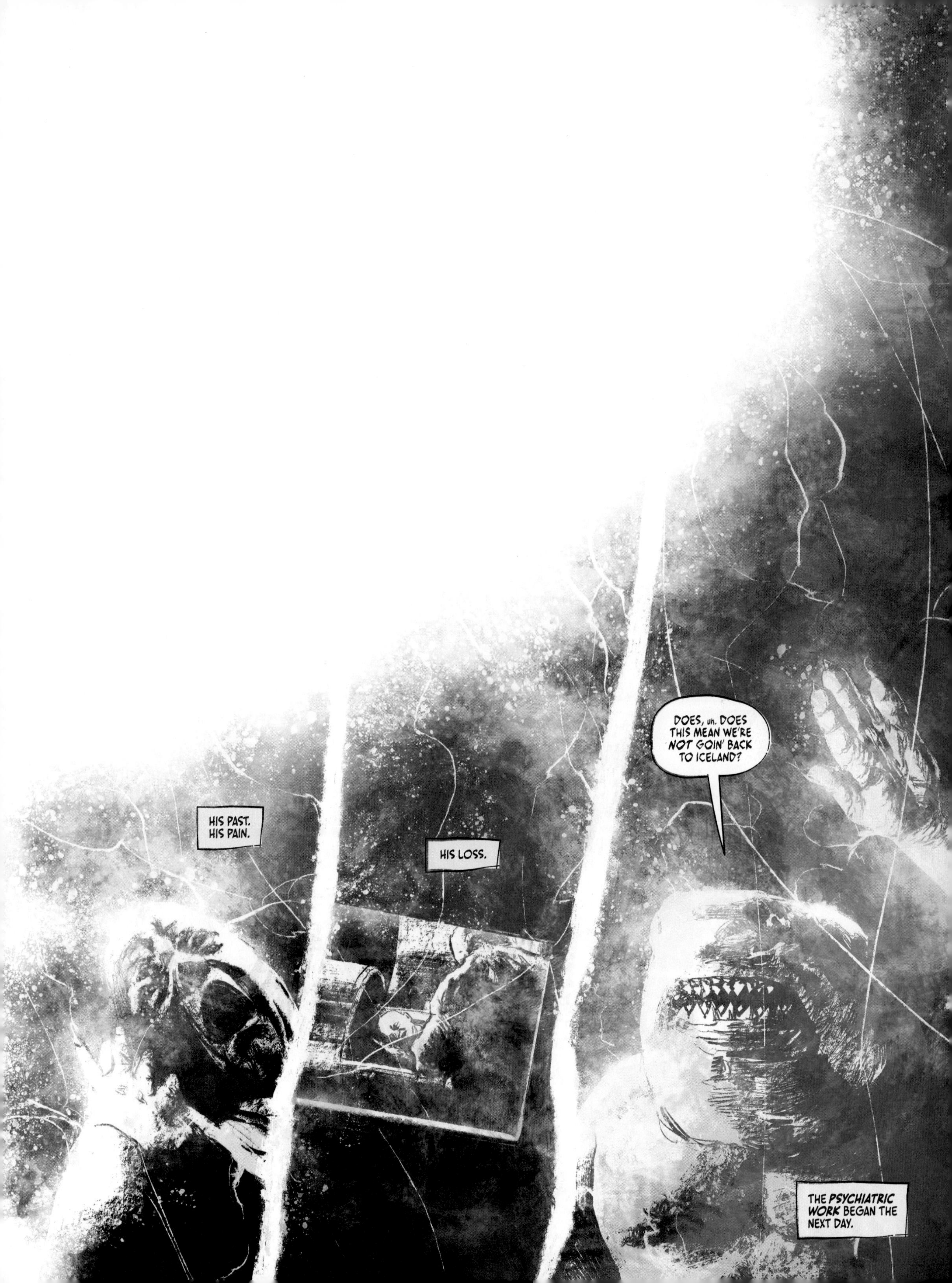
HIS PAST. HIS PAIN.
HIS LOSS.
DOES, uh. DOES THIS MEAN WE'RE *NOT* GOIN' BACK TO ICELAND?
THE *PSYCHIATRIC WORK* BEGAN THE NEXT DAY.

"SUPPORTIVE ANALYSIS," THEY CALLED IT. *"TO PROMOTE EMOTIONAL WELL-BEING AND HELP US GET THROUGH THIS DIFFICULT TIME."*

BUT, *ah...*

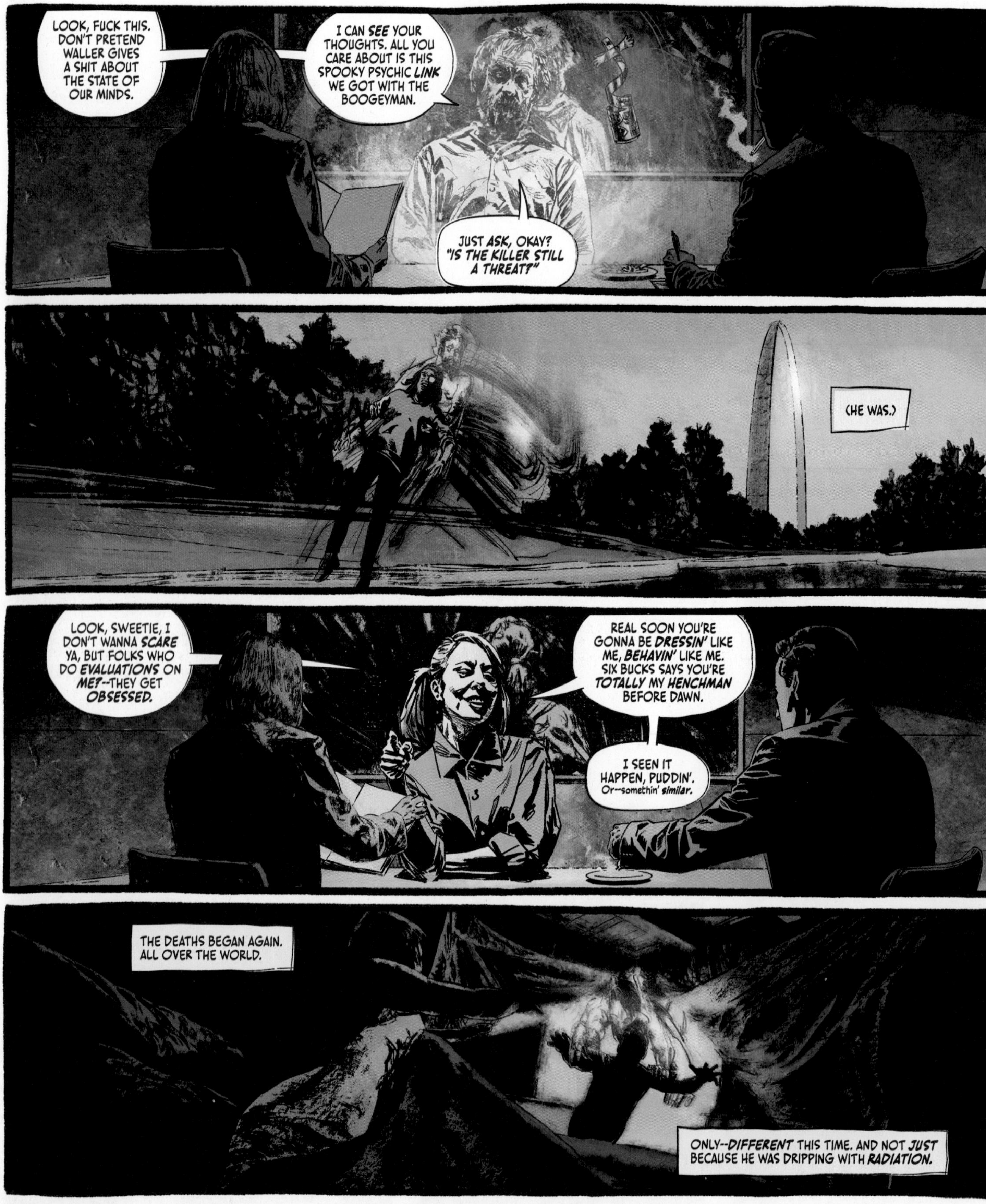
LOOK, FUCK THIS. DON'T PRETEND WALLER GIVES A SHIT ABOUT THE STATE OF OUR MINDS.
I CAN SEE YOUR THOUGHTS. ALL YOU CARE ABOUT IS THIS SPOOKY PSYCHIC LINK WE GOT WITH THE BOOGEYMAN.
JUST ASK, OKAY? "IS THE KILLER STILL A THREAT?"
(HE WAS.)
LOOK, SWEETIE, I DON'T WANNA SCARE YA, BUT FOLKS WHO DO EVALUATIONS ON ME?--THEY GET OBSESSED.
REAL SOON YOU'RE GONNA BE DRESSIN' LIKE ME, BEHAVIN' LIKE ME. SIX BUCKS SAYS YOU'RE TOTALLY MY HENCHMAN BEFORE DAWN.
I SEEN IT HAPPEN, PUDDIN'. Or--somethin' similar.
THE DEATHS BEGAN AGAIN. ALL OVER THE WORLD.
ONLY--DIFFERENT THIS TIME. AND NOT JUST BECAUSE HE WAS DRIPPING WITH RADIATION.

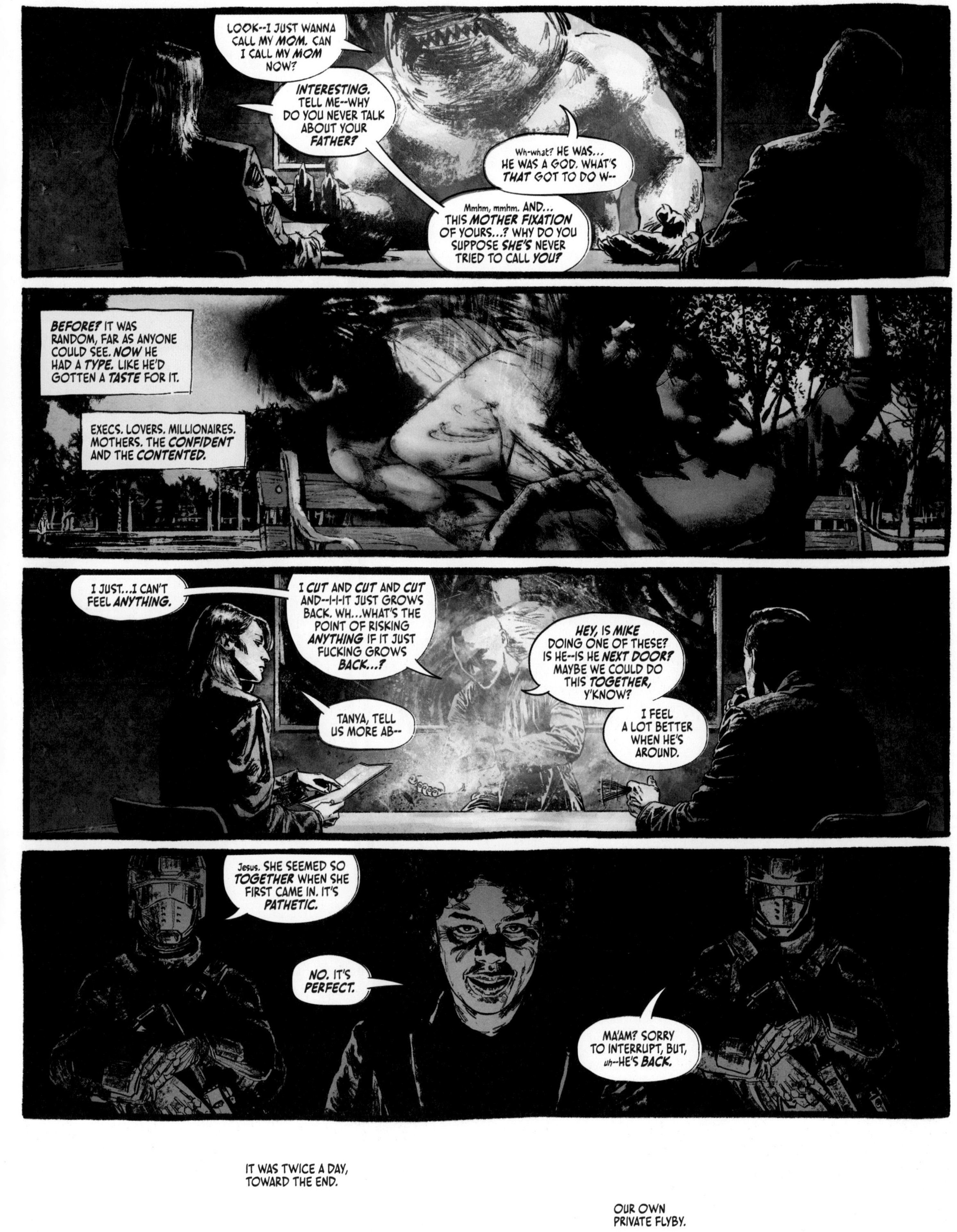
LOOK--I JUST WANNA CALL MY MOM. CAN I CALL MY MOM NOW?
INTERESTING. TELL ME--WHY DO YOU NEVER TALK ABOUT YOUR FATHER?
Wh-what? HE WAS... HE WAS A GOD. WHAT'S THAT GOT TO DO W--
Mmhm, mmhm. AND... THIS MOTHER FIXATION OF YOURS...? WHY DO YOU SUPPOSE SHE'S NEVER TRIED TO CALL YOU?
BEFORE? IT WAS RANDOM, FAR AS ANYONE COULD SEE. NOW HE HAD A TYPE. LIKE HE'D GOTTEN A TASTE FOR IT.
EXECS. LOVERS. MILLIONAIRES. MOTHERS. THE CONFIDENT AND THE CONTENTED.
I JUST...I CAN'T FEEL ANYTHING.
I CUT AND CUT AND CUT AND--I-I-IT JUST GROWS BACK. WH...WHAT'S THE POINT OF RISKING ANYTHING IF IT JUST FUCKING GROWS BACK...?
TANYA, TELL US MORE AB--
HEY, IS MIKE DOING ONE OF THESE? IS HE--IS HE NEXT DOOR? MAYBE WE COULD DO THIS TOGETHER, Y'KNOW?
I FEEL A LOT BETTER WHEN HE'S AROUND.
Jesus. SHE SEEMED SO TOGETHER WHEN SHE FIRST CAME IN. IT'S PATHETIC.
NO. IT'S PERFECT.
MA'AM? SORRY TO INTERRUPT, BUT, uh--HE'S BACK.

IT WAS TWICE A DAY,
TOWARD THE END.

OUR OWN
PRIVATE FLYBY.

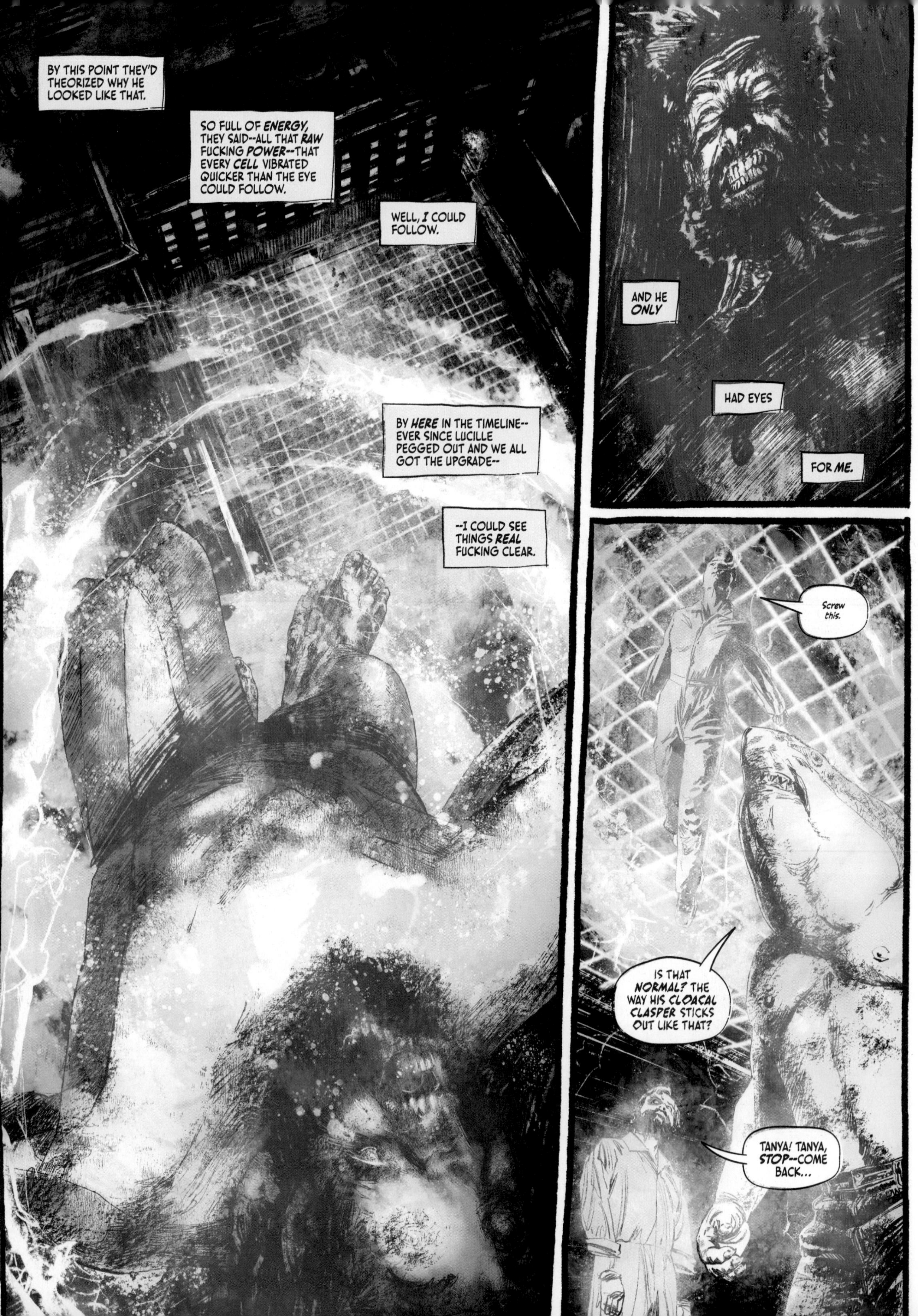

BY THIS POINT THEY'D THEORIZED WHY HE LOOKED LIKE THAT.
SO FULL OF ENERGY, THEY SAID--ALL THAT RAW FUCKING POWER--THAT EVERY CELL VIBRATED QUICKER THAN THE EYE COULD FOLLOW.
WELL, I COULD FOLLOW.
BY HERE IN THE TIMELINE--EVER SINCE LUCILLE PEGGED OUT AND WE ALL GOT THE UPGRADE--
--I COULD SEE THINGS REAL FUCKING CLEAR.
AND HE ONLY
HAD EYES
FOR ME.
Screw this.
IS THAT NORMAL? THE WAY HIS CLOACAL CLASPER STICKS OUT LIKE THAT?
TANYA! TANYA, STOP--COME BACK...

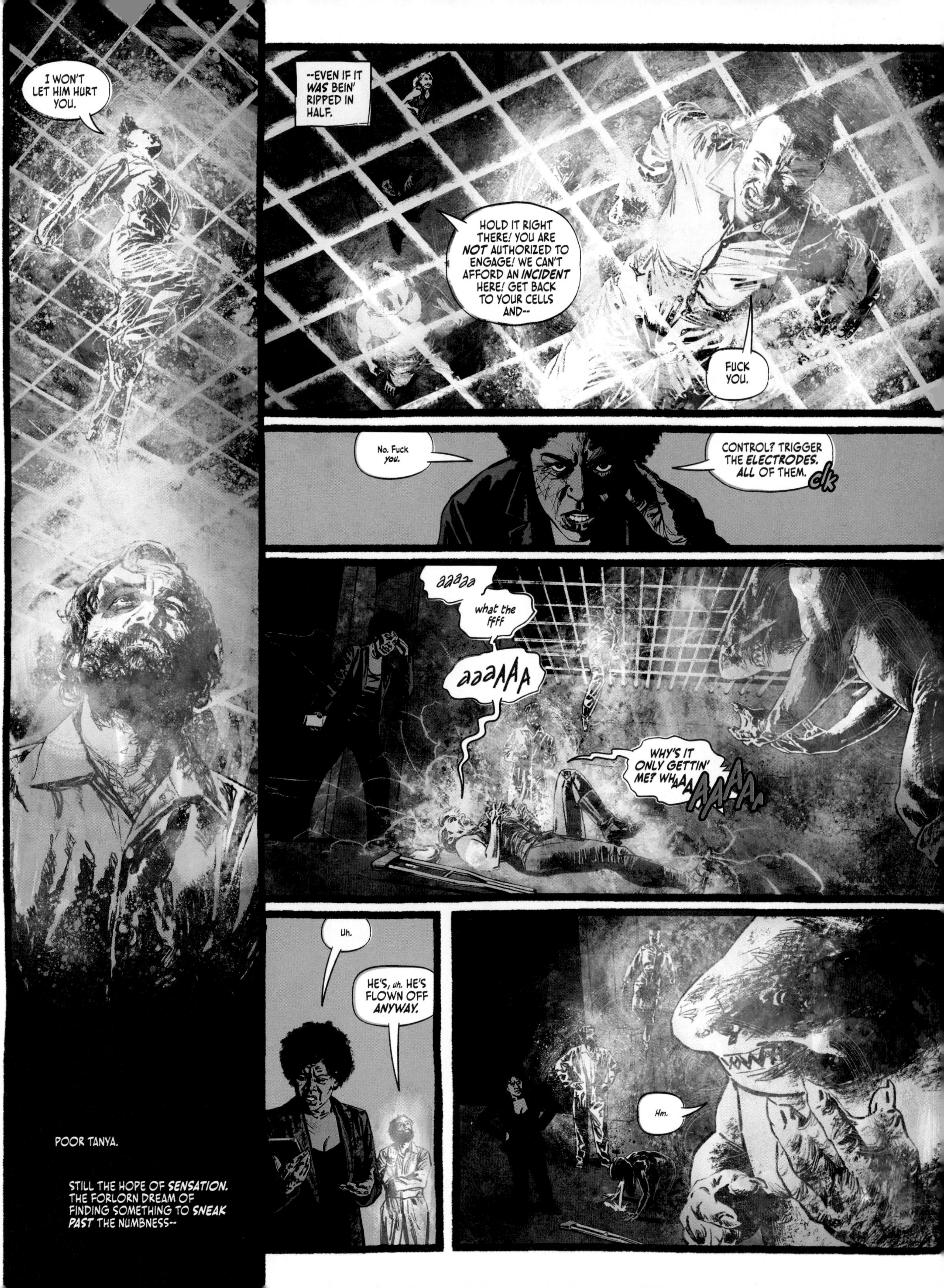
I WON'T LET HIM HURT YOU.
--EVEN IF IT WAS BEIN' RIPPED IN HALF.
HOLD IT RIGHT THERE! YOU ARE NOT AUTHORIZED TO ENGAGE! WE CAN'T AFFORD AN INCIDENT HERE! GET BACK TO YOUR CELLS AND--
FUCK YOU.
No. Fuck you.
CONTROL? TRIGGER THE ELECTRODES. ALL OF THEM.
ck
aaaa
what the ffff
aaaAAA
WHY'S IT ONLY GETTIN' ME? WHAAAAAA.
POOR TANYA.
STILL THE HOPE OF SENSATION. THE FORLORN DREAM OF FINDING SOMETHING TO SNEAK PAST THE NUMBNESS--
Uh.
HE'S, uh. HE'S FLOWN OFF ANYWAY.
Hm.

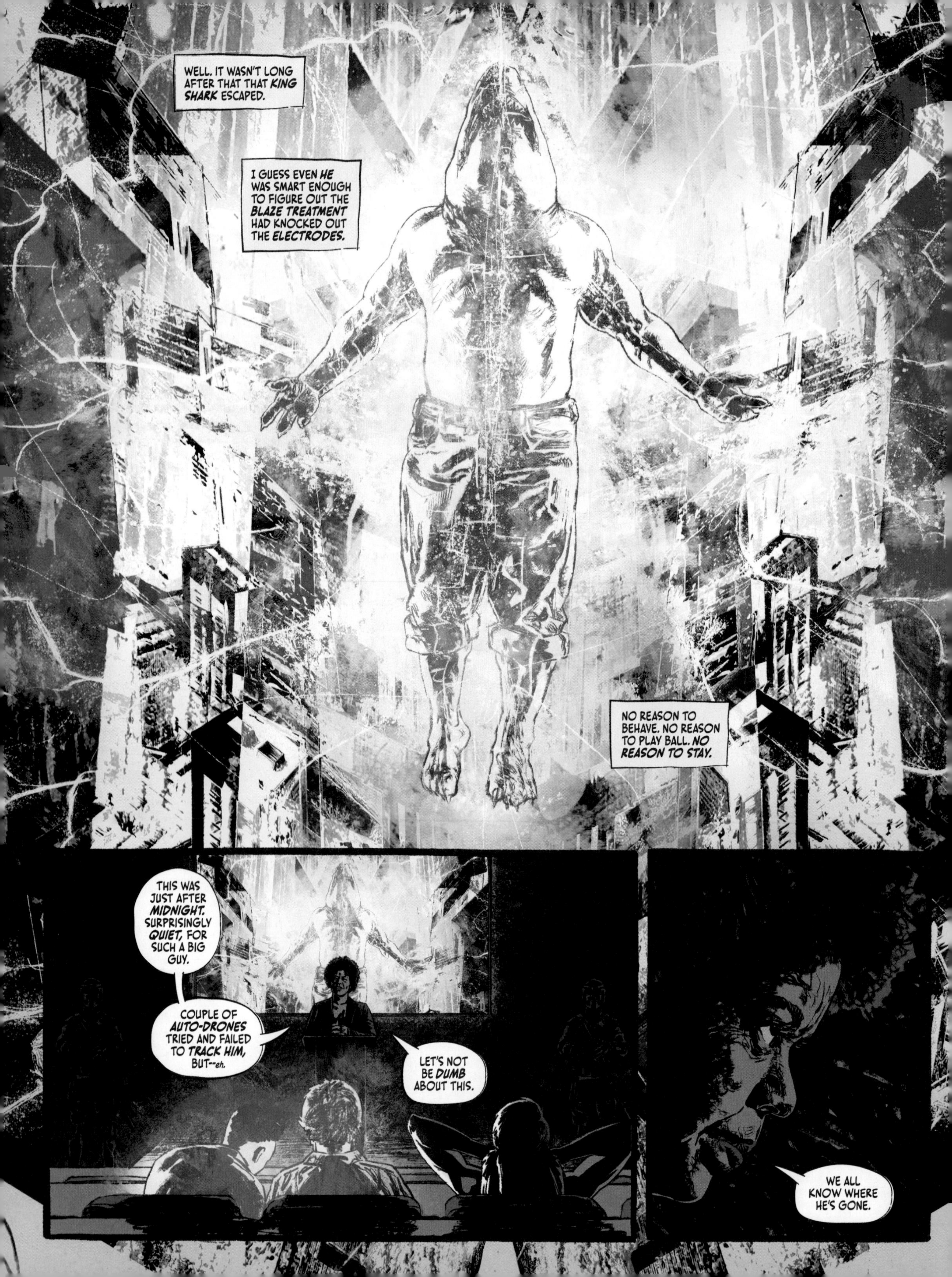
WELL. IT WASN'T LONG AFTER THAT THAT KING SHARK ESCAPED.
I GUESS EVEN HE WAS SMART ENOUGH TO FIGURE OUT THE BLAZE TREATMENT HAD KNOCKED OUT THE ELECTRODES.
NO REASON TO BEHAVE. NO REASON TO PLAY BALL. NO REASON TO STAY.
THIS WAS JUST AFTER MIDNIGHT. SURPRISINGLY QUIET, FOR SUCH A BIG GUY.
COUPLE OF AUTO-DRONES TRIED AND FAILED TO TRACK HIM, BUT--eh.
LET'S NOT BE DUMB ABOUT THIS.
WE ALL KNOW WHERE HE'S GONE.

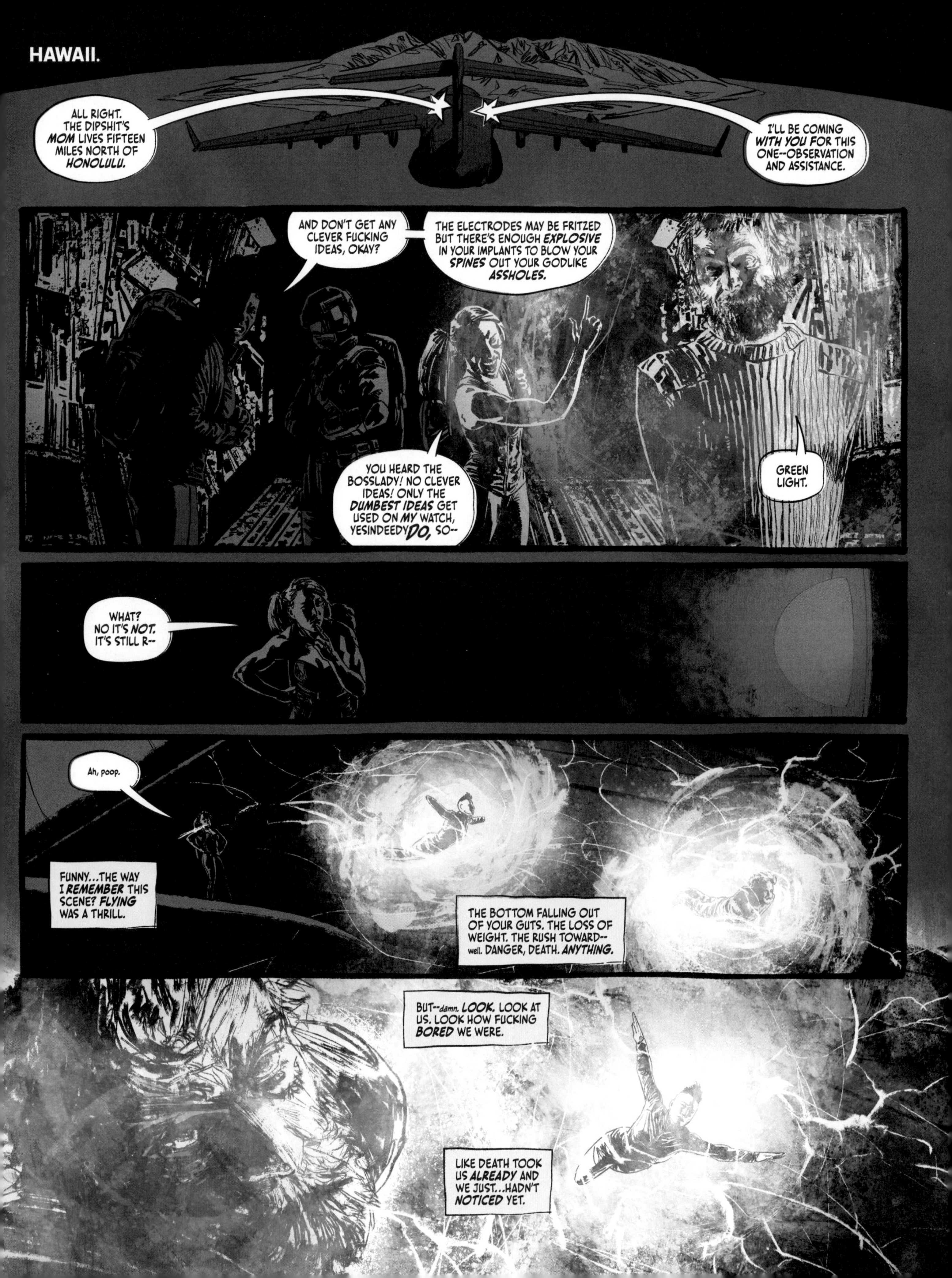
HAWAII.
ALL RIGHT. THE DIPSHIT'S MOM LIVES FIFTEEN MILES NORTH OF HONOLULU.
I'LL BE COMING WITH YOU FOR THIS ONE--OBSERVATION AND ASSISTANCE.
AND DON'T GET ANY CLEVER FUCKING IDEAS, OKAY?
THE ELECTRODES MAY BE FRITZED BUT THERE'S ENOUGH EXPLOSIVE IN YOUR IMPLANTS TO BLOW YOUR SPINES OUT YOUR GODLIKE ASSHOLES.
YOU HEARD THE BOSSLADY! NO CLEVER IDEAS! ONLY THE DUMBEST IDEAS GET USED ON MY WATCH, YESINDEEDY DO, SO--
GREEN LIGHT.
WHAT? NO IT'S NOT. IT'S STILL R--
Ah, poop.
FUNNY...THE WAY I REMEMBER THIS SCENE? FLYING WAS A THRILL.
THE BOTTOM FALLING OUT OF YOUR GUTS. THE LOSS OF WEIGHT. THE RUSH TOWARD--well. DANGER, DEATH. ANYTHING.
BUT--damn. LOOK. LOOK AT US. LOOK HOW FUCKING BORED WE WERE.
LIKE DEATH TOOK US ALREADY AND WE JUST...HADN'T NOTICED YET.

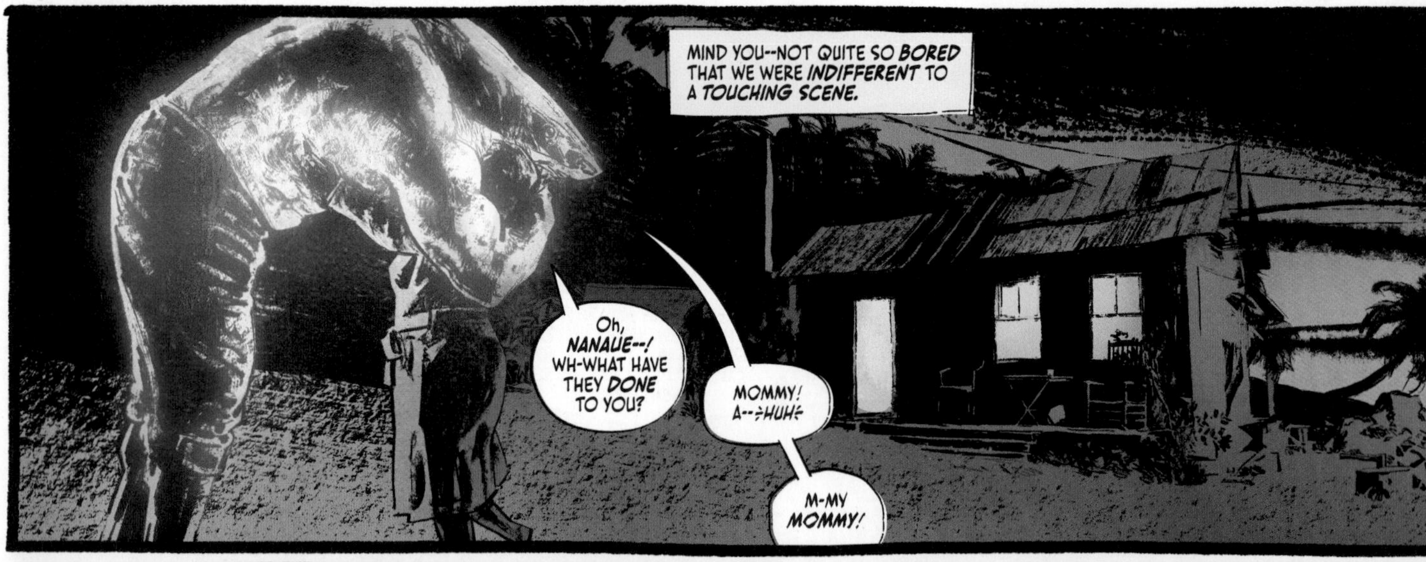
MIND YOU--NOT QUITE SO *BORED* THAT WE WERE *INDIFFERENT* TO A *TOUCHING SCENE.*
Oh, *NANAUE--!* WH-WHAT HAVE THEY *DONE* TO YOU?
MOMMY! A--HUH
M-MY *MOMMY!*

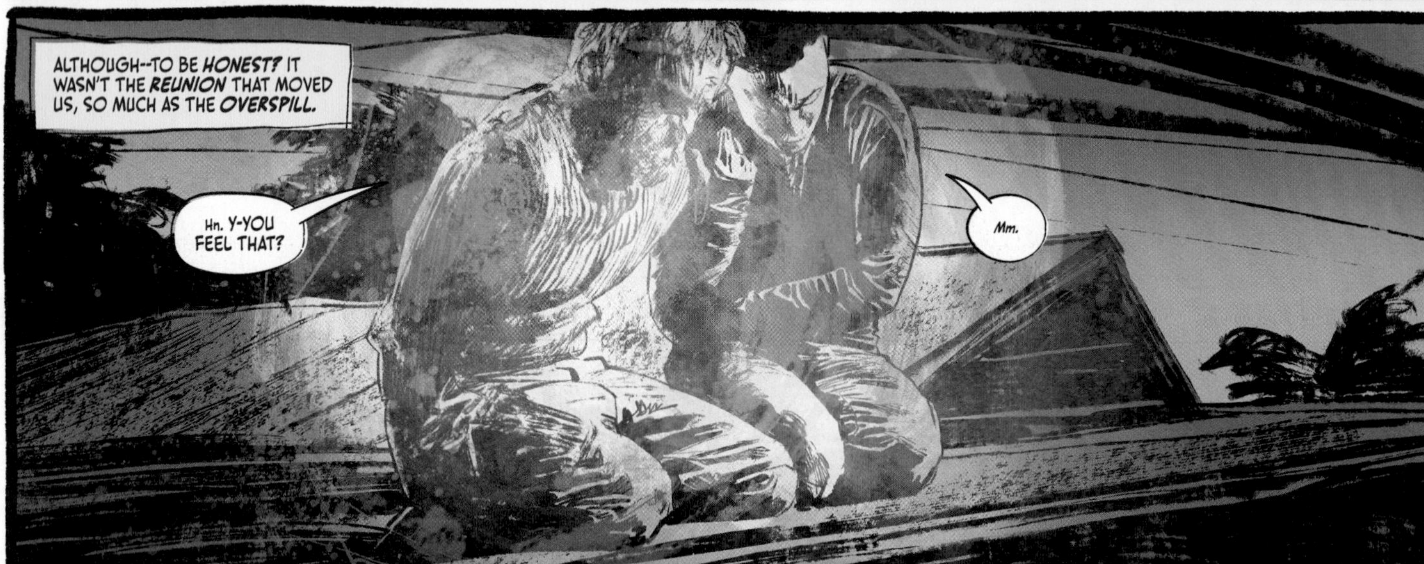
ALTHOUGH--TO BE *HONEST?* IT WASN'T THE *REUNION* THAT MOVED US, SO MUCH AS THE *OVERSPILL.*
Hn. Y-YOU FEEL THAT?
Mm.

SOMETHING ABOUT THE...THE *HAPPINESS?* THE *FULFILLMENT.*

LIKE A *BANQUET* TO A STARVING SOUL.

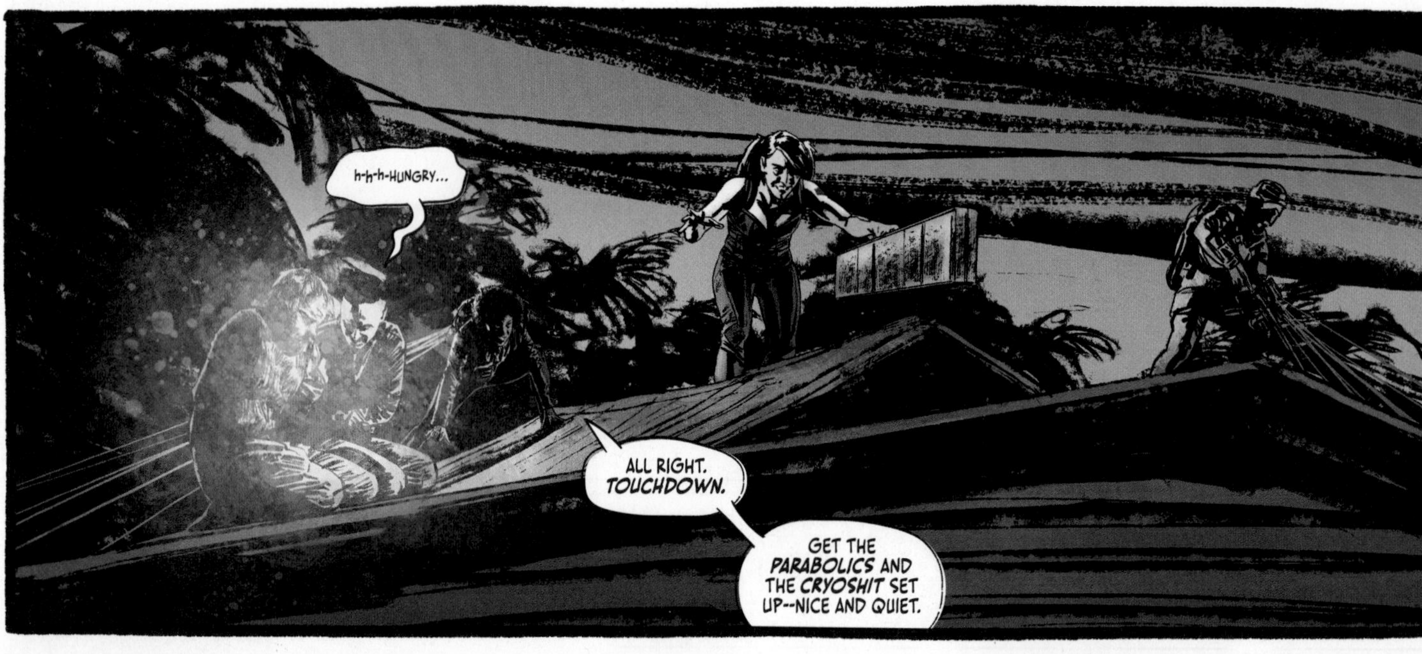
h-h-h-HUNGRY...
ALL RIGHT. *TOUCHDOWN.*
GET THE *PARABOLICS* AND THE *CRYOSHIT* SET UP--NICE AND QUIET.

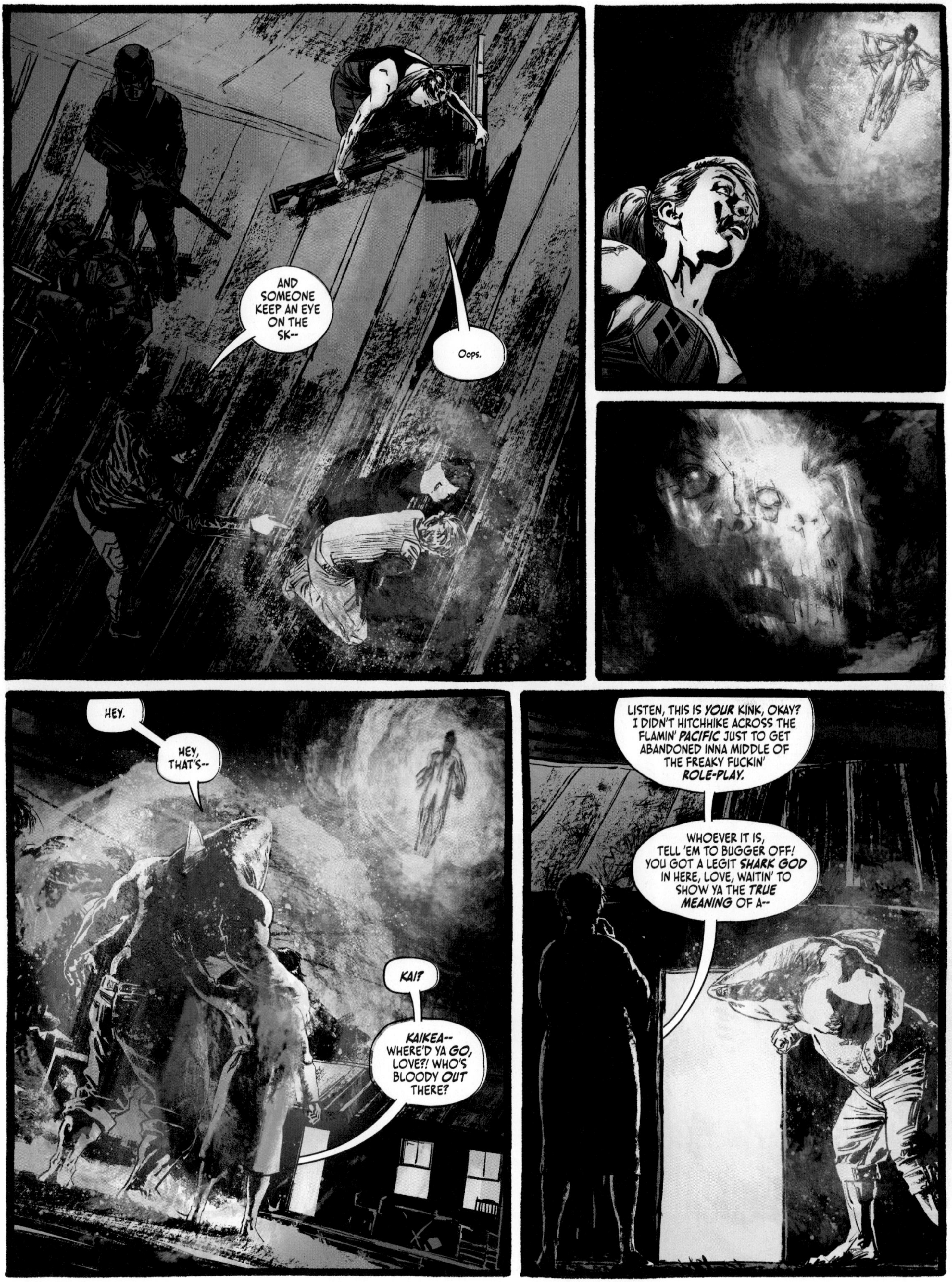
AND SOMEONE KEEP AN EYE ON THE SK--
Oops.
HEY.
HEY, THAT'S--
KAI?
KAIKEA-- WHERE'D YA GO, LOVE?! WHO'S BLOODY OUT THERE?
LISTEN, THIS IS YOUR KINK, OKAY? I DIDN'T HITCHHIKE ACROSS THE FLAMIN' PACIFIC JUST TO GET ABANDONED INNA MIDDLE OF THE FREAKY FUCKIN' ROLE-PLAY.
WHOEVER IT IS, TELL 'EM TO BUGGER OFF! YOU GOT A LEGIT SHARK GOD IN HERE, LOVE, WAITIN' TO SHOW YA THE TRUE MEANING OF A--

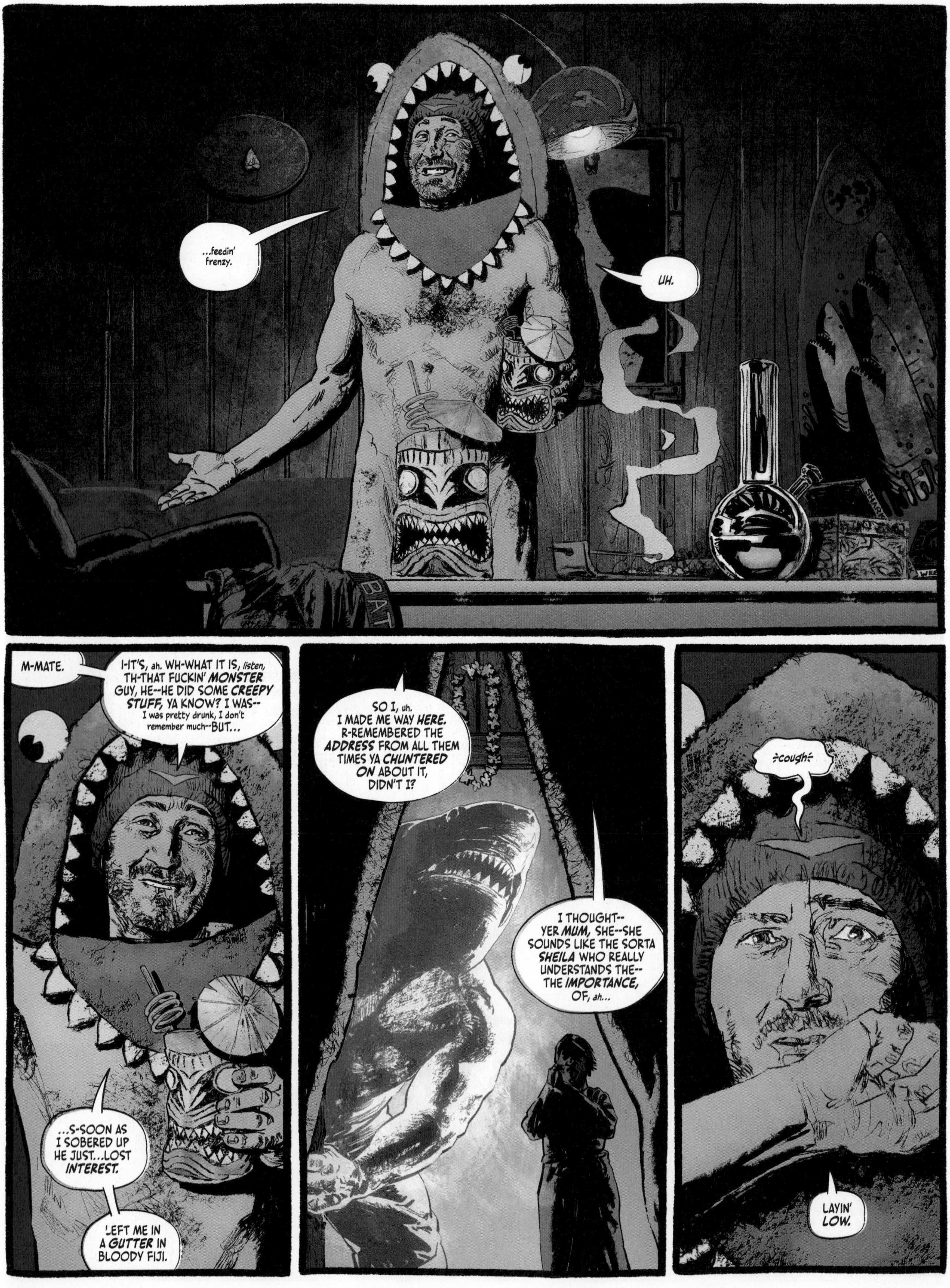

...feedin' frenzy.
UH.
BAT
M-MATE.
I-IT'S, ah. WH-WHAT IT IS, listen, TH-THAT FUCKIN' MONSTER GUY, HE--HE DID SOME CREEPY STUFF, YA KNOW? I WAS-- I was pretty drunk, I don't remember much--BUT...
...S-SOON AS I SOBERED UP HE JUST...LOST INTEREST.
LEFT ME IN A GUTTER IN BLOODY FIJI.
SO I, uh. I MADE ME WAY HERE. R-REMEMBERED THE ADDRESS FROM ALL THEM TIMES YA CHUNTERED ON ABOUT IT, DIDN'T I?
I THOUGHT-- YER MUM, SHE--SHE SOUNDS LIKE THE SORTA SHEILA WHO REALLY UNDERSTANDS THE-- THE IMPORTANCE, OF, ah...
cough
LAYIN' LOW.

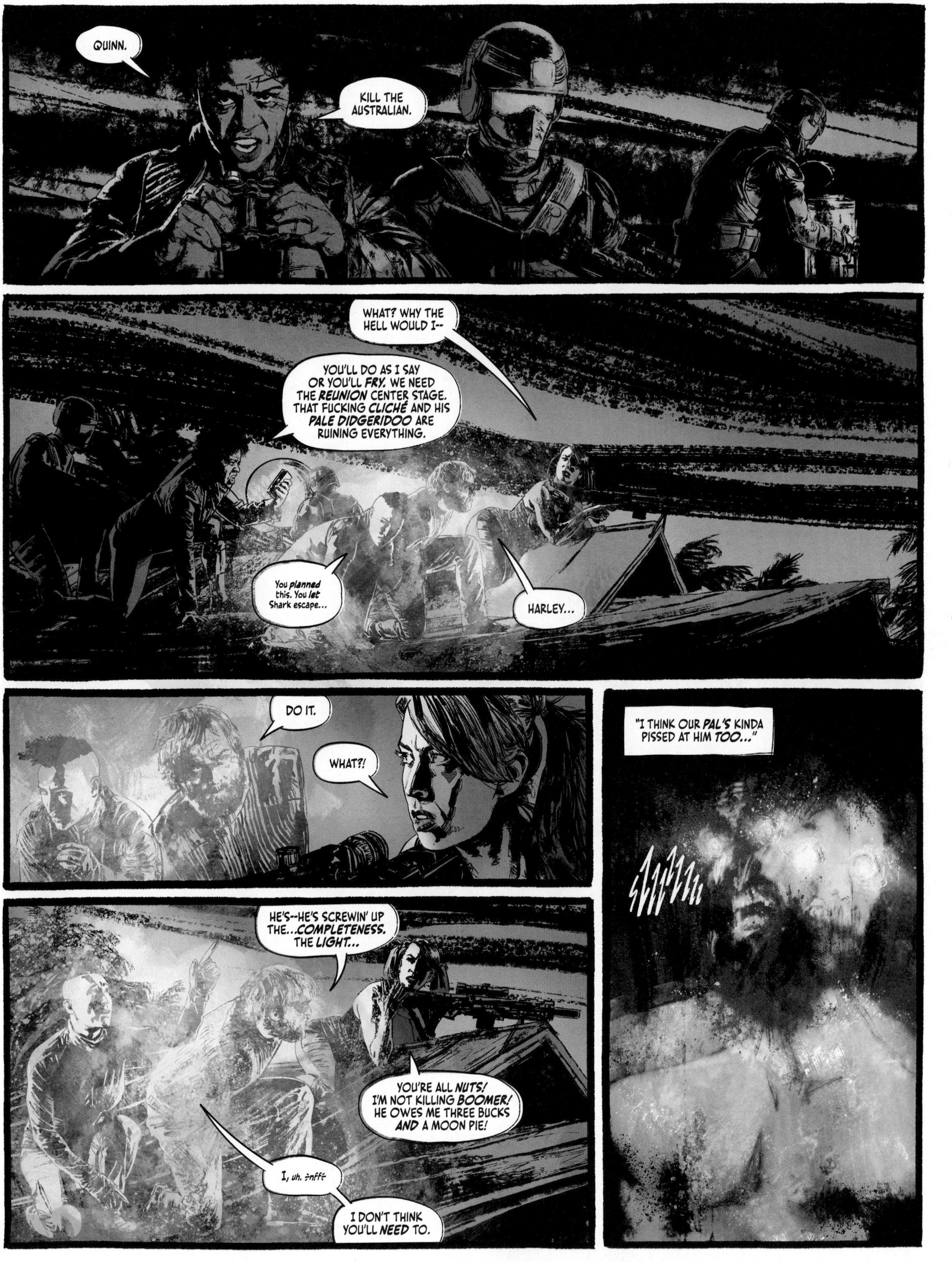
QUINN.
KILL THE AUSTRALIAN.
WHAT? WHY THE HELL WOULD I--
YOU'LL DO AS I SAY OR YOU'LL FRY. WE NEED THE REUNION CENTER STAGE. THAT FUCKING CLICHÉ AND HIS PALE DIDGERIDOO ARE RUINING EVERYTHING.
You planned this. You let Shark escape...
HARLEY...
DO IT.
WHAT?!
HE'S--HE'S SCREWIN' UP THE...COMPLETENESS. THE LIGHT...
YOU'RE ALL NUTS! I'M NOT KILLING BOOMER! HE OWES ME THREE BUCKS AND A MOON PIE!
I, uh. =nff=
I DON'T THINK YOU'LL NEED TO.
"I THINK OUR PAL'S KINDA PISSED AT HIM TOO..."

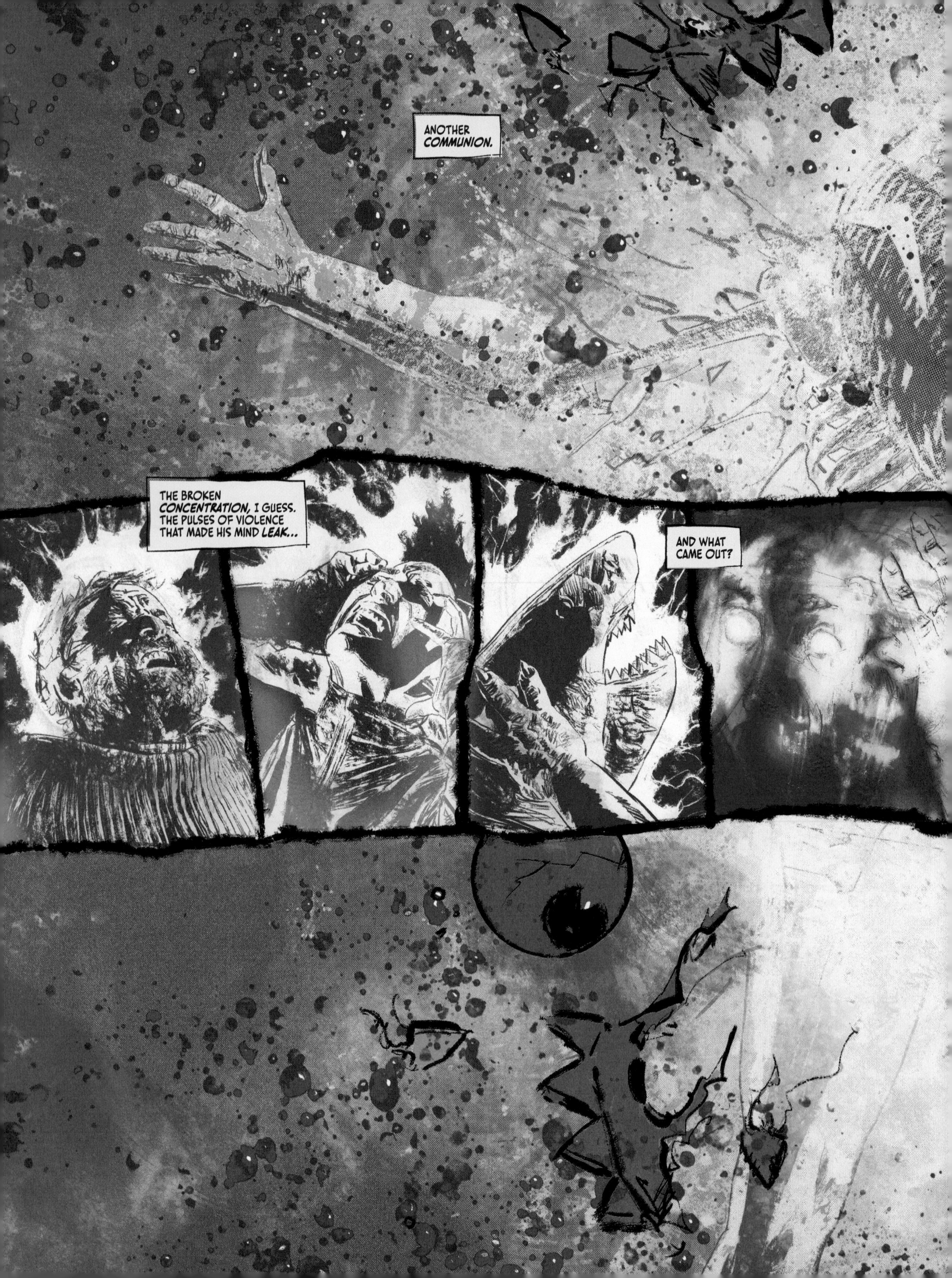
ANOTHER COMMUNION.
THE BROKEN CONCENTRATION, I GUESS. THE PULSES OF VIOLENCE THAT MADE HIS MIND LEAK...
AND WHAT CAME OUT?

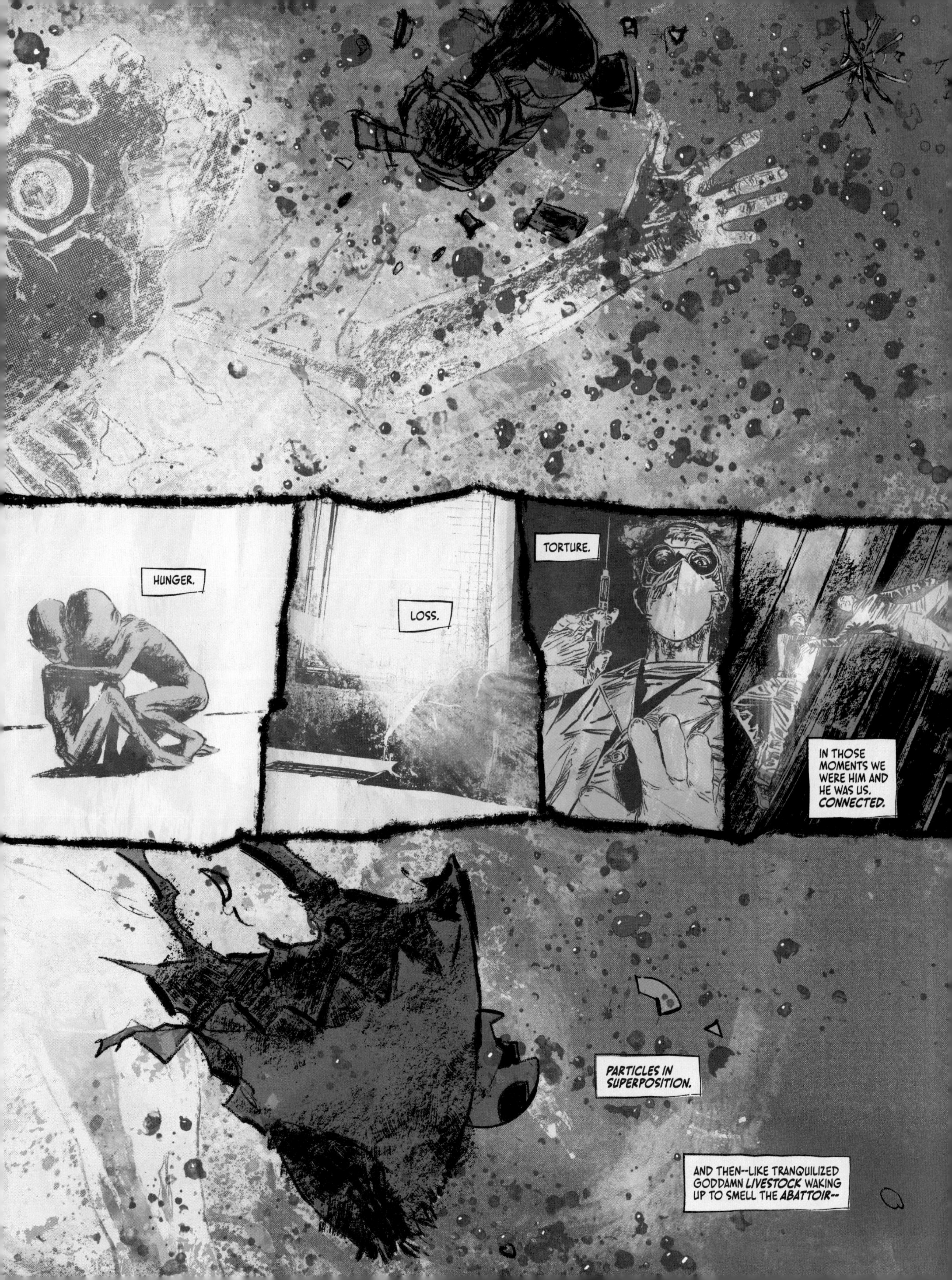
HUNGER.
LOSS.
TORTURE.
IN THOSE MOMENTS WE WERE HIM AND HE WAS US. *CONNECTED.*
PARTICLES IN SUPERPOSITION.
AND THEN--LIKE TRANQUILIZED GODDAMN *LIVESTOCK* WAKING UP TO SMELL THE *ABATTOIR*--

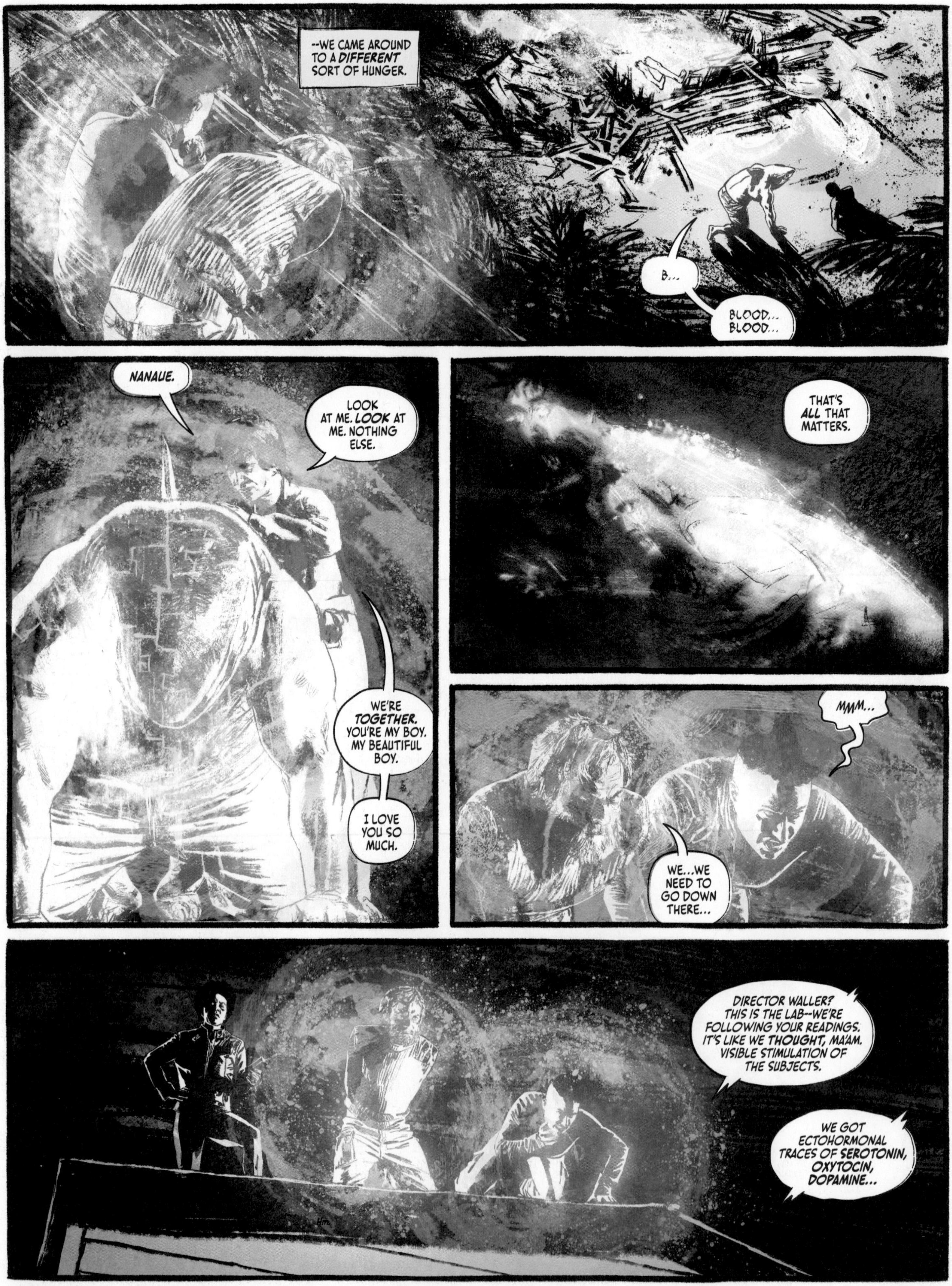
--WE CAME AROUND TO A *DIFFERENT* SORT OF HUNGER.
B...
BLOOD... BLOOD...
NANAUE.
LOOK AT ME. ***LOOK*** AT ME. NOTHING ELSE.
WE'RE ***TOGETHER.*** YOU'RE MY BOY. MY BEAUTIFUL BOY.
I LOVE YOU SO MUCH.
THAT'S ***ALL*** THAT MATTERS.
MMM...
WE...WE NEED TO GO DOWN THERE...
DIRECTOR WALLER? THIS IS THE LAB--WE'RE FOLLOWING YOUR READINGS. IT'S LIKE WE *THOUGHT*, MA'AM. VISIBLE STIMULATION OF THE SUBJECTS.
WE GOT ECTOHORMONAL TRACES OF ***SEROTONIN, OXYTOCIN, DOPAMINE...***

ALL RIGHT, SQUAD, *LISTEN UP.* WE'RE CONFIDENT THAT FUCKER'S GONNA COME SWOOPIN' DOWN HERE ANY SECOND.

TO *HIM* THAT WOMAN'S A MICHELIN-STAR FEAST. YOU CAN FEEL IT TOO, RIGHT?

SO YOU GET YOUR HEADS *STRAIGHT* AND GET SET TO *ENGAGE.*

YOU *GRAB* HIM WHILE HE'S *EATING. INCAPACITATE* HIM HOWEVER YOU FUCKING CA--

H-H-H-H-HARLEY!

I KN-KNOW YOU'RE BACK THERE! I *SMELL* YA!

THERE'S--THERE'S TOO MUCH *BLOOD!* I C-C-CAN'T CONTROL MYSELF! M-M-MY *MOM*, HARLEY.

I NEED YOU TO SAVE MY MOM.

QUINN.

QUINN, DON'T YOU DARE. WE NEED HIM.

I got you, big guy.

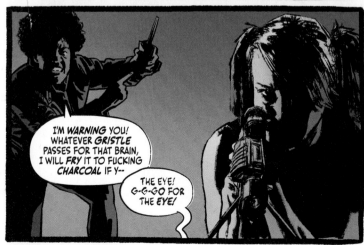

I'M *WARNING* YOU! WHATEVER *GRISTLE* PASSES FOR THAT BRAIN, I WILL *FRY* IT TO FUCKING *CHARCOAL* IF Y--

THE EYE! G-G-GO FOR THE EYE!

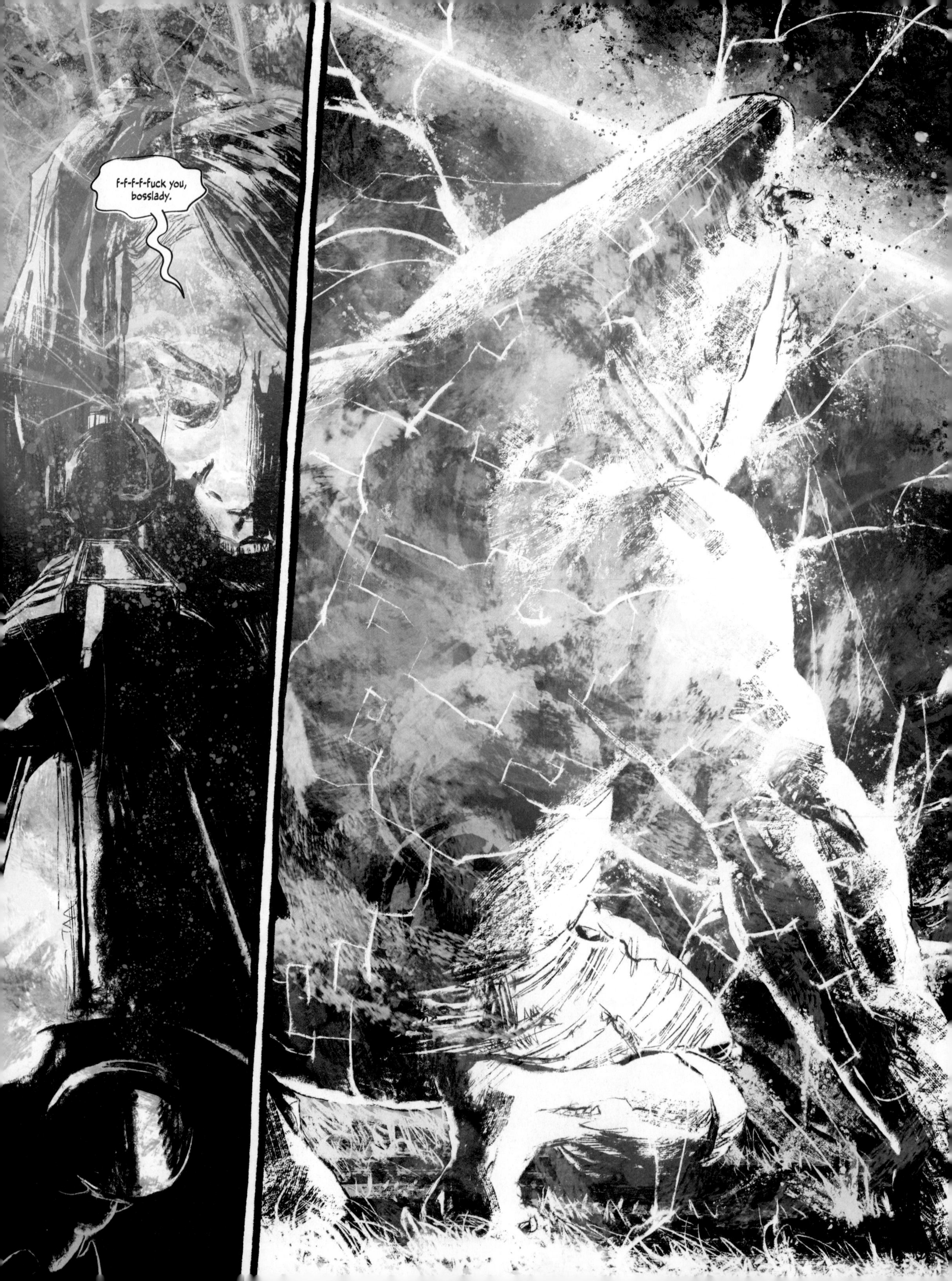
f-f-f-fuck you, bosslady.

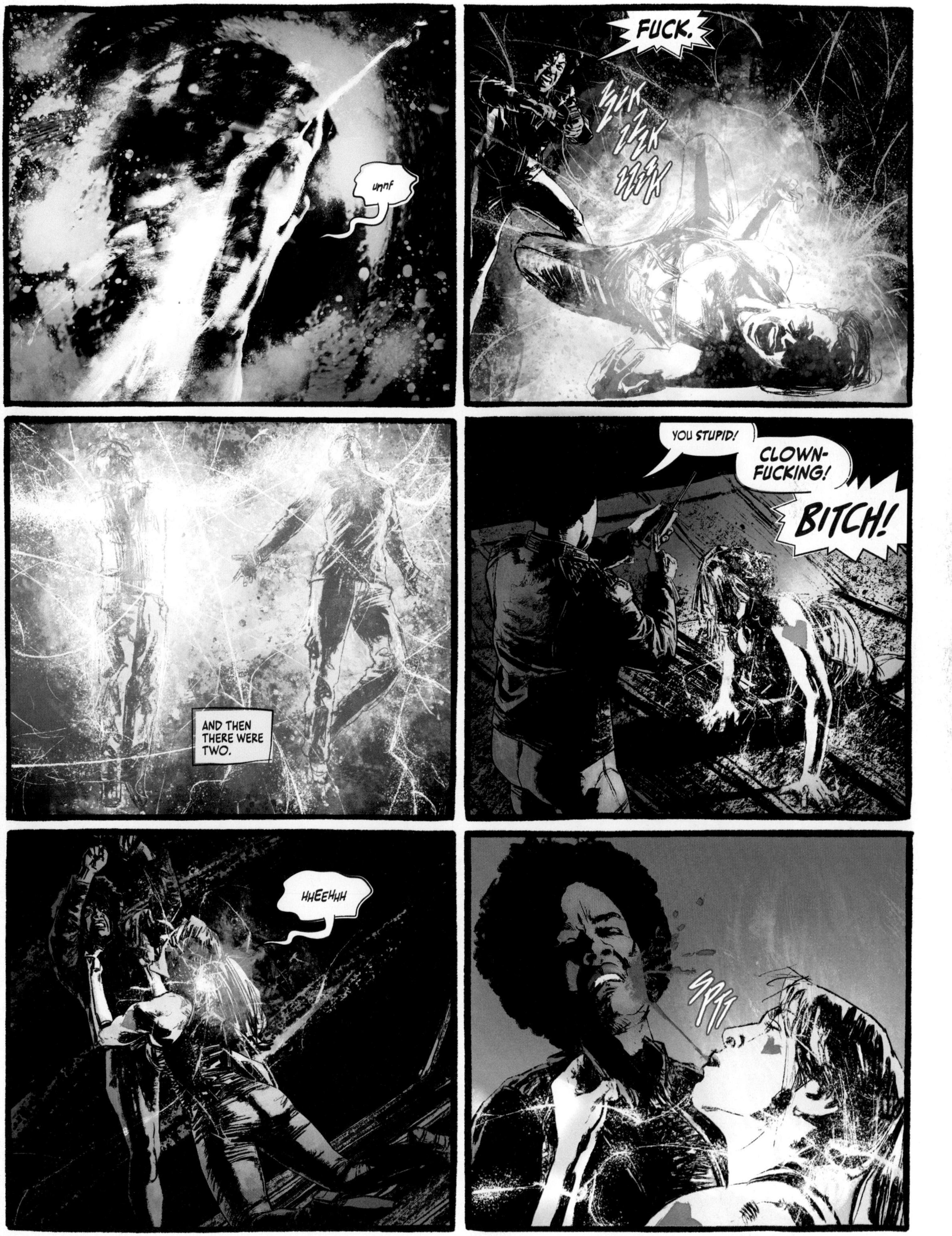
unnf
FUCK.
ZZK
ZZZK
ZZZZK
AND THEN THERE WERE TWO.
YOU STUPID!
CLOWN-FUCKING!
BITCH!
HHEEHHH
SPTT

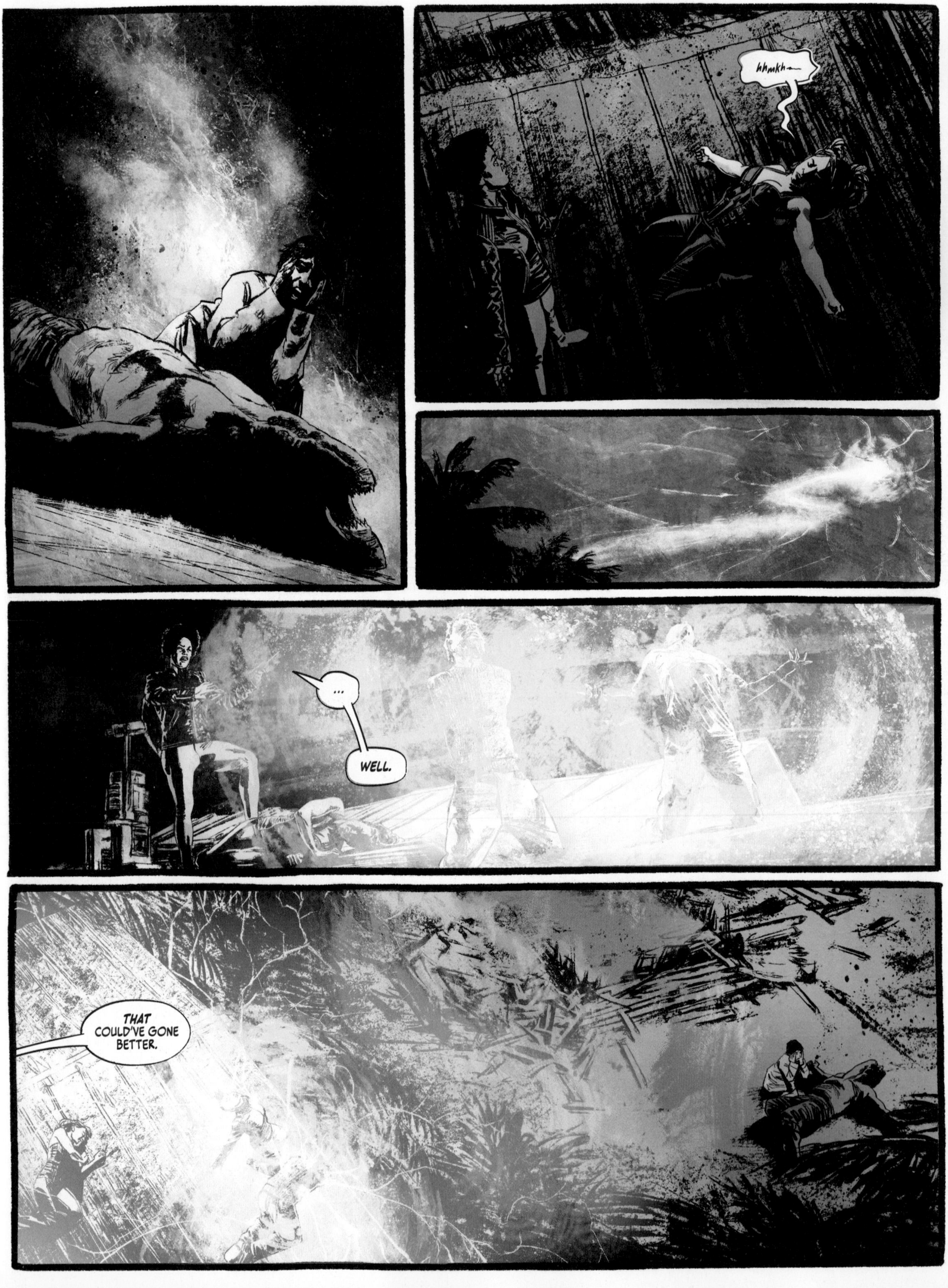
hhmkh—
...
WELL.
THAT COULD'VE GONE BETTER.

FROM OUTSIDE IT ALL, YOU CAN TELL:

IT'S ***HERE*** THAT THE SNOWBALL ***REALLY*** STARTS TO ROLL.

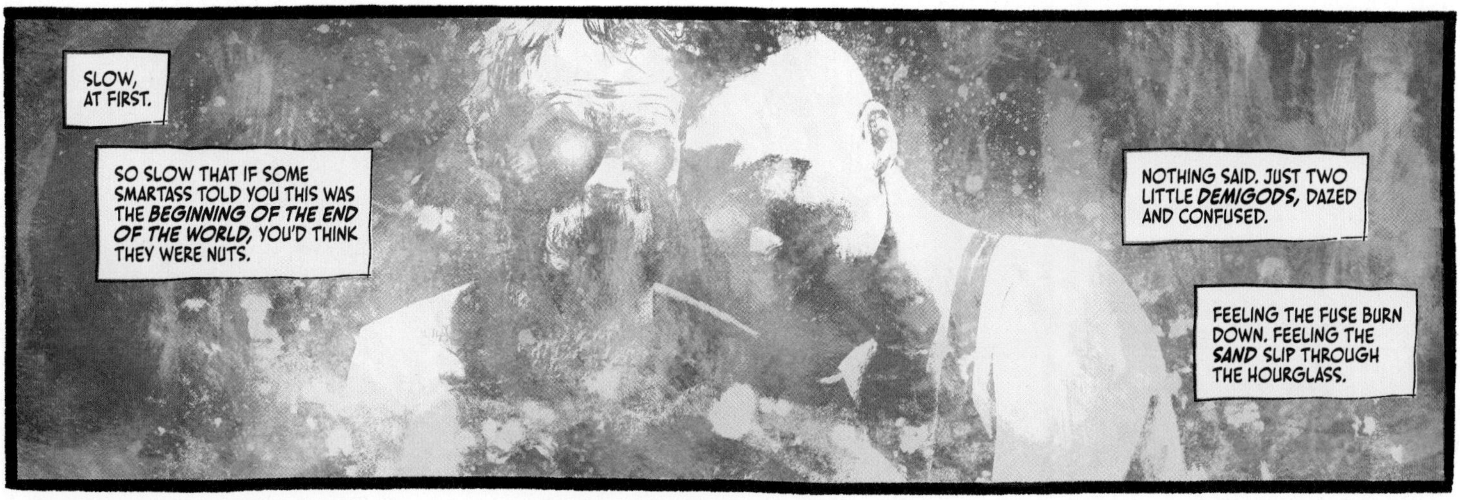
SLOW, AT FIRST.
SO SLOW THAT IF SOME SMARTASS TOLD YOU THIS WAS THE ***BEGINNING OF THE END OF THE WORLD,*** YOU'D THINK THEY WERE NUTS.
NOTHING SAID. JUST TWO LITTLE ***DEMIGODS,*** DAZED AND CONFUSED.
FEELING THE FUSE BURN DOWN. FEELING THE ***SAND*** SLIP THROUGH THE HOURGLASS.

OH, THE SCIENTISTS POKED AND PRODDED, TUTTED AND TALKED. HORMONES OUT, HORMONES IN.

THEY MUTTERED ***LIFE-SPAN ESTIMATES*** WHEN THEY THOUGHT WE COULDN'T HEAR. DAYS OR HOURS.

PLANS WERE DISCUSSED. CONTINGENCIES ARRANGED. IT DIDN'T MATTER. NONE OF IT MATTERED.

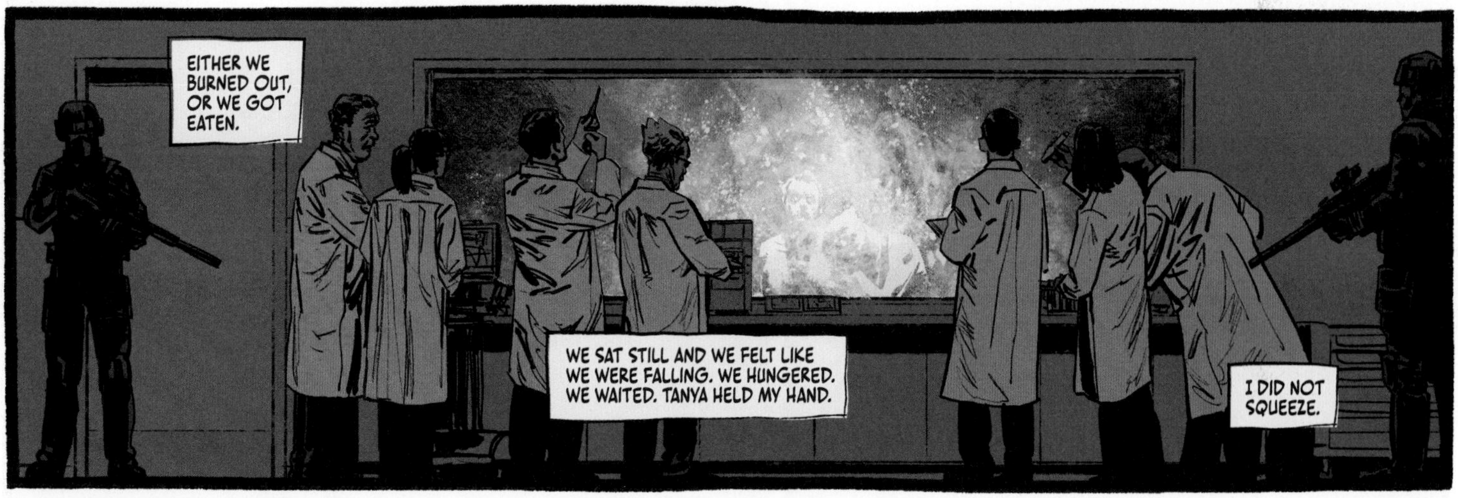
EITHER WE BURNED OUT, OR WE GOT EATEN.
WE SAT STILL AND WE FELT LIKE WE WERE FALLING. WE HUNGERED. WE WAITED. TANYA HELD MY HAND.
I DID NOT SQUEEZE.

IT WAS AROUND THIS TIME, IN THE EMPTY HOURS OF THE LAST NIGHT, THAT HARLEY CAME.

MORE ***SERIOUS*** THAN WE'D SEEN HER. ALL HER ***PERFORMATIVE CRAZY***™ DIALED RIGHT DOWN.

OH, WE COULD'VE LOOKED INTO HER HEAD. WE COULD'VE BENT REALITY JUST TO FATHOM WHAT WAS IN HER HEART. BUT...WE DIDN'T NEED TO.

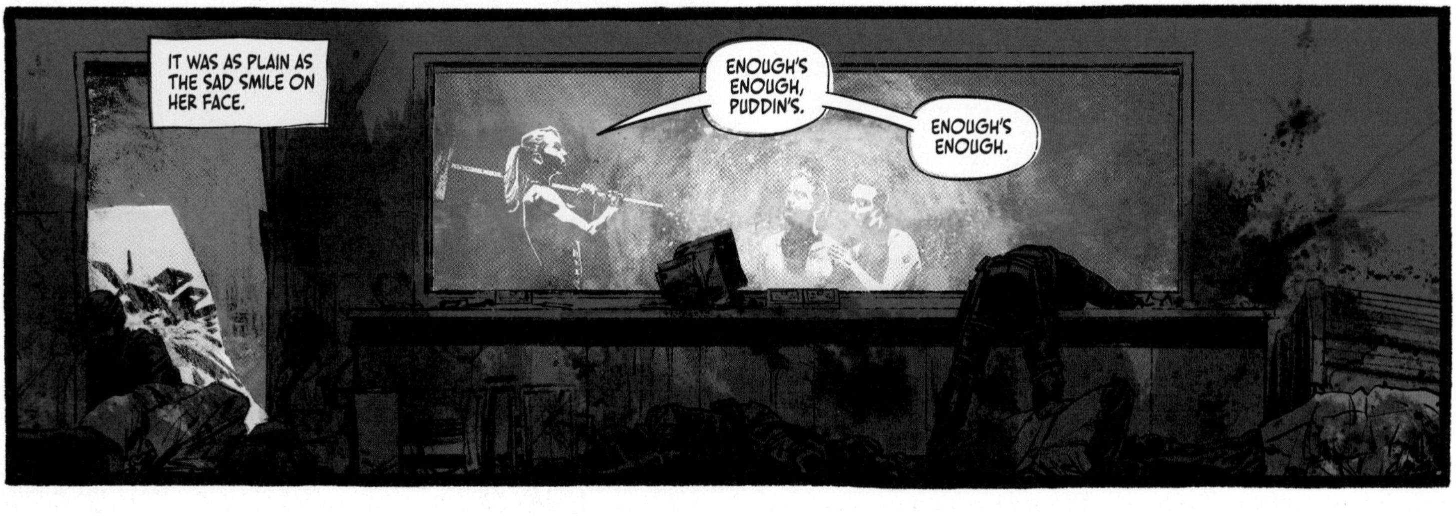
IT WAS AS PLAIN AS THE SAD SMILE ON HER FACE.
ENOUGH'S ENOUGH, PUDDIN'S.
ENOUGH'S ENOUGH.

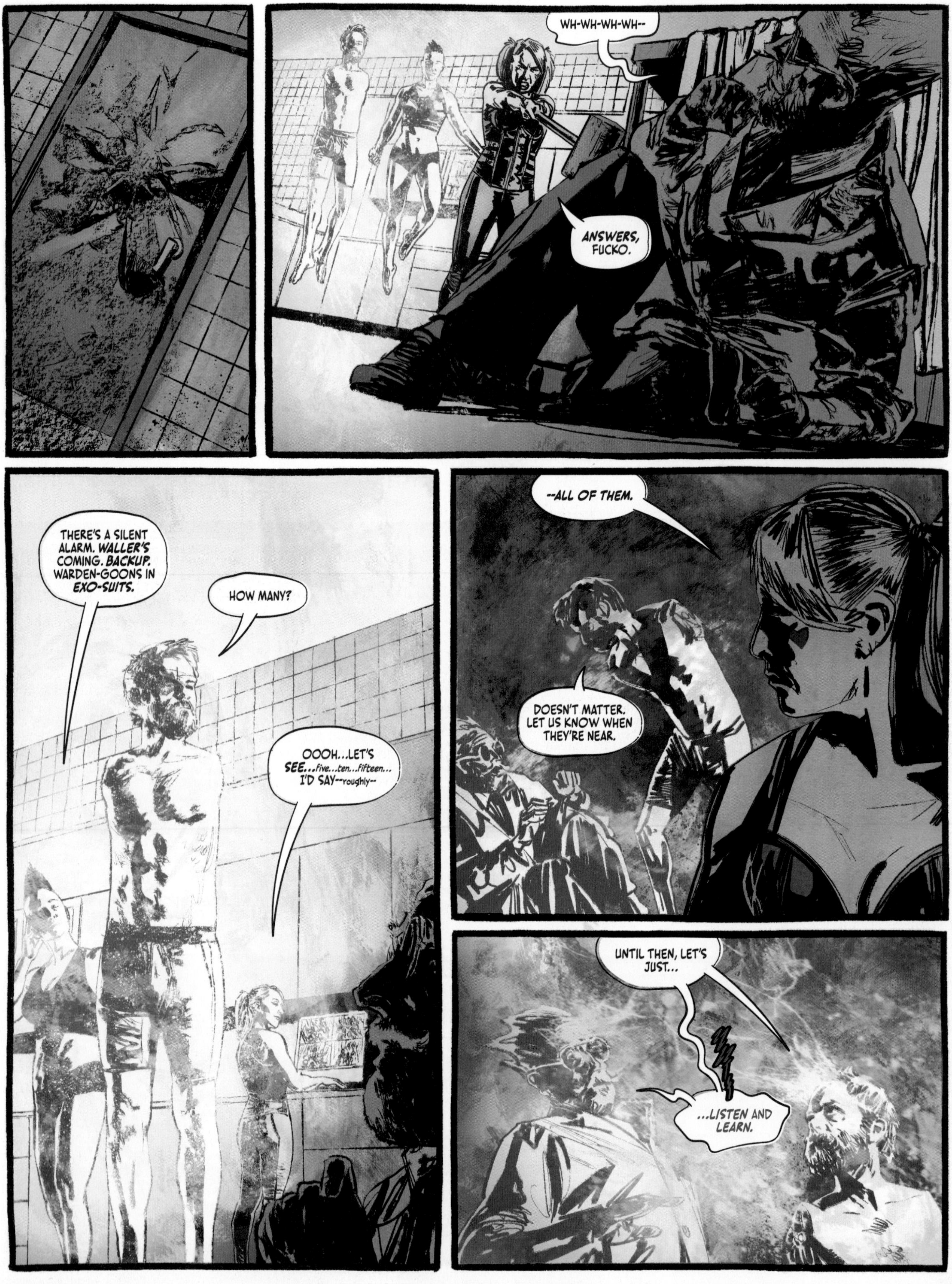
WH-WH-WH-WH--
ANSWERS, FUCKO.
THERE'S A SILENT ALARM. WALLER'S COMING. BACKUP. WARDEN-GOONS IN EXO-SUITS.
HOW MANY?
OOOH...LET'S SEE...five...ten...fifteen... I'D SAY--roughly--
--ALL OF THEM.
DOESN'T MATTER. LET US KNOW WHEN THEY'RE NEAR.
UNTIL THEN, LET'S JUST...
...LISTEN AND LEARN.

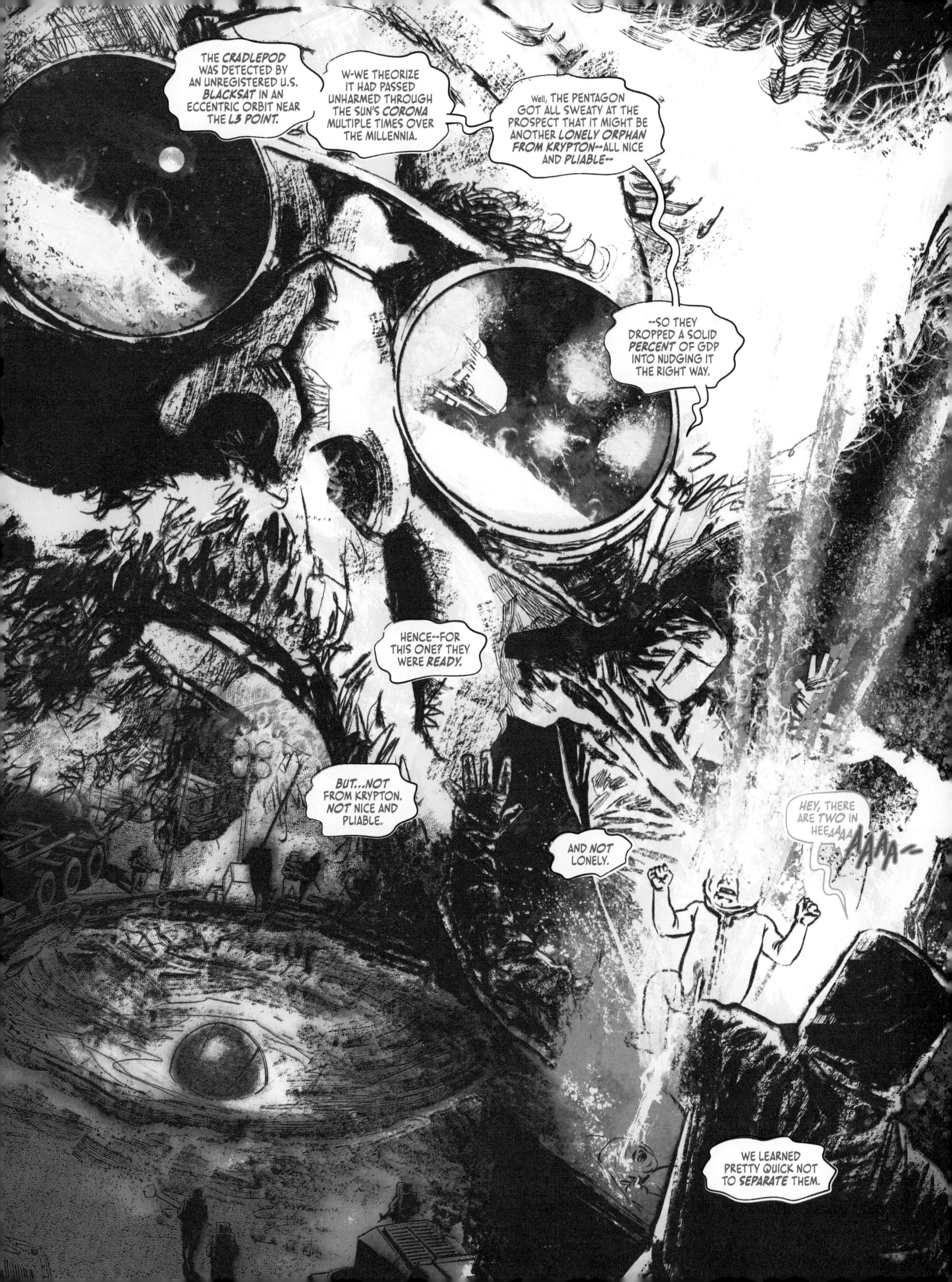
THE *CRADLEPOD* WAS DETECTED BY AN UNREGISTERED U.S. *BLACKSAT* IN AN ECCENTRIC ORBIT NEAR THE *L3 POINT.*
W-WE THEORIZE IT HAD PASSED UNHARMED THROUGH THE SUN'S *CORONA* MULTIPLE TIMES OVER THE MILLENNIA.
Well, THE PENTAGON GOT ALL SWEATY AT THE PROSPECT THAT IT MIGHT BE ANOTHER *LONELY ORPHAN FROM KRYPTON*--ALL NICE AND *PLIABLE*--
--SO THEY DROPPED A SOLID *PERCENT* OF GDP INTO NUDGING IT THE RIGHT WAY.
HENCE--FOR THIS ONE? THEY WERE *READY.*
BUT...NOT FROM KRYPTON. *NOT* NICE AND PLIABLE.
AND *NOT* LONELY.
HEY, THERE ARE *TWO* IN HEEAAAAAAAA--
WE LEARNED PRETTY QUICK NOT TO *SEPARATE* THEM.

CONTAINMENT. TRICKED-OUT COLD WAR BUNKER. TWO HUNDRED FEET DOWN, LINED WITH LEAD.
EVEN THEN THEY COULD'VE CLAWED THEIR WAY OUT ANYTIME--AFTER THEY LEARNED TO CRAWL--IF NOT FOR THE HUNGER PROTOCOL.
TOOK A FEW YEARS OF TRIAL AND ERROR, BUT WE GOT THERE.
A MEAL EVERY THREE MONTHS--NEVER MORE. JUUUUUST ENOUGH TO KEEP THEM GOING...BUT TOO WEAK TO DO MUCH BUT CLING TO EACH OTHER.
Funny thing... THEY ALWAYS WAITED UNTIL THE RATS WERE PLAYING--OR MATING. LIKE THE NOURISHMENT CAME FROM THE CONTENTMENT, NOT THE CALORIES.
OH, THERE WERE CALLS FOR EMOTIONAL INVESTMENT, SURE. SHOW THEM AFFECTION, HARNESS THEIR LOYALTY INSTEAD OF THEIR BIOLOGY...
THAT, uh. THAT NEVER REALLY GOT OFF THE GROUND.
NO TIME FOR HUGS AND BEDTIME STORIES WHEN THERE ARE EXPERIMENTS TO DO. A-AND...BOY DID WE DO 'EM.
GOVERNMENT'S POSITION IS: WE'RE BILLIONS IN THE RED THANKS TO THESE CHUMPS. WE NEED A RETURN.
THEY'RE GODLIKE IMBECILES. FOCUS ON THE FIRST PART, FLUSH THE REST.

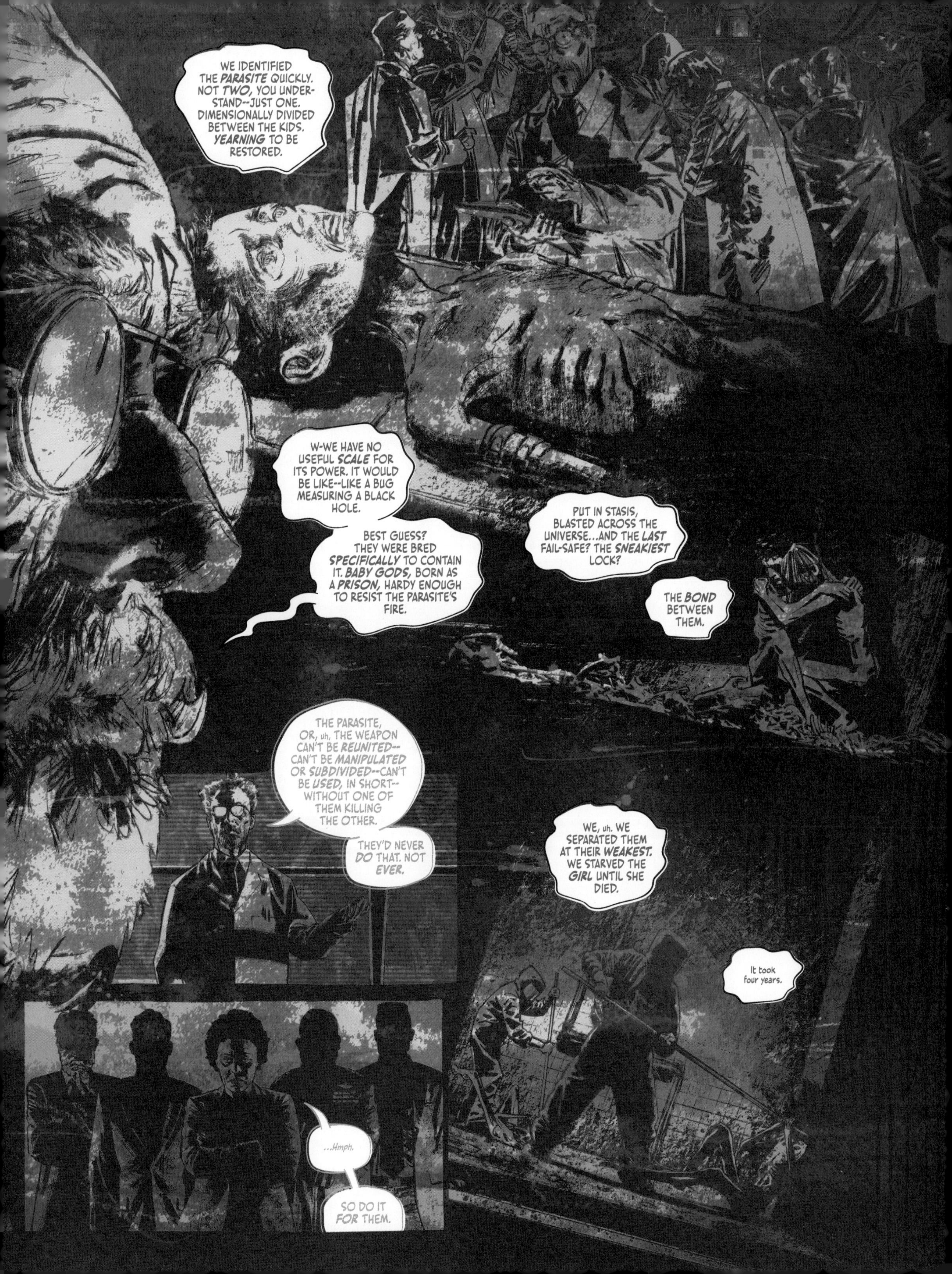

WE IDENTIFIED THE PARASITE QUICKLY. NOT TWO, YOU UNDERSTAND--JUST ONE. DIMENSIONALLY DIVIDED BETWEEN THE KIDS. YEARNING TO BE RESTORED.
W-WE HAVE NO USEFUL SCALE FOR ITS POWER. IT WOULD BE LIKE--LIKE A BUG MEASURING A BLACK HOLE.
BEST GUESS? THEY WERE BRED SPECIFICALLY TO CONTAIN IT. BABY GODS, BORN AS A PRISON, HARDY ENOUGH TO RESIST THE PARASITE'S FIRE.
PUT IN STASIS, BLASTED ACROSS THE UNIVERSE...AND THE LAST FAIL-SAFE? THE SNEAKIEST LOCK?
THE BOND BETWEEN THEM.
THE PARASITE, OR, uh, THE WEAPON CAN'T BE REUNITED--CAN'T BE MANIPULATED OR SUBDIVIDED--CAN'T BE USED, IN SHORT--WITHOUT ONE OF THEM KILLING THE OTHER.
THEY'D NEVER DO THAT. NOT EVER.
...Hmph.
SO DO IT FOR THEM.
WE, uh. WE SEPARATED THEM AT THEIR WEAKEST. WE STARVED THE GIRL UNTIL SHE DIED.
It took four years.

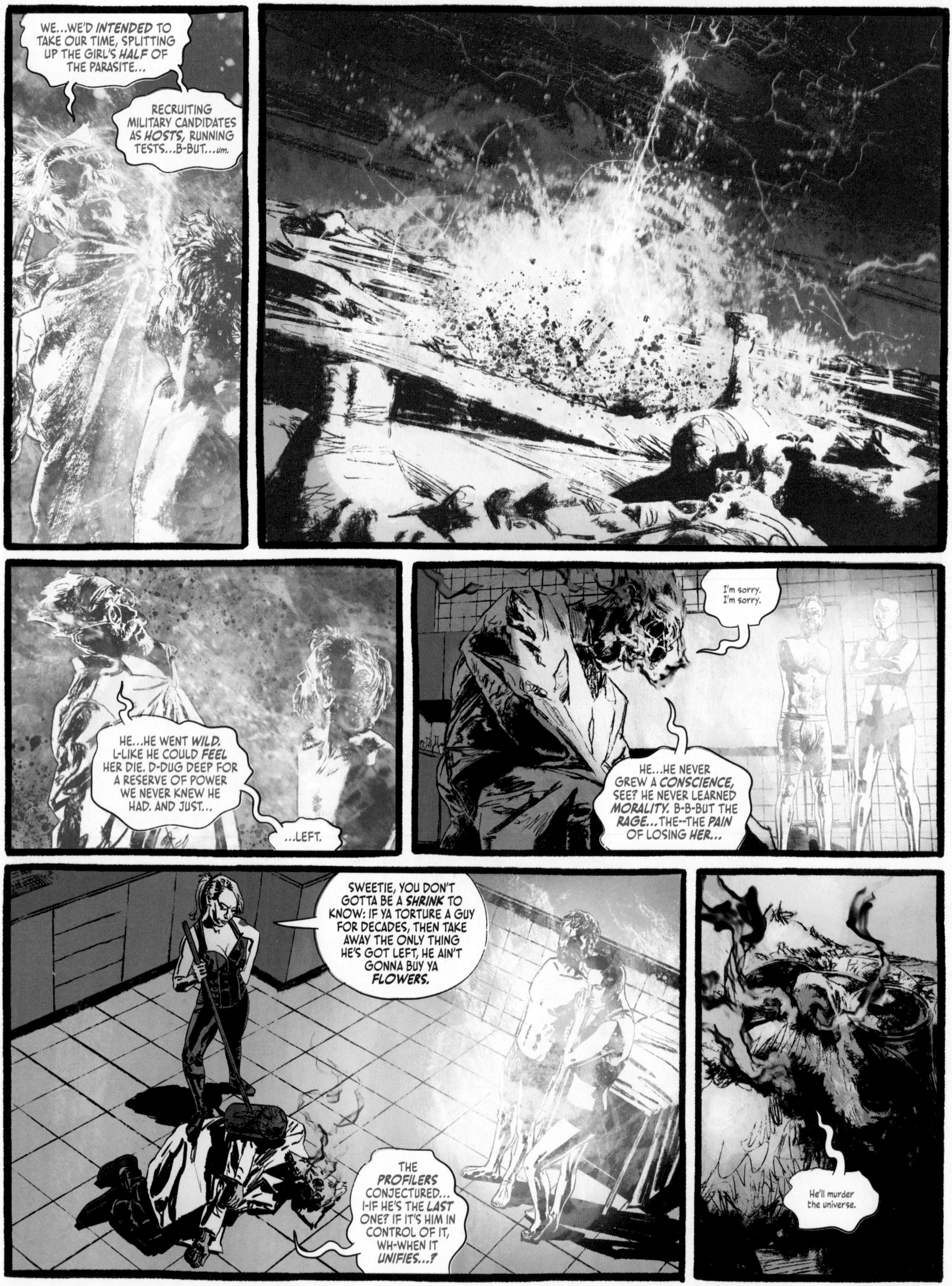
WE...WE'D INTENDED TO TAKE OUR TIME, SPLITTING UP THE GIRL'S HALF OF THE PARASITE...
RECRUITING MILITARY CANDIDATES AS HOSTS, RUNNING TESTS...B-BUT...um.
HE...HE WENT WILD. I-LIKE HE COULD FEEL HER DIE. D-DUG DEEP FOR A RESERVE OF POWER WE NEVER KNEW HE HAD. AND JUST...
...LEFT.
I'm sorry. I'm sorry.
HE...HE NEVER GREW A CONSCIENCE, SEE? HE NEVER LEARNED MORALITY. B-B-BUT THE RAGE...THE--THE PAIN OF LOSING HER...
SWEETIE, YOU DON'T GOTTA BE A SHRINK TO KNOW: IF YA TORTURE A GUY FOR DECADES, THEN TAKE AWAY THE ONLY THING HE'S GOT LEFT, HE AIN'T GONNA BUY YA FLOWERS.
THE PROFILERS CONJECTURED... I-IF HE'S THE LAST ONE? IF IT'S HIM IN CONTROL OF IT, WH-WHEN IT UNIFIES...?
He'll murder the universe.

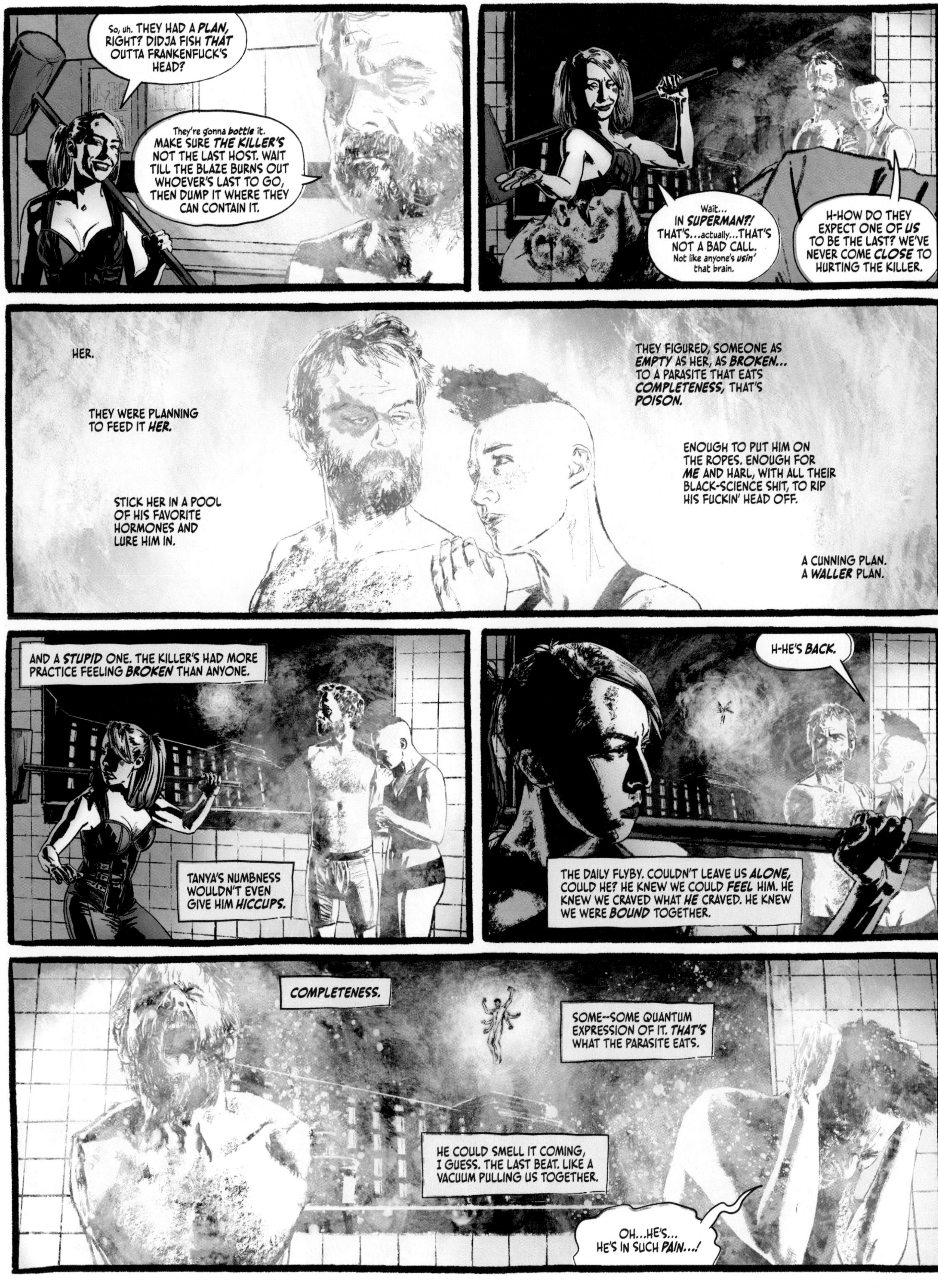
So, uh. THEY HAD A PLAN, RIGHT? DIDJA FISH THAT OUTTA FRANKENFUCK'S HEAD?
They're gonna bottle it. MAKE SURE THE KILLER'S NOT THE LAST HOST. WAIT TILL THE BLAZE BURNS OUT WHOEVER'S LAST TO GO, THEN DUMP IT WHERE THEY CAN CONTAIN IT.
Wait... IN SUPERMAN?! THAT'S...actually...THAT'S NOT A BAD CALL. Not like anyone's usin' that brain.
H-HOW DO THEY EXPECT ONE OF US TO BE THE LAST? WE'VE NEVER COME CLOSE TO HURTING THE KILLER.
HER.
THEY WERE PLANNING TO FEED IT HER.
STICK HER IN A POOL OF HIS FAVORITE HORMONES AND LURE HIM IN.
THEY FIGURED, SOMEONE AS EMPTY AS HER, AS BROKEN... TO A PARASITE THAT EATS COMPLETENESS, THAT'S POISON.
ENOUGH TO PUT HIM ON THE ROPES. ENOUGH FOR ME AND HARL, WITH ALL THEIR BLACK-SCIENCE SHIT, TO RIP HIS FUCKIN' HEAD OFF.
A CUNNING PLAN. A WALLER PLAN.
AND A STUPID ONE. THE KILLER'S HAD MORE PRACTICE FEELING BROKEN THAN ANYONE.
TANYA'S NUMBNESS WOULDN'T EVEN GIVE HIM HICCUPS.
H-HE'S BACK.
THE DAILY FLYBY. COULDN'T LEAVE US ALONE, COULD HE? HE KNEW WE COULD FEEL HIM. HE KNEW WE CRAVED WHAT HE CRAVED. HE KNEW WE WERE BOUND TOGETHER.
COMPLETENESS.
SOME--SOME QUANTUM EXPRESSION OF IT. THAT'S WHAT THE PARASITE EATS.
HE COULD SMELL IT COMING, I GUESS. THE LAST BEAT. LIKE A VACUUM PULLING US TOGETHER.
OH...HE'S... HE'S IN SUCH PAIN...!

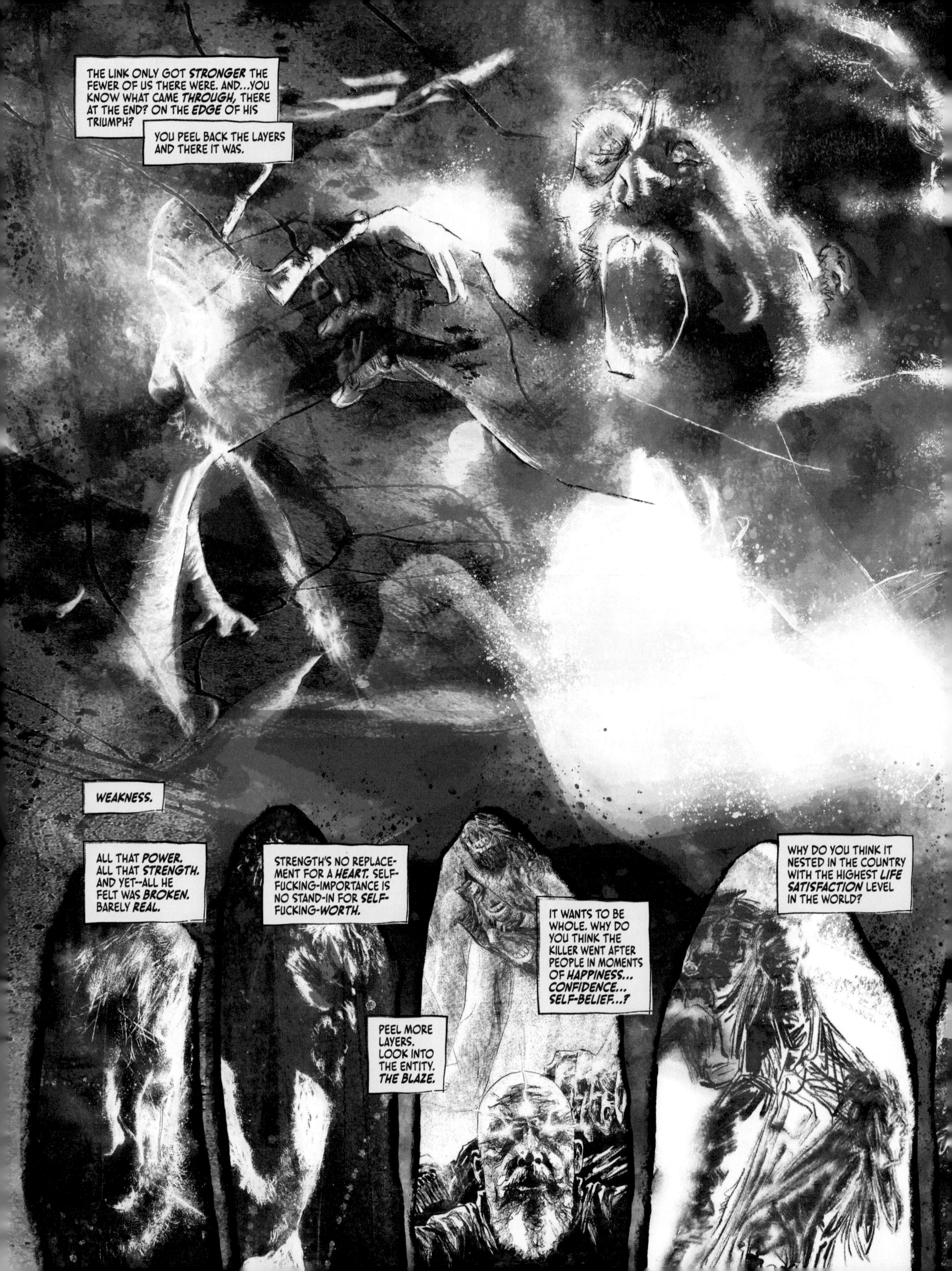

THE LINK ONLY GOT STRONGER THE FEWER OF US THERE WERE. AND...YOU KNOW WHAT CAME THROUGH, THERE AT THE END? ON THE EDGE OF HIS TRIUMPH?
YOU PEEL BACK THE LAYERS AND THERE IT WAS.
WEAKNESS.
ALL THAT POWER. ALL THAT STRENGTH. AND YET--ALL HE FELT WAS BROKEN. BARELY REAL.
STRENGTH'S NO REPLACEMENT FOR A HEART. SELF-FUCKING-IMPORTANCE IS NO STAND-IN FOR SELF-FUCKING-WORTH.
PEEL MORE LAYERS. LOOK INTO THE ENTITY. THE BLAZE.
IT WANTS TO BE WHOLE. WHY DO YOU THINK THE KILLER WENT AFTER PEOPLE IN MOMENTS OF HAPPINESS... CONFIDENCE... SELF-BELIEF...?
WHY DO YOU THINK IT NESTED IN THE COUNTRY WITH THE HIGHEST LIFE SATISFACTION LEVEL IN THE WORLD?

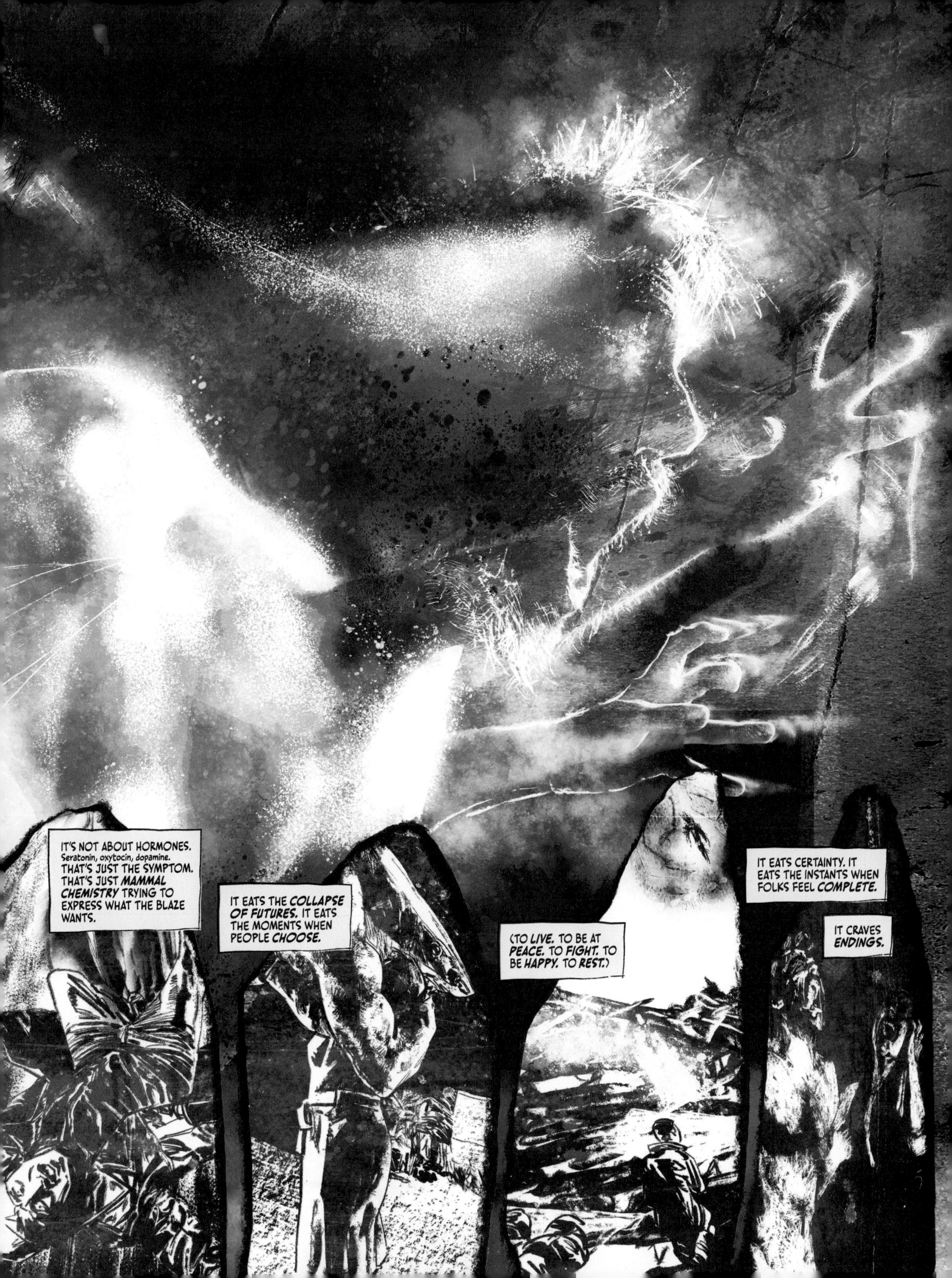
IT'S NOT ABOUT HORMONES. Seratonin, oxytocin, dopamine. THAT'S JUST THE SYMPTOM. THAT'S JUST MAMMAL CHEMISTRY TRYING TO EXPRESS WHAT THE BLAZE WANTS.
IT EATS THE COLLAPSE OF FUTURES. IT EATS THE MOMENTS WHEN PEOPLE CHOOSE.
(TO LIVE. TO BE AT PEACE. TO FIGHT. TO BE HAPPY. TO REST.)
IT EATS CERTAINTY. IT EATS THE INSTANTS WHEN FOLKS FEEL COMPLETE.
IT CRAVES ENDINGS.

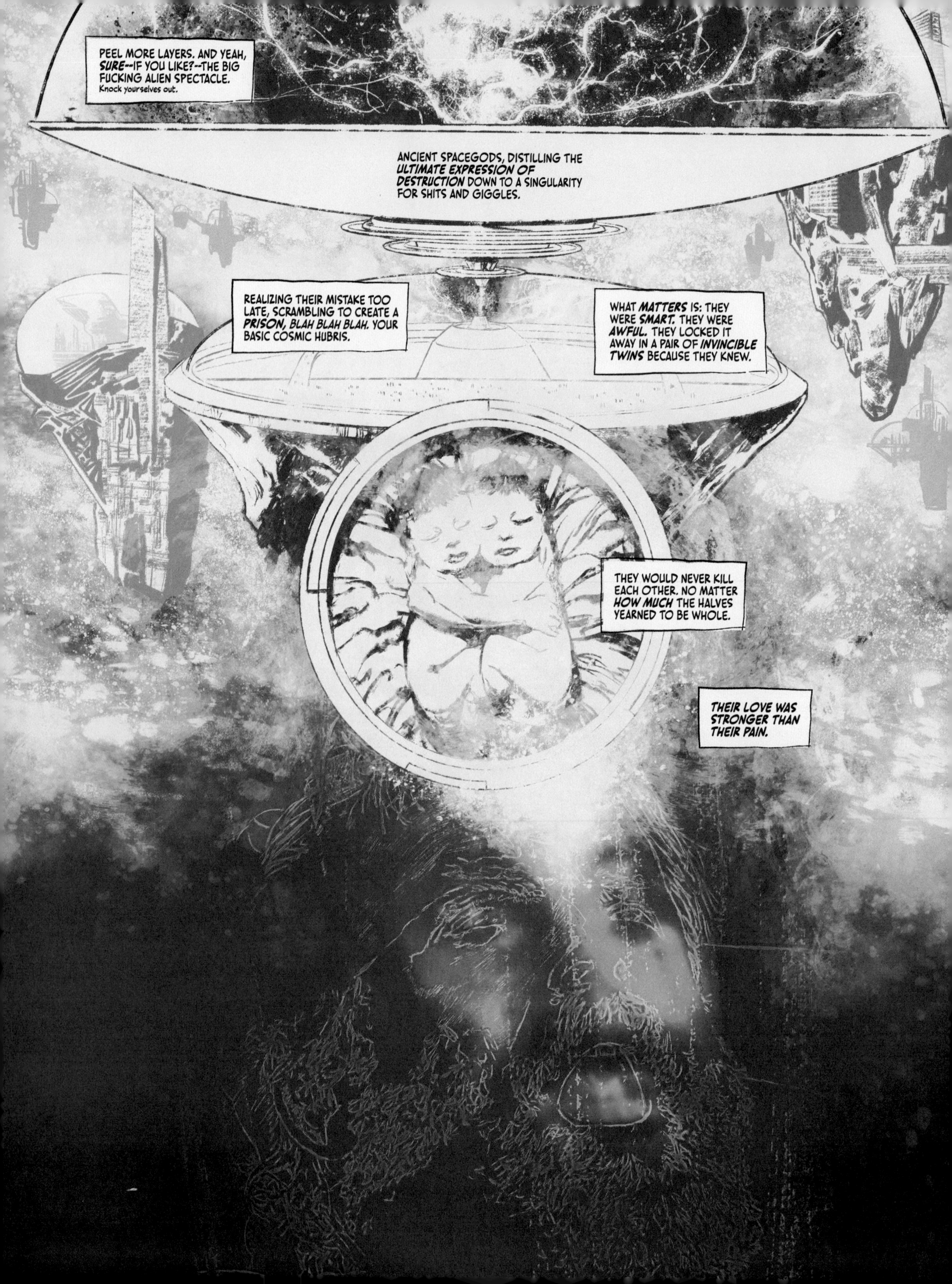
PEEL MORE LAYERS. AND YEAH, SURE--IF YOU LIKE?--THE BIG FUCKING ALIEN SPECTACLE. Knock yourselves out.
ANCIENT SPACEGODS, DISTILLING THE ULTIMATE EXPRESSION OF DESTRUCTION DOWN TO A SINGULARITY FOR SHITS AND GIGGLES.
REALIZING THEIR MISTAKE TOO LATE, SCRAMBLING TO CREATE A PRISON, BLAH BLAH BLAH. YOUR BASIC COSMIC HUBRIS.
WHAT MATTERS IS: THEY WERE SMART. THEY WERE AWFUL. THEY LOCKED IT AWAY IN A PAIR OF INVINCIBLE TWINS BECAUSE THEY KNEW.
THEY WOULD NEVER KILL EACH OTHER. NO MATTER HOW MUCH THE HALVES YEARNED TO BE WHOLE.
THEIR LOVE WAS STRONGER THAN THEIR PAIN.

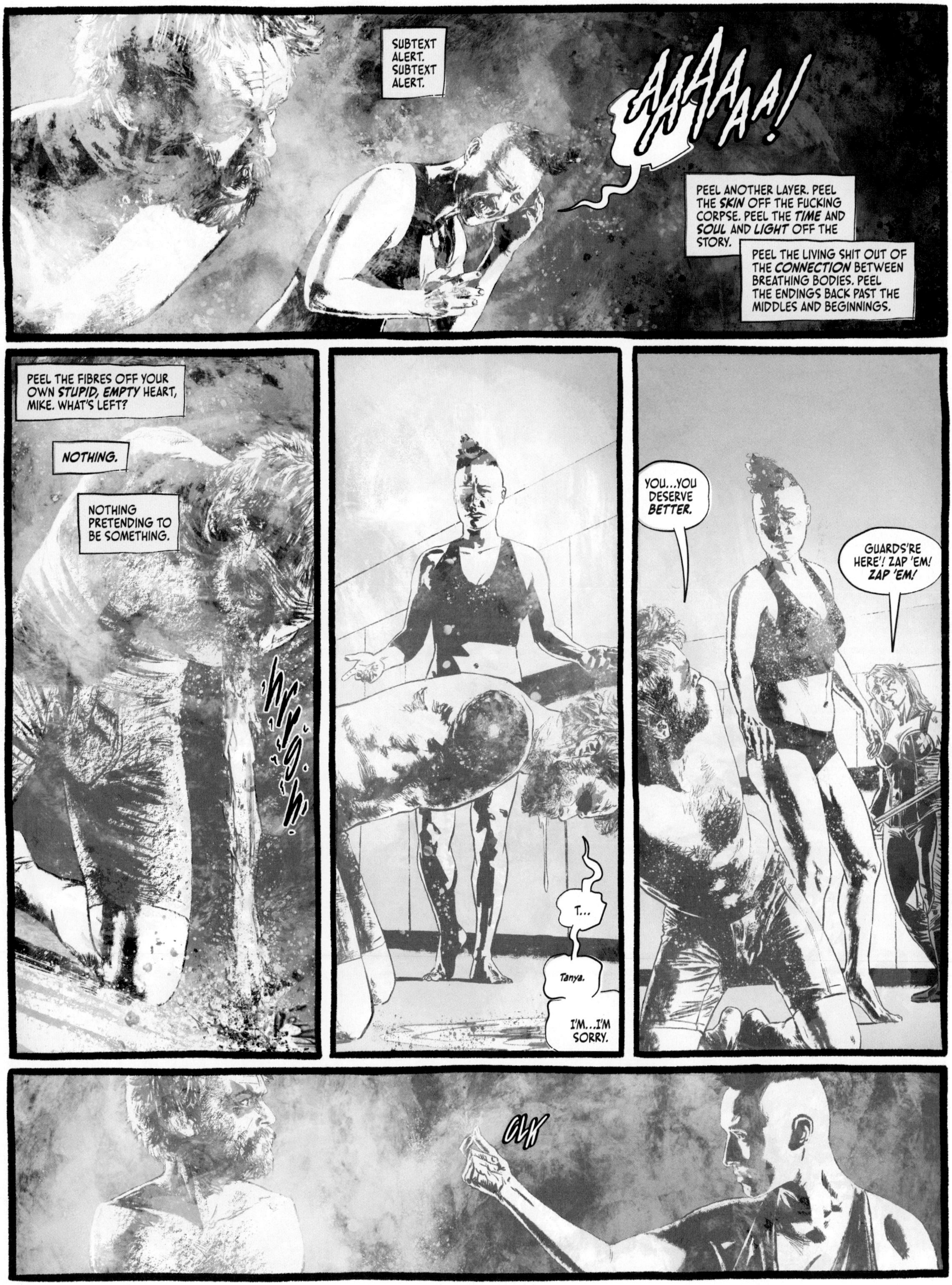
SUBTEXT ALERT. SUBTEXT ALERT.
AAAAAA!
PEEL ANOTHER LAYER. PEEL THE **SKIN** OFF THE FUCKING CORPSE. PEEL THE **TIME** AND **SOUL** AND **LIGHT** OFF THE STORY.
PEEL THE LIVING SHIT OUT OF THE **CONNECTION** BETWEEN BREATHING BODIES. PEEL THE ENDINGS BACK PAST THE MIDDLES AND BEGINNINGS.
PEEL THE FIBRES OFF YOUR OWN **STUPID, EMPTY** HEART, MIKE. WHAT'S LEFT?
NOTHING.
NOTHING PRETENDING TO BE SOMETHING.
hrrgh
T...
Tanya.
I'M...I'M SORRY.
YOU...YOU DESERVE **BETTER.**
GUARDS'RE HERE'! ZAP 'EM! **ZAP 'EM!**
CLK

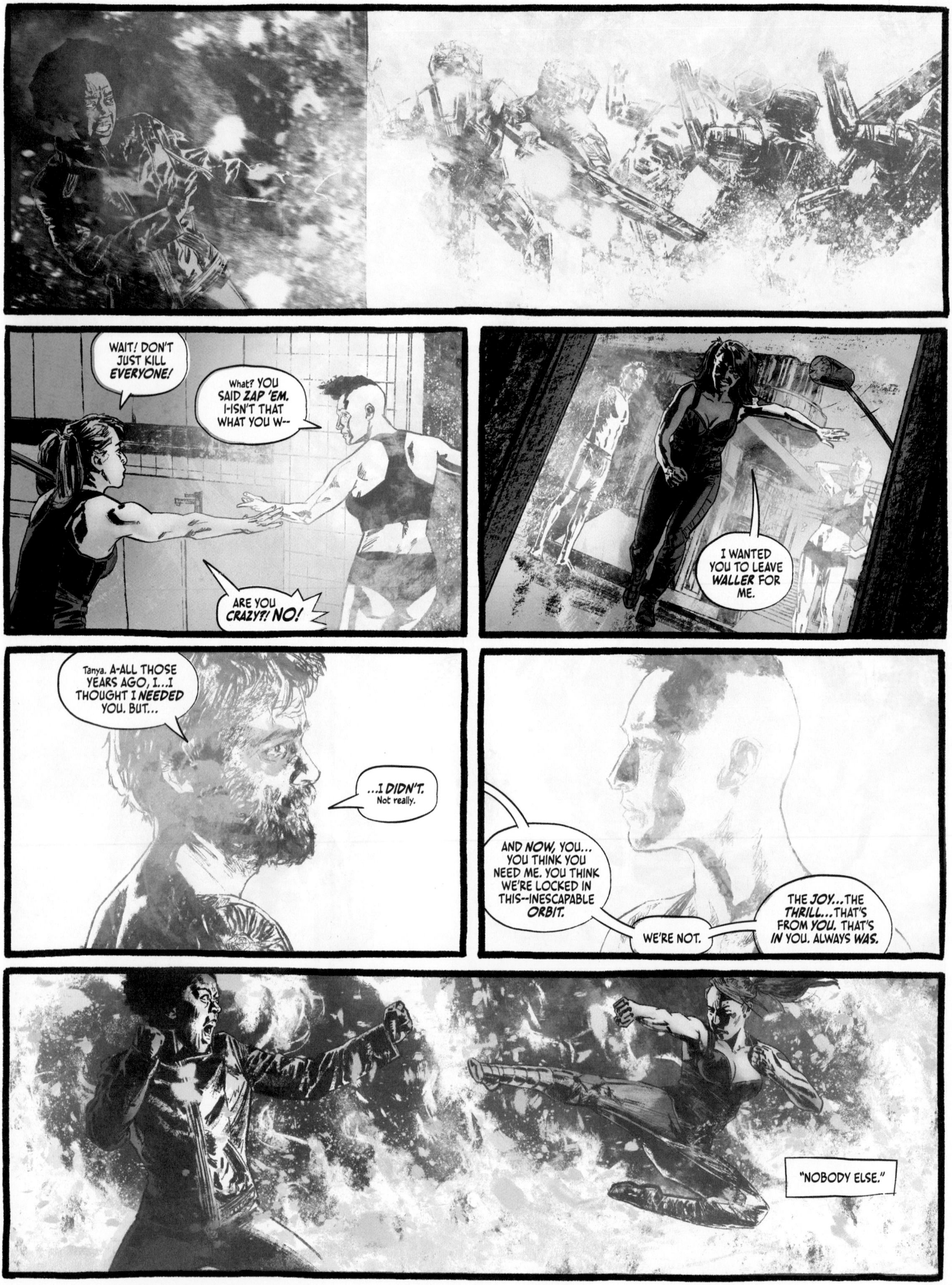
WAIT! DON'T JUST KILL EVERYONE!
What? YOU SAID ZAP 'EM. I-ISN'T THAT WHAT YOU W--
ARE YOU CRAZY?! NO!
I WANTED YOU TO LEAVE WALLER FOR ME.
Tanya. A-ALL THOSE YEARS AGO, I...I THOUGHT I NEEDED YOU. BUT...
...I DIDN'T. Not really.
AND NOW, YOU... YOU THINK YOU NEED ME. YOU THINK WE'RE LOCKED IN THIS--INESCAPABLE ORBIT.
WE'RE NOT.
THE JOY...THE THRILL...THAT'S FROM YOU. THAT'S IN YOU. ALWAYS WAS.
"NOBODY ELSE."

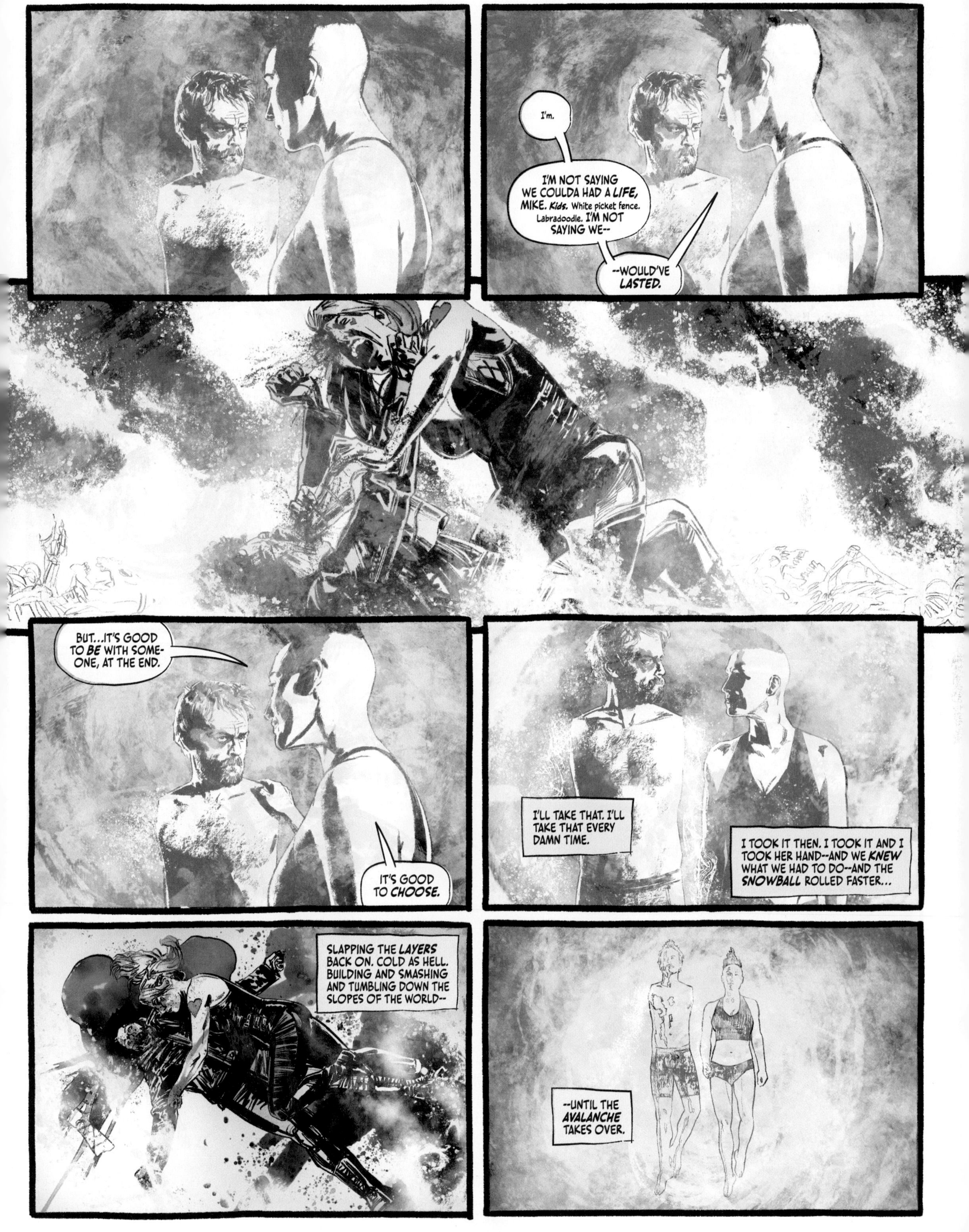
I'm.
I'M NOT SAYING WE COULDA HAD A LIFE, MIKE. Kids. White picket fence. Labradoodle. I'M NOT SAYING WE--
--WOULD'VE LASTED.
BUT...IT'S GOOD TO BE WITH SOME-ONE, AT THE END.
IT'S GOOD TO CHOOSE.
I'LL TAKE THAT. I'LL TAKE THAT EVERY DAMN TIME.
I TOOK IT THEN. I TOOK IT AND I TOOK HER HAND--AND WE KNEW WHAT WE HAD TO DO--AND THE SNOWBALL ROLLED FASTER...
SLAPPING THE LAYERS BACK ON. COLD AS HELL. BUILDING AND SMASHING AND TUMBLING DOWN THE SLOPES OF THE WORLD--
--UNTIL THE AVALANCHE TAKES OVER.

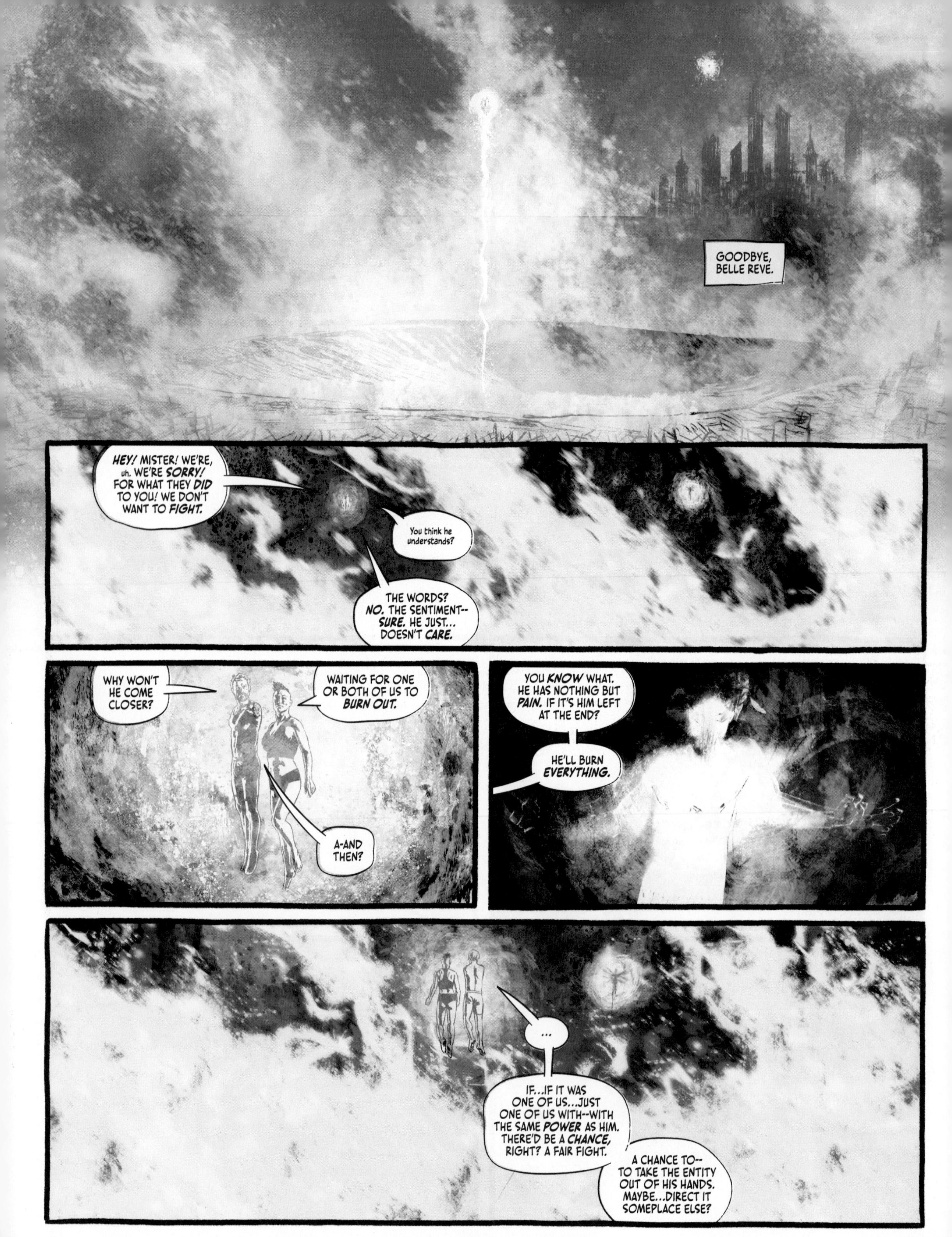
GOODBYE, BELLE REVE.
HEY! MISTER! WE'RE, uh. WE'RE SORRY! FOR WHAT THEY DID TO YOU! WE DON'T WANT TO FIGHT.
You think he understands?
THE WORDS? NO. THE SENTIMENT-- SURE. HE JUST... DOESN'T CARE.
WHY WON'T HE COME CLOSER?
WAITING FOR ONE OR BOTH OF US TO BURN OUT.
A-AND THEN?
YOU KNOW WHAT. HE HAS NOTHING BUT PAIN. IF IT'S HIM LEFT AT THE END?
HE'LL BURN EVERYTHING.
...
IF...IF IT WAS ONE OF US...JUST ONE OF US WITH--WITH THE SAME POWER AS HIM. THERE'D BE A CHANCE, RIGHT? A FAIR FIGHT.
A CHANCE TO-- TO TAKE THE ENTITY OUT OF HIS HANDS. MAYBE...DIRECT IT SOMEPLACE ELSE?

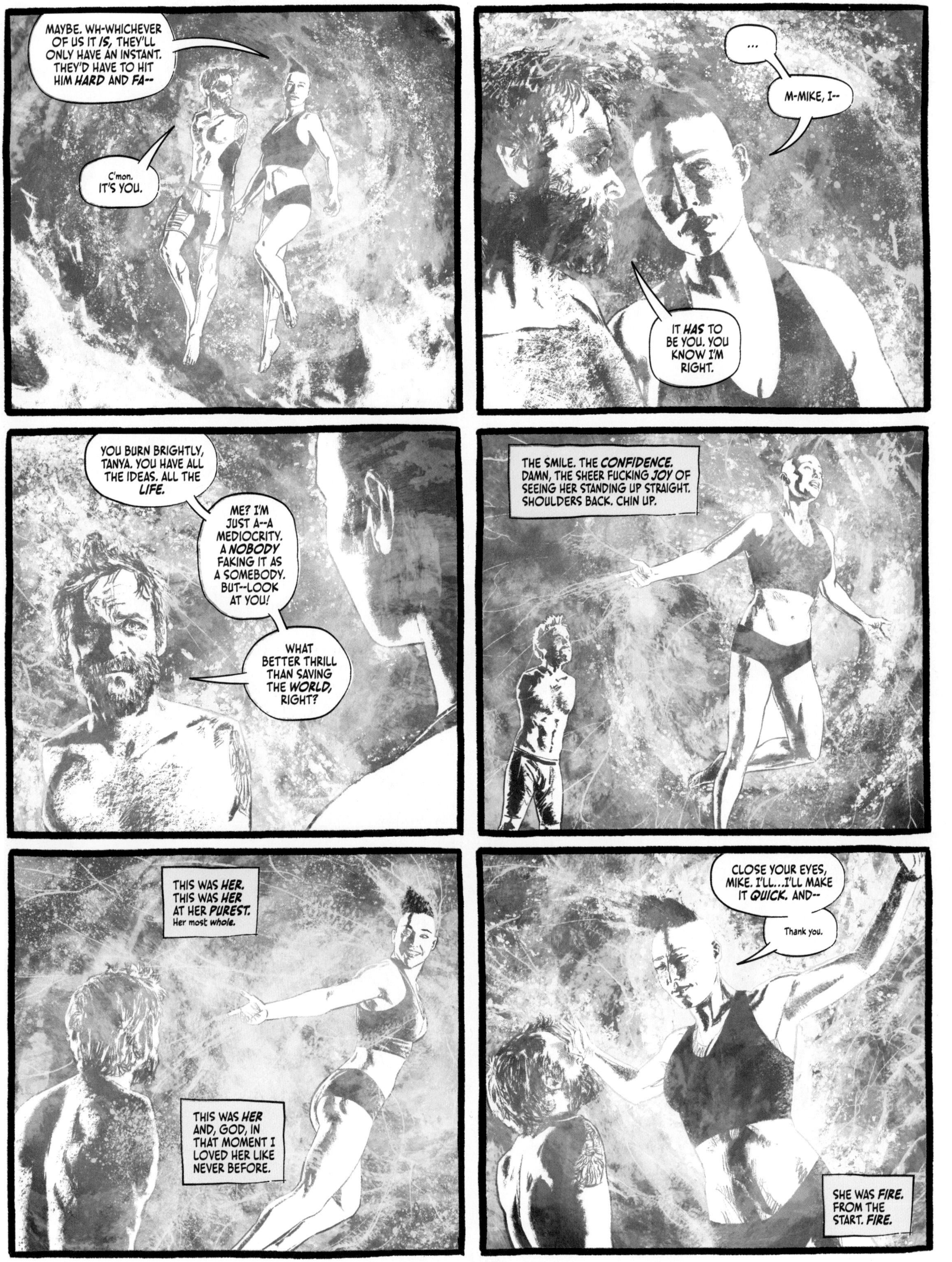
MAYBE. WH-WHICHEVER OF US IT *IS*, THEY'LL ONLY HAVE AN INSTANT. THEY'D HAVE TO HIT HIM *HARD* AND *FA--*
C'mon. IT'S YOU.
...
M-MIKE, I--
IT *HAS* TO BE YOU. YOU KNOW I'M RIGHT.
YOU BURN BRIGHTLY, TANYA. YOU HAVE ALL THE IDEAS. ALL THE *LIFE.*
ME? I'M JUST A--A MEDIOCRITY. A *NOBODY* FAKING IT AS A SOMEBODY. BUT--LOOK AT YOU!
WHAT BETTER THRILL THAN SAVING THE *WORLD,* RIGHT?
THE SMILE. THE *CONFIDENCE.* DAMN, THE SHEER FUCKING *JOY* OF SEEING HER STANDING UP STRAIGHT. SHOULDERS BACK. CHIN UP.
THIS WAS *HER.* THIS WAS *HER* AT HER *PUREST.* Her most *whole.*
THIS WAS *HER* AND, GOD, IN THAT MOMENT I LOVED HER LIKE NEVER BEFORE.
CLOSE YOUR EYES, MIKE. I'LL...I'LL MAKE IT *QUICK.* AND--
Thank you.
SHE WAS *FIRE.* FROM THE START. *FIRE.*

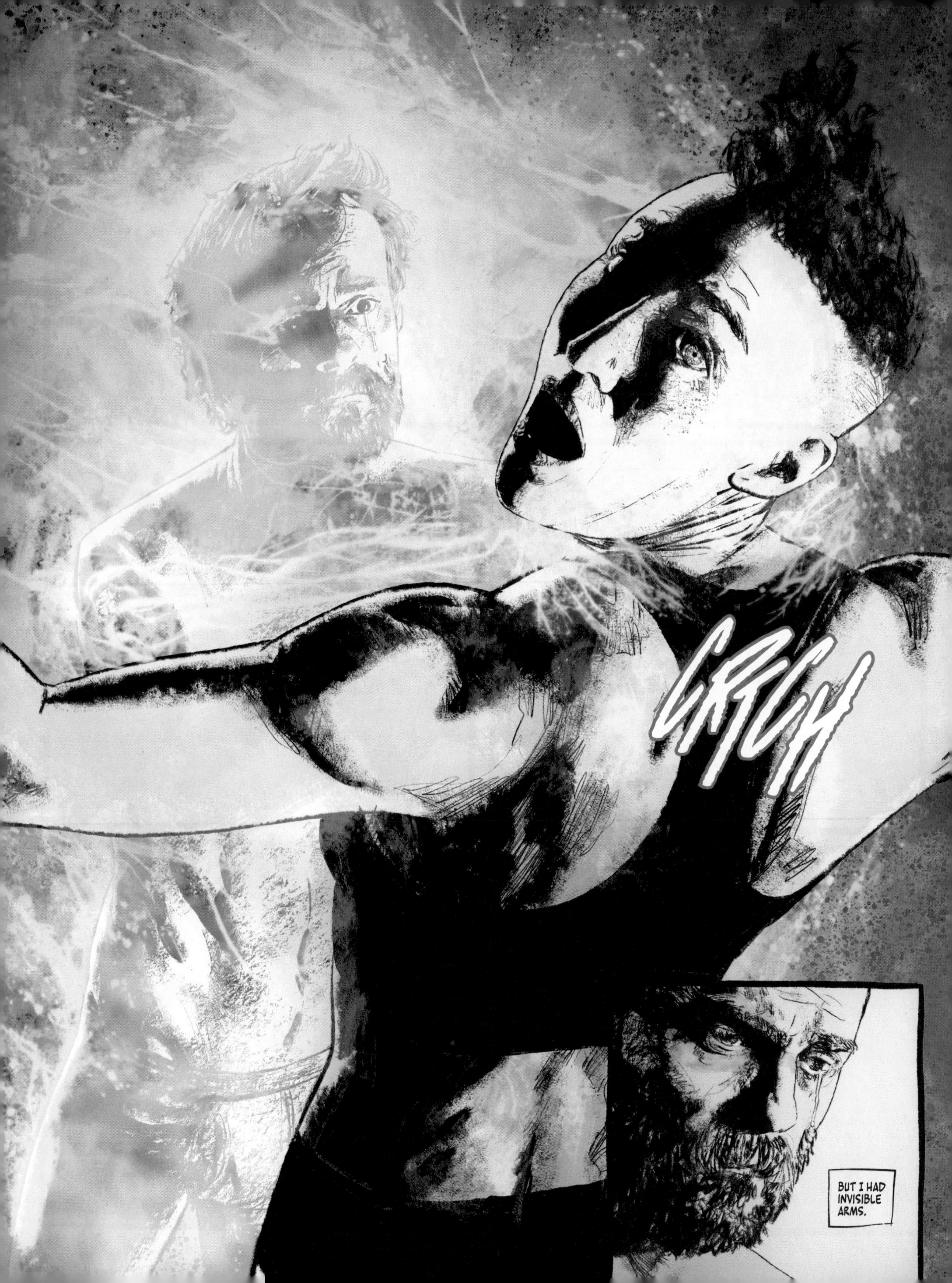
CRCH
BUT I HAD INVISIBLE ARMS.

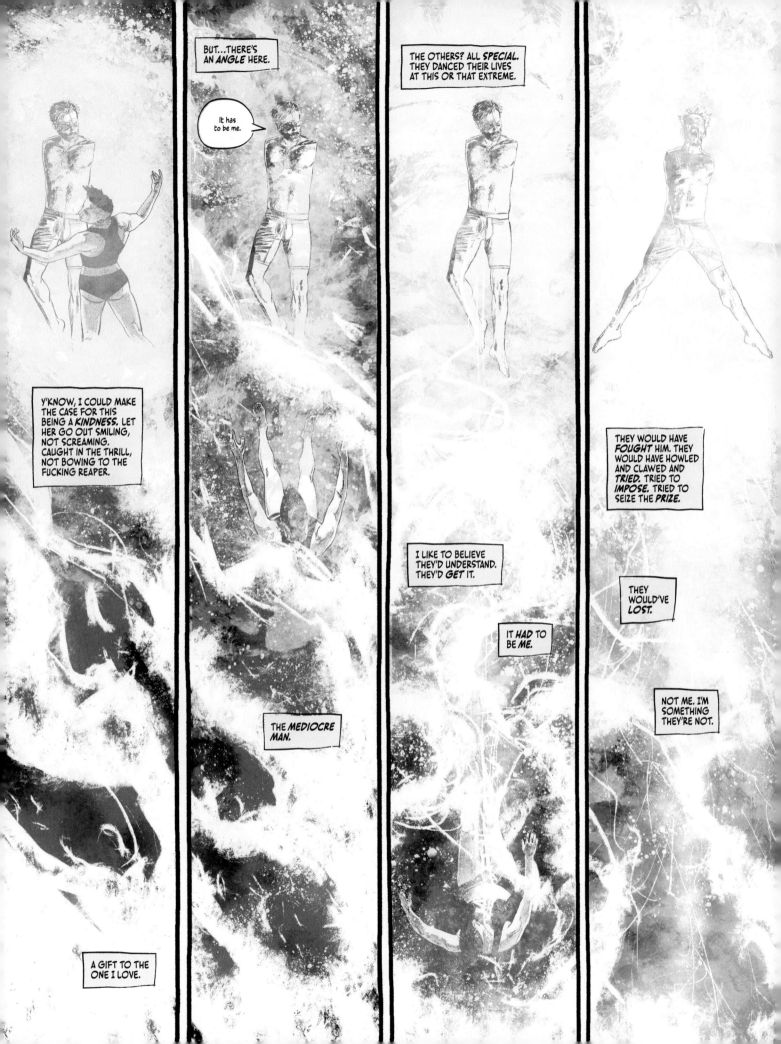

BUT...THERE'S AN *ANGLE* HERE.

It has to be me.

THE OTHERS? ALL *SPECIAL.* THEY DANCED THEIR LIVES AT THIS OR THAT EXTREME.

Y'KNOW, I COULD MAKE THE CASE FOR THIS BEING A *KINDNESS.* LET HER GO OUT SMILING, NOT SCREAMING. CAUGHT IN THE THRILL, NOT BOWING TO THE FUCKING REAPER.

THEY WOULD HAVE *FOUGHT* HIM. THEY WOULD HAVE HOWLED AND CLAWED AND *TRIED.* TRIED TO *IMPOSE.* TRIED TO SEIZE THE *PRIZE.*

I LIKE TO BELIEVE THEY'D UNDERSTAND. THEY'D *GET* IT.

THEY WOULD'VE *LOST.*

IT *HAD* TO BE *ME.*

NOT ME. I'M SOMETHING THEY'RE NOT.

THE *MEDIOCRE MAN.*

A GIFT TO THE ONE I LOVE.

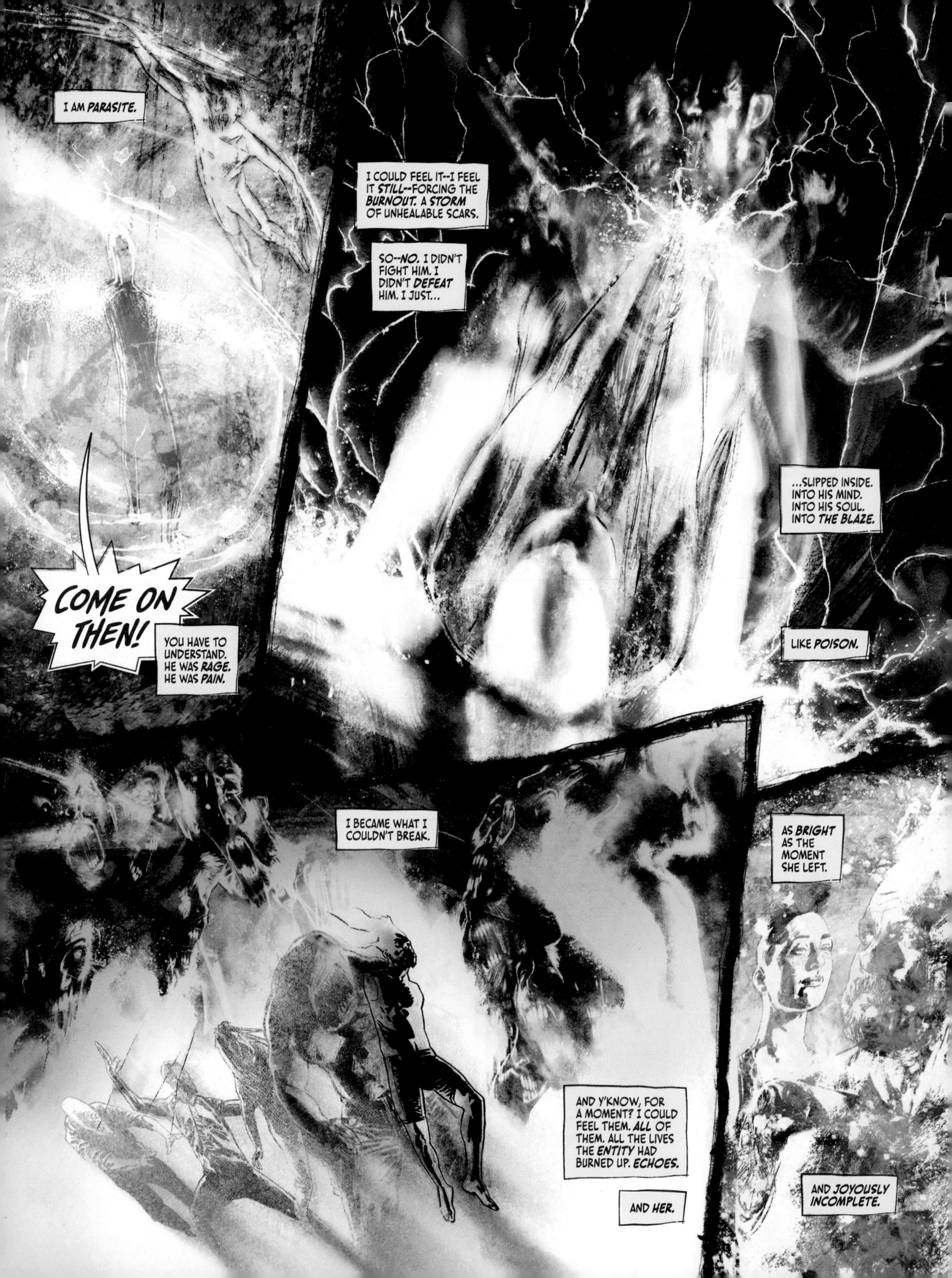
I AM PARASITE.
I COULD FEEL IT--I FEEL IT STILL--FORCING THE BURNOUT. A STORM OF UNHEALABLE SCARS.
SO--NO. I DIDN'T FIGHT HIM. I DIDN'T DEFEAT HIM. I JUST...
...SLIPPED INSIDE. INTO HIS MIND. INTO HIS SOUL. INTO THE BLAZE.
COME ON THEN!
YOU HAVE TO UNDERSTAND. HE WAS RAGE. HE WAS PAIN.
LIKE POISON.
I BECAME WHAT I COULDN'T BREAK.
AS BRIGHT AS THE MOMENT SHE LEFT.
AND Y'KNOW, FOR A MOMENT? I COULD FEEL THEM. ALL OF THEM. ALL THE LIVES THE ENTITY HAD BURNED UP. ECHOES.
AND HER.
AND JOYOUSLY INCOMPLETE.

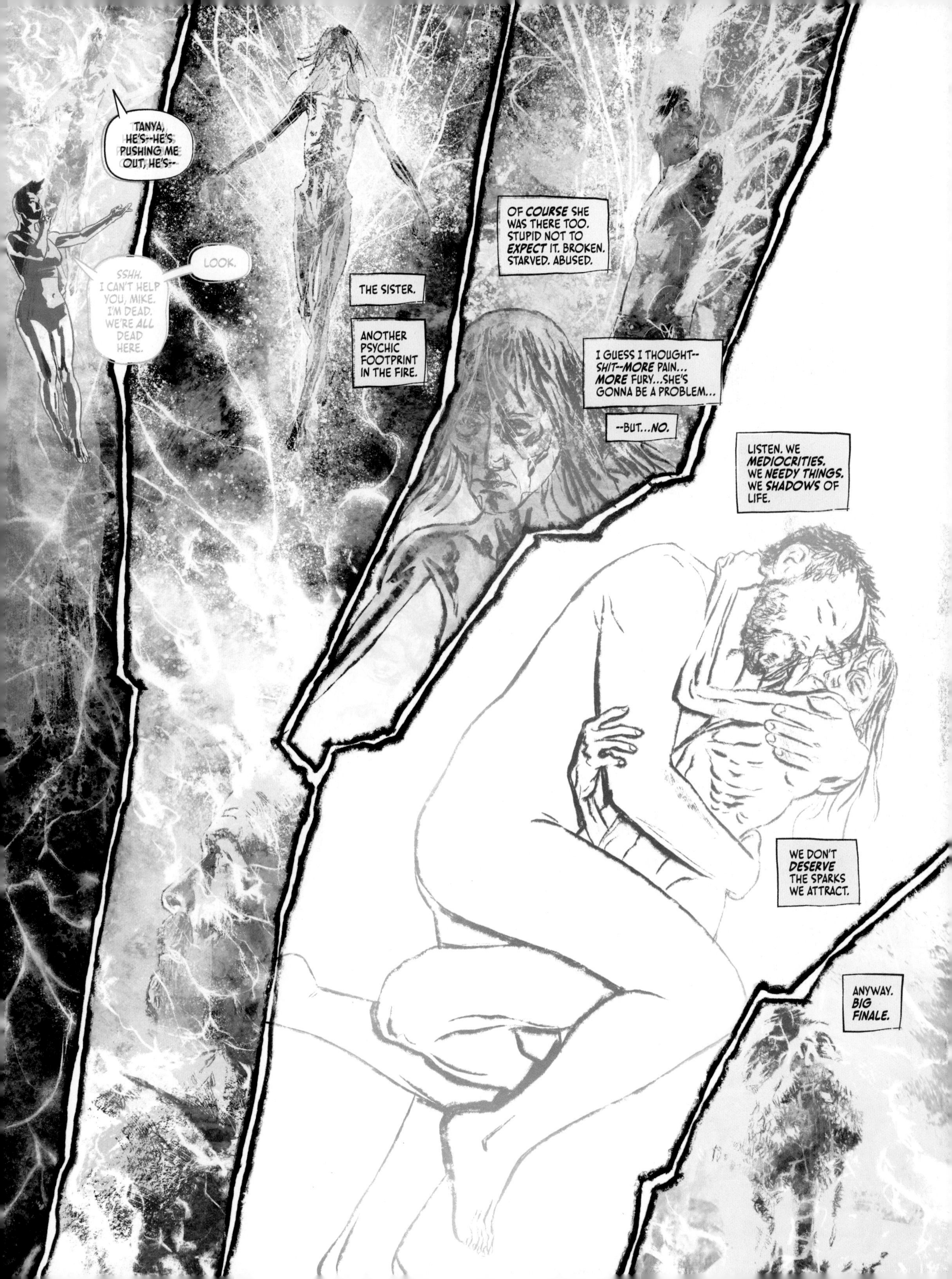
TANYA, HE'S--HE'S PUSHING ME OUT, HE'S--
SSHH. I CAN'T HELP YOU, MIKE. I'M DEAD. WE'RE ALL DEAD HERE.
LOOK.
THE SISTER.
ANOTHER PSYCHIC FOOTPRINT IN THE FIRE.
OF COURSE SHE WAS THERE TOO. STUPID NOT TO EXPECT IT. BROKEN. STARVED. ABUSED.
I GUESS I THOUGHT--SHIT--MORE PAIN... MORE FURY...SHE'S GONNA BE A PROBLEM...
--BUT...NO.
LISTEN. WE MEDIOCRITIES. WE NEEDY THINGS. WE SHADOWS OF LIFE.
WE DON'T DESERVE THE SPARKS WE ATTRACT.
ANYWAY. BIG FINALE.

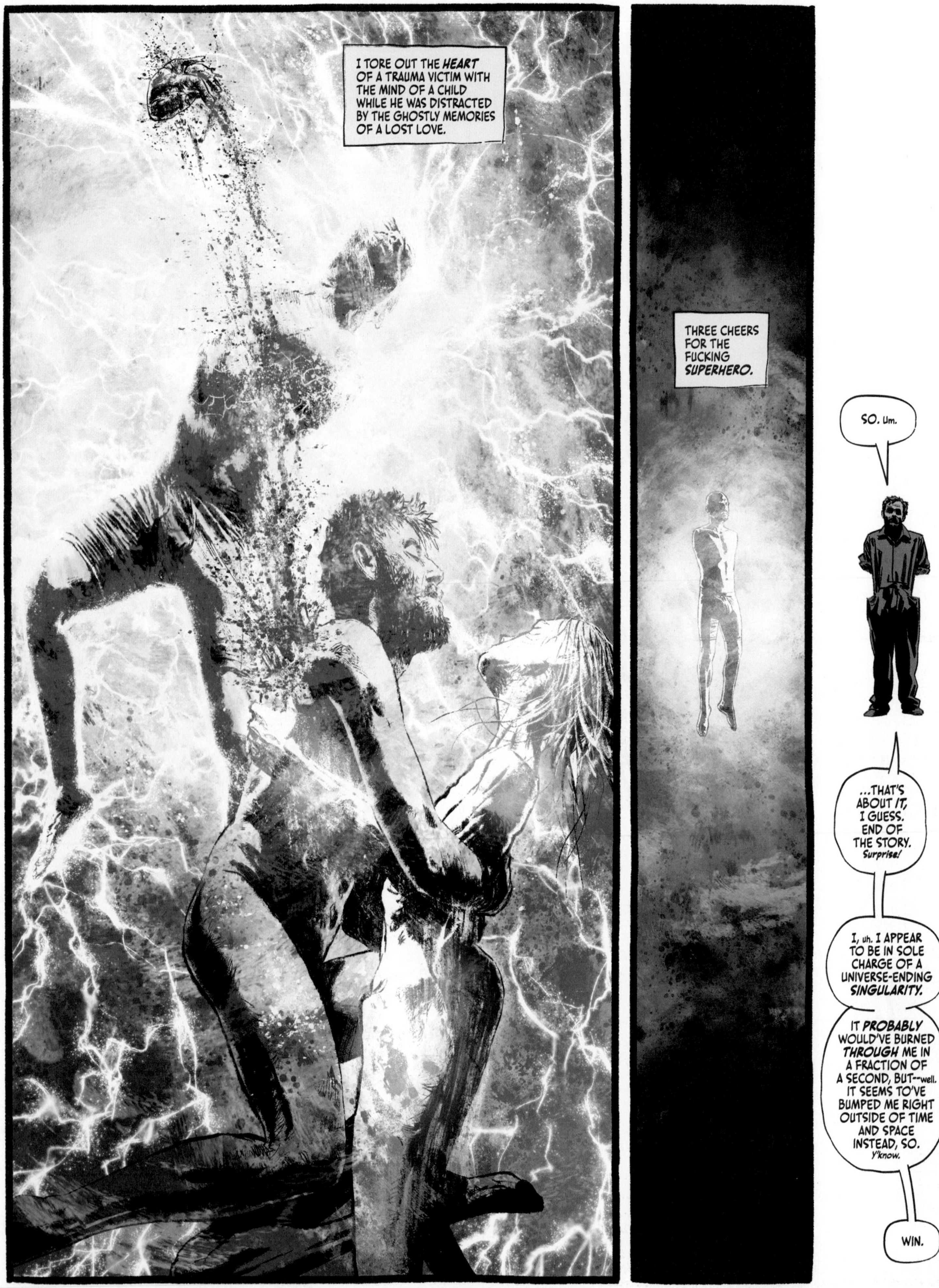
I TORE OUT THE HEART OF A TRAUMA VICTIM WITH THE MIND OF A CHILD WHILE HE WAS DISTRACTED BY THE GHOSTLY MEMORIES OF A LOST LOVE.
THREE CHEERS FOR THE FUCKING SUPERHERO.
SO. Um.
...THAT'S ABOUT IT, I GUESS. END OF THE STORY. Surprise!
I, uh. I APPEAR TO BE IN SOLE CHARGE OF A UNIVERSE-ENDING SINGULARITY.
IT PROBABLY WOULD'VE BURNED THROUGH ME IN A FRACTION OF A SECOND, BUT--well. IT SEEMS TO'VE BUMPED ME RIGHT OUTSIDE OF TIME AND SPACE INSTEAD, SO. Y'know.
WIN.

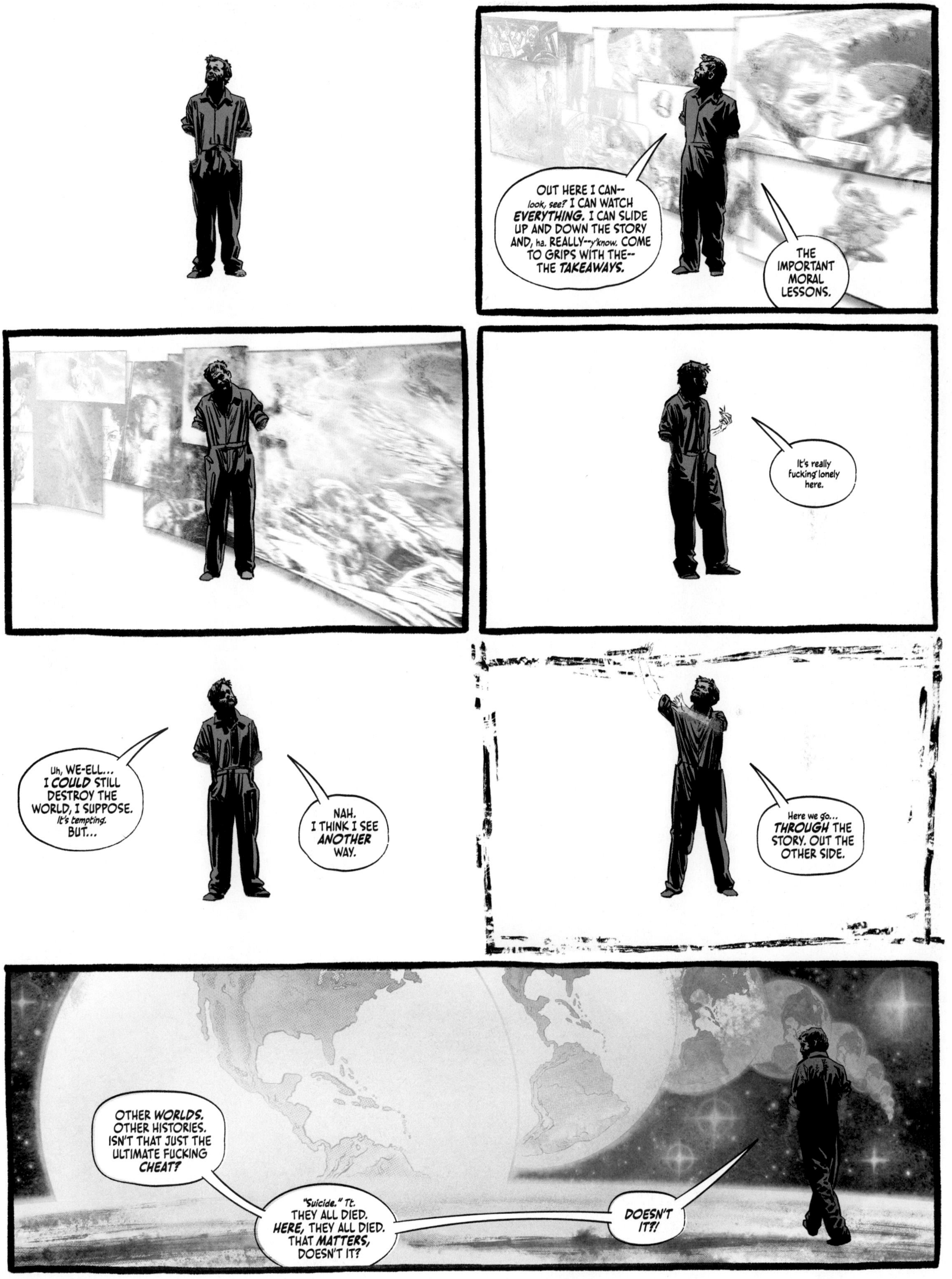
OUT HERE I CAN-- look, see? I CAN WATCH EVERYTHING. I CAN SLIDE UP AND DOWN THE STORY AND, ha. REALLY--y'know. COME TO GRIPS WITH THE-- THE TAKEAWAYS.
THE IMPORTANT MORAL LESSONS.
It's really fucking lonely here.
Uh, WE-ELL... I COULD STILL DESTROY THE WORLD, I SUPPOSE. It's tempting. BUT...
NAH. I THINK I SEE ANOTHER WAY.
Here we go... THROUGH THE STORY. OUT THE OTHER SIDE.
OTHER WORLDS. OTHER HISTORIES. ISN'T THAT JUST THE ULTIMATE FUCKING CHEAT?
"Suicide." Tt. THEY ALL DIED. HERE, THEY ALL DIED. THAT MATTERS, DOESN'T IT?
DOESN'T IT?!

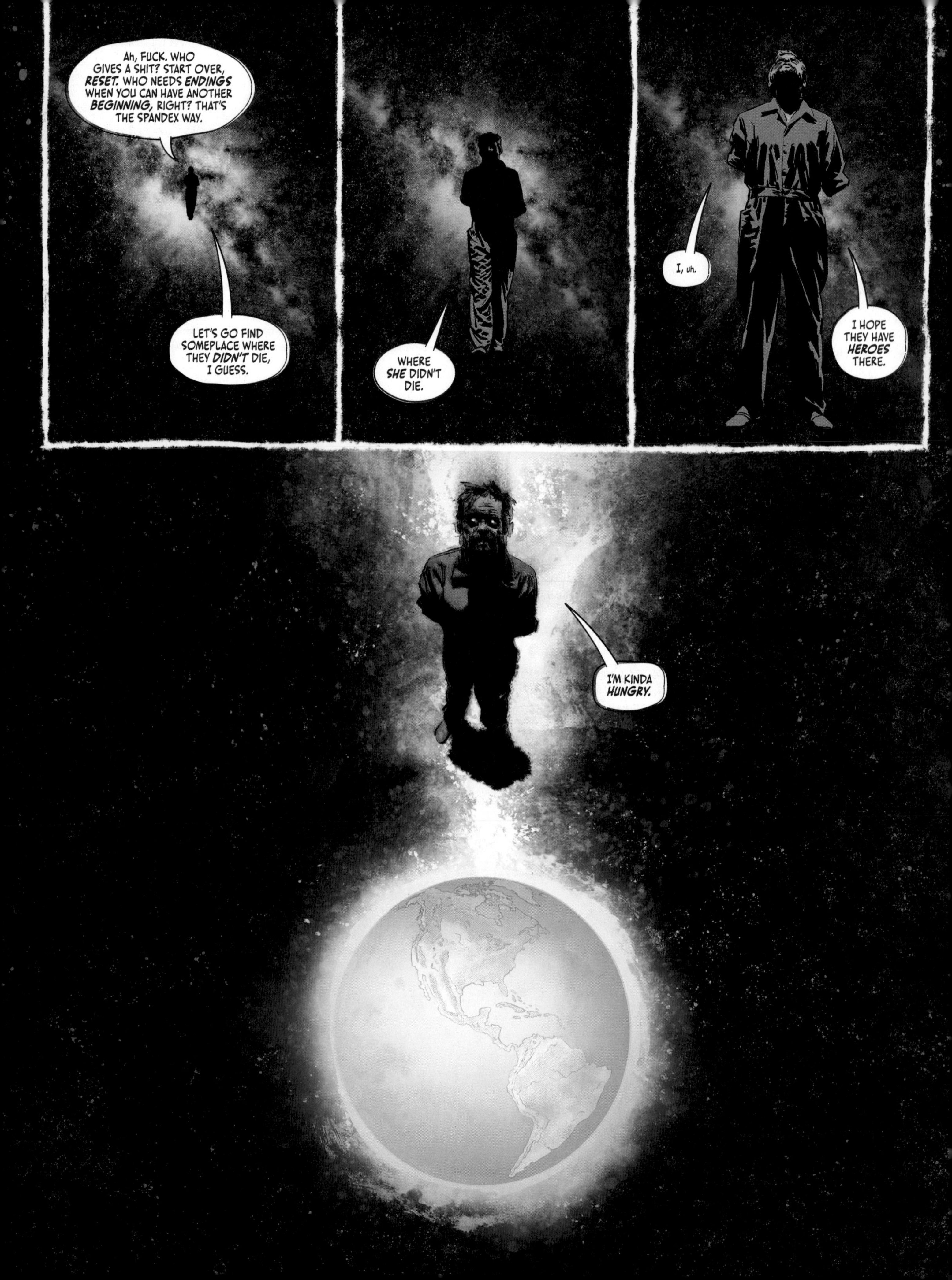
Ah, FUCK. WHO GIVES A SHIT? START OVER, RESET. WHO NEEDS ENDINGS WHEN YOU CAN HAVE ANOTHER BEGINNING, RIGHT? THAT'S THE SPANDEX WAY.
LET'S GO FIND SOMEPLACE WHERE THEY DIDN'T DIE, I GUESS.
WHERE SHE DIDN'T DIE.
I, uh.
I HOPE THEY HAVE HEROES THERE.
I'M KINDA HUNGRY.

THE ART OF SUICIDE SQUAD BLAZE

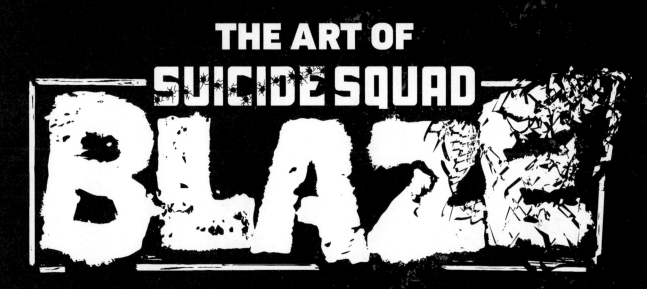

PRESENTED BY AARON CAMPBELL

The cover for issue #3 was loads of fun to do. It was a simple concept. I'd represent the most recognizable accoutrements of the Suicide Squad veterans discarded and bloody in a blazing ruin. This is an "all are dead" moment. In execution, I'd completely indulged my love of still life and model making.

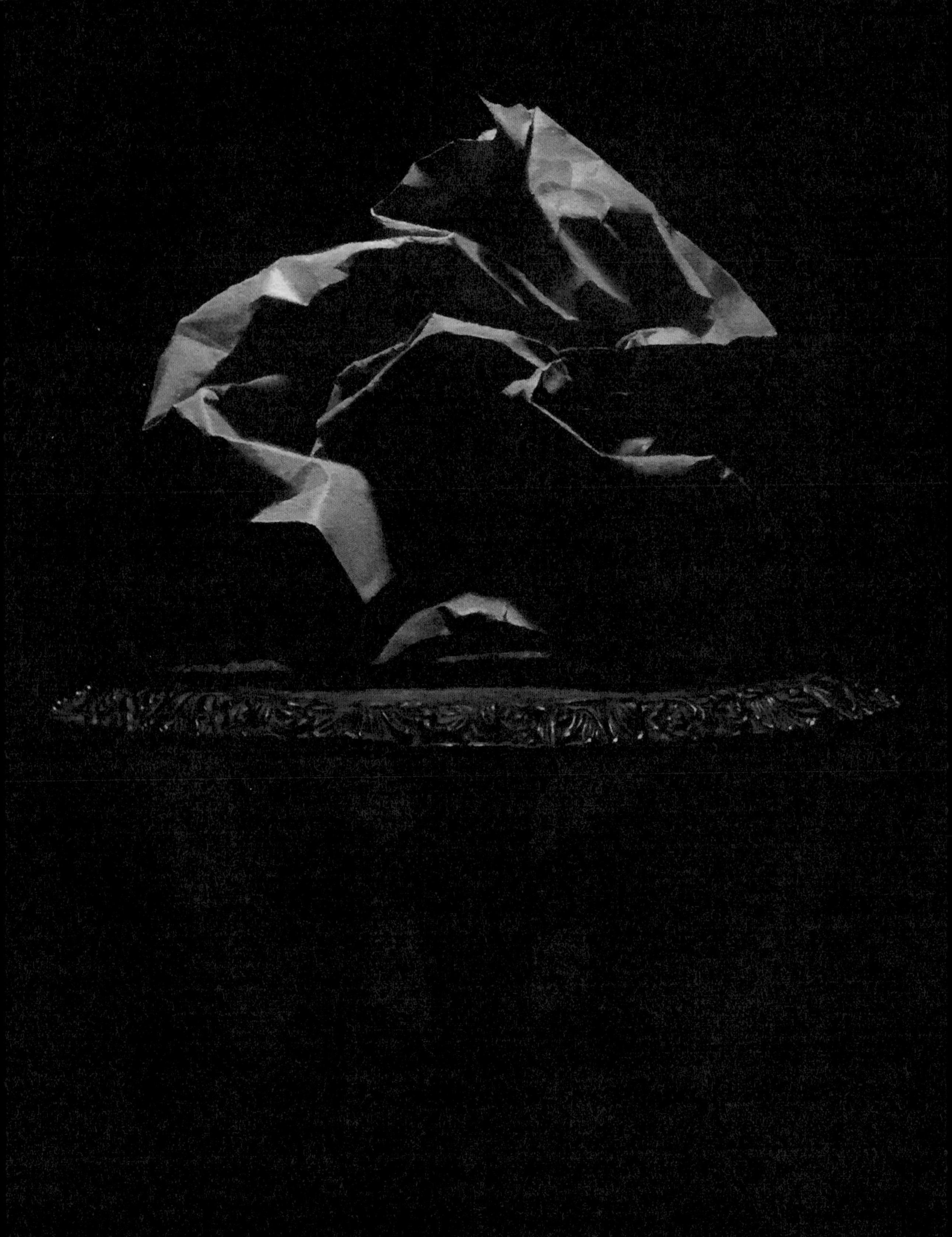

Still life art by Aaron Campbell

First I had to gather all the elements of my macabre little still life. To do so I christened my new 3D printer to make most of the props you see in the reference photos. Harley's club, Peacemaker's helmet, King Shark's teeth, and Boomer's boomerang were all printed using my resin printer. I used a mirror-finish spray paint on the helmet and boomerang to get a reflective surface and hit the mallet and teeth with some off-white primer. None of this needed to be finish quality, just good enough to get me some decent reference.

Then I 2D-printed my reference of the killer's face to use for the reflection in Peacemaker's chrome dome. I also rolled up pieces of paper towels into pea-sized balls and soaked them in isopropyl alcohol. You'll understand why real soon. Finally, I gathered a bucket full of lumpy dirt from my backyard.

Now it was time to put everything together. I spread the dirt out for the ground cover and placed all my 3D elements where I liked them. Then I set lights up on either side of the diorama with some color gels, and I was ready to shoot. This is when I placed the little wads of paper towel soaked in alcohol into the scene. I made sure I was ready go with the camera, lit them on fire, got my shot, and immediately doused them with water. And by the way, don't try this at home. I shot the reflection separately, with my assistant holding the printout right above the helmet to get that reflection just right. And from there I was ready to paint.

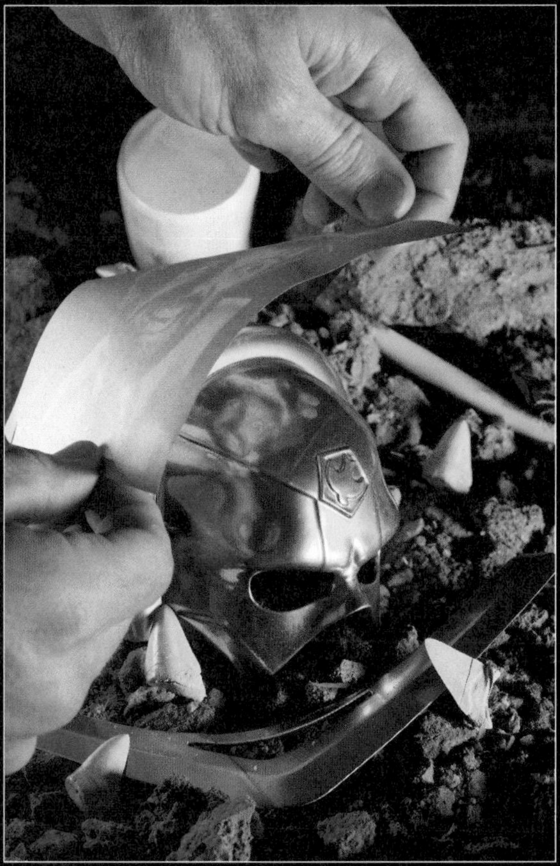

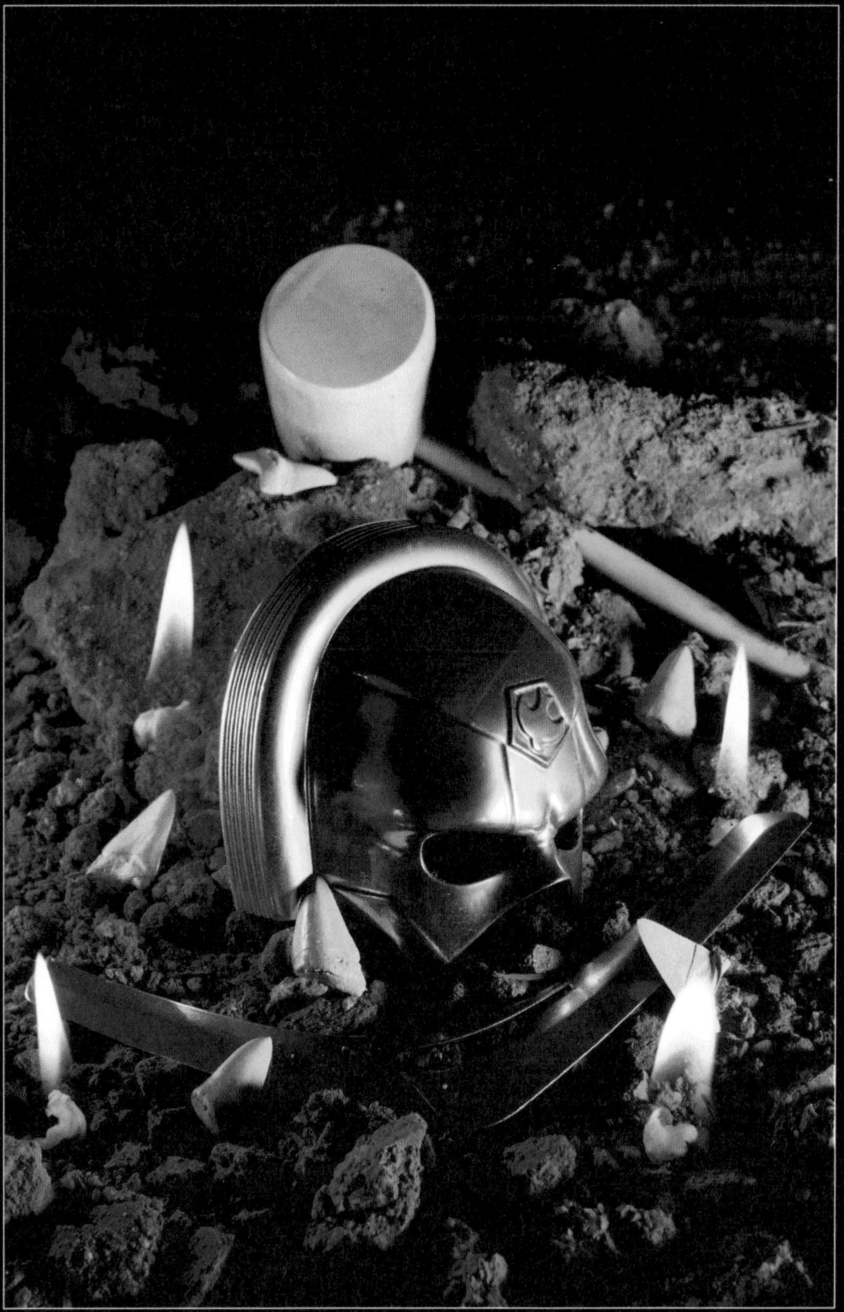

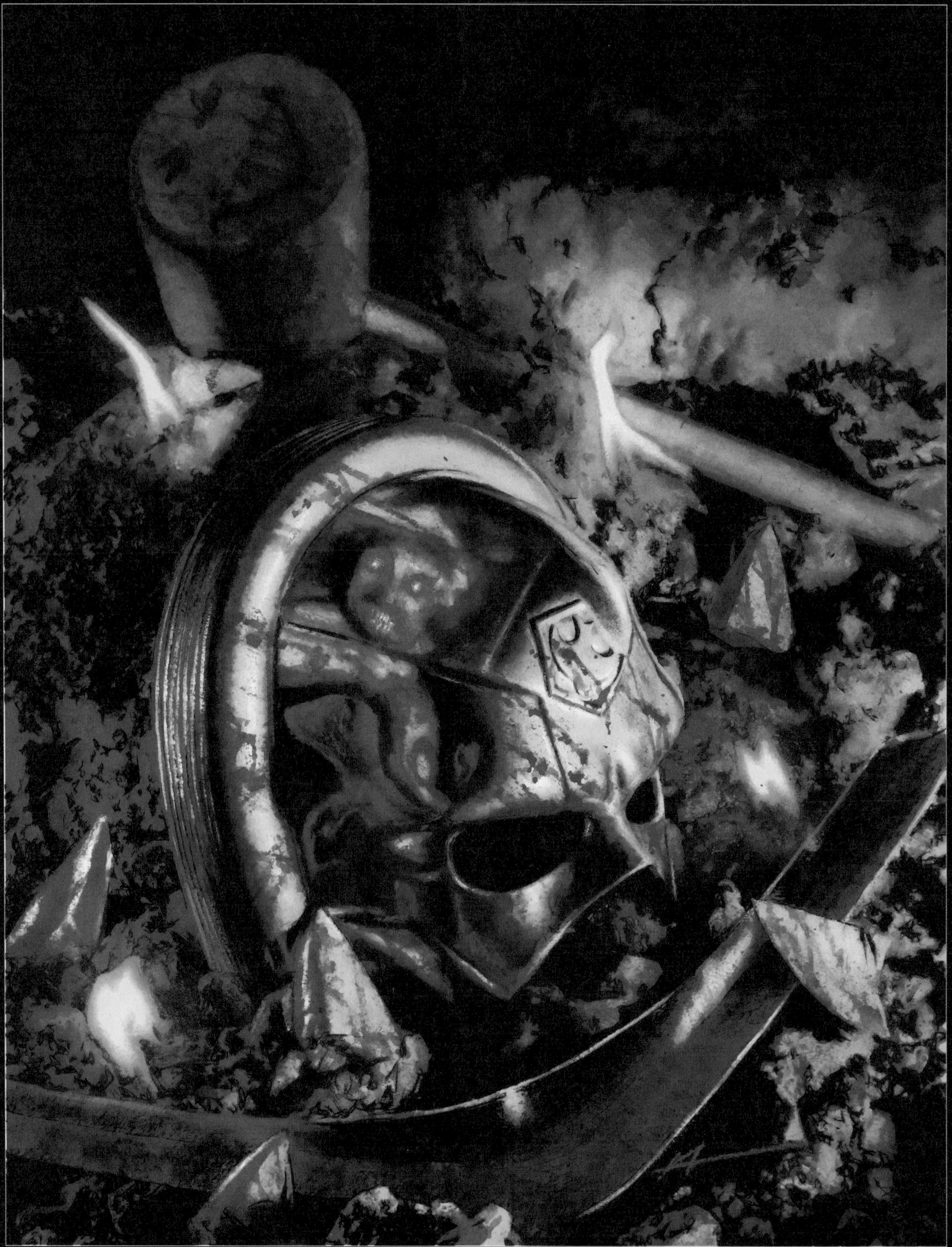

It was always important to the story that, in the beginning at least, we never get a clear look at the killer. And yet it was also very important to see the killer doing his terrible killing things. Silhouettes tend to be the most common solution to this kind of problem, but I obviously enjoy tormenting myself. So I proposed using an old fan theory about Superman. It goes something like this: the reason people don't recognize Superman as Clark Kent is that, as Superman, he vibrates his body at an insane frequency, making him appear all blurry and shit. Now we all know this is not the case, but I suggested, "What if our killer does this?"

For reference I was able to play around quite a bit. I used a combination of strobes and hot lights in conjunction with long and multiple exposures. For each shot I had my model assume multiple poses, usually three to four distinct positions. We would rehearse this beforehand, and then I would count off each position while shooting. The strobes would capture each pose with clarity while the hot lights, which stay on continually, traced the blurry motion between each position. Once I got what I liked, I'd futz with the images in Lightroom and Photoshop until I got something I could draw from.

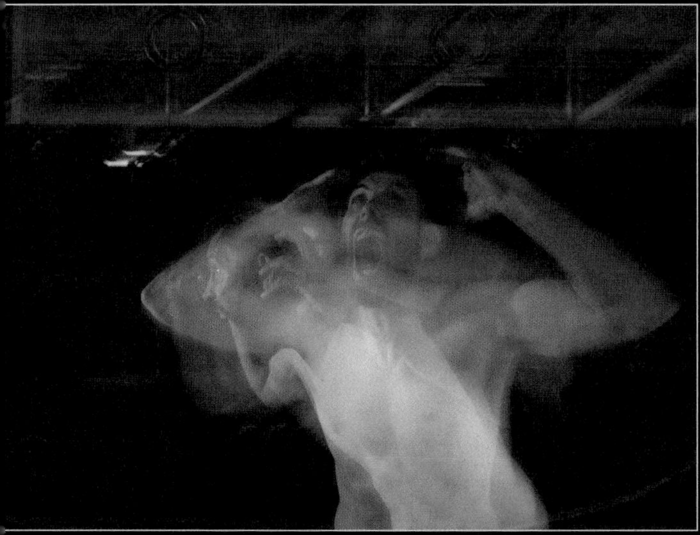

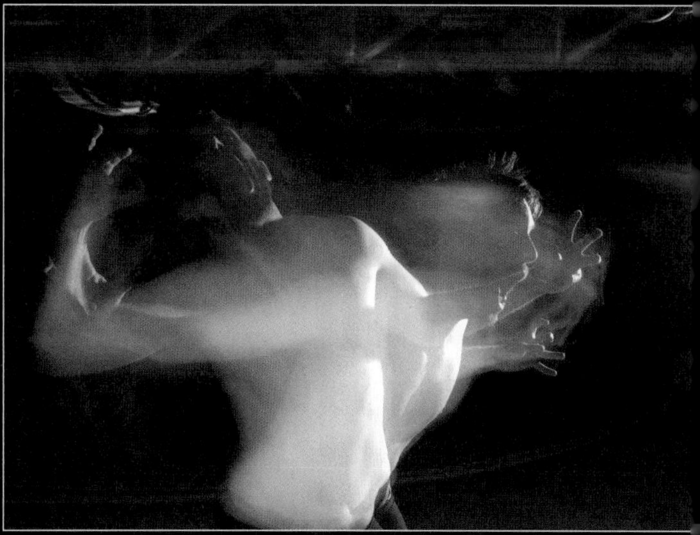

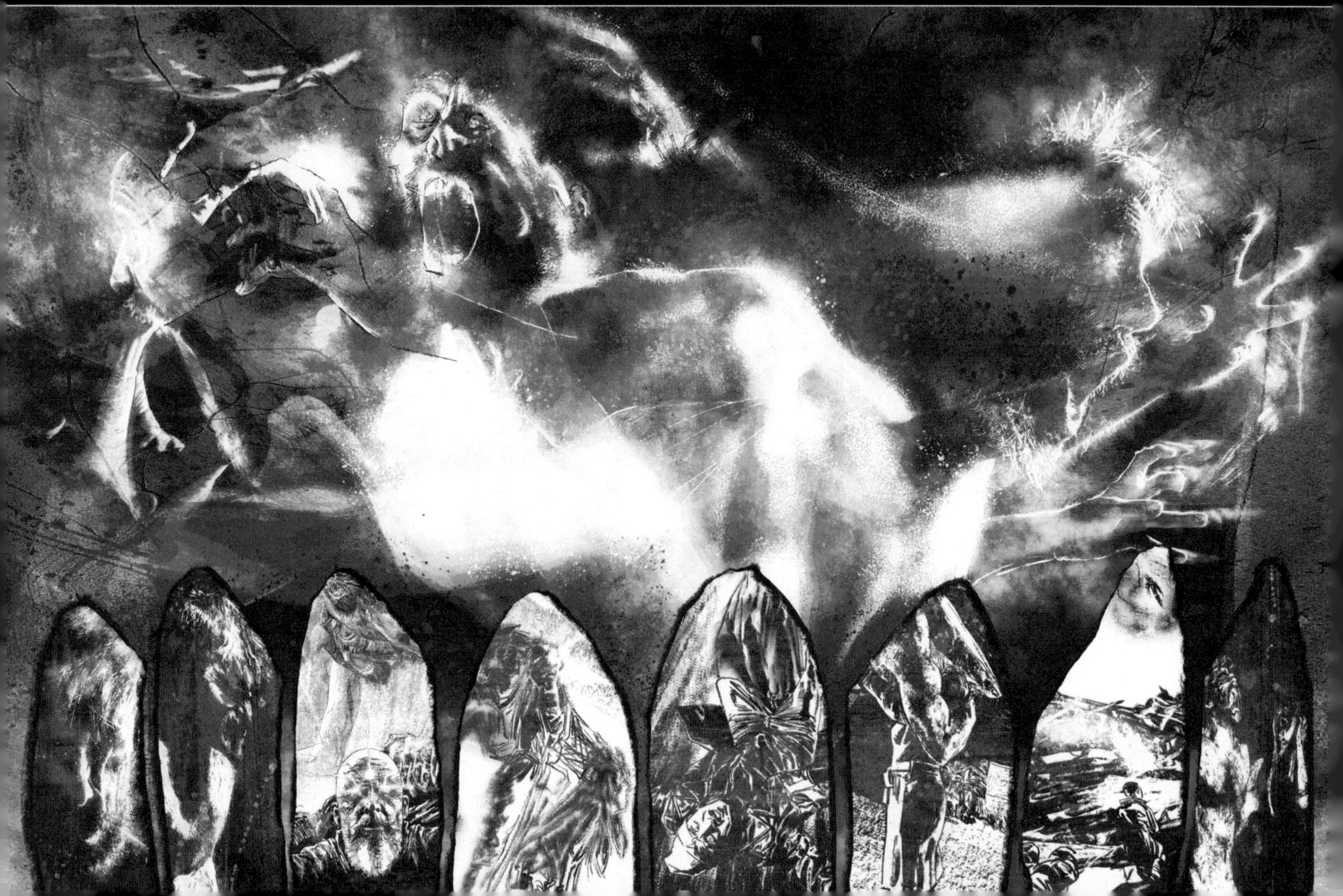

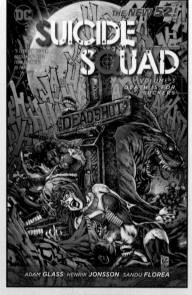